SECOND EDITION

SEARCH STRATEGIES IN MASS COMMUNICATION

JEAN WARD AND KATHLEEN A. HANSEN

University of Minnesota

Longman

New York & London

Search Strategies in Mass Communication, second edition

Longman, 10 Bank Street, White Plains, N.Y. 10606

Associated companies:
Longman Group Ltd., London
Longman Cheshire Pty., Melbourne
Longman Paul Pty., Auckland
Copp Clark Pitman, Toronto

Acquisitions editor: Kathy Schurawich
Production editor: Linda Moser
Text design adaptation: Betty Sokol
Cover design: Joseph De Pinho
Text art: Pompeo Designs
Production supervisor: Joanne Jay

Library of Congress Cataloging-in-Publication Data

Ward, Jean (Jean W.)
    Search strategies in mass communication / Jean Ward, Kathleen
Hansen.—2nd ed.
        p.   cm.
    Includes bibliographical references and index.
    ISBN 0-8013-1035-0
    1. Mass media—Research—Methodology.   2. Communication—Research—
Methodology.   I. Hansen, Kathleen A.   II. Title.
P91.3.W37   1992
302.23'072—dc20   92-8468
                                                                   CIP

1 2 3 4 5 6 7 8 9 10-AL-9695949392

For our families
and for Tren Anderson,
in celebration of his life and his leadership

Contents

Foreword

Professor Jean Ward introduced her students and me to "search strategies in mass communication" a good many years before it became the title of this book. She may not recall, but I sat in on her lectures in an interpretive reporting course at the University of Minnesota during my days as a graduate student and teaching associate there. What I heard was a master teacher exhorting her students to take a more intellectual, rigorous, and systematic approach to conceptualizing their stories and gathering information. For any given story assignment, journalists too often ask "who can I talk to" when their first thought should be "what can I read," she told them. Using a search strategy, she insisted, could help break journalists' overdependence on a relatively narrow group of sources and give journalists a more independent, if not more disinterested, base of knowledge.

Indeed, one of American journalism's most striking characteristics, at least until recently, has been its resistance to change. Journalists have tended to gather information and present it to audiences in much the same way as they have for a century or more. Significant declines in newspaper readership, the fractionalizing of print and broadcast audiences, and the emergence of alternative—and often more individualized and interactive—technologies for information delivery have provided impetus for change, however.

In today's media environment, *Search Strategies in Mass Communication*, second edition, is especially useful. It provides the guidance that should make communicators more cognizant of their changing audiences and equip them to obtain and evaluate better the information those audiences need. But it offers more.

Professor Jean Ward and Professor Kathleen Hansen have produced a book that is as usefully flexible as it is focused. They correctly recognize that search strategy is as relevant to mass communicators in public relations and advertising as to those in print and broadcast news. Therefore this book is genuinely a book about search strategies in *mass communication*, not simply search strategies for news reporters. The authors recognize the need for a book that can serve working professionals as well as students. Consequently

Search Strategies Mass Communication, second edition can serve as a reference book as well as a text.

Search Strategies in Mass Communication, second edition focuses unwaveringly on strategy and links problem definition and solution within the context of practical information about sources and methods. Ward and Hansen address the traditional observational, interviewing, documentary, and survey approaches to information gathering in terms of explaining the techniques and in critically assessing their strengths and limitations. The result is a melding of instruction on information-gathering methods with sound, specific advice on who or what to consult for what type of information. Above all, Ward and Hansen treat information gathering as the deceptively complex and risky matter it is and as a process best regarded only as part of a larger, conscious strategy shaped by careful consideration and development of the questions mass communicators want to address. This is the essence of the important contribution Ward and Hansen make—they offer a conceptual framework and working plans to help professional communicators ask the right questions, use appropriate sources, and evaluate the resulting answers.

Those who have used the first edition of *Search Strategies in Mass Communication* will find that the second edition has been well updated and somewhat reorganized. Fortunately, they will also discover that the heart of the work is unchanged.

Robert E. Drechsel
Professor of Journalism and Mass Communication
University of Wisconsin-Madison

Preface

While the term *information age* may be overused, it does describe contemporary society. Such sweeping changes as those now being labeled part of the information revolution could not fail to change the way communicators work or the demands society places on them. When the production of information is growing rapidly, the challenge for mass communicators is magnified. The clear need is for a fundamental rethinking of the critical role information plays in communication. The first edition of this book introduced the major concepts required for a new approach to information gathering, evaluation, and use. This second edition elaborates on these concepts in the light of recent developments in both technology and scholarship.

Much about mass communication work has changed since the first edition of this book was published. The significance of *information* in mass media messages enjoys better recognition than when we began our studies in this developing subject. Evidence of this growth is easily seen in the following: new partnerships between communicators and information specialists in the production of messages for advertising, public relations, and news; development of new courses about information in mass communication programs around the country; and adoption of new information technologies in media organizations that allow communicators to do more research and do it faster.

While new technology and industry developments have been incorporated into this second edition, the original conceptual framework has been retained. The first edition introduced communicators to the idea of the *search strategy,* which had been used in library science instruction and practice for 30 years. We developed a synthesis of the traditional library science process with the traditional journalistic methods for information gathering and evaluation. This new model of search strategy for mass communication treats the information needs of all mass communicators from a common perspective. Students and professional communicators in various industries may use information in many ways, but the search strategy process allows all of them to proceed securely in developing an information-seeking strategy. For example, a news reporter, an advertising copywriter, and a public-relations specialist may require the same census figure on the percentage of the American population over 50 years of age. The subsequent use of this information by these media professionals will vary, but the process for getting the information is the same.

The original search strategy model, introduced in Chapter One, continues as the organizing principle for Chapters Two through Nine. Each of these chapters expands on one of the components of the search strategy model. Chapter Ten explores the social responsibility and legal obligations of communicators' information use. The advantages of using a model of the information process are even more apparent today than when we wrote the first edition, for the information sources have continued to expand, making it impossible for any communicator or researcher to hold in memory the thousands of specific sources that may be brought to bear in developing a mass communication message. The power of the model includes the fact that its major components can be kept in memory as guides to additional exploration. And a model is comforting, in that information seekers need not feel overwhelmed by the existence of thousands of unknown possible sources. In addition, the search strategy model allows the communicator to identify the major originators and disseminators of information useful for mass communication.

The second edition reflects an expanding amount of scholarship on information and mass communication. This edition includes results from our own research program about the role of the news library in news making. We have included other new research from advertising and public relations perspectives which has enriched our understanding of information functions in those industries. In addition, a growing body of critical research about selection of sources and evaluation of information is incorporated in this new edition.

Technological developments over the past five years have been so dramatic that our treatment of information technologies has expanded from a focus on data-base searching to broader treatment of such technologies as electronic mail, fax, electronic libraries, image data bases, portable video systems, and satellite photography. One of the most significant new entrants for information storage and retrieval is the CD-ROM (compact disc-read only memory) system. This storage medium uses the familiar disc that everyone recognizes from their audio systems, except that what is stored and retrieved can include text, images, and sound together. Computer-assisted journalism has become a major form of news making, in which reporting teams may use data tapes purchased from other institutions or may generate their own data bases from original information gathering. New computer software programs simplify reporters' uses of such information. Communicators have become both creators and users of data bases of information.

Just as technological developments have led us to expand our approach to electronic information systems, so have the needs of two of our groups of readers. Professional communicators and academic researchers have been among those who told us of the usefulness of the search strategy approach for their work. Both of these groups are subject to the same problems of information overload as are our student readers. Academic researchers recognize their need to learn about research from their own and other allied fields. Professional communicators acknowledge their need to expand their approaches for identifying sources and documents. We have incorporated examples that respond to these needs. For some of these individuals, this book serves as a desk reference to which they turn when they encounter an information problem. The "Topical Tool Index," along with the "General Index," is designed to simplify this reference process.

We have tested this generic, process approach to finding and evaluating information for mass communication. More than 3,000 novices at the University of Minnesota have learned to follow the information-seeking path we have set and have successfully applied the principles in their mass communication. We thank them for their receptivity and ingenuity in following the search strategy process. An unknown number of graduate and undergraduate students at other institutions have also been introduced to this method. We have heard from some of them about the impact of this process on their education and their careers. We thank them for writing and calling with their comments.

Among many other debts of gratitude, one of the most significant is to the late Gordon "Tren" Anderson, the Longman editor who took the risk of publishing the first edition of this book when there were no precedents for such an approach and no courses, aside from Minnesota's, in the field. His support was so important to us that we have added his name to the dedication page of this edition.

We are also grateful for the enthusiasm of our faculty colleagues from around the country who recognized the significance of information studies in the mass communication context and who developed new courses for their curricula. Sharing course outlines and course materials with them has been a renewing experience. Similarly, professionals from news, advertising and public relations have been generous in offering their expertise and insight and in opening their "shops" to us as visitors and as researchers.

Several institutions have provided support for our teaching and research efforts. We thank the Freedom Forum Media Studies Center at Columbia University, the McGannon Communication Research Center at Fordham University, the Minnesota Journalism Center, the Poynter Institute for Media Studies, and the University of Minnesota Graduate School for research support and opportunities in professional development.

Among many individuals to whom we owe thanks, we include Colleen Coghlan of Metropolitan State University in the Twin Cities, Robert Drechsel of the University of Wisconsin—Madison, Marion Marzolf of the University of Michigan, Dhyana Ziegler of the University of Tennessee—Knoxville, Ardyth Sohn of the University of Colorado—Boulder, and Randal Beam of the University of Oregon. The editing and production staff at Longman have been most supportive and efficient. We especially thank Kathleen Schura-wich, Communications Editor, and David Fox, Assistant Editor, for their help in bringing this second edition to completion. Linda Sinsheimer Moser, Pro-duction Editor, and Polly Kummel, Copyeditor, have been most helpful in the final stages of the publication process, when time is short and pressures are great. We are pleased to have worked with this Longman team.

SECOND EDITION

SEARCH STRATEGIES IN MASS COMMUNICATION

1

Communicators as Information Seekers: Models of the Search Process

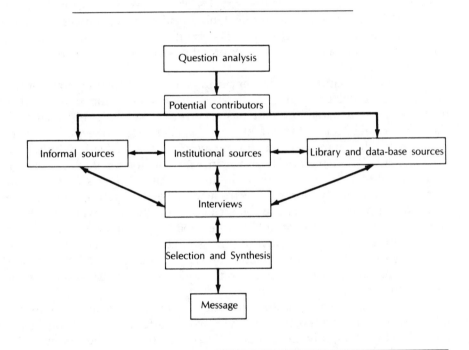

The news assignment: an article or a series of articles on gentrification, or the displacement of the urban poor from old neighhorhoods that are undergoing rehabilitation. The reporter: a generalist who must begin by recognizing her own lack of knowledge of this subject. The challenge: to do a rapid study of gentrification. The sources: knowledgeable people, public records, and reputable books and articles. In conducting her survey of what is known about the subject, the well-prepared reporter will range widely and consult experts in such fields as economics, architecture, insurance, banking, housing, city planning, demographics, race relations, urban affairs, and tax policy. Her choice of people to interview will be influenced by what she learns in her exploration. Her questions will be shaped partly by the need to expand on and update what she first learned.

The advertising assignment: an ad campaign to introduce a new running suit for teenagers of both genders. The advertising professional: an account executive who has no experience with sports apparel accounts and who must recognize his need for background information. The challenge: to do a rapid study of the market for sports apparel, the likely methods for reaching the teenagers for whom the suit is designed, and the advertising trends in the sports apparel industry. The sources: demographic studies of teen interests, incomes, and media preferences; articles about the sports apparel industry and sports apparel advertising; and tools for identifying the costs of the best media in which to place the ads. The creative elements of the advertising campaign will be shaped by the information gathered in the first stages of campaign preparation.

The public-relations assignment: the contribution of the president of an insulation-manufacturing firm to a panel discussion of the safety and effectiveness of home-insulation materials. The practitioner: a public-relations specialist in a fully computerized office. The challenge: to provide the firm's president with comprehensive information on the insulation industry, the safety of insulation materials, and company liability for damages stemming from exposure to chemicals used in the insulation. The sources: reference works in the agency library, electronic-data-base searches, and interviews with company officials. The public-relations practitioner will have to know something about the viewpoints of the moderator, panelists, and audience; the credentials and reputability of the sources to be used; the content of news reports about home-insulation safety; and the setting of the discussion. The information from this background study will be critical to the president's success in representing the firm.

These three communicators pursue essentially similar routines in the information-gathering portion of their work. Information technologies that have developed rapidly in the past decade emphasize the commonality of these tasks. Each communicator has ready access to information and to information-gathering methods once available only to a few specialists. At any moment, all three professionals could be reaching into the same electronic file for information on the same topic. As they search for information, the reporter, the account executive, and the public-relations expert understand what their predecessors always knew: a mass-media message is no better than the information in it.

All messages consist of information and expression. *Expression* is the arrangement of words and images that send the information to the audience, while *information* consists of the facts that support the expression. The challenge for communicators—be they reporters, advertising specialists, or tape or photo editors—is to gather information, to select the relevant portions of it, and to express the information in a way that engages the audience.

In order to produce messages that engage the audience, communicators become experts at gathering material that meets their requirements— accuracy, timeliness, human interest, completeness, and certain legal and ethical standards. Such material must be gathered quickly and efficiently and assessed for its accuracy against increasingly stringent standards. New systems for locating and gathering information supplement the traditional methods of the past century. Interviews, clipping files, library reference works, and other conventional methods have not been replaced. They remain important in the communicator's repertoire of information-gathering devices. However, the new methods discussed in this book enhance the depth, breadth, and speed with which communicators work.

THE SEARCH STRATEGY:
AN INTELLECTUAL TOOL FOR COMMUNICATORS

The essence of the information age is a constantly rising quantity of information, matched by increasingly sophisticated methods of making that information available. Communicators need a conceptual tool that can help them learn where information is located and that offers them a routine for collecting it. A *conceptual tool* is an intellectual device that allows a thinker to apply and use abstractions at a practical, specific level. For example, in the familiar periodic table, the chemical elements, arranged according to their atomic numbers, are shown in related groups. Thus the periodic table is a conceptual tool. Similarly, the search strategy as a conceptual tool provides a coherent overview of information sources. *Search strategy* is a systematic means of acquiring and appraising information that will illuminate a subject.

For the past 30 years, library science has been using the concept of the formal search strategy as a way to organize thought about the information-search process.[1] We have incorporated into the standard library-science models for the search process the standard methods used in news gathering, advertising, and public relations. While the communicator may have worked out a search method that is comfortable and familiar, new technologies that introduce potential additional sources require new research skills.

Any reader of whodunits or watcher of television detective shows probably recognizes the search methods used by such characters as Miss Marple, Sherlock Holmes, Thomas Magnum, and Jessica Fletcher. The writers who create these characters direct them to standard information-seeking routines as part of the plot developments. The characters mostly use investigation and questioning, deductive thinking, and persistent attention to facts.

Uncovering the information needed in mass communication is a process similar to that used by such skilled investigators as Holmes and Fletcher. Communicators may not realize that their own search strategies have these detective-like patterns, but analysis of communicators' information-seeking strategies shows that they rely on methods that they follow fairly consistently. Accuracy, efficiency, and consistency are the goals of the information-gathering routines that communicators have established.

People in any everyday setting use search strategies of sorts for a variety of ordinary tasks—seeking an unlisted telephone number, checking the reputation of a physician or a dentist, learning how to eliminate aphids from house plants. Mass communicators, by the nature of their work, must be more inventive and persistent than most people in their search strategies. At times, they can use ordinary sources—telephone book, city directory, broadcast-ratings books, clippings of previously published material—with relatively little risk of error or loss of time. At other times, they need much more sophisticated sources of information very quickly.

Communicators at work in the information age find a tantalizing—and frightening—amount of material available as they begin to develop strategies to unlock this rich store of information. This chapter presents two models of the search strategy for the mass communicator: the simple model and a more complex, detailed model, which communicators in news, public relations, and advertising can follow for efficient, effective searches for information. A conceptual tool such as the search strategy provides a powerful way to synthesize both new and traditional methods of information gathering.

THE ROLES AND USES OF MODELS

Models have been defined and described by many scholars in a wide variety of fields.[2] For our purposes, we define a *model* as a systematic description in graphic form of the main elements of any structure or process and of the relationships among these elements. There are many advantages and some disadvantages in using models to describe abstract processes.

A psychologist identified some of the advantages of using models in an article written three decades ago.[3] He said that models describe and help us understand complex systems or events, help us learn complex skills, and provide the framework within which experiments are done and theories are tested. Models also help us see new relationships and they amuse us. He also identified some of the disadvantages of models: models invite over-generalization; the relationships among variables in a model may be incorrect; and models often are not tested for their accuracy in representing the processes they mean to represent. Despite these disadvantages, however, the psychologist concluded that models are appropriate and helpful in many situations.

There is a long tradition of using models to describe the communication processes. Most students of mass communication are familiar with the models that identify a sender, a channel, a message, a receiver, a relationship between sender and receiver, an effect of the message, and a purpose for sending or receiving the message.[4] The rationale for using models to represent various communication relationships has been described this way:

> Communication is a binding force in social relationships without at the same time being visible or having tangible and permanent forms. . . . There is, consequently, an attraction in being able to "draw" the "lines" which stand for the links we know to exist but cannot see and to use other devices to show the structure, topography, strength and direction of relationships. So much of the subject of communication has to be dealt with in verbal abstractions that it is an aid and a relief to have at least something "fixed" in graphic form, however much the element of abstraction may remain.[5]

Library and information-science specialists have long studied the process of searching for information. Their focus traditionally has been on the process that a librarian, or intermediary, follows in searching for information requested by a patron or information seeker. The term *search strategy* comes from the work done in this field. In the 1960s and early 1970s, a number of attempts were made to build models of the reference process as practiced by the librarian.[6] These early models of the search process concentrated on the search by the librarian for a fact or an answer in a reference book or another library source. The search by the librarian commenced after an interview with the information seeker about the fact needed or the question to be answered.

More recently, library and information-science specialists have recognized the need for search-strategy models that instruct the information seeker directly in the process of locating and evaluating materials.[7] This is part of a general move toward user competence in every facet of our lives. We all have taken on tasks once relegated to specialists—monitoring our own health more carefully, maintaining our automobiles, handling our own legal or financial activities. Librarians recognized that information seekers should be able to use an information-gathering process just as effective as that used by reference specialists.

The models of this user-oriented search strategy incorporate elements of problem solving to provide a search-strategy process that is broader in scope than previous strategies and more easily adopted by the information seeker. They recognize that in an information-rich environment, it is impossible to remember thousands of specific reference tools that can answer specific questions or help locate specific facts. There are simply too many tools and titles. Instead, the models suggest that the competent information seeker needs a process or method that will provide a map of the pathways into the thousands of information sources.

While the user-directed models of the search process can help the information seeker find needed information independently, there still are times when a consultation with an expert reference staff is appropriate. Just as we recognize when an injury requires stitches rather than a bandage, the skilled information searcher recognizes when an information-search problem requires the expertise of a reference librarian. All the models of the search strategy, whether user-directed or librarian-directed, are informative, but they do not speak directly to the unique information needs of the mass communicator.

One of the most obvious ways in which the mass-communication search strategy differs from others is that the results of the search directly affect the quality of the messages that the public receives. In this sense, the public character of the message and the public need for reliable, relevant material are significant. Errors of fact, inference, or judgment have greater consequences than if the information were presented in a term paper with an audience of one, for instance.

For mass communication, the particular strengths of the search-strategy process are as follows:

1. It allows the communicator to become knowledgeable about a field in general or about a specific topic.
2. It helps the communicator identify segments of the field and select a manageable portion of it for examination.
3. It provides a method for an in-depth examination of the segment selected.
4. It allows the communicator to select the best material, permitting choices based on timeliness, balance, relevance, expertise, authority, human interest, and local, national, or international perspectives.
5. It provides material that can lead to a unified, coherent message.
6. It gives communicators a vocabulary for discussing their information-gathering process.

Various media traditions affect the use of search strategies. A tradition of local reporting of news, for instance, requires that sources from the community be included in a local news report; a search strategy may provide important national or even international material that helps the audience understand the issue, but information from the community is a prerequisite.

A tradition of timeliness also affects the search strategy of media professionals. Although they are not indifferent to the history of laws or regulations, for instance, they cannot accept history as a substitute for accurate knowledge of the law as it stands.

Severe time constraint is another feature of mass communication work that is taken into account by the search-strategy model for communicators. Speed and efficiency in information gathering are useful for anyone, but they are crucial for those who produce mass-media messages.

Mass communicators are especially concerned about the accuracy and consistency of their messages. Therefore, part of their search strategy must include attention to matters in which experts agree or disagree. Inconsistency in facts and figures, prejudice, bias, and incompleteness can be exposed in the search process.

Attribution of information is standard practice in news reports and, to a lesser extent, in advertising and public relations. Much material originates in interviews, for people often provide information that contributes local angles, expertise or authority, or human interest. This is the element of the mass-communication search strategy that most obviously sets it apart from other traditional search-strategy models. The interview as a source of information is built into the mass communication model as a matter of course. In a wide variety of mass-media tasks, some of the researcher's strategy is taken up with asking who should be interviewed and what should be asked. The very process of the search strategy presented in this chapter develops a roster of potential interviewees and an agenda of questions to present to them.

SEARCH-STRATEGY MODELS: SIMPLE AND EXPANDED

Figure 1.1 presents the simple search-strategy model for mass communicators. The model identifies a number of major steps in the mass-communication search process. The steps are linked by lines and arrows that indicate the paths between the steps. That is to say, the interview step follows the search that begins in the three major sources of information. But as the two-way arrows illustrate, the search may include some backtracking in the course of verifying information or raising additional questions.

Information seekers may use the simple model as a map into the various repositories of information that provide the background for a news story, an advertisement, or a public-relations release. Or, they may use it as a strategy for moving through the various steps in the search process—from defining the question, through gathering information, to evaluating the material the

FIGURE 1.1 Simple search-strategy model

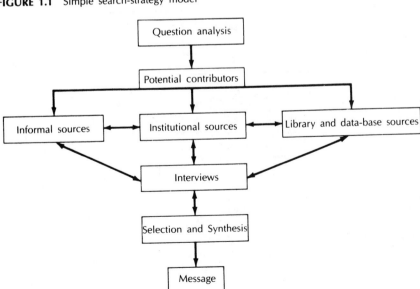

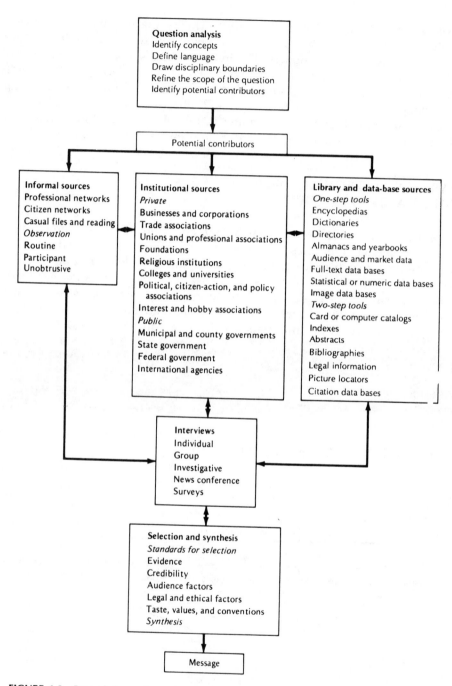

Question analysis
Identify concepts
Define language
Draw disciplinary boundaries
Refine the scope of the question
Identify potential contributors

Potential contributors

Informal sources
Professional networks
Citizen networks
Casual files and reading
Observation
Routine
Participant
Unobtrusive

Institutional sources
Private
Businesses and corporations
Trade associations
Unions and professional associations
Foundations
Religious institutions
Colleges and universities
Political, citizen-action, and policy
    associations
Interest and hobby associations
Public
Municipal and county governments
State government
Federal government
International agencies

Library and data-base sources
One-step tools
Encyclopedias
Dictionaries
Directories
Almanacs and yearbooks
Audience and market data
Full-text data bases
Statistical or numeric data bases
Image data bases
Two-step tools
Card or computer catalogs
Indexes
Abstracts
Bibliographies
Legal information
Picture locators
Citation data bases

Interviews
Individual
Group
Investigative
News conference
Surveys

Selection and synthesis
Standards for selection
Evidence
Credibility
Audience factors
Legal and ethical factors
Taste, values, and conventions
Synthesis

Message

FIGURE 1.2 Expanded search-strategy model

search process has uncovered. As a graphic representation of both the steps to take and the sources of information to refer to, the model serves as an outline of the entire information-gathering process for the communicator. The expanded search-strategy model shown in Figure 1.2 fills in some of the detail not included in the simple model.

Question Analysis

The detailed search-strategy model begins with question analysis and identifies the components of this preliminary step. Question analysis refers to the communicator's approach to narrowing and defining the information need. It is at this point that decisions are made about the scope and focus of the topic. The communicator tries to identify the scope of the problem to be investigated, the appropriate language of the topic, the disciplinary overlap that may give some clues to the rest of the search, and the appropriate strategy to use in gathering information for the message.

Inexperienced information seekers often begin a search for information with a topic or question that is much too broad and undefined. The advertising specialist does not have to know how computers are built in order to write an ad for a personal computer. However, background information about trends in the personal-computer market, data on who buys personal computers, examples of other computer ads, and ideas about where ads may be placed are necessary pieces of the information pie. Similarly, a reporter does not have to find information about how to build a house in order to write a series of stories about housing codes. But solid background information about housing laws, code violators and the types of problems they cause, and the kinds of actions being taken to ensure safe housing are appropriate topics for the information search. Once the communicator has selected a manageable portion of the field to investigate, the potential contributors to the information search can be identified. (Question analysis will be discussed in more detail in Chapter 2.)

Contributors of Information. The search-strategy model proposes three categories of information that can contribute to a mass-communication message: informal sources, institutional sources, and library and data-base sources. It is important to note that the communicator may begin searching for information from any one of these three sources or may investigate two or three types simultaneously. Each category includes a rich variety of sources, perspectives, and further clues in the search. There are distinct and inherent biases in the information that is located by means of each of the three categories, however.

Informal Sources. Informal sources include the communicator's supervisors, colleagues, clients, neighbors, friends, and observations of the world. For the production of messages, much of the needed information will come from the discussions that take place between the communicator and the assignment

Patient May Find His Doctor Taxing as States Seek Revenue

By HELAINE OLEN
SPECIAL TO THE TIMES

WASHINGTON—The states, desperate to ease their mounting fiscal crises, are once again eyeing a seemingly boundless source of additional revenues—imposing taxes not just on the sale of goods but also of services, which now are exempt from most state sales taxes.

And, despite powerful opposition, the move toward taxing services may become an unavoidable trend for a more basic reason: It permits state tax systems to adapt to the fundamental shift in the U.S. economy from manufacturing to services.

Levies on services could affect everything from plumbing repairs to haircuts, from physicians' fees to advertising and interior decorators' bills. They could also net the states hundreds of billions in revenues, depending on which items were taxed.

In the near term, states are likely to move cautiously. Any new tax imposes pain on voters and makes unwelcome changes in the shape of the economic playing field.

All-out lobbying efforts—especially by small businesses and advocates of rapid growth—already have defeated or, in some cases, reversed state taxes on services.

In the longer term, however, many tax specialists believe taxing a wide range of services is inevitable.

"A substantially larger portion of the economic activity each year is taking the form of services," said Hal Hovey, editor of State Budget and Tax News. "Without taxing those, you are hitching your economy to a falling star."

The push toward taxing services already is under way. Although only three states—New Mexico, South Dakota and Hawaii—levy sales taxes on a broad array of services, almost all states have some form of service taxes, mostly on hotel and motel lodging.

And Corena Eckl, a tax policy specialist with the National Conference of State Legislatures, said that, in their current sessions, at least eight legislatures have considered bills to expand their states' sales taxes to cover services. (California was among them, but for now has set the idea aside.)

The path so far has been bumpy.

In one classic turnabout, Florida imposed taxes on a broad array of services—including advertising—in 1987, but was forced to repeal the measure the very next year after the service industries began a massive lobbying campaign that wreaked havoc in the Legislature.

And a services tax on everything from architects to entertainment, adopted in Massachusetts last year, remained in effect for only 48 hours before being repealed. Opponents, including the governor, said the paperwork associated with the tax imposed too big a burden on business.

Opponents of the taxes argue that they make the cost of buying services so high that some firms might begin to turn to in-house staff instead of contracting for services outside—or they might even leave for a state that does not tax services.

They contend also that the impact of any tax on services will fall harder on small businesses than large ones. Without support staffs of their own, smaller firms must rely more on buying services from other companies.

"Everyone who tries it is sorry because it either drives business away or down," Daniel Jaffe, executive vice president of the Assn. of National Advertisers, said about imposing services taxes.

But some states are experiencing success by extending the tax to only a few services at a time.

New York, for example, last year began taxing cleaning and security services, adding to previously existing taxes on auto repairs and appliance installation. But lawmakers scrapped proposals to tax public relations and management consulting services—in the face of heavy lobbying.

Laird Graeser, a New Mexico state tax revenue expert, believes that the gradual approach offers the best hope for success. "When you get too many groups screaming at the Legislature and governor . . . they lose their will to do it," Graeser says.

But Marcia Howard, deputy director of the National Assn. of State Budget Officers, contends that, no matter what the setbacks in the short-run, a tax on services is inevitable. "The states are in such deep trouble," Howard said.

FIGURE 1.3 News story uses many background facts and refers to three associations and numerous state tax and legislative activities (institutional sources) and five interview sources, including one from a specialist publication (library source).

SOURCE: Reprinted by permission of the Los Angeles Times, © 1991.

10

editor, the account supervisor, or associates in the work room. People frequently talk about new projects with co-workers and get examples or ideas that are stimulating and lead to additional questions or topics that may be pursued. In a news office, the assignment editor may have some initial reports of an important event or activity and may share with the reporter whatever is known to that point. Among advertising and public-relations professionals, a good deal of initial information comes from discussions with the client or department requesting the ad or public-relations release. The important decisions about the kind of message needed, the points to be made, and the qualities of the product or service to be emphasized may come from the clients.

Informal discussions with neighbors, friends, or interesting people also are part of the search strategy. Media professionals are known for cultivating friendships with interesting and unusual people. Many of the creative and innovative ideas for messages spring from such sources. At the beginning stages of an information search, the informal interviews with colleagues and friends can lead the communicator to a wide variety of more formal and recognized sources of information.

The communicator's personal library or casual reading also can provide background that can be drawn on in the informal stage of the search process. Observations of the places in which and formats through which people express themselves also are useful. For example, noting the bus stop conversations, bumper stickers, T-shirt messages, billboard copy, and other informal messages that pervade every community can trigger ideas and perspectives for the more formal part of the information search. The files of clippings and tear sheets available in the library of any news, advertising, or public-relations office also constitute some of the informal sources that can help the communicator get a better idea of how a topic or message has been handled before.

Despite the advantages of informal sources, some hazards must be acknowledged. Even at their best, informal sources are likely to be impressionistic and fragmentary, and they may be inaccurate and self-serving. For example, earlier news stories found in clip files may contain errors of fact or interpretation, as well as material that originally was correct but has become outdated. Colleagues and acquaintances often provide information that is incomplete or one-sided. These informal sources are best used as stimulators—the first words on the subject rather than the last words. (Informal sources are discussed in more detail in Chapter 3).

Institutional Sources. The second major category of information sources is institutions, which produce a huge variety and amount of information essential to the functioning of society. Institutions range in size and importance from the neighborhood block association to the United Nations. They collect, organize, and generate information for a number of purposes: to ensure the survival and well-being of the institution, promote the institution's point of view, gain public acceptance or understanding, raise money and enroll new members, communicate information to members in order to maintain solidarity within the group, communicate to the community at large, and keep in touch with people and other institutions with similar interests. Much of the information developed to serve these purposes also is significant for mass communicators' purposes. For example, the United Way, a leading charity in most American communities, generates information for all these purposes. Communicators who work on advertising and public-relations campaigns for United Way can make use of information assembled by the local and national organizations to help them with their work in promoting the campaigns. News reporters also make use of information gathered by this institution as they write stories on its goals, its fund raising, and the manner in which it gives and monitors grants.

There are two major kinds of institutional sources: private and public. Private sources include businesses and corporations, trade associations, unions and professional associations, foundations, religious institutions, colleges and universities, citizen-action groups, and hobby associations. Examples of information from the private sector range from annual reports, house organs, trade publications, and newsletters to research reports and market and opinion studies. Results of industry research sometimes are released in the form of special reports to the public, while other portions are retained as trade secrets.

Governments at all levels constitute the public sources. Examples of information from governments are marriage licenses, birth and death certificates, public health records, arrest and conviction records, and similar information originating in counties and townships across the country. Documents generated at the local, state, and federal levels also include the reports of all activities, hearings, legislative acts, and statistical information gathering that are associated with legislative bodies. Census and demographic information collected as part of governmental data gathering also is included. In addition, reports of recommendations of zoning boards, pollution control agencies, and similar regulatory bodies are governmental information sources.

Just as with informal sources, the communicator must be aware of the biases and structure of information generated by institutions. Reflecting again on the purposes of institutions helps us to recognize their biases. Information is developed that will support and enhance the institution. Organizations as different from each other as the U.S. Department of Defense and the Women's International League for Peace and Freedom share this characteristic.

Organizations also disclose information selectively. Some material may reach the eyes and ears of only the inner circle of leaders. Other information may circulate to members generally but not to outsiders. And some information may become part of a publicity campaign designed to influence attitudes and opinions of the public.

Communicators get information from institutions directly or through various indexing tools. For example, a medical researcher who presented a paper on new treatments for diabetes might be located either through the research institution where the work was done or through a print or computer reference source such as *Index Medicus* (Institutional sources are discussed in more detail in Chapter 4).

Library and Data-Base Sources. Library and data-base sources of information constitute the third major category of information for communicators. Libraries and the new technology of electronic data bases are storehouses of recorded knowledge. The information in these repositories is collected, organized, and made accessible for a great variety of purposes and in a great variety of ways. Just as communicators, in the question-analysis step, must define the problems and identify the disciplines involved, they must employ decoding skills to unlock the rich collections of information in libraries and data bases. One important decoding trick involves understanding that not all libraries and data bases are the same. Finding the *right* library or data base for a particular information need is an important first step in approaching these sources. The type of information collected in a public library is very different from the type of information collected in a university law library. An archive has a vastly different type of collection than does a government documents library. A popular-magazine data base will yield information different from that provided by a data base of audience and demographic statistics.

The model identifies two types of sources available from library and data bases: one-step tools and two-step tools. The one-step tools contain the information itself, and the searcher is able to quickly locate the material needed by referring to these sources. The model identifies such familiar library resources as encyclopedias, dictionaries, directories, and almanacs and yearbooks in this category. Encyclopedia articles are very useful for a solid overview of an unfamiliar topic. Information on major events, people, and phenomena can be located quickly by referring to encyclopedias. Dictionaries can help with the decoding process mentioned earlier in the chapter by defining new language or jargon for the communicator. Directories are perhaps the most widely used one-step tools because they include addresses, telephone numbers, and information on memberships, publications, and many other vital data about people, organizations, or institutions. Almanacs and yearbooks are one-volume compendia of information, facts, figures, events, and activities covering a single year. They are especially useful when information has to be found quickly.

Less familiar, but equally important as one-step tools, are the library sources that provide audience and market data. In these sources, the searcher can locate such things as the age and media preferences of people who purchase 35 mm cameras, the number of people who read a particular magazine or watch a particular television program, and the characteristics of a community or market for products and messages. Another one-step tool is full-text data bases, which are electronic files that contain the complete text of every article in the newspapers, magazines, or journals included in the data base. The communicator can get a complete copy of every article about acid rain that appeared in the *New York Times*, for instance, by tapping into a full-text data base. Numeric and statistical data bases also are included in this category. They provide audience and market data, demographic information, and a variety of other statistical information in electronic form. Image data bases, another of the one-step tools, allow the communicator to search for and retrieve maps, meteorological data, photographs, animated images, charts, reproductions of documents and other visual materials that can be used in messages.

The two-step tools do not contain background material, facts, and figures but list the sources that do—hence the designation *two-step*. Indexes and abstracts are among the most important two-step tools. An index lists the magazines, newspapers, and books in which articles or information on various topics have appeared, giving the title of the publication, the title of the article, the name of the author or authors, the date, and the page numbers. Indexes may be arranged by subject and may list articles in popular magazines, scholarly journals, and newspapers; plays or short stories in collections; essays in magazines; or even pictures in books. Abstracts list the same information as indexes and include a short summary of the article or book. An abstract can be a timesaver for communicators because the summary may give enough information to alert the communicator that it is not worth the time to track down the actual article or book.

Card or computer catalogs, bibliographies, and publications like *Books in Print* are also two-step tools. The card or computer catalog in a library is the key to all the books, journals, records, and audiovisual materials in the library. Bibliographies deal with specific topics and provide citations to books, magazine and journal articles, dissertations, and other kinds of printed or audiovisual sources. For instance, a bibliography on city parks may include citations of government documents, books on the development of parks, articles in city-planning magazines, and surveys done by city managers of the public's use of parks. *Books in Print*, a major two-step tool, is a set of reference books that gives information about what is currently in print and for sale. Issued annually, it includes author, title, and subject volumes. By using the *Subject Guide to Books in Print*, a communicator could learn, for instance, the titles, publishers, and prices of all books still in print on the topic of acid rain.

Legal information is another category of two-step tools. Many legal periodicals are indexed by special tools, and legal cases and court decisions are located through an elaborate system of library reporting or digest services. Some of these services may be available only through a law library or a legal office.

Mass communicators often need access to visual materials. Libraries have a variety of two-step tools that help locate the whereabouts of pictures, photographs, collections of visual materials, and even sources of free stock photography.

Citation data bases are other types of two-step tools. Unlike full-text data bases, citation data bases do not contain the complete text of every article in the newspapers, magazines, or journals included in the data bases. Instead, they give the title of the publication, the title of the article, the name of the author or authors, the date, the page numbers, and, in some cases, a short summary of the article.

These one- and two-step tools make up the bulk of information available in libraries and data bases. The communicator must choose from an overwhelming amount of information on any conceivable topic in the many kinds of libraries and data bases in our information society. However, effectively mining library and data-base sources requires considerable skill. The decoding process becomes crucial as the communicator approaches the unfamiliar organizational and labeling schemes used by the organizers of these sources. (Library and data-base sources are discussed in more detail in Chapters 5 and 6).

Interviews. Communicators in the early stages of their research may pursue any or all of the informal, institutional, and library and data-base sources as starting points. Moving from one source to another, the communicator might consult a special dictionary to check the definition of an unfamiliar term, ask colleagues a few questions about their knowledge of the subject, consult a legal document, and look up demographic data. In mass communication, however, most paths lead sooner or later to interviews.

Interviews are basic sources of information for mass communicators because they help to meet the requirements of mass communication for timeliness, human interest, authority, and localism. For example, a communicator might read a researcher's paper on new treatments for diabetes. But an interview with that researcher also would be desirable, since it would give the communicator an opportunity to ask if even more recent results of research are available. The interview might provide human-interest material as well. Further, the interviewer could elicit an explanation of new findings about diabetes in the researcher's own words and could ask for clarifications if they were needed for the lay audience. If the communicator's earlier research had uncovered conflicting information, he or she could seek an explanation for the discrepancies.

The greatest error that communicators make in conducting interviews is to do so without sufficiently preparing for them. Indeed, in journalistic interviewing, failure to prepare and to ask the important questions is overwhelmingly cited as the reason for errors in news stories. For the most part, this is understandable. Talking to people is a quick and pleasant method of getting information. Unfortunately, misunderstanding the answers and inaccurately reporting them are not pleasant consequences for the communicator. Preparation is imperative, and the position of the interview step in the search-strategy model reflects the fact that preparation must precede the interview.

Various types of interviews are common in mass communication: individual, group, investigative, news-conference, and survey interviews. The individual interview takes place with one interviewer and one interviewee. It is the most wide-ranging in its possibilities. It applies in advertising, public

REDUCE YOUR CHANCES OF GETTING HEART DISEASE, KIDNEY DISEASE OR GOING BLIND.

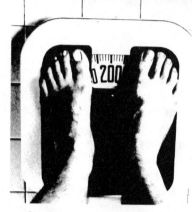
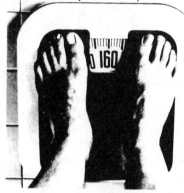

Obesity can start a chain reaction to poor health that can be devastating.

To begin with, most physicians and researchers consider obesity to be the major cause of diabetes in adults. Up to 90% of adults diagnosed as having diabetes, in fact, are overweight.

Of course, once you have diabetes your chances of developing heart disease, kidney disease, or going blind increase dramatically.

As a person with diabetes you'll be twice as prone to heart disease. 17 times as prone to kidney disease. And 25 times as prone to blindness, if you are insulin-dependent.

Diabetes, in fact, can shorten your life expectancy by one-third.

Fortunately, diabetes in adults, in most cases, can be prevented with careful weight control, healthy eating habits, and regular exercise.

So if you're overweight, doesn't it make sense to take off the extra weight?

Instead of years off your life?

FIGHT SOME OF THE WORST DISEASES OF OUR TIME.
Support the American Diabetes Association.

FIGURE 1.4 Advertising copy is rich in specific facts and ideas. As this example illustrates, the factual base of a successful ad rests on varied sources. A rich factual base allows the advertising specialist to tell a story with effective dramatic touches. Unlike news stories, most ad copy does not attribute factual matter to the original sources. But the contribution of library sources to this ad is clear.

SOURCE: Reprinted by permission of the American Diabetes Association.

relations, and news work. In advertising, the client may be interviewed about the product or service to be advertised. In public relations, department heads may be interviewed about their plans to present a new service to the public. In news, the county attorney may be interviewed about a new strategy for prosecuting forgers.

Group interviews usually take place with one interviewer and a number of participants. An example is the focus-group interview, in which the interviewer takes advantage of the participants' interest in a topic and encourages them to respond freely to one another's statements about the subject. For example, grade-school children might be assembled to sample new snacks and to state their preferences and the reasons for them. Or, the marketing department of a newspaper might assemble community leaders in a series of focus groups, asking what qualities make a great newspaper. Some focus-group interviews are followed by studies, such as survey research, in which the ideas brought up in the group interviews are subjected to additional analysis for verification. Such polls and surveys may be conducted by media organizations on their own behalf or may be commissioned, using firms that specialize in the scientific study of opinions and attitudes. (Polls and surveys are discussed in more detail in Chapter 8.)

News conferences are familiar forms of interviews. The most familiar, of course, is the presidential press conference televised by the major networks. Most news conferences, however, bear little resemblance to presidential news conferences. More typical news conferences involve a handful of journalists and public-relations specialists gathered in a small room. Often a prepared news release is available with routine and basic information set down for journalists by the public-relations staff. Journalists ask questions in a calm, orderly way. Inexperienced journalists have to prepare for their first news conferences, but usually need not fear going into an atmosphere like that of the televised presidential news conference. (Interviewing is discussed in more detail in Chapter 7.)

Selection and Synthesis.   Perhaps the most complex task for the mass communicator is the selection and synthesis of all the material gathered. At this point in the search-strategy process, all facts, ideas, and perspectives come together in the mind of the communicator. What follows is the direct link between the search strategy of the information gatherer and the expressive act of the writer.

In analyzing the material gathered, the communicator begins to shift mental gears and takes on a more critical perspective. Now it is important to eliminate any erroneous material, to update whatever facts are not current, to identify differences in viewpoints, and to put into context information that reflects special interests. For example, if the subject is adult illiteracy, the communicator will review all material for accuracy, recognizing that some statistics may reflect the bias of an organization trying to attract potential donors to its campaign against illiteracy by presenting alarming statistics about its prevalence in the population. If the statistics on adult illiteracy are not consistent, the communicator will go to additional sources, perhaps retracing earlier steps taken in the search strategy, in pursuit of more reputable materials. The communicator also will consider the reputation of the sources—whether they are popular or scholarly, for example. Popular sources, such as newspapers and weekly magazines, are considered less reliable than scholarly sources, which are published in less haste and with more reviewing and editing of content than is the custom with popular materials. All the considerations of bias that were mentioned in connection with informal sources, institutional sources, and library and data-base sources again become part of the picture when the communicator evaluates the materials collected and selects from among them.

The traditional tests of evidence are useful measures for communicators engaged in selection and synthesis:

1. Clarity: Does the material have one unmistakable meaning?
2. Verifiability: Can the information be verified?
3. Accuracy: Has the correctness of the information been established?
4. Recency: Is the information the most recent available?
5. Relevance: Is the information relevant to the subject?
6. Reputation: What is the reputation of the information or those who have provided it?
7. Sufficiency: Is there enough information for each main point?
8. Internal consistency: Is the information consistent with itself, or are there internal contradictions?
9. External consistency: Are the pieces of information consistent with one another, or does some information contradict other information?
10. Comparative quality: How do the pieces of information compare in quality? Is some material clearly inferior to other material?
11. Context: Has the information been placed within the true context?
12. Statistical validity: Does the information meet tests of statistical validity?

The 12 points can be considered an automatic checklist that communicators can adopt at this point in their work. With each red flag that goes up in the communicator's mind during this checkup procedure, the communicator can return to a tool or resource suggested by the model. (Appraisal of information is discussed in more detail in Chapter 9.)

When the information is as solid and reliable as possible in the time available, the communicator has successfully resolved doubts and filled gaps. The message can be produced and distributed. The responses to the message—from editors and from the public—will give additional insight about the quality and comprehensiveness of the communicator's information-gathering skill.

Within the limits of mass communication, bearing in mind the time and space constraints in the field, the communicator strives for a message that gets and keeps attention, tells a story well, and presents accurate information to the audience. The search strategy presented here in overview helps the communicator produce the message as effectively and accurately as possible. With practice, the communicator can follow the process and learn to make it a routine that becomes automatic.

LITERARY CONVENTIONS: STORY-TELLING AND THE MEDIA

The long literary traditions of the human race influence ideas about what a message must—or must not—be. Information, then, is collected with an often unconscious understanding of these literary traditions, which require that communicators signal to an audience whether the material is to be taken as fact or as fiction. The rules for telling the literal truth are suspended in fictional messages but must be adhered to in factual messages.

Literary traditions for both fact and fiction have common underlying elements. While the news story traditionally includes only verified facts, it presents those facts in "story" format, as the term suggests. The story elements—character, setting, motive, suspense, conflict, and resolution—are dramatic staples that give life, color, and movement to the message. They are found in newspaper stories, television commercials, broadcast news, and events staged for advertising and public-relations purposes.

Reuven Frank, while an executive producer of NBC-TV news, explained the story and dramatic requirements to his staff, using slightly different terminology.

> Every news story should, without any sacrifice of probity or responsibility, display the attributes of fiction, of drama. It should have structure and conflict, problem and denouement, rising action and falling action, a beginning, a middle and an end. These are not only the essentials of drama; they are the essentials of narrative.[8]

Sociologist Gaye Tuchman stresses that factual and fictional stories have much in common.

> To say that a news report is a story, no more, but no less, is not to demean news, nor to accuse it of being fictitious. Rather, it alerts us that news, like all public documents, is a constructed reality possessing its own internal validity. A selective reality, rather than a synthetic reality as in literature, news reports exist in and of themselves. They are public documents that lay a world before us.[9]

Advertising, as well as news reporting, relies on story-telling elements. For their preliminary presentation of an ad, advertising specialists prepare what they call a *story board*, in which all the major dramatic, visual, and audio components of the ad are laid out in cartoon form. Martin Esslin identifies the television commercial as a dramatic form possessing all the important qualities of classical drama.

> I think it can be shown that most, if not all, TV commercials are essentially dramatic, because basically they use mimetic action to produce a semblance of real life, and the basic ingredients of drama—character and story line—are present in the great majority of them, either manifestly or by implication.[10]

Communicators consider story-telling traditions when they collect material for their messages. The verbal, visual, and audio cues that are part of the traditional codes are embodied in communicators' links to their audiences and in the shaping of story elements. The search strategy helps communicators identify information that contributes to the story-telling aspect of news, advertising, and public relations.

CONSTRAINTS ON COMMUNICATORS

Legal and Social Constraints

Communicators are constantly aware of the legal and social context in which messages are received. Thus they recognize the need to adhere to legal requirements concerning privacy and libel, regulatory constraints, and verifiability. Regulations for some commercial messages may require the communicator to have full and verifiable information on hand before the message is delivered. The advertising substantiation rule, for instance, requires an advertiser to substantiate or to have evidence to substantiate any claim that an ad makes about a product or service.

Warner-Lambert, the company that produces Listerine, claimed in its advertising that by using its mouthwash, people could reduce the number and severity of colds they caught. Challenged by the Federal Trade Commission (FTC) to prove its claim, the company failed to produce adequate evidence. The FTC required Warner-Lambert to run a corrective advertising campaign in which it retracted the claim.[11]

An advertising campaign that withstood the challenge of substantiating its claims involved the celebrated "burger wars." Burger King, in its television commercials, claimed that its hamburgers were 20 percent larger than those of McDonald's and that people preferred Burger King burgers over McDonald's and Wendy's by three to one. McDonald's and Wendy's filed suit, demanding that Burger King substantiate its claims. Burger King was able to produce evidence, in the form of a customer survey, that the court found acceptable. Because Burger King met the requirements for substantiation, the firm saved the cost and embarrassment of running a corrective ad campaign.[12]

News reporters take into consideration libel laws and rights to privacy as they collect information for use in their stories. Any information about a private citizen or a public official must meet specific standards of accuracy and public interest before being used in a news story. Since there is no prior restraint on publication in the United States, communicators run the risk of publishing material that might defame people. Even a libel suit that is successfully defended is very costly to a media organization.

Ethical constraints also enter the picture for information gatherers. Some information may be regarded as useful, even essential, for a communicator but may not be obtainable by ethical means. Misrepresenting one's identity or purpose in order to gain information, rifling through files in an unattended office, or eavesdropping on private conversations are considered unethical means of gathering information. Other material may be obtainable through legal and ethical means, but the use of that material in a message would violate ethical standards. Revealing information from the proceedings of juvenile courts, publishing the names of rape victims, and printing charges about a political candidate on election eve usually fall into this category. When ethical constraints prevail, locating alternative material that can be used without violation of ethical standards is the communicator's information-finding challenge.

Accuracy is a major concern for communicators. When searching for information—whether for an ad, a public-relations release, or a news story—the communicator has a greatly enlarged universe in which to search. Care must be taken that the information selected is the most accurate available. The old custom of attributing all the information included in the message as a way of escaping responsibility for its accuracy grows less acceptable in an age when fact checking is fast and simple.

The way mass communicators do their work also is recognized as a concern of society as a whole. Communicators are among the significant information brokers of society. They process ideas, facts, and fantasies into media messages. They hold great power as directors of the public's attention in some directions instead of others. They provide the public with some scenes and plots rather than with others and shine a spotlight on some facts, while leaving others in the dark. The more adept the communicator is in using information sources with skill and responsibility, the better the public will be served. Many complaints about media performance in our society claim that the information used is flawed by bias, incompleteness, or inaccuracy. As interpreters for society, communicators have an obligation to use the best information available.

Using long-standing, literary and social conventions, communicators are among the constructors of a culture's social realities. That is, they help to designate what is ordinary and what is extraordinary. They impute significance to facts, values, policies, and events. Because mass communication affects the view of the world that people perceive as real, communicators bear a heavy responsibility. Chapter 10 provides additional discussion.

Time and Resource Constraints

As the sources and types of information expand, communicators face issues of time and resource management. The communicator cannot explore all information available for every message on every occasion. Constraints of deadlines and of costs involved in collecting some information force the communicator to make choices about when it is appropriate to use particular sources. The longer, interpretive news story should be based on many information sources. It stands in contrast to the story about a fire that starts nearby an hour before deadline. The advertising campaign that will run over many months and include ads in several media also is likely to rest on a large information base. But one ad placed in the newspaper by a local shoe store does not benefit from such an extensive information search. The media organization must make choices about the management of both time and money involved in the use of sources.

Some information can be obtained only at great expense, and media organizations may not provide their staffs with the financial support needed to acquire high quality information. Other information can be obtained at little cost by those who are skilled at using available resources. In most mass-media organizations, time and money are regarded as the major constraints on the quality of work. Time factors in broadcast news, for example, may be the major information constraint. In newspaper news, the costs of paying a highly trained staff and of maintaining a library with interactive data-base services may be considered to be the major constraint. Whatever their settings, communicators are coming to view the efficient information search as an essential component in the production of a mass-communication story that meets the audience's expectation of interesting story-telling and the organization's requirement for economy in producing a message. Media organizations analyze how their staff members use time and money to produce the messages that they distribute.

INFORMATION NEEDS OF THE AUDIENCE

Communicators have the responsibility and, with the new technologies, the resources to anticipate the breadth and depth of the information that is appropriate for their audiences. Audiences vary considerably in the depth of their information needs and in their appetites for various amounts of information. For instance, news releases about a new medical product, the insulin pump, will differ from one another depending on the audience. For a daily newspaper, the material must be nontechnical, easily understood by the general public, and geared to questions that potential users of the insulin pump might have. A news release for an endocrinology journal, however, should contain material directed to physicians that meets their need for technical, detailed background on the pump.

Some members of the mass communicators' audience have high levels of education and substantial amounts of professional or technical experience, but this audience also includes a substantial number of poorly educated, information-deprived people whose needs must be kept in mind in the writing of advertisements, news stories, and public-relations releases. While a small minority of Americans may use electronic-data-base searching as a way to get the information they want, most people probably spend their television time as viewers seeking news, entertainment, and escape. To meet their information needs as citizens, consumers, and neighbors, the vast majority will continue to rely on mass communicators as their information providers and story-tellers.

THE SEARCH-STRATEGY MODEL IN A MASS-COMMUNICATION CONTEXT

The mass communicator's world is more complex today than in earlier times for three principal reasons. First, the explosion of information has dramatically increased the potential information base for mass-media messages: enormous amounts of information are created daily. Second, communicators now recognize the necessity of selecting appropriate information from the widest possible range of sources. Third, information is now stored in many new formats, such as data bases and compact discs, as well as in traditional paper documents. These complexities have created a need for communicators to develop information skills greater than those of their predecessors.

The search-strategy method is designed to help communicators meet the constraints and requirements of this new, more complex world. As in the past, communicators today compete to capture audience attention, to interpret the world for their readers and listeners, and to present stories that inform, entertain, and persuade. In this competition, the search-strategy method will help communicators meet standards of accuracy, completeness, relevance, and responsibility as they shape their messages. Communicators can use the search-strategy method when they have a tough information problem and don't know where to turn.

Search strategy is not a magic method to cure all the ills of which mass communicators have been accused. It treats the information component of mass-media messages, recognizing that responsibility for the expressive component is equally significant. Search strategy can help communicators be responsible professionals, but it must be employed by those who have the motivation to be responsible. Search strategy can help communicators to work rapidly and efficiently, but the rapidity with which information can be collected should not be an excuse to take shabby shortcuts. To the contrary, the very abundance of information requires that communicators exercise discretion and judgment in gathering information for their messages. Some information tasks become quicker and easier in the new information age. Some become more challenging. The search-strategy model for locating and evaluating information is designed to assist communicators in meeting the growing demands they face. It is a conceptual tool to be carried in their heads to all information-gathering tasks.

One of the most challenging of these information tasks is raising appropriate and original questions to be addressed in the search strategy. Chapter 2 examines the process of question analysis through which a communicator begins defining the information needs intrinsic to a message.

NOTES

1. Jesse Shera, "Automation and the Reference Librarian," *RQ* 3 (July 1964): 3–7; Norman J. Crum, "The Librarian–Customer Relationship: Dynamics of Filling Requests for Information," *Special Libraries* 60 (May–June 1969): 269–277; Charles A. Bunge, "Reference Service in the Information Network" (Paper delivered at the Interlibrary Communication and Information Networks Conference, 1970), 8.
2. K.W. Deutsch, "Some Notes on Research on the Role of Models in the Natural and Social Sciences," *Synthese* 7 (1948–1949): 506–533; A. Rosenblueth and N. Wiener, "The Role of Models in Science," *Philosophy of Science* 12 (1945): 316–321; Roy Lackman, "The Model in Theory Construction," *Psychological Review* 67, (1960): 113–129; F. C. Johnson and G. R. Klare, "General Models of Communication Research: A Survey of a Decade," *Journal of Communication* 11 (1961): 13–26.
3. Alphonse Chapanis, "Men, Machines, and Models," *American Psychologist* 16 (1961): 113–131.
4. See, for example, C. David Mortensen, *Communication: The Study of Human Interaction* (New York: McGraw-Hill, 1972); Stewart Tubbs and Sylvia Moss, *Human Communication* (New York: Random House, 1977).
5. Denis McQuail and Sven Windahl, *Communication Models for the Study of Mass Communications* (New York: Longman, 1981).
6. Shera, "Automation"; Crum "Librarian Customer–Relationship"; and Bunge "Reference Service."
7. For example, Rao Aluri and Mary Reichel, *Information Literacy: Critical Skills for a Changing World* (Chicago: ALA, 1990); Patricia Senn Breivik, "Literacy in an Information Society," in *The White House Conference on Library and Information Services, July 9–13, 1991, Discussion Papers* (Washington, D.C.: The White House Conference on Library and Information Services, 1991); Anita Kay Lowry, "Beyond BI: Information Literacy in the Electronic Age," *Research Strategies* (Winter 1991) 8: 22–27; Cerise Oberman and Katina Strauch, eds., *Theories of Bibliographic Education: Designs for Teaching* (New York: Bowker, 1982); Hannelore Rader, Billie Rienhart, and Gary Thompson, *Evaluating Information: A Basic Checklist* (Chicago: ALA, 1990).
8. Quoted in Edward J. Epstein, *News from Nowhere* (New York: Random House, 1973), 4–5.
9. Gaye Tuchman, "Telling Stories," *Journal of Communication* 26 (Autumn 1976): 97.
10. Martin Esslin, "Aristotle and the Advertisers: The Television Commercial Considered as a Form of Drama," in *Television: The Critical View*, 3d ed., ed. Horace Newcomb (New York: Oxford University Press, 1982), 261.
11. Warner-Lambert Co. v. FTC, 562 F.2d 749 (D.C. Cir. 1977); *cert. denied*, 435 U.S. 950 (1978).
12. Richard Kreisman and Christy Marshall, "Burger King's 'Challenge' Set for Heavy Drive," *Advertising Age*, 13 September 1982, 1, 74; "McDonald's Sues to Halt BK Effort," *Advertising Age*, 27 September 1982, 1, 80; Christy Marshall, "Burger King Thinks It's Found the Sizzle," *Advertising Age*, 27 September 1982, 4, 80.

2

What's the Question?

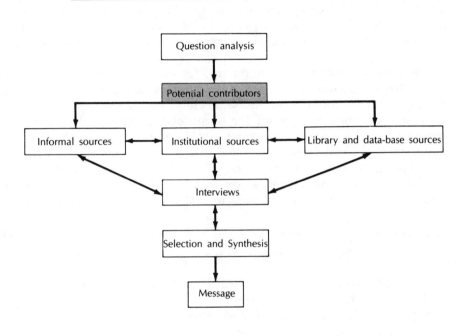

The network TV journalist began the program with his first question to the guest expert. The expert responded, "That's not the question. The question is . . . ," only to be cut off with a snarl from the interviewer, "I'm asking the questions here!" While such rude assertions of authority are rare in TV journalism, the exchange illustrates the idea that the nature of the question often is in dispute. Raising questions that are real and right frequently involves give and take among a number of interested parties, each of whom has a stake in how the question is presented. In the example of the journalist and the expert, the way the question is stated also may reflect discussions by the interviewer with the assignment editor and with a researcher who provided background material. In advertising, such an issue may arise when researchers seek evidence, such as statistics, that can be used to support claims to be made in an ad campaign. In academic settings, student researchers need to develop research questions that fit the focus of the course for which the paper is required. For example, for a course in economics of the broadcasting industry, appropriate questions might be: How has Congress regulated the amount of commercial time allowed on children's TV programs? How has the broadcast audience changed since the widespread use of cable? TV markets of what size are likely to invest in satellite news gathering equipment? How have requirements for public access changed since the early years of cable TV? Questions that do not fit a broadcast economics course include: Does MTV promote sexist attitudes? Do soap operas portray a realistic view of life? Does TV news contribute to street violence in metropolitan areas?

In question analysis, the communicator raises questions that will help to define the information needed. These questions help determine the scope of the topic and the focus of the message. How broadly the questions should be construed depends in part on the scope of the project. For example, if a reporter for a national news magazine and another reporter for a city newspaper each planned stories on Lyme disease, the national magazine would raise questions about the incidence of the tick-borne disease across the country, whereas the local newspaper reporter would concentrate on questions of concern to people in its circulation area. Both, however, would need similar

---

BOX 2.1   Question Analysis: Too Little, Too Late

REPORTER: I was just calling to see if you have done any research on the effects of the media on crime.

INTERVIEWEE: I haven't done that kind of research.

REPORTER: Well, do you know of anyone who has?

INTERVIEWEE: Yes, there is quite a lot of research on that theme. (She then goes ahead to summarize a variety of findings. The interviewer cuts her off.)

REPORTER: That's not what I'm looking for. What I want to know is if headlines in newspapers and, maybe also stories about crime tend to cause people to commit the crimes they read about.

INTERVIEWEE: I'm afraid I can't help you. Perhaps that is more of a criminology topic than a media topic.

What happened here? The reporter called a researcher who studies the mass media and society and asked about "media." But his question was much more narrow—he wanted to know about newspaper crime headlines and stories, not media generally. In addition, his interest was what motivates individuals who commit crimes, not in media–society relations, which is considered more broadly. Question analysis could have saved the reporter a time-consuming and useless call.

material on the symptoms, treatment, and prevalence of the disease. Box 2.1 shows another example of how question analysis can be useful. In an advertising example, the question may be how we can legally and ethically promote the use of a new drug available only by prescription. In community-action public relations, the question may be how our neighborhood can fight crime and drug dealing and communicate to potential home buyers that the neighborhood also has potential. For an application of question analysis to a job search see Box 2.2. The question-analysis stage, then, may occasion discussion and conflict as questions to be raised are negotiated. Carefully focused questions are an essential prelude to the communicators' subsequent information-finding actions.

For reasons of time saving and other economies, communicators often are advised to concentrate on the obvious and narrow questions, to avoid global questions. Undeniably, narrow questions save time. But some critics point out that questions drawn too narrowly may fail to raise important issues. For example, journalists trying to explain the Jonestown, Guyana, massacre, in which close to a thousand members of the colony died in a mass suicide, concentrated their questions on the character of the colony leader, Jim Jones. Having asked their question this way, reporters selected their sources narrowly, from among relatives and friends of victims and former members who were acquainted with Jones. A sociologist, John R. Hall, concluded that journalists had mistakenly narrowed their question to "How could a madman lure his victims to the jungle and brainwash them into committing suicide?" A better question, according to Hall, would have been, "What are all the possible reasons that could account for mass suicide

---

BOX 2.2   Question Analysis in the Job Search

Question analysis can be used in a variety of settings and for a variety of purposes separate from academic research and research for media messages. For example, a person seeking a professional position in the communication industries might use question analysis to locate all the material needed to decide whether to apply for or accept a position. Some relevant questions might be:

What can be learned about ownership? Is the organization nonprofit or for-profit? Is it a subsidiary or division of another organization? Where is the headquarters?

Who are the organization's leaders and what are their achievements?

What is the financial condition of the organization?

What is the organization's record as an employer? Have lawsuits been filed alleging discrimination? If so, how did the suits end?

What is the organization's reputation?

What is an accurate description of the corporate culture of the organization?

What salary, benefit, and professional training policies does the organization have?

by Jones and his followers?" By asking the broader question, Hall argued, journalists would have called upon sources with more varied expertise and backgrounds, including those knowledgeable of similar historical events.[1] Special circumstances might require even broader preparation. For example, free-lancer Richard O'Regan prepared to write stories from Africa for National Public Radio, *Mother Jones,* and the *Atlanta Journal* and *Constitution* by putting historical and statistical information on a computer disk. During his travels through a number of African countries, he carried the disk with his background information in his shirt pocket. Thus, he was prepared for producing a variety of stories without having to seek background material from one of his home-base organizations.[2]

Question analysis, an essential and critical early step, then, forms an intellectual foundation for the work that comes throughout later steps in the search strategy. And, as with other points in the strategy, communicators can return to the question-analysis step to reconsider their original question-analysis decisions.

HOW TO TALK ABOUT THE TOPIC

The language of a topic is the key that opens the door to discussion of most subjects. Early in their exploration of question analysis, communicators are likely to discover that the topic may have varied levels of terminology. For example, one student seeking examples of coverage of a religious service used the term *eucharist* for his search in a news data base. That was the term he took from a discussion with the participants at the service. However, he did not locate news stories on his subject, since the event could be found only under the more popular term *communion* in the newspaper data base. Language, then, is the access code through which all collections of information are indexed and organized. The communicator needs to recognize, however, that varied degrees of formality and technicality may affect access to material. In addition, terminology shifts over time as new words are added and as some language falls out of favor and is replaced. Language related to nations, landmarks, occupations, technology, ethnicity, race, gender, and sexual orientation has changed over time.

Political perspectives also play a role in decoding language. One researcher sought information about coverage of a territorial war between Great Britain and Argentina, using the term *Falklands Islands* in her search to refer to the disputed territory. She forgot that those islands are called the Malvinas by Argentines, and many items about the war were indexed under the Argentine term rather than the British one. Similarly, a body of water in the Middle East is called the Persian Gulf by some and the Arabian Gulf by others, depending on their political perspective.

Reference works are convenient early steps for learning the vocabulary of a field. Dictionaries, general and special encyclopedias, directories, and annual reviews often are used to get specific information on topics. For example, a student beginning research on a project about magazine audiences seeks a definition of *pass-along audience*. A specialized dictionary (*Dictionary of Advertising Terms*) provides a brief definition that can help the student researcher understand general material about the topic, as well as assist the student in narrowing the topic and framing research questions.

Language and definitions, then, are arbitrary and change over time. The specialists who organize repositories of information develop their own logic and translate the concepts of the topic into language that they believe is the best available for encoding and decoding the material to be stored. Language is the key to all the encoding and decoding that allows an information-retrieval system to work, whether the system is a conventional paper one or an electronic system. The communicator needs to learn the overall process of decoding the language of each topic, since it is language that unlocks all collections of information.

For example, the news reporter working on a story about health-care costs will encounter such terms as *HMO, fee for service, cost sharing, cost shifting, primary-care networks, third-party payers,* and *preferred provider organizations*. Similarly, communicators working on an advertising or a public-relations campaign for a health insurer or a hospital must have a grasp of the same terminology. The introduction of such terms into the health-care system reflects developments and issues in the field; doing an adequate job of selecting information in this field requires that the communicator understand the terminology and its significance.

Communicators might want to understand new terminology in terms of an *abstraction ladder*. S. I. Hayakawa describes the process of decoding the language of a topic as a trip up or down an abstraction ladder. Hayakawa uses the following example to explain how the abstraction ladder works. If we regard the word *Bessie* (the name of a particular cow) as occupying the lowest rung on the abstraction ladder, then the word *cow* is one rung higher; *livestock* is one step further up; *farm assets* is higher still; *assets* is yet more abstract; and *wealth* is as far from Bessie the cow as we might get.[3]

The conceptual skills required at this stage of the information search are crucial. The communicator must identify the words that are used to describe the topic and must understand the concepts to which those words refer. The communicator might draw on knowledge of the specific topic or of the entire field, discussions with the editor or account executive who assigned the task, or another way of clarifying the scope of the topic. As information searcher, the communicator must have a clear idea about exactly what is being sought and why. For instance, in order to write the story on rising health-care costs, the communicator must know about denial of health-care to poor people, the roles of insurers and big business in keeping costs down, the health-care professionals' role, and so forth. By first understanding the scope and range of the overall topic, then subsequently defining and limiting the topic, the communicator can save much time in the next stages of the information search.

DRAWING DISCIPLINARY BOUNDARIES

Another step in the question-analysis stage of the search strategy involves identifying the disciplines that contribute to the topic under examination. Most information is produced, collected, and arranged according to subject areas, or disciplines, which are knowledge-producing and -disseminating systems. Looking through a college course catalog gives clues to discipline structure. Such fields as political science, biology, history, and mathematics can be identified as unique disciplines with their own patterns of information development, arrangement, research, and dissemination.

Older, fully developed disciplines, such as literature and history, are based on accepted information that remains fairly stable, even though methods and interpretations change over time. New disciplines emerge from social, political, and technological developments. Women's studies grew out of a grass-roots movement to recognize the contributions and perspectives that women bring to society and the way that society is studied. Genetic engineering is a highly technical field with a rapidly changing core of information, made possible by new technologies and by substantial dedication of federal research money, as well as intellectual breakthroughs by scientists. The relative age of the discipline or disciplines that contribute to any topic affects the kinds of information available on the topic.

Over time, a definite pattern in the evolution of the disciplines becomes evident. Three stages of discipline development can be identified: the pioneering stage, the elaboration and proliferation stage, and the establishment stage.[4] The important developments that characterize the different stages are accompanied by specific types and modes of communication among members of the discipline. This, in turn, affects the kinds of information available to the communicator trying to formulate an accurate picture of the discipline.

In the *pioneering stage*, the discipline is coming into being. A group of significant thinkers or a maverick intellectual leader may be the driving force behind the development of original ideas, new insights, and important theories in a field of study. The struggle to attract attention and followers to the new discipline characterizes this stage of development. Practitioners develop terminology that allows them to talk about their world and begin to both dispute and agree upon appropriate language for their discussions. Much communication among the innovators is interpersonal, via correspondence, newsletters, and computer bulletin boards. The modes of communication among proponents of the new discipline and between them and the public are often informal and unstructured. In its pioneering stage, the discipline now called women's studies involved the development of theories concerning roles of women throughout history, in various cultures, in private and public life, and in the disciplines themselves.

The *elaboration and proliferation stage* is characterized by an increased number of followers, the formation of national and international associations concerned with the topics of the discipline, and a more formal mode of communication among proponents. At this point, newsletters become journals, and the caucus of an organization may develop into a division of that organization or into an entirely separate association. Journal articles and books proliferate, signaling some acceptance of language and perspectives among the innovators. Typically, as in the case of women's studies as a field, advocates work to establish academic departments, institutes, or centers in their colleges and universities. It is no longer possible for all the principal thinkers in the new discipline to personally know one another, as it was during the pioneering stage.

In the *establishment stage*, the discipline gains legitimacy by becoming part of the recognized academic establishment. University departments teach the principles and practices of the discipline; graduate training is introduced; research centers are established; and textbooks, reference books, and other printed sources become available. In fewer than 20 years, women's studies grew from a pioneering movement to an established academic field with its own academic departments, journals, abstracts, and jargon.

Since communicators work in a number of disciplines, they need to understand that each discipline is not in the same stage of development. Communicators are confronted continually with the task of producing messages on topics that cross the boundaries of disciplines and cover many aspects of any subject. Different kinds of information will be available, different information-finding tools will be used, and different types of experts or practitioners will be interviewed, depending on the stage of the discipline or disciplines that contribute to the topic.

The stage of evolution of the relevant disciplines is not the only important consideration, however. The distinctions among the sciences, the humanities, and the social sciences also are important. The clearest distinction is between the sciences and the humanities. These are the best-established disciplines with the longest traditions of information generation and organization. The scientist and the humanist use different sorts of research methods and study different phenomena. They publish their findings in forms that are characteristic of their disciplines and make these documents accessible through a variety of indexes, abstracts, and electronic files.

Scientists seek experimental validity by studying the natural world and examining the regularities or irregularities that seem to govern natural phenomena. Their methods must be open to scrutiny and, in the best of circumstances, must be reproducible by others following the same procedures. Experimental validity, rather than individual interpretation of events or phenomena, is paramount. Immediacy in sharing results is very important for professionals in the scientific fields, so scientists rely on the research report and journal article, both of which can succinctly describe work in progress, as their major vehicles of communication. Journal articles make up 80 percent of the research literature in the sciences, and scientific research is a cooperative venture, with coauthoring the primary form of authorship.

The humanist's method is shaped for interpretive validity; that is, the humanist tries to interpret a poem, a painting, a novel, or a musical score by presenting an interpretation that will be considered valid. Humanists study the products of human imagination and combine a personal, unique perception with the framework of accepted concepts and knowledge that their disciplines provide. Humanists rely on the book as the primary method of expressing their knowledge of a field because the book allows the in-depth exploration of context that characterizes humanistic investigation. One third to three-quarters of the literature in the humanities is in book form, and single authorship of books is most common.

Social and policy scientists rely on a combination of experimental and interpretive methods. They have adopted the scientific method for much of their work and exhibit the same concern for openness and validity exhibited by scientists. However, because the subject of much of their study is human social activity, social scientists work interpretively as well. For the most part, they are concerned with the present and with the implications of their work in social organizations and in public decision making. Social and policy scientists publish their findings in a number of forms. Quarterly journals, as in the sciences, are important. However, research reviews and yearbooks are prominent as a type of book material, along with books and monographs. Coauthoring is prevalent.

The distinctions among fields as disciplinary information-producing and -disseminating systems become imperative as the communicator is formulating the search strategy. If a topic is concerned primarily with an event or a subject in the sciences, it is necessary for the researcher to become familiar with the methods of locating journals and technical reports because the most recent and appropriate scientific findings are presented in them. But if a topic is concerned primarily with an event or a subject in the humanities, identifying the most recent books on the topic probably will lead the researcher to appropriate information.

In decoding information from the disciplines, researchers can rely on some basic rules about how information is produced, published, organized, and made accessible. The stages of information production correspond, in some ways, to the stages of discipline development. A *bibliographic chain* of events can be identified. The four links in the bibliographic chain correspond to the stages in the development of printed materials and substantive information among the knowledge generators. When a new idea or set of ideas is being introduced and worked on by a community of scholars, the link in the bibliographic chain is loose and informal. Scholars may talk to one another on the telephone, exchange letters, participate in an electronic bulletin board, review first drafts of one another's papers, share progress reports at conferences, and publish informal newsletters for an in-group of people working on the idea. This constitutes the "invisible college" of scholars and insiders who know one another's work. Libraries and data bases rarely penetrate into this invisible college. One special problem with information generated at this first link in the bibliographic chain is that it may contain gross errors, inconsistencies, and misinterpretation of data, since it represents the very first view of new research and new ideas. An example of this problem is the publicity about cold fusion advancements at the University of Utah. On the day of a university's declaration that cold fusion had been achieved experimentally at low temperatures, a Salt Lake City TV station devoted more than seven minutes of its evening newscast to the announcement, using sophisticated computer graphics to show the experimental results. However, as time went on, the results were challenged by other scientists who were unable to replicate the Utah experiments. Because new developments are so significant for most mass-media messages, the communicator is greatly handicapped when potential information sources are part of an invisible college. It is unusual for an outsider to be allowed within the magic circle; researchers generally are especially guarded about premature disclosure of their ideas or results.

The second link in the bibliographic chain consists of the first formally published results of new research, including the journals, magazines, books, recordings, and other materials that make up the bulk of library collections. The sources of information also can include the proceedings of conferences, the papers delivered at conventions, and other such formal presentations as musical scores and works of art. Electronic data bases of the complete texts of newspapers, magazines, or journals also can be included. The important characteristic of this kind of information is that it usually has gone through some kind of review process. Experts in the field have examined the scholarly material for errors, gaps, misinterpretations, and problems. Popular materials, such as newspapers and magazines, have been edited and scrutinized for obvious errors and inconsistencies, although this scrutiny is less thorough than that of scholarly publications. These review processes help promote accuracy and completeness, although neither the scholarly or popular reviewing and editing treatment can be said to eliminate all errors.

The third link in the bibliographic chain involves access tools for library and data-base information. Examples of tools in this category include periodical indexes, abstracts of articles and books, articles reviewing major research findings, and bibliographies of subjects or authors' works.

The fourth link in the bibliographic chain includes works that provide overviews or summaries that are useful to communicators seeking basic information about a subject. Articles in encyclopedias, dictionary entries, and textbooks fall into this category. These items are the most removed in time from the original research or ideas of the field; for that reason, communicators should recognize that these access tools are likely to be outdated in some respects.

Understanding this bibliographic chain can help the communicator decode the structure of information in any discipline. Since each field of study has an identifiable pattern of information generation, publication, and organization, the communicator can tap into the link in the chain that is most relevant to the task at hand. If the subject is very new, the best method of gathering information about it is through discussions with researchers and thinkers in the field, since there is not yet a formal publishing apparatus. This might involve keeping in touch with informants who work in universities, research centers, and think tanks, people who have an overview of current ideas in their fields. A more established subject area offers the communicator a wide variety of summary or review publications to use as background information. In this case, it may be appropriate for the communicator to start with the fourth bibliographic link (overviews and reference works) and move to the more recent material after gaining solid background knowledge. The information in libraries and data bases becomes more understandable when these patterns are recognized.

The question-analysis stage of the search-strategy process, then, is an important one for the communicator, who must identify the appropriate language of the topic, the scope of the problem to be investigated, the disciplinary overlap that may give some clues to the rest of the search, and the appropriate strategy to use in gathering information for the message. Because communicators usually are confronted with topics that cross disciplinary boundaries, they face special challenges in their information gathering. They need, therefore, to develop a search process that will allow them to confidently cross disciplinary boundaries, providing a methodological approach that is appropriate for any topic and any type of message.

In the example of the article about rising health-care costs, for instance, the communicator might decide that the relevant disciplines include law, economics, business, insurance, sociology, medicine, and health-care planning and administration. Fortunately, only limited segments of each field need to be considered. That the scope of the topic has been limited allows the communicator to do a more complete job with the rest of the search. Whether the communicator is preparing to write an interpretive news story, a series of ads for a health-insurance company, or a public-relations release for a hospital, these first steps in the search-strategy process are crucial for ensuring that the background for the message is sufficient and appropriate for the audience.

NARROWING THE TOPIC

A series of questions designed to assist the communicator in narrowing the topic can be useful. These include probes about the disciplines that produce information related to the subject, complexity of the topic, geographic limits, time period limits, the depth of the treatment, the nature of the audience, and the kind of message that will be produced. If, for example, the broad question is "What are the causes of the growing rate of homelessness in the United States?" the formula for narrowing the question might work this way:

- Which disciplines contribute information to this topic? Sociology, politics, economics, banking, and urban affairs, are places to start.
- What factors make this topic complex? Homelessness is a relatively recent concept; academics, politicians, and advocates for the homeless have entirely different ways of approaching the issue; the

social and political climate affects lawmakers and policy officials in subtle and frequently unknown ways.

• What are the geographic limits of the topic? While homelessness exists throughout the United States, how the condition is understood and approached varies from community to community, from state to state. The area in which messages are distributed may be important in establishing geographic boundaries for the topic. On the other hand, the pervasiveness of homelessness is considered an overall context of the topic that must be considered in any locale.

• What time period factors can be used to limit the topic? Much of mass communication emphasizes recency. Therefore, the newest information is likely to be stressed, with older material used to establish context or to provide contrast to the recent material. Trends in homelessness in the recent decade will be important.

• How in-depth will the message be? Communicators and their organizations may make major research efforts for some projects, while others are quite primitive and perfunctory. A major magazine article on homelessness requires extensive research, using varied print, data-base, and interview sources. A short news story concerning the takeover of vacant houses by advocates for the homeless, produced on short deadline, allows only a cursory background search. Question analysis helps the communicator specify the detail and depth required in the search strategy, permitting the search for the most essential information.

• What is the nature of the audience? Two important ways of analyzing audiences are using demographic factors—income, education, age, race, gender, and so on—and psychographic factors, which involve such psychological factors as values, lifestyles, interests, and self-concept. Other useful knowledge about audiences includes the information sophistication of likely audience members, the importance of a topic to the audience, and whether it is an issue to the audience either directly or indirectly in audience members' roles as community residents. Few of the homeless are likely to be among the audience for stories about their condition. However, most of the policy actors and shapers of public opinion are likely to be potential audience members for this topic.

• What kind of message will be produced? Will it be a news story, part of a public relations or ad campaign, an editorial, a research report to be used in the communication industry, a term paper for a college class? What standards for evidence and documentation are important for the message? A research paper on public opinion about homelessness requires different information on the subject than does a public relations campaign, although some material will overlap.

Once these question-analysis probes have been examined, the communicator is in a position to focus selectively on some aspects of the larger question and develop an exacting standard for raising questions and seeking information to address those questions. Completing these probes frequently allows the communicator to revise or refine the question, based on information and insights gained during the question analysis.

In addition to the question-analysis work that involves the topic of the research, communicators in various industries also keep in mind the standard questions asked routinely in their fields. Perhaps the most well-known question routine for news reporting is the formula of who, what, where, when, how, and why? In advertising, a set of related questions to be asked is:

- What should our advertising accomplish?
- To whom should we advertise?
- What should we say?
- How should we say it?
- Where should we say it?
- How much should we spend?
- After the campaign, did we accomplish our ad goals?

A public-relations version for strategic planning research uses similar concepts in this fashion:

- Defining the problem: What's happening now?
- Planning and programming: What should we do and why?
- Taking action and communicating: How do we do it and say it?
- Evaluating the program: How did we do?[5]

WHAT'S NEW ABOUT THE TOPIC?

Originality, or at least a fresh slant, is a prerequisite for much media work. Therefore, the search is intense for information and ideas that support that demand. The question-analysis routine can support the writer's desire for a fresh angle or a new twist on a topic. In addition, the search-strategy process itself provides the communicator with material that illustrates conventional wisdom, traditional perspectives, and examples of other communicators' work. This material helps the information searcher and the writer to recognize stale, hackneyed approaches, to steer clear of copyrighted material, and to avoid plagiarism. Sometimes, however, it seems that examination of previously published material contributes to imitation rather than to originality. The communicator may get lost in the wealth of material that emerges from a solid search strategy.

In general, media writing is criticized for lack of originality and for accepting conventional wisdom without questioning its accuracy or relevance. Some examples of conventional wisdom about human achievements are that males are naturally better at mathematics and science than are females, that older people are poor drivers, that African-Americans are superior athletes, and that artistic talent is inherited. If communicators identify conventional wisdoms and challenge the basis for them, they may be able to present new and interesting perspectives on old topics, especially since specialists who study such subjects continually learn more about the conditions under which people achieve well. Once the communicator suspects that an unsupportable conventional wisdom is at the basis of the research, it is relatively simple to locate the researchers who have challenged that conventional wisdom and brought new information into the field.

Another way of criticizing media for lack of originality involves the creation of stereotypes and the imitation of successful patterns and formulas in advertising, news, and entertainment. In addition, media industries are growing more alert to the substantial amount of outright plagiarism in their industries and are taking action against communicators who present the work of others under their own names. Questions that can help the searcher are: Does this idea adopt a conventional wisdom that has little or no basis in fact? Has this concept been used previously? Does this idea perpetuate an existing stereotype? Is there a copyright conflict? What am I contributing that is new, original, and fresh?

QUESTION ANALYSIS AND INFORMATION SUBSIDIES

As communicators raise questions to be answered during their search strategies, they find it tempting to raise questions that they know can be answered efficiently. Generally, this means that a willing individual or institution is at hand to provide answers to the questions, making it unnecessary for the communicator to consult primary sources or to do original research. Gandy describes the exchange this way: "An information subsidy is an attempt to produce influence over the actions of others by controlling their access to and use of information relevant to those actions. This information is characterized as a subsidy because the source of that information causes it to be made available at something less than the cost a user would face in the absence of the subsidy."[6] Seen within this framework, everything from the United States census to a politician's media packet to a public-relations release for a concert can be viewed as an information subsidy. However, some information subsidies are more likely than others to directly affect media researchers' work in unfortunate ways. An example of a relatively innocuous subsidy is to be found in a state's public-relations releases on traffic deaths. Of greater concern are successful attempts to provide communicators with phony or manipulated data designed to convince communicators and the public on a particular public policy question.

Few communicators can avoid contact with or use of information subsidies. But recognition that information subsidies influence the body of material available at low cost can enhance the communicator's sophistication and skill in the question-analysis phase. Census data often present some problems of bias and accuracy; when reprocessed for specific purposes by organizations hoping to direct attention in a particular way, the data may become problematic in additional ways. The communicator working on question analysis can ask: Who is responsible for providing this information? How do people supplying me with information hope to influence the way I raise questions and develop answers to these questions? Identifying these information subsidy issues during question analysis helps researchers anticipate problems that might arise later in the evaluation and synthesis steps described in Chapter 9.

LINKS TO THE SEARCH STRATEGY

In this step of the search strategy, communicators work through the tasks in the question-analysis box: they identify the concepts and language associated with their topic, they draw disciplinary boundaries, they refine the scope of their questions, and they begin to identify potential contributors of information.

The investments of time and resources in developing a media message are considerable. Question analysis, as an integral part of search strategy, allows the communicator to move among disciplines and subject areas, to select a segment of a larger topic or issue, and to focus the major questions sharply. Question analysis has the capacity to help the communicator stay on track, to avoid getting lost in the many subtopics that can be found in a larger topic, while continuing to see the selected subtopic in context.

Chapter 3 examines the way that informal sources and observation contribute to the search-strategy process.

NOTES

1. Jeanne Abbott, "Useful tools for analysis," *The IRE Journal*, Fall 1988, 17–18.
2. Gib Johnson, "The Compleat Reporter: With a Few Essentials, The Journalist Is Wired to the World," *Washington Journalism Review*, May 1990, 19.
3. S. I. Hayakawa, *Language in Thought and Action*, 4th ed. (New York: Harcourt Brace Jovanovich, 1978), 155.
4. Michael Keresztesi, "The Science of Bibliography: Theoretical Implications for Bibliographic Instruction," in Cerise Oberman and Katrina Strauch, eds., *Theories of Bibliographic Education: Designs for Teaching* (New York: Bowker, 1982), 13–21.
5. Glen M. Broom and David M. Dozier, *Using Research in Public Relations: Applications to Program Management* (Englewood Cliffs, N.J.: Prentice Hall, 1990), 23–24.
6. Oscar Gandy, *Beyond Agenda Setting: Information Subsidies and Public Policy* (Norwood, N.J.: Ablex, 1982), 61.

3

Consulting People
and Observing the World

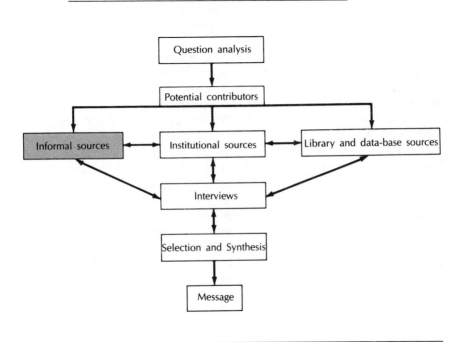

Getting started on a new subject and grounding the information in "reality" are two challenges that the communicator faces early in the search strategy. For these purposes, communicators consult people informally and observe the world around them. As do social scientists, media professionals recognize that the methods for understanding the world and for knowing "reality" vary considerably and are subject to dispute. Some people approach reality through faith, relying on authority and sacred texts to guide them to truth. Custom and tradition are guidelines for others. Experience and experiment are additional approaches to learning about the world. As communicators seek to understand the world, they gather information that seems to help them explain and interpret the world for their audiences. They are aware that what seems to be truth and reality to some may be sham, sensationalism, and blasphemy to others.

Observation and conversations with a cross section of the public are limited, but useful, measures for developing a first approach to a subject and for creating a "reality check" on the content of messages. Communicators appreciate that their first observations and uses of informal sources may produce false starts and faulty ideas, along with brilliant beginnings. Nonetheless, many important news stories, bright feature stories, clever ads, and moving opinion columns begin with an observant communicator.

Noticing the long lines in front of automatic teller machines, for example, may be the start of a news story on fundamental changes in bank services. Observing that the lakeshore has been eroded by runners can lead to a series of articles on conflicts between the goals of recreation and preservation in park systems. Seeing "teachers wanted" classified ads may signal the education reporter that a decade of teacher layoffs is ending. Standing in the grocery check-out line behind teenage shoppers can alert the advertising researcher to do further study on which family members purchase the groceries.

Informal sources and observation produce much of the information that forms the basis of mass-media messages. This chapter illustrates the relationship of these sources to the search-strategy process and to the development of media messages. Informal sources may be consulted at any point in the search strategy; they often are used during a preliminary survey of a topic. However, the communicator may return to them at a variety of points in the search strategy. Observation, especially random and casual observation, also is used early in the process. More formal and strategic observations are undertaken after the communicator is fully prepared by study of other sources. Along with generating ideas for a story or an ad, informal sources and observation can lead to additional sources, especially institutional sources.

NETWORKS OF INFORMAL SOURCES

Without exception, mass communicators operate in numerous networks of people. Some networks are connected with the communicators' professional roles, and others are part of the communicators' private lives. Among the professional networks are, of course, the colleagues in the news room, ad department or agency, or public-relations office. In a news operation, for example, a reporter's colleagues include other reporters, editors, photographers, graphic artists, copy assistants, and librarians and their assistants in the news library.

The professional network of a member of one media organization also includes people who work in other media organizations. For example, a staff

member of a public-relations office has professional dealings with news reporters for print and broadcasting. An advertising specialist knows many
other specialists, both in the home community and in other cities. The networks are both formal and informal. News workers may belong to such
associations as the Society of Professional Journalists, National Association of
Black Journalists, Asian-American Journalists Association, or Women in Communications. Editorial writers, science reporters, travel writers, and free-lance
writers and editors join associations of those with similar specialties. Public-
relations specialists may affiliate with the International Association of Business Communicators or with Public Relations Society of America. Advertising
professionals join such organizations as the American Advertising Federation.

Formal memberships help communicators keep in touch with one another and to meet people who are just entering the field. Associates in these
networks are accustomed to helping one another. They are particularly useful
at the start of the search strategy, when the communicator is casting about to
gain a preliminary understanding of the subject. Communicators in competing organizations often help one another in these informal ways, unless
doing so directly conflicts with their competitive advantage. For example,
creative staff members of ad agencies form an informal network in most
communities. They know one another's strengths and specialties and share
some sources and methods of finding information.

Another kind of network involves those outside the profession but connected with the communicators' regular "rounds" of activities. In news, this
network includes the vast numbers of news contacts and sources known to
reporters and editors. For editors who have held a number of news positions,
the network can be extremely wide, since it consists of people from many
fields whose paths converged with that of the editor at numerous times in the
past. For reporters, all current and previous beat sources are part of the network. For example, a reporter may begin on general assignments, move to
police and courts beats, then cover religion, and later specialize in ecology
reporting. As part of each beat assignment, the reporter accumulates sources
and contacts who are knowledgeable in their fields. People from these networks assist reporters in the first phase of investigating a new topic.

In advertising, account executives keep in close touch—perhaps daily
contact—with clients whose accounts their office handles. They discuss general news that affects the client's product or service, as well as business
developments, events in their market, and the overall condition of the economy. More specifically, the client shares some information about sales, potential new products and services, and competitors' activities, as well as other
information directly affecting the advertising approach. Information from the
advertising client plays a major part in the planning of advertising campaigns. Advertising media buyers (who purchase commercial time or ad
space for clients) have regular contacts with the media representatives, or
"reps," with whom they bargain for the best rates. The reps offer information about ad-buying patterns, "hot" television programs, and recent trends
in commercial placement.

Public-relations specialists have well-established and wide networks. For example, a public-relations worker for a utility company may have been a newspaper or broadcast reporter. From this earlier association, as well as from current work, the public-relations person is acquainted with many reporters and editors. In addition, the network includes members of state and local regulatory commissions; politicians; city, county, and state planners; demographers; and public-opinion pollsters. As with reporters and advertising specialists, they keep in close touch with those in the network and strive to maintain cordial relations.

As well as being members of professional networks, communicators are members of personal networks that relate to their roles as citizens, community residents, and, in some cases, parents. While these networks are much less formal than professional ones, communicators use them to stay in touch with developments that affect their audiences. Even everyday routines and errands bring a variety of people together. Those who ride buses to work see the same people at the bus stop. In casual conversation with other travelers, communicators can survey ideas and viewpoints on current topics. Visiting the laundromat or the barber shop offers similar opportunities. Waiters and bartenders are potential sources.

Residential networks offer additional contacts. These range widely from committees that organize neighborhood festivals, to associations that issue community newsletters and newspapers, to advocacy groups with a variety of purposes. Parent and teacher groups concerned with schooling typically organize around a particular school or in response to issues affecting education. Churches are the sites of social and political activities, as well as religious ones. Food banks, overnight shelters, and sanctuary for political refugees from abroad are services that churches offer in the community. Connected with these activities are numerous individuals who can become part of the communicator's network of sources.

Tips, suggestions, and volunteered ideas are other informal sources. These frequently come from those who are part of the communicator's networks and who are interested in how media messages are produced. Reporters find that acquaintances tip them off about new developments that might be newsworthy. Sometimes these "tips" clearly are motivated by self-interest on the part of the tipster. But on other occasions, they are provided by those who enjoy seeing their story ideas in print.

Magazine, feature, and free-lance writers use networks to locate people who have interests or hobbies that relate to topics they want to pursue. These interests might include bluegrass music, antique autos, herb gardening, calligraphy, Tennessee walking horses, exploring caves, and rafting down wild rivers. The individuals who join hobby clubs become important informal contacts for writers who rely on casual discussions to generate ideas in addition to their own and decide if the topic is worth further investigation.

Family and other personal acquaintances also help communicators with preliminary research on subjects. A reporter interested in investigating conditions in day-care centers may ask family members and friends about their experiences with day care—for example, if they have removed a child because of unsatisfactory treatment of children in a center and what their own standards for assessing centers are. These preliminary questions give the reporter some rough ideas about the potential for a story and a number of strategies for pursuing the subject. Such preliminary discussion may—or may not—be useful for the serious research that follows.

INFORMAL FILES AND REFERENCES

In approaching a new subject, many writers begin with a survey of what has been published on the topic. Despite the acknowledged risk that the earlier messages will undermine a fresh approach to the material, referring to files is standard practice. In advertising, for example, when an agency begins to work on a new account, the agency library collects tear sheets of ads previously published for the product the agency is advertising. If the agency acquires as a new client a firm selling stereo equipment, it comprehensively analyzes the content of other stereo ads—both print and broadcasting—their placement, and the evident marketing strategy involved in the campaigns. In news work, a business reporter or feature section reporter might be preparing a story on stereo equipment. The reporter would seek any clips from the newspaper library that show what had been published in the paper thus far. Some newspaper libraries also file stories printed by competing newspapers, making it easy to check on what has been published by others. Public-relations news releases also might be available and would be compared with earlier news stories. If the material published earlier is substantially the same as the reporter's story idea, the reporter would seek a new angle or decide against going on with the story.

Most communicators maintain a reference shelf and files of material they consult frequently, even though these materials may be duplicated in the organization's formally maintained library. These personal files come into play during the informal search. Colleagues may share material from their personal files. For example, a public-relations writer keeps a file of news releases, organized by subject, that she or he has produced. A news reporter maintains clippings files of major stories, especially those that are likely to merit follow-up stories. Communicators keep their own lists of frequently called telephone numbers and files of sources, including the sources' official positions, telephone numbers, and mailing addresses. Some keep cross-filed systems, filed by last name of source in one file and by subject in the other file. This is useful for those who frequently forget names of people or institutions. Special directories of sources are useful personal resources. Membership lists of organizations help communicators in a hurry to make contact with specialists in a field or with individuals active in a social movement. Reporters and editors typically keep a "tickler" file to remind them of ideas and upcoming events and keep a list of situations that need periodic monitoring.

Many communicators use their work computers to create and maintain the personal files that are so necessary for making good use of informal sources. Communicators may create a calendar of upcoming appointments, name, phone, and address information, personal notes about individuals or institutions frequently consulted, and other information that may help in the first stages of a search. Idea files can be stored in the computer as well. Some news rooms keep a master source file in a computer, a practice especially helpful to new staff members who are trying to learn the community's human resources.

CASUAL READING

Billboards, bumper stickers, and T-shirt messages are among casual information sources that reach out to attract attention and to persuade passers-by. While workers in other fields may find no use for such intrusions, mass communicators recognize their usefulness in helping them to keep in touch with what is going on. Of course, bumper stickers alone will have little or no significance. But in combination with numerous other signs and signals in the community, they can alert the communicator to ideas and issues that deserve attention. Many such messages seem purely personal, even whimsical: "Black Holes Are Out of Sight"; "Insanity Is Inherited—You Get It from Your Children"; "Have You Hugged Your Goldfish Today?" Others present social and political issues: "War Is Not a Substitute for an Energy Policy"; "Buy American"; "I'm Pro-Choice and I Vote." Such public slogans tell the communicator that people have organized to try to get public attention. The existence of a newly organized group merits investigation by those who try to read the community's pulse.

Members of the public who seek attention for their viewpoints use a variety of methods other than bumper stickers, of course. They make signs to tack up on utility poles, kiosks, and bulletin boards: "Save Our Park"; "Stop Hwy. 35E"; "Form a Blockwatch." They print flyers to distribute door to door: "Anti-Pornography Rally Saturday." They advertise public meetings devoted to issues that concern them: "Neighborhood Council Meeting on Aircraft Noise." They publish newsletters and newspapers for free distribution to the audiences they wish to reach. Communicators wisely attend to these messages and, in some cases, collect copies for their own files. The information in them may prove useful at a later time but will be very difficult to retrieve by ordinary search methods, for such informally published and circulated materials generally are not collected and indexed by libraries. Nor will new and local associations be listed in such reference works as the *Encyclopedia of Associations*.

Direct-mail advertising and various promotional appeals are additional sources available through casual reading. Direct-mail advertising brings news of national and international associations and their actions that may interest communicators and their audiences. A mailing seeking donations to help fund scholarships for minority-group students asserts that the percentage of minority-group students in American colleges is dropping. Another asking for contributions to help the poor heat their homes in winter reveals the number of people who are too poor to pay for heating oil or gas. Another promoting a new resort community appears to be violating state law in its inducements to visit the resort. Communicators are likely to open and casually read much of what other people consider junk mail because they recognize it as a source of ideas and an opportunity to monitor events.

Most professional communicators are heavy readers and consumers of media offerings. Their own imaginations are stimulated by casual reading. They attend to the advertising and editorial content of leading national magazines, newspapers, and broadcasting, as well as local news and magazine content. Those with national audiences find cues in local and regional publications that can lead to national stories. For example, watching fire and drought reports from the western states suggests planning for coverage of federal disaster-relief plans—a national news story. A public-relations department of an insurance firm also watches the weather and fire reports for their implications in the insurance industry.

For local audiences, information appearing at the national level can be reshaped to reflect city or regional conditions. A new national policy on eligibility for treatment in veterans' hospitals probably would be announced from Washington. But every community in the United States in which a veterans' hospital is located would be affected by the decision. Communicators at the local level may get their alert about this story by way of an Associated Press story from Washington or an article in a New York or Washington daily newspaper. Other potential informal sources are the public-relations office of the hospital or the staff of a senator or representative.

Casual reading also inspires stories that expand on brief treatments. For example, two reporters for the *Pittsburgh Press* found themselves reading a number of press releases and news stories about kidney transplants. They also were writing stories themselves about local and national problems and trends in the procedures for selecting kidney recipients and matching donated organs with waiting patients. Over a four-month period, the two reporters wrote a number of short pieces for the newspaper on the topic. This alerted them to the potential for a lengthy and exhaustive treatment of the subject. They got permission to conduct a year-long investigation that resulted in a six-part series in the newspaper. Their initial recognition of a pattern of problems, as evidenced by the reports they were reading and writing, led to the remainder of the search-strategy steps. They then were able to conduct an information search for the more formal and appropriate information for an extensive series.

Informal sources have limitations, however. Using them as stimuli and "get started" devices is safe. But more authoritative and reliable sources generally must be consulted if the communicator wants to deliver a complete and accurate message. The family members of a patient who was turned down for a kidney transplant might claim that the donated organ was given to a wealthy foreign patient instead. But the physician in charge of the organ donation program at the hospital might explain that the real reason for the choice of kidney recipient had to do with tissue and blood compatibility of the donor and the recipient. National computer files with information about organ donations and waiting recipients might show a pattern that an individual family member or physician would not be able to see. Understanding the limitations of informal sources in the search process helps the communicator avoid errors and distortion.

PERSONAL MEMORY AS AN INFORMAL SOURCE

Most people recognize that personal memory is an important and rich source of information for individuals' daily lives and decision making. However, carefully used personal recollections also can serve as informal sources of information for communicators. An editor at a major newspaper says that one way to spot trends in the community, and thus get ideas for trend stories, is to pay attention to how things used to be. How has the community changed in the past few years? Even though a reporter may not have the hard facts at this early stage of the information search, using personal memory of things that the communicator knows to be true can be very helpful starting points.[1]

Personal memory also can inform current reports that may lack the perspective of treatment over time. For instance, a number of columnists and reporters recalled, from personal memory of covering the events at the time, that the Kurds (an Iraqi minority group displaced and threatened by the Iraqi army in the aftermath of the Persian Gulf War) had sought help from the United States much earlier. In fact, Kurdish insurgents had been alternately aided and abandoned by the United States government over a period of two decades.

Columnist Daniel Schorr recalled the numerous United States–Kurd dealings from covering the stories at the time. His personal memory was very vivid, since he lost his job at CBS over the issue. A United States House of Representatives committee investigated dealings with the Kurds in 1976, but the full House suppressed the committee report. Someone leaked the report to CBS Washington correspondent Schorr, who gave it to the *Village Voice*, which published it. Schorr lost his job. In his 1991 column, he supplemented his personal recollections of the events with reference to House documents and government reports, however.[2] Other columnists writing about the 1991 Kurdish situation compared it to the defeat of the Cuban Bay of Pigs soldiers in 1961 and the destruction of the Hungarian freedom fighters in 1956. All these events were recalled from the personal memories of the writers.

Personal memory also can aid communicators trying to create advertising messages. For instance, an advertising team member might recall a particular joy as a child in playing with a classic toy such as roller skates. For a current campaign for the modern version of the toy, roller blades, the creative effort of the team might focus on recapturing some of that simple, childhood joy, supplemented by current market research about who is using roller blades now (mostly adults).

COMMUNICATORS AS OBSERVERS

All the content of mass communication originates with observation. In news reporting through most of the nineteenth century, a high percentage of the information originated with the reporter as the observer. Today, reporters and other mass communicators rely on others—often specialists in various fields—as their observers for much more of the information that is transmitted. A variety of factors accounts for this change. Today, much research—itself rooted in observation—is conducted on subjects that formerly were approached casually. Another factor is the growth of government bureaucracies, many of which are organized as information providers. Still another is explained by the prominence of interviewing as a reporting method, prized as a means of introducing authority and human interest into the story.

When three tardy whales became stranded in the fall ice off the coast of Alaska, journalists from around the world converged on the area to cover the story. They described, taped, and photographed what they saw. But for additional sources, to cite a few, they used local villagers, marine biologists, state historians, engineers who knew about equipment to keep ice from forming, ice-breaking ship experts, meteorologists, and economists who could talk about the effect of so many visitors on the local economy. Together, these varied and expert observers undoubtedly gave a more complete and accurate account of the stranded whale situation than reporters could give without them.

Nevertheless, the major difficulties with observation are scarcely eliminated merely because the number and expertise of the observers have increased. Observation takes place within a context. Observers often see what they expect to see or are prepared to see and fail to perceive equally visible elements that are not part of what they expect. Another factor is that observers have limits in their own sense organs—one with an acute sense of smell may detect a natural-gas leak that others might not notice; one may see a boat sinking across the lake, while three or four others see nothing.

Observation seems inseparably linked with inference. The observer at the scene of the stranded whales might infer that this was an unusual situation. However, local villagers might tell the observer that every fall a few tardy whales are trapped by ice and die or are killed by hunters. The villager might add that any whale so unwary as to stay too long in waters that freeze should not be freed to propagate its defective genes. The possibility of faulty inference is a problem for both the mass communicator as an observer and other observers on whom communicators rely.

Bias on the part of the observer invariably affects the observation process. Professional communicators try to be aware of bias in themselves and in others upon whom they rely. They are aware that all individuals have assumptions about the world—beliefs about what is ordinary and normal, as well as convictions about what "ought" to be. These convictions influence what is perceived and how the perceptions are interpreted. Recognizing the role of bias in observation, communicators hope to limit the effect of bias by developing better techniques for observation and by sharing the responsibility with other observers.

The effect of the observer on the scene is an additional factor to be reckoned with. The presence of observers changes the event being observed. This is most clearly seen in confrontations that take place specifically for the purpose of attracting media attention. But even in so mundane an event as a parade, the bands make sure they are playing when they pass the television cameras. When the observer comes to the schoolroom, even kindergarteners adapt their behavior to the presence of a stranger. A most striking example of an institution that has changed as a result of observation is the American presidential nominating convention. After 50 years of broadcasting coverage, the conventions now bear no resemblance to the nineteenth- and early-twentieth-century smoke-filled-room negotiations. Party managers learned to arrange the conventions to take account of—and advantage of—television coverage. The institution that broadcasters found so significant and fascinating gradually changed, in large measure because of the attention that broadcasters were directing its way.

For some kinds of observation, observers may have a reasonable hope that their presence can be, in part, neutralized as an effect. For example, the reporter in the kindergarten might devise methods to counteract the intrusion. However, at the institutional level, such as the nominating conventions, individuals and media organizations are powerless to counteract their effect. They are inextricably intertwined with the event itself. The best they can do is recognize that they, the observers, are part of the activity.

Observation, then, is affected by the inherent perceptual limitations of the observer, expectations, inference, bias, and the effect of the observer on the action. The mass communicator as an observer may be more or less affected by these factors than others who supply information to the communicator. Skill, experience, and awareness of the problems in accurately observing events can help to counteract the inevitable difficulties of observation.

Types of Observation

Communicators rely on three kinds of observation: routine, participant, and unobtrusive.

Routine Observation. The most frequently used type of observation is so routine as to be habit. It involves simply going to the scene of the action. Professionals in all fields of mass communication perform these routine observations. Advertising specialists attend the unveiling of new auto models. Public-relations practitioners go to events they have sponsored as attention getters in order to observe the effect of the event. News reporters go to meetings, conventions, accidents and disasters, parades, fairs, speeches, and countless other kinds of events.

Being on the scene of a dramatic event helps the communicator to give a credible report. Although, as we have noted, an observer's accuracy and interpretations may be flawed, no one questions that the observer can be more accurate in most emotional settings than a nonobserver. For example, eyewitness accounts and news photographs provided a moving account when Germany was reunited. The *New York Times* printed photographs of women planting flowers at the Reichstag building and Berliners crowding the street before the Brandenburg Gate, along with a by-lined account by Serge Schmemann:

> BERLIN, Wednesday, Oct. 3 — Forty-five years after it was carved up in defeat and disgrace, Germany was reunited today in a midnight celebration of pealing bells, national hymns and the jubilant blare of good old German oom-pah-pah.
>
> At the stroke of midnight Tuesday, a copy of the American Liberty Bell, a gift from the United States at the height of the cold war, tolled from the Town Hall, and the black, red and gold banner of the Federal Republic of Germany rose slowly before the Reichstag, the scarred seat of past German parliaments.
>
> The state President, Richard von Weizsacker, declared: "In free self-determination, we would like to fulfill German unity in freedom. We are aware of our responsibility for these tasks before God and people. We want to serve peace in the world and a united Europe."
>
> With that, a throng estimated at a million broke into the German national anthem—whose first verse with the words " 'Deutschland, Deutschland uber alles' was banned after the war. The anthem now opened, "Unity and justice and freedom for the German fatherland. . . ."[3]

Conferences, meetings, and governmental activities at all levels usually are covered with observation as a prominent technique. Before conferences, public-relations staff prepare much advance material to assist those who cover the sessions. The staff provides press credentials and assists with facilities for transmitting the reports. Reporters receive packets of background material to help them on routine aspects of their work. The lead of even a straight news story usually reflects some details that can be accurately gathered only by an observer. The Associated Press account of the opening of a United Nations conference illustrates this convention:

> NAIROBI, Kenya (AP) — Singing "We Are The Women Of The World," some 11,000 delegates opened a series of workshops Wednesday to mark the end of the United Nations Women's Decade.
>
> Dame Nita Barrow of Barbados convened the delegates, warning that the session was their "last chance" to press the United Nations to set up a

permanent women's forum and to "recognize us as an asset and not a liability."[4]

Observation can give human interest to an otherwise routine story about changes in services and facilities offered to the public. Larry Rohter of the *New York Times* filed this story, which includes observations designed to interest the reader:

> When summer arrived and classes let out in late June, 10-year-old Angelique Medrano looked forward to two whole months without having to set foot in school. But yesterday, Angelique, who will enter fifth grade in the fall, was once again at Public School 2, at 122 Henry Street on the Lower East Side.
> She was lured back into the lunchroom with friends and classmates from her neighborhood by the Board of Education's free summer lunch program.
> For lunch, there was a bologna and cheese sandwich on a kaiser roll, potato salad and a cup of grape juice. For dessert, there was a strawberry ice pop made from fruit juice.
> "To tell the truth, I'd rather be swimming," Angelique said before heading out to play with her friend Evie Pena. "But this is a pretty good lunch."[5]

The subsequent paragraphs gave routine information on the administration and cost of the program, information readily available from public-relations staff in the school district. But the human-interest lead and the on-the-spot interviews are the responsibility of the reporter, and observation makes the difference between a routine, bureaucratic story and an engaging interpretation of the lunch program.

Annual events, such as civic festivals, parades, contests, and announcements of awards, often seem repetitious and lack the novelty needed for a good news or public-relations message. However, an observer who carefully records details at such events can give them a quality of freshness:

> HANNIBAL, Mo.—A stiff breeze off the Mississippi River ruffled the pinafores of five rosy-cheeked Beckys as they posed Thursday before a battery of photographers.
> Slouching nearby, five mischievous Toms—on stage in the Tom and Becky contest—clutched their straw hats and smirked. After all, Tom Sawyer was no prissy.
> And when Elizabeth Brown and Eric Durr, both 13, were announced as winners, the crowd erupted into cheers for this year's goodwill ambassadors from Mark Twain's hometown.
> The annual contest was the 29th sponsored by the local chamber of commerce. As the boyhood home of author Samuel Clemens—known worldwide as Mark Twain—Hannibal will send Tom and Becky across the nation to promote the town's tourism industry.[6]

Interpretive and investigative articles and series also rely heavily on reporters' observations. For these reports, particularly, writers need the authenticity and details that observation can provide. For a radio investigative reporting piece, WBBM reporter Phil Rogers started his report about O'Hare airport's security problems with these authentic sounds and words:

ROGERS: The Achilles heel of O'Hare security is the Mount Prospect Road entrance to the field from Touhy Avenue. When you get to the guard house there, procedure is for your vehicle to be escorted to wherever you're going. We drove in aboard a semi-trailer truck making a regular delivery, were asked by the guard if we knew the way, and went in unescorted. [truck sounds]

From there we had a free ride around the service road, which leads to active taxiways and the runways. [runway sounds] Our driver makes regular deliveries through that entrance. He says his load is *never* checked and he is *never* escorted.

DRIVER: Not if you appear to know what you're doing, know where you're going. They will let you just *go*. You say, "I've got a delivery for such-and-such"; they say, "Have you been there before?" You say, "Plenty of times"; they say, "Go ahead."

ROGERS: Although we told the guard we had a delivery for American Airlines, in fact our truck could have contained dozens of men and hundreds of pounds of explosives. And from that taxiway, we could have rammed aircraft taking off, the terminal itself, or could have pulled up next to any aircraft at virtually any gate.[7]

Play-by-play sports coverage also makes extensive use of reporters' observation. Sally Jenkins's coverage of the U.S. Women's Open golf tournament is an example:

SPRINGFIELD, N.J., July 11—One thin dime deprived Jan Stephenson of a tie for the lead with Nancy Lopez, Kathy Baker and Janet Anderson today after the first round of the U.S. Women's Open at Baltusrol Golf Club.

Lopez, who has struggled with nerves in this event, shot a two-under-par 70 on the hilly upper course to put herself in a tie with 24-year-old Baker and Anderson, the 1982 winner.

But Stephenson provided most of the day's drama when she was assessed a one-stroke penalty on the 11th hole after her ball marker, a dime, stuck to her putter. It gave her a bogey six, and cost her a share of the lead. Angry and apparently close to tears, she finished at a one-under 71, tied with six others in second place.[8]

The reporter's powers of observation are critical to the effective coverage of sports, as illustrated in the golf story. In this case, the reporter's conclusion about the golfer's state of mind and the drama of the sticky dime contributes to the reader interest of the story. Such details and interpretation of their significance also play an important part in articles in which the writer openly expresses opinion: reviews of films, concerts, plays, dance, and other performance, as well as commentary on art exhibitions, architecture, and landscape design. The skill of the observer in such opinion columns is an essential part of the opinion-making process, and it aids clear expression once the opinion is formulated.

Columnists for newspapers and magazines must create some of their content by their powers of observation. Keith Schneider of the *New York Times* began his "Louisiana Journal" column with these observations:

> BURNSIDE, La.—The avenue of oaks leads from the bank of the Mississippi River to the white Doric columns of the Houman House Plantation, a shaded path through the history of battle and blood, dreams and dust at what was once Louisiana's largest sugar plantation.
>
> But missing from this quintessential Southern scene of wealth derived from sugar cane and the sweat of 1,000 slaves is the curtain of Spanish moss that once draped these elegant trees in extravagant abundance.
>
> All over Southern Louisiana, from the silent swamps of the Atchafalaya basin to the green marshes west of Lafayette, the plant that is a symbol of Southern pain and mystery has vanished from its former range.[9]

Routine observations also play a part in the work of public-relations and advertising professionals, who are less likely than reporters to incorporate their observations as part of the messages they produce. Nonetheless, their observations about the needs, habits, and life styles of clients' audiences are important to their work. For example, either an advertising or a public-relations specialist who had a hotel or restaurant as a client would visit the facility frequently, observing the customers, the atmosphere, and the response to the service offered. Similarly, working for a candidate for public office would require public-relations and ad staffs to observe the candidate's contact with voters, reporters, and party officials.

Watching how people interact with the product has become another important observation method for marketing and advertising professionals. The Gallup Organization has been using equipment that helps newspaper marketers learn how individuals read the newspaper. Two miniature, light-weight videocameras mounted on headgear record the time readers spend with each item in the newspaper. One camera focuses on the eyes, the other on the printed page of whatever material the subject is holding. A research director at Gallup says, "This is a whole lot different from asking what people read. Now we can watch them do it."[10] The information can help marketing and design experts understand how best to draw readers' attention to the content of the newspaper. Marketing or advertising professionals may regularly bring in a group of average consumers and ask them to cook a package of food or try a new product, all under the gaze of observers who record their comments and watch what they do.

Participant Observation.   Participant observation involves joining or living with a group and becoming a part of the action. Members of the group—for instance, prison inmates—may not know the observer's true identity, but he or she clearly is a part of the group. This method of observation is common in sociological and anthropological research, as well as in communication research. It allows the information gatherer to get direct experience and to reduce reliance on the expertise or testimony of others. In becoming part of "the scene," the observer begins to understand it as an insider, to decode the various systems at work, and to interact casually with members of the group. Participant observation is an expensive technique, requiring a substantial amount of time in the field. For that reason, among others, it is less frequently used in mass communication than is the routine observation of single events. However, when a community problem is very pressing or perplexing or when a publication has the resources to devote to the topic, participant observation may be a major technique.

The Minneapolis *Star Tribune* was going to run a front-page story about the Red Lobster restaurant chain, owned by General Mills, Inc., a major corporate member of the community. In preparation for the story and to add human interest, a business reporter, Josephine Marcotty, joined the waitress-in-training program at the newest restaurant. Her story began:

> ST. CLOUD, Minn.—The vegetable of the day was buttered carrots, and the earnest staff-in-training at the newest Red Lobster restaurant in St. Cloud was pushing deep fried cheese sticks—"nice and warm and gooey"—as an appetizer.
>
> The word for the day was fabulous. Not just "Fabulous!" but "FABU-LOUS!" In the middle of a sunny Saturday afternoon two days before the grand opening, 130 of us gathered in the dining room and shouted it loud enough to raise the roof. I began to understand how Red Lobster has become the largest, most successful dinner-house chain in the country. What this is all about is building a team spirit dedicated to service.
>
> And the best way to understand it was to participate—which is how an individualistic, mildly cynical reporter prone to wearing pink socks when the dress code says black (more about that later) found herself wearing the floppy bow tie, white shirt, black pants and maroon apron of a Red Lobster waitress.[11]

Participant observation has been a major information-gathering method for numerous celebrated reports. Gloria Steinem worked as a Playboy Club bunny and wrote about the working conditions that bunnies face. John Howard Griffin, a white man, underwent treatments so he could pass as a black and wrote a book about how he experienced life as a member of another race.[12] Others have entered prisons and mental hospitals in attempts to understand life from the perspective of those in such institutions. A few have joined the corps of a city's homeless, seeking shelter in emergency quarters and meals in soup kitchens. A student journalist confined himself for a time in a wheelchair, in order to write an account of the barriers, both architectural and emotional, that the disabled face. Another joined a religious group that he suspected of illegal and unethical methods of recruiting students as members.

Participant observation generally begins only after the communicator has made a thorough study of the event or group to be observed. The observation will, of course, include interviewing other group members. As well as being costly, participant observation can be dangerous. Solid preparation helps to prepare the observer for the situation to be faced. It prepares the observer intellectually to interact on the scene while maintaining sufficient social and emotional distance so that an independent perspective remains.

Even excellent preparation may not prevent every false move, as one Wisconsin high-school student learned. With help from a corrections official and a social worker, he posed as an offender in a boys' correctional institution, an experience he reported in his high-school newspaper. However, when his first meal tray was placed before him, he forgot his new identity and politely said "Thank you" for the tray. This lapse immediately marked him as an outsider; the noisy room fell silent, and other inmates stared suspiciously. The student had reason to worry that his experiment was seriously undermined. He did, however, manage to complete his 24 hours in the institution. And his story won a high-school press award.[13]

Unobtrusive Observation. In some circumstances, unobtrusive observation may be more effective than participant observation, especially if the observer's presence will change the situation to be observed.

A team of reporters may be working on a series of articles on drunk drivers. People who drive while drunk cannot be expected to volunteer their testimony. Bartenders are unlikely to want to go on the record about the amount of drinking that may be done before patrons get into their cars. However, reporters could station themselves in bars and, as a team, carefully record what patrons drink and if they drive away from the bar. The observers would have to pay careful attention to the details: the time at which drinking begins, the number and kinds of drinks consumed, the approximate weight of each drinker, and so on. The observers would have to hear the actual drink orders, rather than assume they could identify the drinks by sight. Nonalcoholic beers look like alcoholic ones; ginger ale resembles some mixed drinks; and mineral water with a lime slice looks like gin and tonic. With these and other precautions, however, the observers could develop well-documented evidence for their series on drinking and driving. A table showing the level of intoxication for people of various weights consuming alcohol at specific rates per hour is available to assist in calculating driving impairment. The researchers could use such a table to illustrate the condition of patrons under observation before they began driving their cars.

Unobtrusive observation has a place in public-relations work, particularly in connection with special events and exhibits. Public-relations staff frequently design and set up exhibits at conferences, shows, and fairs. They observe the visitors' use of the exhibit, the attention the exhibit attracts, and the public interest in handouts and other evidence of success. They evaluate the usefulness of the exhibit to their overall strategy in public relations. In order to make such an evaluation, they may place themselves in positions where they can overhear candid remarks about the event, analyze the demand for materials distributed to passers-by, and observe the interaction of public-relations staff members with exhibit visitors.

When a company representative is giving a speech or a demonstration, public-relations staff often assist with evaluating the response to the presentation. They may observe if the speaker can be heard easily, if the audience is attentive and engaged, and if the audiovisual materials are effective. Often the public-relations department has helped to draft the speech, arrange for the setting and the audiovisual materials, and analyze the potential audience. Thus as informed observers, they can view events in the light of planning and strategy and improve subsequent performance in similar situations.

Unobtrusive observation techniques also are being adopted by advertising professionals. A very large Chicago agency has an ongoing research project in a town of 8,000 to 12,000 about 150 miles from Chicago. Advertising researchers visit the town on a regular basis and politely listen in on conversations in coffee shops and churches, hairdressers' shops, and taverns. The agency professionals are trying to learn what is important to average folks, what occupies their hearts and minds. In the process, they think they will gain clues to why people don't always follow cooking directions for frozen pizzas or what they really think about prunes. The advertising professionals have learned to prepare themselves well for their visits. One advertising agency employee's too-hip hairdo marked her as an outsider, and another researcher learned to drive a pick-up truck rather than his Audi to town.[14]

Everette E. Dennis has presented a series of "touchstones" through which communicators can keep tabs on community realities. Many of the methods he advocates require sensitive observation: learn how people live and work by observing housing standards, neighborhoods, and primary work places. Monitor such public gathering places as laundromats, beauty parlors, restaurants, and bars. Use public transportation at various times during the day and night. Watch facilities such as emergency rooms, jails, and shelters for the homeless—action at these sites helps the observer understand the community's pressure points. Observe popular culture, from fast food to pop art. Note fads and trends that affect life styles and leisure time.[15]

Developing Observation Techniques

Skilled observers are trained, rather than born. With observation, as with other skills, practice precedes proficiency. The novice can practice observing, making notes, and drawing conclusions without risking mistakes or embarrassment. Television affords the learner numerous opportunities to practice. During a televised sports event, parade, or similar nonverbal production, the novice can turn off the sound, observe, make notes, and summarize the main points. This version of the event can then be compared with the next day's newspaper account.

Novice observers typically experience a number of difficulties. One is their inability to organize their perceptions, to see anything interesting or important. They have neglected to prepare their perceptual apparatus before getting to the scene of the action. Veteran observers, though, arrive ready to see, hear, smell, and sense the activity. Skilled observers have an established system of items they have learned to put into play. They use—although many do not know the term for it—a heuristic. *Heuristics* are intellectual tools for discovering subject matter. The familiar news formula of who-what-when-where-why is one heuristic.

For observers, the news heuristic is a reasonable beginning. But each opportunity for observation offers much more than the news formula might ordinarily elicit. For example, consider the communicator who has to observe a speaker. The speech might be attended by a news reporter who intends to write an account of the talk, a public-relations specialist who helped to arrange the speech, and an advertising staff member whose clients are interested in what is being presented. Each of these observers would have a slightly different focus in the observation. Thus each might arrive with a slightly different heuristic. The following heuristic covers much that each would want to record:

1. *The event:* What is the occasion? What is its significance? Is anything unique? Who sponsored the event? Why?
2. *The speaker:* Who is the speaker? What are the speaker's credentials? Is the speaker an expert, a celebrity, or an ordinary person? What is the speaker's purpose? How are the speaker and the sponsor related to each other?
3. *The message:* What is the main idea? What are the supporting points? Does the speaker cite evidence? From whom? Does the speaker illustrate with examples? How are they significant?
4. *The delivery:* What style or tone does the speaker use? What rhetorical devices are employed? Does the speaker use humor, repetition, emphasis? What nonverbal language is noticeable? Does it support or contradict the verbal message? Does the speaker use audiovisual aids?
5. *The audience:* For whom is the speech intended? Are there social, political, and psychological factors among audience members that the speaker plays to? Are there some unfavorable psychological elements between speaker and audience? How does the speaker adapt the main idea to this audience? Does the speaker approach this same subject similarly or differently with a different audience? How does the immediate audience respond? How can other audiences—for example, those hearing a broadcast of the speech—be analyzed for their response? What evidence is there that the speaker affected the audience or motivated it to action?

To prepare for a competent observation, communicators can develop heuristics for any occasion. For example, the student reporter who entered the juvenile detention center would have found some of the heuristics listed useful but would have concentrated also on questions about physical conditions, behavior of inmates and staff toward one another, inmates' concerns about their present and their future, biographical factors connected with the boys' trouble with the law and their families, and legal implications of their detention in the center. Before arriving at the observation site, the communicator naturally would have completed much of the search strategy that involves institutional, library, and database sources.

Recording the Observations

Making a record of observations presents a variety of challenges. For ordinary observations, the communicator often is expected to make notes or record details on a small tape recorder. Examples include the sports reporter covering a game, the reporter at the scene of an accident or a natural disaster, and the advertising specialist observing the opening of a new restaurant on behalf of a client. But in many circumstances, openly recording or making notes interferes with the action being observed. For example, the audience at a play or concert expects to enjoy the performance without hearing pencil scratching by reviewers. Communicators devise a variety of strategies for such circumstances. One is training the short-term memory for excellent recall. The arts critic, for example, can wait until intermissions and note observations at that time and at the end of the performance. Participant observers may, in some circumstances, make notes in the presence of group members but more often try to do so without calling attention to their note taking. They may resort to taking notes in the privacy of bathrooms or even—in the case of observers in prisons or mental hospitals—under the bedcovers. Unobtrusive observation requires the same kinds of ingenuity. For example, the observers studying typical alcohol consumption in the bar cannot stare at other patrons and openly tabulate their orders on a chart atop the table. They might be able to make notes using a pocket recorder. For example: "8:19, A orders scotch and soda, B an eight-ounce beer. 8:45, A and B order another round." Once out of the bar, the observers could tabulate the material recorded at the scene. (Note taking is discussed in more detail in Chapter 7.)

RECOGNIZING CONDITIONS FOR DISTORTION

Since communicators constantly rely on informal sources and observations made by a variety of people, including themselves, they have to recognize the potential for distortion by these sources. Distortion is relative. Ideas about what is "real" differ from culture to culture, from time to time, and from place to place. Communicators who live in a given culture in a specific place and time should understand that the conditions of their culture influence their own definitions of a situation, as well as the definitions of their sources and their audiences. Within their cultural framework, communicators hope to avoid the most obvious and serious distortions.

Prominent causes for distortion include:

1. *Source reactions to the communicator.* Those who give tips to communicators or who serve as informal sources are familiar with the content of mass communication. Often they know, or think they know, what the communicator is looking for. Based on these ideas, sources select

what they disclose and what they withhold. In other instances, sources deliberately obscure information that they suspect is better kept secret by the organization of which they are a part.

2. *Selective perception.* Both communicators and their sources are, like all other humans, prone to perceive selectively. Selective perception is rooted in our experiences, our prejudices, and our expectations. Overcoming some of the distortions caused by selective perception lies in training, as well as in understanding the occasions when such selectivity is most damaging to accuracy. Communicators using ideas from informal sources learn, with experience, to avoid consulting those most prone to selective perception.

3. *Selective recall.* Recalling events, conditions, and factual information is tricky in many respects. Memory fades quickly. What remains may have been selected for its interest value, its amusement quotient, its quotability, or its sensationalism. Taking the most complete notes possible helps the communicator overcome some of the problems of selective recall. But sources whom the researcher consults may be relying on a selective memory when they talk to the communicator. Some are aware of the need for accuracy and offer to consult records that may aid their recall or, at least, warn that memory may be incomplete or faulty.

4. *Institutional bias.* Informal sources and communicators themselves owe allegiances to a variety of institutions. Some of their perceptions inevitably are shaped by institutional factors. Recognizing that this is so is the first step to reaching beyond the bias of the institution. (Institutional bias is discussed in more detail in Chapter 4.)

5. *Ego-involved bias.* Human beings naturally protect their egos and identities. Their testimony and observations frequently reflect strategies, conscious or unconscious, of self-protection. Communicators watch for signs that their informal sources are excessively ego-involved in their subjects. And they frequently decide not to take on topics in which they suspect their own ego is likely to interfere.

6. *Inaccurate observation.* Mechanical or technical errors abound. Each moment in the day presents us with more stimuli than we can possibly perceive. With so much around us to observe, errors are inevitable. Communicators check with as many observers as possible as one method of eliminating ordinary errors. They give more credibility to trained observers with no obvious personal or institutional biases and attempt to verify what observers tell them, especially when precision is critical.

LINKS TO THE SEARCH STRATEGY

In this step of the search strategy, the contribution of informal sources is spelled out. These include the communicator's use of personal files, casual reading, and personal memory as they relate to the topic of the search. In addition, the communicator's own professional networks and access to other community networks are included as informal sources. Observations—routine, participant, and unobtrusive—are included in this part of the search strategy.

Despite the potential hazards and limitations of informal sources and of various observation techniques, their use is highly valued in mass communication. And with good reason. They offer the communicator methods of approaching a subject, learning from others, and checking on situations and conditions as they currently exist.

Chapter 4 examines the contributions and complexities of private and public sector institutions. Access to institutional information may come through many other parts of the search-strategy process, but the next chapter has a strong emphasis on institutions as *creators* of information as well as disseminators.

NOTES

1. Amy Eisman, "How to Spot Trends and (in the Process) Spark Up Your Hard-News, City-desk Report," *Gannetteer*, October 1987, 8.
2. Daniel Schorr, "Kurds Relied on U.S. Help Before, But to No Avail," column reprinted in the *Star Tribune*, 11 April 1991, 13A.
3. Serge Schmemann, "After 45 Years Divided, The Two Germanys Unite," *New York Times*, 3 October 1990, A1.
4. "Singing 'We Are the Women,' Delegates Open U.N. Forum," *St. Louis Post-Dispatch*, 11 July 1985, 10A.
5. Larry Rohter, "Free Summer Meals Lure Children Back to School in City's Poverty Areas," *New York Times*, 11 July 1985, B1.
6. Eric Johnson (special correspondent), "New Tom, Becky to Promote Twain's Hometown," *St. Louis Post-Dispatch*, 5 July 1985, C4.
7. "Closing the gate," *The Quill*, June 1990, 31–32.
8. Sally Jenkins, "Lopez, Baker, Anderson Share U.S. Open Lead," *Washington Post*, 12 July 1985, E1.
9. Keith Schneider, "Trying to Resurrect Shades of the Old South," *New York Times*, 9 December 1990, A1.
10. Gene Goltz, "The Eyes Have It: Another Readership Research Tool Is Introduced," *presstime*, September 1987, 14–15.
11. Josephine Marcotty, "True Fish Story: Red Lobster Hooks Staff on Concept of Team Spirit," *Star Tribune*, 9 December 1990, 1A.
12. Gloria Steinem, "A Bunny's Tale," *Show*, May–June 1963; John Howard Griffin, *Black Like Me* (Toronto: Signet, 1961).
13. Douglas McLeod, "Exclusive: The Loneliness of a Lock-up, Or a Night in Detention," *Regent Review*, 24 February 1977, 8–9.
14. Andrew Stern, "Ad Agency Seeks Small-town Guide to Consumer Taste," *Star Tribune*, 29 April 1991, 3D.
15. Everette E. Dennis, "Touchstones: The Reporter's Reality," *Nieman Reports*, Autumn 1980, 40–45.

4

Digging into Institutions

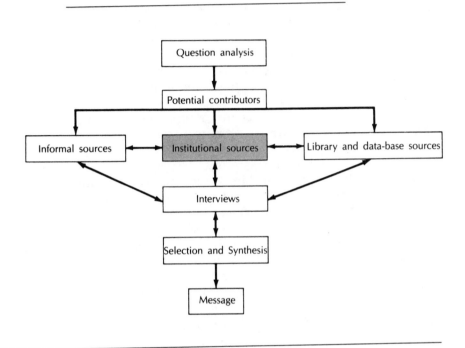

"The fabric of society" is a common metaphor that sociologists use to suggest the rich patterns and the complex interweaving of social institutions. The metaphor is both compelling and illustrative. One need only picture the cloth emerging from the loom in order to appreciate many truths about social institutions. They coexist and overlap, forming countless interlacements. They are not fully appreciated outside the context of the neighboring strands. Viewed in isolation from the other strands, they may seem confusing and distorted.

The term *institution* covers highly diverse concepts and organizations. One way to think about institutions is to view the enduring practices and relationships as the warp of the fabric. In weaving, the warp threads stretch lengthwise on the loom, while the weft is the filling threads that run crosswise, creating the specific textures, patterns, and novelty effects. Like the warp, some long-enduring social institutions are the essential threads stretching from the past to the present. All societies have conventional social arrangements, such as marriage, and legal and economic arrangements, such as property-inheritance standards and free-market behavior. All individuals exist, during much—if not all—of their lives, in relation to these fundamental institutions. But beyond that, people also relate to the more specific and visible institutions of their particular societies: governments, religious organizations, unions, political parties, schools, corporations, neighborhoods, and hobby groups, among many that might be cited.

At the junction of every thread with another in the social fabric—where the warp of the fundamental institution meets the weft of a specific institution—information is generated. Each individual in society leaves an information trail that represents interaction in the social fabric. For example, a man and a woman who marry begin a series of interactions with many institutions, which keep records that reflect the couple's married status: a marriage license is purchased; sworn witnesses confirm the alliance; insurance beneficiaries, property registration, and surnames may change. When land and a house are acquired, records establish the sales price, method of payment, and terms of ownership. When children are born, their births are recorded, and, more often than not, files relating to the births are kept by hospitals, health-insurance companies, and the attending physician or midwife. The federal government requires that all children have a Social Security number. If a savings account is established for the child, another set of tax and income records is generated. For the children and their parents, these records are just the beginning of paper—or electronic—trails of information that accompany them through their lives in society: public and quasi-public records confirm that they attend school, play tennis in the public park's league, buy a car, acquire driver's licenses, are arrested for speeding, apply for a credit card, go to the hospital emergency ward in an ambulance, receive a scholarship, earn money and pay taxes, and inherit money from a relative.

Just as individuals leave traces behind, so specific institutions leave distinctive marks. Institutions affect individuals and, simultaneously, the larger social arena. Their decisions, policies, and administrative styles are felt by individuals and by other institutions. Later in this chapter, some paper and electronic trails through institutional information will be followed.

Institutionally generated information is evident in many settings. It exists as primary evidence in the institution that developed it. It also may exist as primary material in other institutions, notably libraries and data bases. In addition, much institutional information is available as the content of many secondary sources: news, advertising, and public-relations messages that incorporate the institutional information for their own purposes, for example.

Whenever possible, communicators prefer getting information as close to its source as possible. Thus a communicator seeking information about a corporation's actions or a union's bargaining position would seek original material from the corporation or the union. Another route, however, would be to use sources available through libraries and data bases. These may be primary materials—National Labor Relations Board documents, for example—or they may be secondary ones—such as news and public-relations reports.

Communicators find themselves moving in circles during many searches. They use a library's resources, such as directories and yearbooks, to learn the names and addresses of institutions that are relevant to their information needs and key people in them. They use additional library research techniques to discover more about those institutions and people. Next, they select institutions to approach directly. Later, they return to library and data-base sources for additional material to supplement, verify, and interpret the information they have gathered. The search-strategy model, with its interplay among elements, encourages such routing among varied institutions. (Library and data-base sources are discussed in Chapters 5 and 6. However, this chapter mentions some library and data-base sources that provide searchers with the reference tools that help to locate institutional materials.)

Interplay among elements is a key concept in the search-strategy model. Communicators learn of institutions as part of question analysis, through their informal and observational methods, during interviews, and through library and data-base sources. Subsequently, communicators rely on their knowledge of institutions and their motives for and methods of producing information.

HOW AND WHY INSTITUTIONS
PRODUCE INFORMATION

Institutions—and the people who labor in them—produce a staggering amount of information. Much of it is produced for internal use only, but some is produced for use both inside and outside the institution. Some of the major reasons why institutions generate information are:

- to operate the institution itself;
- to cooperate with other institutions, including governments at all levels;
- to make decisions and set policy;
- to justify policy and operational decisions; and
- to administer policy.

For example, a retail store keeps many records for its own use. The inventory of goods ordered, received, and sold is essential for the orderly conduct of business. So are records of employees' work hours and pay rates. Generally, records of this sort are for private use in the firm. However, records of taxable goods and the amount of sales tax collected are kept and forwarded to tax collectors. Then sales-tax data are compiled and become a measure of economic activity in the community. Records of employees' work hours and pay rates may become part of the public record if there is a dispute about whether an employee was properly paid for hours worked or a dispute about payroll taxes. Thus even the relatively simple and straightforward information generated by a small retail store has some public dimensions and larger significance.

More complex information production takes place when organizations develop information for policy making. A state agency may, for example, consider closing a facility for the mentally retarded and sending residents back to their home communities for support. To properly evaluate the proposal, the agency would need a substantial amount of information. Some may be available already, but undoubtedly much more would be needed. Therefore, the agency would create "new" information to use in considering the change. Having studied the matter internally, the agency might ask other interested agencies, institutions, and citizens to comment. The information process that begins within the agency inevitably takes on a public character whenever any sensitive policy is proposed.

Justifying a policy change brings on another round of information development. In the case of closing the facility for the mentally retarded, the agency must produce information that will convince state legislators and relatives of retarded people that the change is appropriate. New audiences for the information are involved at this point, and their questions and potential objections must be addressed. Again, some new information is generated.

If the proposal is adopted, the agency must plan for administering the new program. Again, much new detailed information must be developed and communicated before the policy can go into effect. Some is directed to the information needs of administrators and people in the communities that now will serve retarded residents. Some information is related to the public-relations efforts of the agency making the change, in seeking consent of the parties most affected. Throughout these processes, information development has played a critical part in effecting a social change. The example illustrates that institutions develop information for use both internally and externally and that information plays a critical role in policy making and administration. The institution needs information in order to make a decision, justify the decision, seek consensus about the decision, administer the policy coherently and consistently, and maintain good public relations with various constituencies.

Communicators enter the picture when they understand the process through which information is produced and take advantage of the fruits of that process. Voluminous records result from the process outlined above. Many of these records are available for the asking. Some are kept within the institution. And some are publicly promoted by the agency through news releases, letters to editors, and advertisements.

PUBLIC AND PRIVATE INFORMATION

No hard and fast lines separate public information from private information. Generally, public information is that material produced at public expense for the conduct of public business and in which society has an interest in principle. Private information includes that which individuals and associations produce for their own use and for which society has no interest in principle. For example, private information includes personal diaries, correspondence, and appointment books; proprietary information—the recipe for a soft drink or a fast-food chicken product—and marketing information, of the kind used to promote a product or service.

Some public records are, by law, open for inspection by any person: licenses to drive, marry, establish businesses, and own guns, boats, cars, and airplanes; records of real-estate transactions and taxes; certificates of birth and death; minutes of meetings held by governmental bodies at all levels; records of political-campaign contributions and expenditures; records of property ownership and taxes; files of the courts and police. For most open records, however, there may be exceptions. For instance, while birth records generally are available, some governmental units have a policy of not releasing records of "illegitimate" births. And although adoption records fit the definition of public records, they are in most areas sealed so that access is available only through a court order. Similarly, minutes of meetings in which public business is conducted may be held confidential if discussion concerns personnel matters, such as evaluation of individual workers. Conversely, such a purely private item as a diary or an appointment book may become a public document. Both defendants and plaintiffs in either civil or criminal suits may offer such material as evidence, or it may be found by investigators and introduced as evidence in a trial. Through these processes, private information becomes public information.

Overall, access to various records and documents reflects long-held ideas about the role that information plays in the healthy functioning of the social and political systems. Democratic theory is based on the belief that citizens must have access to information that helps them to be members of an informed public. Most information that is made available to the public rests on this premise. In addition, governments at all levels produce volumes of information for distribution to individuals, businesses, and associations. Some of this material is consumer-oriented, while some is designed to promote good public relations for an agency or to influence public opinion in a particular direction. Indeed, the United States government is the world's largest publisher.

Additional records are produced as by-products of government business: contracts, minutes of legislative hearings, research reports filed before legislative committees, transcripts of meetings, ordinances, bills, and laws. Formats vary. Sometimes meetings are tape-recorded. If so, the tapes are available, as is such printed material as the official agenda for the meeting, the secretary's minutes, and a collection of handouts given to those who attended the meeting.

Communicators have legal and legitimate access to much more information from both private and public records than they ever think to request. Their failure to harness the information power in society's institutions arises chiefly from their neglect to request, rather than from denials of their requests. Among the communicators who effectively use information from institutions are those who comprehend the workings of institutions and bureaucracies. They understand what is legitimately considered public and what appropriately remains private. They have a clear picture of institutions in the overall fabric of society and recognize that information is generated at most of the interlacements that make up the fabric.

INSTITUTIONAL BIAS IN INFORMATION

As we have seen, institutions generate information that helps them to conduct their activities and to perpetuate their own existence. In that sense, information that serves their purposes inevitably has a bias that communicators should understand. In addition, being closely woven into the social fabric, institutions naturally reflect prevailing social values and assumptions about the world. For example, the gross domestic product (GDP) is the United States government indicator that reports the total national output of goods and services valued at market prices. It is widely cited as a measure of overall economic activity in the nation. It reflects purchases of goods and services by consumers and government, along with investment and net export figures. However, many goods and services—but especially services—are not purchased, but provided for free. Recently, with many social and economic changes taking place in society, the measure of "work" has been challenged. For example, volunteers work in schools, hospitals, nursing homes, recreation centers, political parties, civic associations, and countless other facilities and groups. Their unpaid efforts do not show in the gross national product. The same activities would register as productive activity if wages were paid. The same is true in households. If someone is employed to clean, cook, and maintain the house and equipment, the GDP includes that work. If members of the family do these tasks, their work is not officially a part of the indicator. The example is offered not as a criticism of the GDP, but to illustrate the principle that all information reflects some kind of bias that is rooted in assumptions about the world. In this case, the assumption is that if it is not paid for, it is not work. Challenges to this assumption have come from other institutions, which criticize the bias that is evident and produce information in support of their objection.

The communicators' responsibility is not to resolve the arguments but to be alert to diverse viewpoints and to the significance of institutional bias in the information they collect. Communicators can reasonably expect institutions to be reliable, accurate, and complete in their information-producing and -disseminating functions. But they should not expect the information to be neutral in respect to social values and social structures. Nor should they expect that institutions will not alter their methods as laws change and as social values and social structures evolve. Rather, they should, when they use information from institutions, recognize the biases, assumptions, and vested interests inherent in the information.

There is, in fact, competition among institutions that try to produce a "definition of the situation" that will be broadly adopted in society. As part of such competition, institutions provide information to mass communicators as they attempt to influence prevailing ideas. Despite the competition, the most powerful of the institutions often have overwhelming advantages in having their perspectives adopted. For measuring national economic conditions, for example, there is no close competitor to the United States government. The *information subsidy* provided to communicators by any institution (see Chapters 2 and 9) may significantly affect the perspective the communicator adopts in treating the subject. It is important that this information subsidy be recognized and acknowledged.

Since communicators play significant roles in distributing information in society, they naturally adopt much of the information produced by institutions. Their skill in making full use of what is available from many sources, as contrasted with simply using what an association promotes, can make an important difference in how residents and consumers are informed and in how members of society understand their common life together. Nevertheless, some information produced in the private sector is not available to communicators, however resourceful they may be. While access to information is a generally conceded social value, so is privacy. Frequently, the two values conflict. That being the case, communicators learn to use a variety of routes in seeking information that institutions in the private sector are willing to make public.

Institutions devote substantial resources to organizing and maintaining the information they have generated. They keep their collections in libraries and archives run by knowledgeable staff members. They also have a staff that provides information to communicators from outside the organization who request material. For example, a corporation, trade association, or foundation is likely to have both a library and a public-relations or public-service office. These are early stops on the communicator's routes, in most instances. The staff in these offices assist the communicator as far as their own expertise permits and make referrals to other offices and staff members in the institution. In addition to maintaining libraries, large organizations may produce data bases that are available to communicators. These resources supplement the institutions' publications and news releases.

Small institutions, of course, have less elaborate services available to communicators than do large institutions. The National Council of Churches, at its headquarters, naturally provides more easily for communicators' needs than does the small-town church with one or two staff members. Despite the shortage of staff, communicators find that even small institutions try to cooperate with requests for information.

MAJOR TYPES OF INSTITUTIONS

Institutions are divided, broadly, into two sectors: the private and the public. Private institutions are those funded with money and other resources from private individuals, acting singly or in association with one another. Public institutions are those funded with tax money and other resources from local, state, and federal governments. Thus the corner drug store is in the private sector, while the police precinct station next door is in the public sector. The elementary school maintained with tax revenues is part of the public sector, while the church-affiliated school is in the private sector. The lines are hardly neat, however. Almost all private colleges have students whose financial support comes partly from state and federal sources. And the dormitory they live in may have been built with public support. Most corporations are in the private sector, but some are joint ventures with the federal government, as is COMSAT, the communication-satellite company.

Both private and public sectors produce information that heavily influences collective life. The information-producing industries are significant not merely for their capacity to issue statistics and to produce facts. More importantly, they contribute to the conventional wisdom, to the collective sense of reality, and to public sentiment and opinion on a wide variety of topics. Understanding the context in which institutions gather and disclose information is an important part of the communicator's obligation to the audience.

Private-Sector Institutions

Businesses and Corporations. Businesses produce proprietary information, which is used to enhance their competitive advantage, as well as information they are willing to make public. For example, a corporation that is building a headquarters is not only willing, but eager, to have the public learn about the project—the firm of architects, the cost of construction, the number of jobs it provides in the community, the materials used in construction, the expected completion date. This information is available through the public-relations department of the firm. However, some facts about the project are not available for public consumption—for example, details about the computer system and the security systems safeguarding it and information about equipment that gives the company its competitive advantage over others.

Businesses issue many publications designed to inform various groups about their products, services, and activities. Among the types of publications that communicators find useful are news releases, annual reports, house organs, newsletters and magazines distributed to clients and customers, and reports circulated to others in the industry. Because they are directed to different audiences, a single firm's publications present different information and varied perspectives.

Generally, businesses are willing to provide information from their own research if doing so does not undermine their competitive advantage. For example, a sporting-goods manufacturer may disclose some statistics that it compiled about changes in American life styles. It would not, however, be likely to reveal those portions of the research on which it is basing a new product line or marketing plan. Beyond the research information, however, firms also offer to provide a wide variety of publications and services about their activities. Typical offerings include industry statistics, biographies of officials, photos, press kits, bibliographies, brochures, information searches, and interview arrangements. The public-relations office typically handles preliminary requests from communicators.

Another example of business information subsidies to communicators is the company information service. For example, the Aerobic Information Bureau is actually a division of the Reebok athletic shoe company. The service issues a monthly newsletter discussing the physiology and health benefits of exercise. The Gatorade Sports Science Institute, a division of the beverage company, hired nutritionists, professors, and trainers to produce sports and nutrition information in a bimonthly bulletin sent to 13,000 sports medicine professionals. Part of the purpose of such information services is to promote the use of certain products and reinforce the brand names of the sponsoring company.

In addition to the information that businesses disclose voluntarily, either as a courtesy or for their own advantage, communicators are aware that the law requires many disclosures. Businesses intersect with governments at all levels. In many instances, a license is required in order to conduct business. This "permission" to do business affects business people from the ice-cream vendor on the street to executives of aerospace firms that have contracts with the Defense Department. Many public records, which are generally available to communicators and other residents, result from the licensing power of governments at the local, state, and national level. The inspection power is another example of government and business intersection. To monitor safety and health standards, governments inspect restaurants, hospitals, nursing homes, factories, elevators, and countless other facilities operated in the private sector. The inspections result in public records setting forth the inspectors' findings. For example, a major metropolitan television station examined the city board of health's restaurant inspection records for a variety of food establishments and then visited those restaurants with a camera crew. Their surprise visits documented food preparation and handling problems on tape. The series was so popular that the station instituted a regular feature: the anchors report twice a month on all restaurants that failed their health inspections. Disclosure of relevant public information is another point of intersection between government and business. For example, federal law requires that publicly held corporations file quarterly and annual reports on their financial condition. The reports include the names of corporate officers along with their salaries, bonuses, and certain fringe benefits. Additional typical content includes information on new products and services, acquisitions, sales, divestitures, mergers, major lawsuits, and government regulations that affect business. Annual reports are available through the firm itself and through stock-brokerage houses.

Privately held businesses are not required to file such reports. However, both privately held and publicly held corporations get involved in law suits and criminal complaints that bring them into courts of law. And court decisions, along with records introduced as evidence, are publicly accessible. Court records, then, reveal much information that was hidden. For example, a communicator might find the following in the record of a patent-

Corporations and Their Public-Relations Officers

Dun & Bradstreet directories
O'Dwyer's Directory of Corporate Communications
O'Dwyer's Directory of Public Relations Firms
Predicasts F & S Index United States
Predicasts F & S Index of Corporate Change
Standard & Poor's Register of Corporations, Directors and Executives
Thomas Register of American Manufacturers

Corporate Publications

Standard Periodical Directory
Working Press of the Nation

Public Records about Corporations

Corporate annual reports

The Internal Revenue Service requires that nonprofit organizations file IRS Form 990, which details how an organization raises and spends money each year. The Revenue Code allows for more than 20 categories of nonprofit organizations, including some nonprofit corporations, investment partnerships, and businesses. These records are open to the public; in some states the records are available through a computer data base.

Public reports filed with the Securities and Exchange Commission (SEC)—such as those identifying stockholders and officers, disclosing significant changes in ownership or finances, and alerting the agency to the possibility of takeover by another firm—can be monitored regularly using either the printed reports or the data-base versions.

Public reports filed with the Federal Trade Commission (FTC)—such as those that must be filed when a corporation is under investigation, when a merger occurs, or when advertising claims are being challenged—are available.

Public reports filed by the Consumer Products Safety Commission—such as those about public hearings on product safety, defect notices, and injury and illness data related to consumer products—can alert the communicator to important activities.

Foreign Markets and International Corporations

Overseas Business Report
Predicasts F & S Index Europe
Predicasts F & S Index International
Principal International Businesses

The International Trade Administration, a division of the United States Department of Commerce, is responsible for helping United States firms develop their export markets. However, the agency will provide profiles of foreign-based companies and can offer analysis of the economic and commercial situation in a particular country.

FIGURE 4.1 First steps for locating information on businesses and corporations

infringement suit: financial standing and strategy, product design and manufacturing technique, advertising and marketing tactics, franchise and dealership data.

Trade Associations. Individual business firms generally belong to associations of companies in the same industry. Through the association, they exchange information, lobby for favorable legislation and administrative rules,

Encyclopedia of Associations
Standard Rate and Data Service: Business Publications volumes

Contact the American Society of Association Executives

FIGURE 4.2 First steps for locating information on trade associations

and promote their industries as a whole. They produce an enormous amount of information useful to communicators and have offices whose task is to make it easy for communicators to get the information they offer. For example, the Aerospace Industries Association of America represents American manufacturers of missiles, aircraft, and spacecraft. Through its public-relations office, communicators can get statistical data, the industry's positions on aerospace issues, and similar material.

Virtually every powerful commercial and business interest is involved in trade associations. Information is collected and released to the public cautiously, since the various members of any trade association have different vested interests and methods of protecting certain kinds of information. Communicators should be aware that trade associations share voluminous amounts of information, but what is released publicly is carefully negotiated with an eye toward protecting members' interests.

Unions and Professional Associations. Workers in every field from the arts to zoo keeping are organized into trade unions and professional associations. Typically, these groups conduct and sponsor research, lobbying, organizing, and public-relations activities. Like other associations, they offer communicators facts and views on issues that concern them. They provide biographies of their leaders, statistics on wages and benefits, press kits, newsletters, pamphlets, position papers, annual reports, and assistance in gathering information at their conventions or during labor negotiations. Some communicators qualify to be placed on the associations' or unions' mailing lists and regularly receive bulletins and newsletters from them. Large organizations have public-relations officials who maintain contact with media people.

Foundations. More than 27,000 foundations fill a variety of roles in American life, spending billions of dollars on activities they deem important. These nonprofit organizations not only wield substantial power but also vary in purpose. Some support causes and classes of people, conduct or sponsor research, promote viewpoints, and subsidize activities that are not supported in the marketplace. They issue annual reports on their expenditures, invite grant submissions, and report to the federal and state governments on their financial affairs. Foundations are under close scrutiny because, as nonprofit organizations, they sometimes are used by individuals or corporations as tax-sheltered means to pursue personal interests. Regulation is designed to ensure that foundation expenditures are in the interest of the larger society, rather than in the personal interest of those donating tax-exempt money.

Encyclopedia of Associations
Occupational Health and Safety Letter
Occupational Safety and Health Reporter
Register of Reporting Labor Organizations

Professional organizations have their own directories and/or yearbooks, such as the *American Medical Directory, Directory of Environmental Scientists in Agriculture,* and *American Library Association Yearbook.*
Union offices in all communities provide information on bargaining, contracts, constitutions, and membership.
The National Labor Relations Board is an independent federal agency that issues decisions each year that relate to collective bargaining, unfair labor practice, and other labor relations issues. NLRB files may be available through the regional office where the case arose.

FIGURE 4.3   First steps for locating information on unions and professional associations

Religious Institutions.   Among the oldest institutions are religious organizations, which touch the lives of many individuals and intersect with other institutions at all levels. In the local congregation are found records of births, deaths, and such rites of passage as baptism, confirmation, bar and bas mitzvah, and marriage. Other records preserve details about selection of clergy, financial matters, membership, and synagogue- and church-run groups, such as youth clubs, missions, and prayer and study groups. Locally, regionally, and nationally, religious institutions hold conventions, keep minutes of their meetings, and issue news releases, publications, and position papers. In doing so, they create detailed records useful to communicators and to scholars.

Religious organizations affiliate in a variety of common-interest associations. For example, the National Council of Churches of Christ has 32 denominations as members and speaks on their behalf on matters ranging from theology to justice and liberation. The National Conference of Christians and Jews, B'nai B'rith International, the American Jewish Committee, and the National Association of Evangelicals are examples of other national religious associations that provide information to communicators and seek to influence opinion through their public pronouncements. These, and others, produce the usual collections of publications, news releases, statistics, and position papers.

FIGURE 4.4   First steps for locating information on foundations

Foundation Directory
Foundation Grants Index
Foundation Grants to Individuals
International Foundation Directory

The Internal Revenue Service requires private foundations to file annual reports about their financial activities with IRS Form 990–PF. The Foundation Center, with offices in New York, Washington, D.C., Cleveland, and San Francisco, collects foundation tax records from the IRS and makes them available to the public.

Directory of Religious Organizations in the United States
Handbook of Denominations in the United States
Religion Index
Yearbook of American and Canadian Churches

FIGURE 4.5   First steps for locating information on religious institutions

Colleges and Universities.   The research universities in the United States are among the most prolific of information-producing institutions. Most can be thought of as part of the private sector, even though many are public institutions in some sense of the word. Some are privately endowed and operated, but rely on public research-and-development funds. Some are partly supported by state or local taxes but are viewed as independent of executive and legislative branches of the government. Public colleges and universities, by law, disclose much more about their operations than do private ones. In a private college, for example, such information as staff salaries is not available, whereas it is available in a public institution.

Research conducted by faculty in colleges and universities constitutes a treasure for society and communicators. Most of the basic study in all fields of knowledge in the United States takes place under the auspices of higher education. Information concerning this research finds its way to the public through a variety of routes. One is the public-relations office of the college or university. Another is the papers presented by individual researchers at conferences and their findings published in books and scholarly journals. Teaching faculty present their research in classes, in talks in the community, and in applications for research grants. In addition, communicators can locate research topically and regionally by consulting research directories.

Additional significant information about colleges and universities involves their curricula. Course catalogs, faculty biographies, and the campus telephone directory give significant clues to the organization and conduct of the teaching program.

Political Parties, Citizen-Action Groups, and Policy Associations.   Political parties have been significant almost since the birth of the United States. They are not provided for in the Constitution, but they vitally affect local, state,

FIGURE 4.6   First steps for locating information on colleges and universities

American Men and Women of Science
American Universities and Colleges
Directory of American Scholars
Directory of Postsecondary Institutions
Education Index
Research Centers Directory

The Office of Educational Research and Improvement, a division of the United States Department of Education, operates an Education Information Branch, which disseminates statistics and publishes studies related to all levels of education.

and federal government. Political-party offices at each level reflect party activities and disseminate information concerning their actions. This is particularly the case during election campaigns. Communicators contact these
offices directly and monitor the publications and documents they issue.

The mission of citizen-action groups is to monitor the life of communities
and the nation and to suggest and argue for changes that they think will
benefit society or some segment of society. These groups may ask for change
in such private-sector institutions as corporations and colleges and in public-
sector institutions. Like all other institutions, they are in the information-
producing business. They study issues, conduct research, engage in
advertising and public-relations campaigns, and try to influence policy wherever they think change is needed.

Innumerable associations that promote ideals of good government operate at all levels in the United States. In some organizations, local groups that
operate at the township, city, or county level are linked at the state and
national levels. One example of this form of organization is the League of
Women Voters, which conducts research at all levels and presents its findings
to voters. The league also sponsors the televised debates between the presidential and vice-presidential candidates.

Some organizations have much narrower and more specific goals than do
good-government groups. Among these are associations that monitor the
private and the public sectors for infringements of laws or constitutional
rights. The civil liberties of Americans are the special interest of the American Civil Liberties Union, for example. This national association has state and
local affiliates, all of which work with the national organization to discover
violations of historic civil liberties. In addition to publicizing civil-rights violations, the association assists individuals in filing lawsuits related to them.
The National Organization for Women (NOW), the National Association for
the Advancement of Colored People (NAACP), the Urban League, and many
other organizations operate similarly.

Countless groups fulfill similar roles on behalf of innumerable ideologies
and causes. Wildlife and ecology issues, for example, are the concern of such
associations as the Izaak Walton League, the Sierra Club, the Audubon Society, and the National Wildlife Federation. Some national organizations are
devoted to a single idea—Mothers Against Drunk Driving (MADD) is one
example. Some controversial laws stimulate the sprouting of clusters of associations to either support or oppose legislation or court rulings. Examples
include groups defending and opposing legalized abortion, gun control, tobacco subsidies, and protective tariffs.

Policy and public-affairs groups resemble other private-sector organizations in many ways. For example, they typically conduct research and publicize results selectively as they seek to influence public opinion, legislation,
and administrative actions. They also make use of information produced by
others, extracting from government documents material that is useful for
their perspectives and sharing with their members and the public information
produced by associations with views similar to their own. They maintain

America Votes: A Handbook of Contemporary Election Statistics
Directory of Newsletters
Encyclopedia of Associations
Newsletters Directory
Washington Representatives Book

Federal lobbyists must register with the Secretary of the Senate or the Clerk of the House of Representatives in the United States Congress. The registration reports include the name and address of the lobbyist, the name and address of the employer in whose interest the lobbyist is working, duration of employment, salary paid and by whom, and types of expenses allowed by the employer. The House of Representatives' reports also are available in a computer data base.

The Federal Election Commission requires all presidential and congressional candidates to file reports about their campaign finances, including lists of individual contributors' names, contributions from political action committees (PACs) and political parties, and bank loans. The FEC has a public records office and a press office that can provide records within a few days. Some FEC data also are available in electronic-data-base form.

FIGURE 4.7 First steps for locating information on political parties, citizen-action groups, and policy associations

offices in state capitals and in Washington, D.C. They lobby in the capitals, either with their own staff members or with the assistance of lobbying firms. They keep in touch with their own members through publications and with the mass-communication industries through news releases and personal contact. Communicators find these groups eager to remain in contact with them and willing to contribute information that helps them to tell their story to the public. The cautions about the potential bias of information apply to that produced by these organizations as much as to information produced by groups not so explicitly concerned with public affairs and public policy.

Interest and Hobby Associations. In addition to the policy-oriented groups, the private sector includes thousands of associations whose members pursue more personal interests. Some people join to indulge their interest in a sport or travel; others, to associate with like-minded button collectors, restorers of antique cars, and breeders of toy poodles; still others, to share skills and equipment. Such hobby groups maintain organizations chiefly to serve their members, rather than to promote an organizational ideology or influence public opinion on issues. Thus they are less active in seeking attention from communicators. They may enter the public arena in rare instances. The car-restorer association may oppose a drastic rise in the fees charged for license plates for classic cars, for example. Or, the poodle breeder may become concerned with maintaining standards for pedigrees. But for the most part, these associations have fewer reasons to seek communicators' attention than do the policy and citizen-action associations. Thus communicators may have to make relatively greater efforts to get information from these associations than from those whose mission includes influencing opinion.

Public-Sector Institutions

Institutions in the public sector—governments, particularly—are among the most prolific producers of information used in mass communication. There are a number of reasons why governments are such enormous information factories. Some information is collected for internal record keeping and decision making and for creating a permanent record of government activities. Some is collected on behalf of other institutions: the statistical material produced by the federal government alone is critical to the operation of traditional commerce, manufacturing, and services, as well as to the new information economy. Much information is generated as a way of keeping track of government-sponsored or -commissioned research. Also, some government agencies serve as clearinghouses for the collection and dissemination of information that is produced by other institutions in society. The National Technical Information Service is an example of a clearinghouse at the federal level.

Some of the information generated by governments is available only to those who are aware of its existence and who request it. But some is advertised for consumers ("Write for your free booklet from Pueblo, Colorado") and is made available to them either for free or at nominal cost. The federal government actively promotes distribution of these materials: books and pamphlets on child care, nutrition, health and safety, insurance, retirement, national parks and forests, horticulture, and lawn care—to name but a few.

One way to picture the complex organization of public-sector information is to visualize a grid with nine boxes, like the table pictured here. Information is generated at each level and in each branch of government. The information sources are so voluminous that it would require a book for each of the nine boxes to discuss comprehensively the material available at each level and in each branch. For instance, at local levels of government—township, municipality, county—legislative decisions are made by an elected council or board. Much complexity at the local level results from the overlapping political jurisdictions that are typical in American government. A person who resides at 2345 Elm Street in Anytown, U.S.A., may have to comply with legislative decisions made by a city council, park board, school board, county board, metropolitan council, water-quality board, port authority, mosquito-control district, sanitation district, board of estimate and taxation, and a variety of additional bodies that legislate for local governments.

Each piece of information collected or produced by a public institution has either a public or a private character. By definition, some information must be public. The clearest example is laws. Obviously, laws enacted and

Branch	Local	State	National
Legislative	Council	Legislative	Congress
Judicial	Municipal courts	State courts	Federal courts
Executive	Mayor	Governor	President

interpreted cannot be obeyed unless they are made public. Thus even societies in which the public cannot observe the making of laws at least follow the practice of making the laws public. However, much greater openness is the rule in democratic systems, in which public-affairs information is expected to be accessible. Conversely, some material has little or no significant public character. For example, public clinics treat medical patients who have no way to pay their own medical bills, but these patients' medical records are considered private. There is no public interest in revealing medical information about individuals, even if their treatment is at public expense. But medical information about individuals is aggregated into statistics that register the state of public health at all levels. In each local area, contagious diseases and causes of death are recorded, tabulated, and analyzed. Thus the communicator has access to government-produced documentation about public-health matters in the community, the state, and the nation.

Information produced by governments is widely available not only from governments, but also from other institutional sources. As original material of a public character, it is obtainable from the governmental unit that produced it and, often, in libraries and data bases. In addition, news, public-relations, and advertising messages sometimes include governmentally produced information. A news account may include a table of the federal figures on estimated mileage for all cars sold in the United States. A public-relations release may include census figures, and a car manufacturer's public-relations release may also include the most recent federal figures on estimated mileage for all models built by the firm. A car advertisement may include the federal figures on estimated mileage for the model advertised.

Generally, communicators prefer to use original materials, rather than secondary sources. And they may prefer to get the information from the governmental producer, rather than from a library or data base. Convenience, location, and cost are factors in this decision. Some local agencies may be the only repositories of certain local government information. In addition, many communicators habitually rely on staff members in public agencies to help them with their information-gathering tasks. They find that the personal contact facilitates their collection of information. Finally, mass communicators traditionally have not used libraries and data bases extensively. Too often in the past, they were unaware of the tools available in public and academic libraries. These customs are changing, however, as communicators broaden their approaches to information search. The search strategy helps communicators discover a variety of paths that lead to information from governments.

Municipal and County Governments. Since it is impossible to commit to memory all the sources of governmental information, communicators have to learn how governments operate, how they produce information, and what portion of the information is available in public records, documents, and publications. In addition to general background on governmental operations, it is useful to maintain a file of material that is specific to a local area of interest. Such a file should include organization charts of municipal and

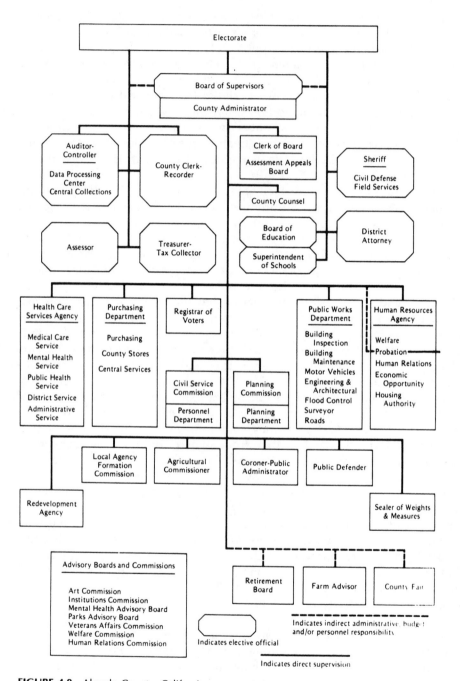

FIGURE 4.8 Almeda County, California, government

The chart shows the following organizational structure:

Electorate

Board of Supervisors
County Administrator

Auditor-Controller
Data Processing Center
Central Collections

County Clerk-Recorder

Clerk of Board
Assessment Appeals Board

Sheriff
Civil Defense
Field Services

County Counsel

Assessor

Treasurer-Tax Collector

Board of Education
Superintendent of Schools

District Attorney

Health Care Services Agency
Medical Care Service
Mental Health Service
Public Health Service
District Service
Administrative Service

Purchasing Department
Purchasing
County Stores
Central Services

Registrar of Voters

Public Works Department
Building Inspection
Building Maintenance
Motor Vehicles
Engineering & Architectural
Flood Control
Surveyor
Roads

Human Resources Agency
Welfare
Probation
Human Relations
Economic Opportunity
Housing Authority

Civil Service Commission
Personnel Department

Planning Commission
Planning Department

Local Agency Formation Commission

Agricultural Commissioner

Coroner-Public Administrator

Public Defender

Redevelopment Agency

Sealer of Weights & Measures

Advisory Boards and Commissions
Art Commission
Institutions Commission
Mental Health Advisory Board
Parks Advisory Board
Veterans Affairs Commission
Welfare Commission
Human Relations Commission

Retirement Board

Farm Advisor

County Fair

Indicates elective official

Indicates indirect administrative budget and/or personnel responsibility

Indicates direct supervision

county governments, such as that of Alameda County, California, illustrated in Figure 4.8. Each office is, in effect, an information factory and repository. Many, if not all, offices have staff members assigned to provide information to those who seek it from these offices. News, advertising, and public-relations professionals are among those who routinely gather information from the county and other local government offices. Using Alameda County as an example, a public-relations staffer for the state dental association may seek information from the Public-Health Service and from the office of the Superintendent of Schools before organizing a Dental Health Week geared to elementary-school children. General-assignment news reporters might require information from any of the offices, depending on an editor's assignment. Specialists in medical, environmental, education, welfare, law-enforcement, and political reporting would have more specific contacts with offices on their beats. Advertising professionals might work with staff members in those offices directly related to their specific assignments. Governments do a substantial amount of advertising. The Redevelopment Agency, the County Fair, and the Planning Department are among departments likely to advertise to the general public.

Communicators receive some information when local governments want to publicize their actions or decisions. For example, when a paving crew plans to interrupt traffic for a week, the city or county Public Works Department will issue a news release to the media. When a public immunization campaign is scheduled, the Public Health Service will try to get the word out. Public-service advertisements on radio and television might be used, along with news releases to the media. In addition, public-relations staff members may schedule news conferences and public meetings, send letters or postcards, visit or telephone officials in government departments, and offer to help the news media with spot coverage.

In other instances, communicators take the initiative. They monitor the schedule of public meetings, making sure that significant ones are covered. They attend to conflict over proposed ordinances and problematic enforcement of laws. As part of their surveillance of the city and county, they learn to interview knowledgeable residents and public officials. They learn to read

FIGURE 4.9 First steps for locating information on municipal and county governments

Congressional District Data Book
County and City Data Book
Index to Current Urban Documents
Municipal Yearbook
PAIS International In Print
Urban Affairs Abstracts

Municipal government libraries provide information about city or county policies, along with documents issued by local government agencies.

Municipal public records from 12 major metropolitan areas may be searched in an on-line data base called *Information America*. Civil suit information, real property filings, and limited partnership information are just some of the records that may be located through the system.

and get the main idea from a wide variety of public records. They are interested in taxes and budgets, licenses and inspections, arrests and lawsuits and the judgments rendered in them, decisions of the medical examiner's office, demographic shifts in the local population, statistics relating to the business climate and marketing opportunities.

Information seekers at the local level can make the best use of available material if they understand the assignments and the limitations of each government office. For those offices they deal with directly, communicators also know what records are kept, how they are kept, who is responsible for record keeping, and who supervises the office. Communicators also keep abreast of changes in state and federal laws that enlarge or limit their access to public records at the local levels.

Local governments provide substantial help to communicators and community residents who search for information. Many maintain municipal reference libraries, which exist chiefly to help public employees do research on topics connected with their departmental jobs. But communicators and private persons also frequently have access to the materials. Through the use of such a reference collection, communicators can conveniently compare local statistics and policies with those in similar municipalities.

State Governments.   Local governments frequently operate at the direction of state governments. Although births and deaths are recorded locally, for example, the format and method for recording them is prescribed by the state. This is so with many local government actions. State governments resemble the federal government more than they do local governments. A simplified model of the executive branch of state government is shown in Figure 4.10. Much more complex ones exist; for example, that of North Carolina has 189 boxes specifying such agencies as the Tobacco Seed Committee and the Armory Commission. State governments, of course, also include the legislative and judicial branches. All three branches of state government are rich sources of information for communicators.

Typically, state governments employ many public-relations staffers who help provide information to residents and to media representatives. In addition, advertising agencies have contracts with state governments and produce print, radio, and television ads for such purposes as promoting tourism. Like local governments, states actively disseminate some information. Each state maintains a legislative reference library that is open to both officials and private individuals. States issue numerous publications, many of which grow out of research done in state agencies. These publications include reference works that are useful to individual communicators and have a place in the libraries of media organization. For example, a state law-enforcement directory lists the names, addresses, and telephone numbers of law-enforcement offices in each city, county, and state. An international-trade directory lists the state manufacturers that export their products abroad, while the state manufacturers' directory notes companies, their locations, and their products.

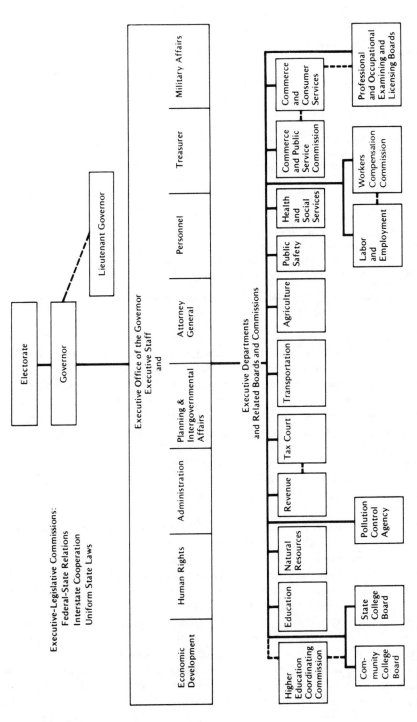

FIGURE 4.10 State government

Book of the States
Monthly Checklist of State Publications
State and Metropolitan Area Data Book
The State Publications Index

Each state publishes a *Blue Book*, or legislative manual, that compiles state government data. Or, the searcher may consult *State Blue Books, Legislative Manuals and Reference Publications: A Selective Bibliography* (1990).
    Legislative activities for all 50 states may be tracked using one of several electronic-data-base systems: Commerce Clearinghouse, State Net, and Legislative Information Network Corporation (LINC) allow searchers to identify bills introduced in any state legislature, check the status of legislation, and track activities in each statehouse. Searchers also may consult *Access to Electronic Records: A Guide to Reporting on State and Local Government in the Computer Age* (1991), published by the Reporters Committee for Freedom of the Press, to learn whether a state has its own electronic system for public use.
    State legislative reference libraries collect information to meet legislators' needs, but these libraries sometimes serve other patrons.
    State government publications sometimes are listed in a state publications catalog available from the state government printing office.

FIGURE 4.11   First steps for locating information on state governments

Communicators generally seek information from a limited number of state offices, rather than from a wide range of them. The ad agency that has the tourism account might do most of its business with the departments of economic development and natural resources. A public-relations staff member with the Association for the Blind may have frequent contact with the health and education administrations. Legislative reporters, of course, have to be broadly familiar with the legislature as an institution. They frequently seek information from both the legislative and the executive branches concerning a single issue. For example, if the legislature is considering a radical change in the method of distributing financial aid to schools, the story requires comment from the governor and from staff in the state education department.

Public meetings are additional sources of information. Countless public meetings take place, called by the legislative and executive branches and by citizen-action groups and business associations that seek to have their views heard. In some cases, minutes or other forms of records are available. But in many instances, communicators must be alert and attend the meetings in order to write satisfactory accounts of events.

The state constitutions specify the system of courts for each state. The systems differ substantially from one another. Thus communicators must become acquainted with the provisions of the state constitution and learn the court system of the states in which they are serious about gathering judicial information. Some courts, of course, operate at the municipal and county levels as prescribed by the state constitution. The decisions of lower courts can be appealed up the ladder of a state's system of appellate courts. (Locating legal materials is discussed in Chapter 5.)

Federal Government.   The federal government of the United States probably has no close competitor as a generator of information. Its information production takes place not only in the nation's capital, but also in federal offices in all 50 states and at diplomatic posts and military installations around the globe. It is willing and, in some cases, eager to provide some information to all who seek it. This is especially the case with consumer information and with statistical material that is collected specifically to monitor such important economic indicators as agriculture, manufacturing, and commerce. Other information is difficult to extract, and some is impossible to obtain, such as documents that are classified on national-security grounds.

Federal offices employ staff that is responsible for assisting communicators and other information seekers, such as the general public, business people, and employees of foreign governments. The general title for such individuals is public information officer. A solid understanding of the relationships within and among the three branches of the federal government allows communicators to make the most speedy and effective use of the vast resources of the federal government.

As with local and state governments, an organization chart of the national government helps the communicator identify the major departments and the lines of authority and responsibility (see Figure 4.12). A novice needing introduction to the federal government discovers that the government itself publishes comprehensive manuals and handbooks that specify how each agency operates, what its responsibilities are, and how to contact it. In addition, organization charts showing, in more depth, the specific offices that can provide needed information are useful reference tools. For example, a Washington correspondent covering Congress must have extensive knowledge of the organization of the Senate and the House of Representatives. Each member of Congress has an office and staff that constitute a separate information factory. Each legislative committee has a research staff that gathers existing information and produces new reports on behalf of the committee. Each committee publishes the official record of the hearings it holds before making a recommendation or sending a bill to Congress. It also publishes a report explaining its recommendations and its intent in supporting proposed legislation. Congress has extensive research services at its command. The facilities include the Library of Congress, which was founded in 1800 and is now open to the public, and the Congressional Research Service (CRS), which serves the legislators and their staff members exclusively. While CRS services are not open to the public, communicators sometimes can get copies of needed reports through the office of a legislator. CRS also issues reports and magazines and maintains reading rooms, reference centers, and computer services, all of which the researcher in Washington finds invaluable. Two other major research arms of the Congress are the Office of Technology Assessment (OTA) and the General Accounting Office (GAO). These agencies have reputations in both the public and private sectors for their meticulously produced, independent, and nonpartisan studies of any subject for which a request from Congress or any other agency has been made. Their

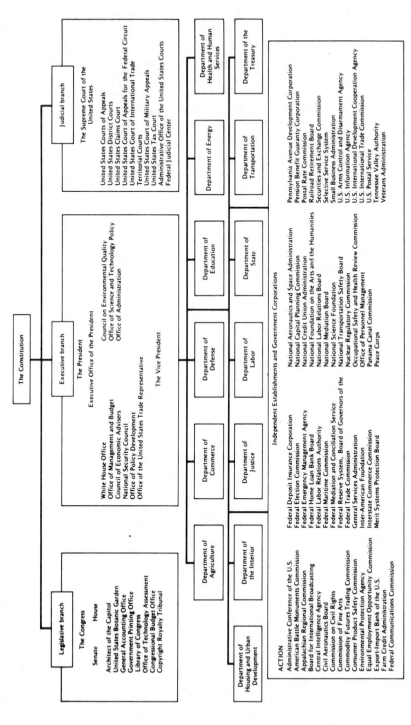

FIGURE 4.12 The government of the United States

The Constitution

Legislative branch

The Congress

Senate   House

Architect of the Capitol
United States Botanic Garden
General Accounting Office
Government Printing Office
Library of Congress
Office of Technology Assessment
Congressional Budget Office
Copyright Royalty Tribunal

Executive branch

The President

Executive Office of the President

White House Office
Office of Management and Budget
Council of Economic Advisers
National Security Council
Office of Policy Development
Office of the United States Trade Representative

Council on Environmental Quality
Office of Science and Technology Policy
Office of Administration

The Vice President

Judicial branch

The Supreme Court of the
United States

United States Courts of Appeals
United States District Courts
United States Claims Court
United States Court of Appeals for the Federal Circuit
United States Court of International Trade
Territorial Courts
United States Court of Military Appeals
United States Tax Court
Administrative Office of the United States Courts
Federal Judicial Center

Department of Agriculture
Department of Commerce
Department of Defense
Department of Education
Department of Energy
Department of Health and Human Services
Department of Housing and Urban Development
Department of the Interior
Department of Justice
Department of Labor
Department of State
Department of Transportation
Department of the Treasury

Independent Establishments and Government Corporations

ACTION
Administrative Conference of the U.S.
American Battle Monuments Commission
Appalachian Regional Commission
Board for International Broadcasting
Central Intelligence Agency
Civil Aeronautics Board
Commission on Civil Rights
Commission of Fine Arts
Commodity Futures Trading Commission
Consumer Product Safety Commission
Environmental Protection Agency
Equal Employment Opportunity Commission
Export-Import Bank of the U.S.
Farm Credit Administration
Federal Communications Commission

Federal Deposit Insurance Corporation
Federal Election Commission
Federal Emergency Management Agency
Federal Home Loan Bank Board
Federal Labor Relations Authority
Federal Maritime Commission
Federal Mediation and Conciliation Service
Federal Reserve System, Board of Governors of the
Federal Trade Commission
General Services Administration
Inter-American Foundation
Interstate Commerce Commission
Merit Systems Protection Board

National Aeronautics and Space Administration
National Capital Planning Commission
National Credit Union Administration
National Foundation on the Arts and the Humanities
National Labor Relations Board
National Mediation Board
National Science Foundation
National Transportation Safety Board
Nuclear Regulatory Commission
Occupational Safety and Health Review Commission
Office of Personnel Management
Panama Canal Commission
Peace Corps

Pennsylvania Avenue Development Corporation
Pension Benefit Guaranty Corporation
Postal Rate Commission
Railroad Retirement Board
Securities and Exchange Commission
Selective Service System
Small Business Administration
U.S. Arms Control and Disarmament Agency
U.S. Information Agency
U.S. International Development Cooperation Agency
U.S. International Trade Commission
U.S. Postal Service
Tennessee Valley Authority
Veterans Administration

reports and testimony transcripts are available to the public, sometimes for free. Many of the tools in Figure 4.13 include citations for OTA and GAO reports.

Washington correspondents enjoy a number of courtesies that help them as information gatherers. Official accreditation as a journalist opens doors of the congressional galleries, the White House, and various executive departments. Working space is provided for accredited reporters. More informally, communicators receive assistance in gathering background information and arranging interviews from many personal contacts who are in their orbits— public-relations and news colleagues; congressional staff members; political-party workers; lobbyists; and librarians, archivists, and data-base professionals. In addition, they are guests at the rounds of social events that are viewed as essential information-swapping sessions in the nation's capital.

Many federal functions take place in regional jurisdictions: Veterans Administration hospitals, appellate courts, Internal Revenue Service offices, and Federal Reserve Banks. Again, communicators need solid understanding of the government structures at all levels.

FIGURE 4.13   First steps for locating information on the federal government

Indexes

American Statistics Index
Congressional Information Service/Index and Abstracts
Congressional Record Abstracts
CSI Federal Index
Encyclopedia of Governmental Advisory Organizations
Federal Register Index
Index to International Statistics
Index to U.S. Government Periodicals
Monthly Catalog
PAIS International In Print

Directories

The Federal Database Finder
Federal Executive Directory
Federal Information Sources and Systems: A Directory Issued by the Comptroller General
National Journal's White House Phone Directory
Official Congressional Directory
United States Government Manual
Washington Information Directory

Almanacs and Yearbooks

Almanac of American Politics
Congressional Quarterly Almanac
Statistical Abstract of the United States

Much federal government information is available in on-line or CD-ROM format. Many of the tools listed here are available in both print and electronic form. Each federal department or agency may have an electronic information system that is available for public use, as well.

Anything published by the federal government qualifies as a government document. Thus a "document" can have virtually any format: print, map, graphic, film, photographic, and data base. Popular government documents include cookbooks and textbooks, magazines and compilations of statistics, bibliographies and handbooks. All of the executive departments produce voluminous documents. For example, the Department of Agriculture publications range from pamphlets on nutrition to handbooks on avalanche control and magazines on forest-fire control.

Libraries that receive federal material are called *depository libraries.* The federal government describes the depository library as a "library within a library," reflecting the fact that the documents in the federal depository system are distinct from those in ordinary library collections. Both federal documents and selected international documents are forwarded to depository libraries. More than 1,350 libraries receive federal material judged to be of public interest and educational value. At least one library in each state, the library of the state capital, receives federal documents. Other recipients may include two libraries in each congressional district, two libraries selected by each senator from each state, and libraries in public colleges and universities and government agencies. Libraries having government documents require staff who can assist users, since the cataloging system for these materials differs significantly from those most users are familiar with. Instead of the Dewey decimal classification or the Library of Congress numbers, government documents are cataloged with what are called Sudoc (Superintendent of Documents) numbers. Since the logic of the Sudoc system is radically different from that of other classification systems, those who use government-document collections take advantage of the documents library staffs to help them locate the materials they need. Tools such as the *Monthly Catalog,* the *Congressional Information Service,* and many of the other sources listed in Figure 4.13 can help the communicator locate government documents, reports, and testimony transcripts.

Federal government data bases also are available in on-line or CD-ROM format. These data bases are available directly from several federal offices, as well as from vendors. Many of the data bases include the complete texts of the reports or documents being sought, thus eliminating the need to locate a document in hard copy or microform format. (Using data bases is discussed in Chapter 6.)

Census data are among the most extensively used offerings of the federal government. The first census was held in 1790, and subsequent population tallies have been conducted every 10 years. In addition, some figures are updated periodically between major census taking. Public-relations, advertising, and news organizations rely heavily on census studies. Demographics, population trends, mobility, and housing characteristics are among the major types of information of interest in mass communication. Of special interest in advertising and marketing are current census data on businesses, industries, and manufacturing. The Census Bureau has 12 regional offices where users can get help with information needs, either in person or by telephone. The 1990 census information also was issued in CD-ROM format, so the data could be analyzed and manipulated with a personal computer. (Census data are discussed in more detail in later chapters.)

Researchers frequently use the telephone to locate information in the federal government. For example, the Library of Congress and the Bureau of Labor Statistics are among many agencies that answer factual inquiries over the telephone. In addition, there are regional Federal Information Centers (listed under "United States Government" in a local telephone directory, or in the *United States Government Manual*) staffed by individuals who have a good understanding of the responsibilities of all federal government agencies and departments. These staff members may be able to answer communicators' telephone questions directly or know who can. Additionally, many internal telephone directories of federal government agencies and departments are available for public purchase at reasonable prices from the Government Printing Office.

International Agencies and Foreign Governments. Communicators occasionally need information from international agencies—such as the United Nations, the World Court, and the World Bank—and from regional agencies—such as the North Atlantic Treaty Organization (NATO) and the European Community (EC). International agencies and commissions meet

FIGURE 4.14 First steps for locating information on international agencies and foreign governments

---

The Encyclopedia of the Third World
Europa World Year Book
International Yearbook and Statesmen's Who's Who
Statesman's Year-Book
U.N. Demographic Yearbook
U.N. Directory of International Statistics
United Nations Documents Index
U.N. Statistical Yearbook
World Statistics in Brief
Worldwide Government Directory
Yearbook of International Organizations
Yearbook of the United Nations

The United Nations and its affiliated bodies issue more than 1,800 serial publications and 1,000 books every year. They maintain 900 information data bases and produce hundreds of official and non-official documents. They operate television and radio services around the world. Communicators may use the tools listed here or contact the United Nations Department of Public Information.

Most countries with which the United States government has ongoing relations establish consulates and embassies in the United States. These consulates and embassies can assist searchers with questions about many aspects of their countries' activities and interests. Both the United States State Department and the United Nations maintain lists of names and addresses of embassy and consulate personnel.

Many foreign governments have retained the services of United States public relations agencies or private consulting firms to represent them and their interests in the United States. Political lobbying activities must be registered with the congressional offices mentioned in Figure 4.7. Public-relations firms working for foreign governments can be identified using *O'Dwyer's Directory of Public Relations*.

---

regularly to deliberate on such subjects as agricultural production, the world's money supply, labor, nutrition, and disarmament. Each agency or organization produces information about its decisions and the reasons for its actions. The agencies commonly publish periodicals, statistics, and news releases. Information officers assist communicators who request material from these agencies. For example, the Organization of Petroleum Exporting Countries (OPEC) maintains the OPEC News Agency, which has a mission to "provide information on OPEC to about 77 countries and counteract inaccurate reporting by some other sources." Many international documents are available in the depository libraries that have United States government documents.

With the internationalization of the economies of the industrialized world and with governmental upheaval and change, it is useful for the communicator to know how to locate information about foreign governments and countries quickly. Many institutional resources may be tapped. For instance, the Library of International Relations in Chicago (founded in 1932) is one of the premier research and reference centers for international study. It is an official repository for United Nations, European Community, and OPEC documents, and it contains yearly banking reports and materials about the economic, social, demographic, and historical backgrounds of countries around the world.

FOLLOWING THE PAPER
AND ELECTRONIC TRAILS

A *Miami Herald* reporter called the news library director to see what library staffers could find out about Eric Dubins, a man who wounded his girlfriend, killed her sister, and then shot himself. In less than an hour, the library director, Nora Paul, had traced Dubins' personal trail through institutional, library, and data-base sources. This is what she learned about him and how she found it:

- Using county property records from a service called *Redi-Real Estate* (in microfiche and on-line format), she found information about the location and value of the homes of Dubins and his victims.
- Using the *LEXIS* full-text legal data base, she found record of a lawsuit Dubins had filed against a former fellow corporate officer. The suit had gone to the state appeals court, and the record of that hearing gave Paul the name of Dubins' lawyer.
- The *Vu/Text* full-text newspaper data base included a *Fort Lauderdale Sun-Sentinel* society column about Dubins and an ex-girlfriend's amorous activities at a local charity auction.
- Dubins' previous addresses (one in California), employers and years of employment, ex-wife's name, his date of birth, and Social Security

number all were located using the *National Address Identifier* data base, a service provided through W.D.I.A. Credit Information Network. All Paul needed to locate this information was Dubins' name and address.

- Since the search in the credit file gave the library director Dubins' date of birth, she could use the Florida driver's license records to locate information about his height, eye color, and the fact he had to wear glasses.
- Using Prentice-Hall's public-records data base, Paul located records of Dubins' default on his California mortgage three years earlier and an ex-girlfriend's personal bankruptcy filing the previous year.
- Paul located information about ten corporations in which Dubins was a corporate officer, three of them with former girlfriends, using the Florida secretary of state's listing of corporate officers.[1]

This example illustrates how almost every activity we undertake as individuals in a modern society generates an institutional record. Not all the information generated as a result of Nora Paul's search through institutional, library, and data-base sources ended up in the story written by *Miami Herald* reporters, but it turned up a number of leads and sources for interviews. The search-strategy model identifies, implicitly or explicitly, all the stops that Paul made in her search along the paper and electronic trail left by Dubins.

Organizations, industries, and institutions also leave paper and electronic trails. A 1989 Pulitzer Prize-winning series called "The Color of Money" is an example of how one reporter, Bill Dedman at *The Atlanta Journal-Constitution*, followed the paper and electronic trails of a major industry in Atlanta. The savings and loan and banking industry in the city was examined in a five-month project that sought to determine how well the city's financial institutions were complying with the Community Reinvestment Act, a federal statute that says deposit-gathering institutions have an "affirmative obligation" to solicit borrowers and depositors in all segments of their communities. Dedman and the project team used lenders' reports and real-estate records to track home-purchase and home-improvement loans made by every bank and savings and loan in the Atlanta metropolitan area for a six-year period.

Major institutional information resources helped the team track the performance of this industry:

- Federal Freedom of Information Act (discussed later in this chapter) requests yielded lender reports compiled by the Federal Financial Institutions Examination Council. Reports generated by the Federal Home Loan Bank Board, the FSLIC and the FDIC (the insurance programs for depositors), the Federal Reserve Board, and the Home Mortgage Disclosure Act were also examined. A Freedom of Information Act request also generated records from the Small

Business Administration about every bank loan made to small businesses in Georgia over the same six-year period.

• Census Bureau reports on population characteristics in Atlanta, and updated census figures from the Atlanta Regional Commission were used to match lending data with demographic data. The findings disclosed that banks and savings and loans financed four times as many home purchases and five times as many home loans in middle-class white neighborhoods as in middle-class African-American neighborhoods.

• Federal appeals court decisions, Justice Department suits, federal laws and statutes regarding housing discrimination and financial institutions' obligations, records of testimony before Congress, and interviews with United States senators and representatives helped the team identify what was supposed to be happening under the law.

• The team discovered that annual reports prepared by Georgia banks and savings and loans are compiled in one directory, called *Sheshunoff's Banks of Georgia.* As mentioned, annual reports are excellent windows into what corporations and businesses are doing and what is important to them.

• Industry associations (such as the Mortgage Bankers Association of America, the National Association of Realtors) were identified, and the team read their publications and interviewed their members and officers. Neighborhood activism and community-action associations, watchdog associations, and citizens' councils also were identified and their publications and officers consulted.

• Trade publications such as *Savings and Loan News* and *American Banker* were identified and back issues were combed for insight into the industry and inside news about recent activities of Georgia and Atlanta banks and savings and loans.

These examples were only a fraction of the information identified through the paper and electronic trails that the banking and savings and loan industry generated in the conduct of its affairs. The news team also hired the services of an independent data analysis firm to conduct studies of the information generated by this wealth of institutional, library, data-base, and interview resources. Once again, many of the methods and resources identified by the search-strategy model were reflected in this four-part series.[2]

PUBLICITY AND PRIVACY

Information is power. Communicators share their appreciation of this fact with other professionals and with ordinary people. On the whole, communicators are successful at finding and using information from both public and private sources. Virtually every information-generating institution provides for sharing some information with the public. Nonetheless, other information is beyond the reach of communicators. For news reporters and editors, familiar examples come easily to mind: the Central Intelligence Agency, Department of Defense, and county prosecutor are sanctioned to withhold certain information from the general public and the news media. In addition, government and military officials frequently suppress material even though the information should be accessible. Such major institutions as corporations, foundations, and universities release information selectively as part of their public-relations activities.

The distinction between public and private information in the United States is reflected in legislation that provides both for access to information and for privacy for individuals and institutions. Legislation at the local, state, and national levels specifies what is protected as private and what must be disclosed as public. Nonetheless, much information falls ambiguously between the two designations.

At the federal level, for example, the Freedom of Information Act (FOIA), passed in 1966 and amended in 1974, and again in 1986, ensures that individuals can secure information in federal executive agency files. It does not apply to records of Congress or the federal courts. The FOIA is strongly defended by all communicators. There is much argument over what constitutes a "record" under the FOIA, especially as concerns information that is stored electronically. Some information that is electronically gathered and stored has been deemed by the courts to be out of reach of FOIA requests. Also, the 1986 amendment instituted a "public interest" test, which requires requesters to show that disclosure of the information is likely to contribute to public understanding and is not solely in the commercial interest of the requester. Authors working on books for which they will receive royalties and freelance writers who cannot prove their material will be published suffer a particular hardship under these new rules. This is an area of much contention between communicators and some agencies of the federal government.

Requests for information under FOIA provisions must be specific enough that the agency can identify what is being requested. Communicators and ordinary persons can invoke the FOIA when they believe that information is wrongly concealed from them. The act identifies substantial exemptions designed to safeguard national security, trade secrets, law-enforcement investigations, foreign-policy actions, and privacy rights of government officials.

Another federal law, the Government in the Sunshine Act, is designed to provide for open meetings of some 50 agencies and commissions. Agencies are expected to announce scheduled meetings one week in advance and to publish meeting agendas so that interested persons may attend.

The privacy issue is governed by the federal Privacy Act, passed in 1974 and amended in 1986. The Privacy Act is intended to give individuals some control over the personal information that is collected by the executive branch of the federal government. The act guarantees two rights: the right of individuals to see files about themselves, and the right of individuals to sue the government for permitting others to see information about them without their permission. The 1986 amendment seriously diminished the effectiveness of the Privacy Act, however, with a new provision that allows the FBI to have access to individuals' financial records and telephone logs if the person is suspected of espionage or other federal felony offenses. The amendment also allows the FBI to share information about individuals with any other government agency (such as the IRS, the Selective Service, the federal student loan programs, and so on) that might have an interest in the information. Communicators' abilities to collect information about individuals from the federal government are affected by both the FOIA and the Privacy Act, as well as by a number of other federal statutes and regulations.

States also have privacy, sunshine, and freedom-of-information legislation. Communicators have to study the laws that apply to privacy and access in the communities in which they work.

LINKS TO THE SEARCH STRATEGY

This step of the search strategy illustrates the richness and complexity of the communicator's encounters with institutions. Private and public sector institutions generate enormous amounts of information for their own purposes and much of it is of value for communicators. Associations, foundations, and corporations in the private realm and governments from the municipal level to the international agency level may be contributors in this step of the search process.

Getting information from institutions constitutes a major portion of the search strategy of mass communicators. Inasmuch as institutions are major strands in the social fabric, they intersect with one another at many points. Thus the search-strategy model graphically shows how information generated by any single institution may be gathered in other institutions. For example, government is the largest generator of information, and communicators get much information directly from government. However, government-produced information is found through other sources: libraries, data bases, and interviews. Frequently, it also comes to the communicator's attention by way of informal discussions with officials at the county or state level of government. State officials presenting statistics on health and safety in the work place probably will cite the federal standards that apply, along with the state's requirements. Further, as we have seen, government-produced statistics find their way into countless secondary sources, such as news reports and public-relations releases.

Since institutions share information, whether in adversarial or cooperative contexts, and build their own information bases partly from material developed in other institutions, learning the origin of a particular fact can be a demanding, but stimulating, process.

Chapter 5 examines the process of identifying and retrieving the myriad materials available from libraries. Specific tools appropriate for a variety of topics also are introduced.

NOTES

1. Nora Paul, "The Killer Left a Paper Trail," *IRE Journal*, Winter 1990, 11.
2. "The Color of Money," *The Atlanta Journal-Constitution*, May 1–4, 1988.

5

Approaching Libraries:
Tactics and Tools

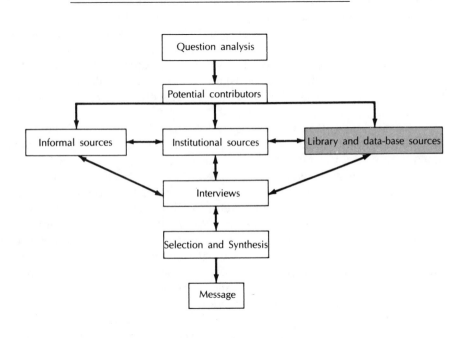

For him that stealeth, or borroweth and returneth not, this book from its owner, let it change into a serpent in his hand and rend him. Let him be struck with palsy, and all his members blasted. Let him languish in pain crying aloud for mercy, and let there be no surcease to his agony till he sink to dissolution. Let book worms gnaw his entrails in token of the Worm that dieth not, and when at last he goeth to his final punishment, let the flames of Hell consume him for ever.
Monastery of San Pedro, Barcelona

The monastery librarian who wrote these words in the front of each book in the library of the Monastery of San Pedro was reflecting the attitudes of his era. It may be difficult for the inhabitants of the information age, over-whelmed by an enormous amount of available information, to imagine a time during which each item in a library was a rare and treasured thing.

We know little about the origins of the first libraries.[1] In many Western and Eastern civilizations, the library was reserved for the priestly or scholarly castes. The average resident of Alexandria, Athens, Rome, Constantinople, or Baghdad did not have access to the materials stored in library collections. Knowledge was recorded in clumsy ways. The papyrus scroll was unwieldy and fragile. Clay tablets were cumbersome and difficult to transport. The shift from the use of papyrus or clay to the use of parchment as the writing surface led to the "codex," or physical form of books familiar today. During the Middle Ages in Europe, however, monastery libraries had little more than a handful of guarded manuscripts that had been copied by hand—sometimes beautifully adorned with illustrations, but usually carelessly scrib-bled by monks working under the worst of conditions. The introduction of paper from China, brought to the Islamic world around 800, greatly increased the ability of societies in the West to record, store, and organize knowledge in libraries.

The invention of movable type by Johannes Gutenberg at Mainz in about 1450 significantly affected the development of libraries. For the first time, the book supply could grow with ease. The scriptorium, or room in a monastery in which manuscripts were hand-copied, was no longer the only source of books. The volumes no longer had to be chained to the table or shelf to prevent theft, and even the architecture of libraries reflected the change by moving book shelves into the public areas of the building. The invention of printing opened the world of learning to many more people than ever before.

In the following centuries, the great universities, seats of learning, and their attendant library collections evolved. Research libraries began to collect not only books, but also periodicals—a publishing artifact related to the development of scientific inquiry and the scientists' need to quickly share information.

We have to look to a unique characteristic of American society, however, to explain one important milestone in the history of libraries. The American *public* library as we know it is a creature of the strongly held belief by the founding citizens of the new country that universal education and an in-formed electorate were absolute necessities for a democratic society to flour-ish. In 1731, Benjamin Franklin founded the Philadelphia Library Company. Members bought stock in this voluntary association, whose book collection was available to all those who subscribed. No library was truly public, to the extent that it was freely open to all residents of a community and supported by tax dollars, until 1803, when a Boston bookseller gave 150 books to the town of Salisbury, Connecticut. The town board voted $100 from the public treasury to support the library, and the collection was open to all residents of the community.

The Boston Public Library was established in 1852 and opened its doors in 1854. Other towns followed Boston's example and began to build their own public libraries. Library development spread across the country, greatly aided around the turn of the century by the gifts of Andrew Carnegie, who donated the money to build a library if a community agreed to continue its support. Many communities still have a Carnegie library building as a reminder of the early days of library development in the United States.

Libraries, then, have a long history and an established reputation as the repositories of culture and knowledge. While the libraries of ancient societies were impressive and unique beacons of learning and wisdom in their respective ages, the libraries in this information-rich era have an expanded role to play. It is no longer just the priests, scribes, and scholars who have access to the vast collections of information housed in modern collections. Every person who can read (or wants to learn to read) can tap the wealth of material housed in libraries anywhere in the country. However, the key to successfully using libraries in the information age may be recognizing that no two types of libraries are quite the same. It is especially important for the communicator—who is working under a deadline and who has special needs for accurate, appropriate, and verifiable information—to understand how libraries differ from one another and how those differences affect the search strategy.

It is possible to identify five types of libraries that are useful to communicators: public libraries, academic libraries, special libraries, archives, and media-organization libraries. These types of collections do have a few characteristics in common. All libraries, no matter the type, are set up to preserve, collect, and make accessible recorded intellectual products. Most libraries have a card or computer catalog that lists the contents of their collections. Most libraries have both book collections and periodical collections, and they have the tools (indexes, abstracts, bibliographies) to help searchers find what they need in the collections. More and more often, libraries have access to data bases, or machine-readable files. And, of course, all libraries have the most important resource of all, the librarian or archivist, the person who knows the most about the collection and about how best to use it. Beyond these superficial similarities, though, each type of library is unique.

PUBLIC LIBRARIES

As stated earlier, public libraries in America exist to serve a very special function. The need for an informed electorate is considered so important that residents are willing to tax themselves to make libraries available to the entire community. The public must be served by the collections in these libraries. Many collections reflect the history and the make-up of the neighborhoods in which they are situated. They may include materials in the languages of the most dominant ethnic groups of that section of the city. Public libraries offer many services that are not available from other types of libraries. Reader-counseling services (helping patrons decide what the best mysteries are this week), reference and referral programs (a central telephone number that community residents can call for referral to appropriate community agencies that can handle their problems), story hours for children, and résumé-writing workshops are not unusual.

Public-library collections reflect this community characteristic. The books and periodicals are of a popular, ephemeral, topical, and conventional nature. There might be 10 or 15 copies, for instance, of the most recent entries on the *New York Times* best-seller list. The collection reflects the library's attempt to meet the recreational and day-to-day informational needs of the general public. Most public libraries are not equipped to handle the in-depth or technical research project or question, although the collection may be the best available for such things as local telephone books and city directories, electoral-district maps, photographs of city landmarks over the years, and other community-related material. Since most public-library directors must answer to a library board composed of community residents, it is difficult, but not impossible, for very controversial materials to make their way onto public-library shelves. Public libraries are continually under attack from groups that want to censor what their tax dollars are supporting.

For the communicator, it is important to recognize that public libraries are a major community resource and may have local information that is not available from any other source. It is also necessary to caution that for the in-depth, complicated, and national or international research question, a public library (unless it is of the caliber of the New York Public Library) is not likely to fill the bill.

ACADEMIC LIBRARIES

Academic libraries serve a very different function from the other types of libraries. These collections exist to support the teaching and research needs of the scholars, students, and researchers of the institution with which they are affiliated. Large academic libraries collect scholarly materials published in many languages and from all over the world. Even small academic libraries reflect the teaching mission of the institution. Specialized, technical, detailed materials are the norm in most academic collections of any size.

Unlike use of public libraries, use of academic-library collections may be restricted to some extent. The communicator may have to apply for a special privilege card or pay a fee in order to check out materials or may be able only to use materials without checking them out. In extreme instances, unauthorized users may not even be able to enter the building. However, if the topic being researched is of a national or an international nature, if it involves specialized or technical subject areas, or if it is likely to cover controversial ideas, then an academic-library collection is probably one of the best places to look. For instance, for a series of stories on the development of nuclear power in the United States, an academic library connected with an institution that has an engineering school would have much material, includ-

ing current and back issues of special journals devoted to the topic, compilations of scientific papers, public-policy information, and all the indexes and
reference tools necessary to locate information quickly.

SPECIAL LIBRARIES

The term *special* refers to a broad category of various kinds of libraries. The
collection, the clientele, or both may be special. For instance, most companies
have some kind of library or information center that houses the books,
journals, documents, and material relevant to that industry. Historical societies usually support libraries. Museums have libraries that are geared to the
subject matter of the museum collection. The Folger Shakespeare Library is a
special library in the sense that it collects books and materials by and about
Shakespeare. Public and academic libraries often have special collections or
rooms to house rare, fragile materials or to distinguish a particularly strong
subject collection. The Kerlan Collection of children's books, manuscripts,
illustrations, and research materials about children's literature is an example
of a special collection at the University of Minnesota.

A communicator may have to use these special libraries for the kinds of
unique materials available. For instance, if an advertising campaign for a
brand of beer is being prepared, the communicator may wish to use the
library collection at the brewery in order to get an understanding of the
history of the company and the nature of past campaigns. If the information
is not proprietary (that is, held by the company to be private because it
involves trade secrets or financial information), the communicator may want
to look for clues about the unique brewing process or chemistry that sets that
brand of beer apart from its competitors ("It's the water," declares Olympia
beer ads).

Special collections are usually not organized in quite the same way as
other collections. Because the materials in the collection are about the same
topic or industry or company, there is likely to be an internally designed
organization system that fits the needs of the clientele. In addition, special
collections may or may not be open to the public because corporate secrets
often are housed alongside the usual industry or company information. The
best rule of thumb for the communicator is to call ahead, since the hours and
visiting policies are likely to differ from collection to collection.

ARCHIVES

An archive is an institution responsible for keeping the permanent record of
an organization or a movement, and thus the collections do not circulate.
Rather than seeing books arranged on shelves, the visitor to an archive is
likely to see acid-proof boxes filled with letters, documents, office records,

photographs, scripts, manuscript copies, and so forth. As historical resources, archives are invaluable. For instance, the Immigration History Research Center archive at the University of Minnesota is a treasure trove of information about the immigration of Eastern Europeans to the United States. Ships' logs, letters, photos, newspapers in the immigrants' native languages, and much more of historical interest are included. The National Archives, in Washington, D.C., is responsible for keeping the permanent record of the United States government. Treaties, maps, photographs, motion pictures, sound records, correspondence files, and other documentation of the operations of the administrative branch of the federal government are kept.

An alternative source of government information is found in the National Security Archive, a nonprofit, nonpartisan organization that attempts to collect internal government documentation for research by journalists, policy makers, public interest groups, and the public. The records in the collection are unclassified or declassified government reports, oral histories, congressional testimony, court records, and materials released under the Freedom of Information Act. The archive attempts to put together as complete a documentary record of recent and contemporary public policy making as possible within the constraints of security classification.

Corporations and businesses house archives that serve both a public-relations function and provide historically accurate information about the company and clients. For instance, the Coca-Cola archive includes such materials as original Coke bottles, print and broadcast ads, drugstore signs, decal-covered serving trays, toy Coke trucks, and Coke clocks. The manager of the archive is called upon regularly by the legal department to produce documentation to protect the Coca-Cola trademark.[2]

Purdue University provided an invaluable service by creating the Public Affairs Video Archive in 1987. The archives record, preserve, and distribute all programming on both channels of the Cable-Satellite Public Affairs Network (C-SPAN) exclusively for education and research. Before the advent of the Public Affairs Video Archive, hundreds of hours of cable-cast public debate, speeches, panel discussions, and policy making were lost for future reference because no method was available to comprehensively capture and preserve the programs.

Archives are not organized the way libraries are. There are special methods for recording and making accessible the files, documents, videotapes, and materials housed in boxes and vaults. This does not mean that the communicator must despair of finding what is needed. On the contrary, the archivists in charge probably have personally organized and housed the materials in the archive and are therefore the most well-versed in how to unlock the information. Printed guides or catalogs may outline the contents of the archive collection. As the best source of primary materials about a person, an organization, a movement, or an institution, archives form some of the most valuable, if little used, collections available to the communicator.

MEDIA-ORGANIZATION LIBRARIES

The libraries supported by media organizations are types of special libraries. Both the materials and the clientele are unusual. As the likely first stop for the communicator during the library stage of the information search, media libraries are crucially important. Most media organizations—whether in the business of producing a newspaper, a national magazine, a local television news broadcast, advertising campaigns, or public-relations materials—have some sort of library collection.

The in-house library of a newspaper office may have a small, current collection of major reference tools (dictionaries, directories, almanacs), may subscribe to a handful of magazines and journals, may have access to a number of remote electronic data bases, and most likely is staffed by a professional librarian. But by far the most important resource, in the opinion of a newspaper staff, is the backfiles of the newspaper itself. Many smaller newspapers still use clippings files in which are kept handclipped articles from each edition of the paper.

During the 1970s, most newspapers switched their mode of production to computers. Instead of banging out each story on a typewriter and editing it by hand, the newspaper staff prepares each story, ad, obituary, and column on a computer screen. The material is edited on the screen, and the information is sent to computers that set the type and print the paper that is delivered to the subscriber's doorstep.

Newspaper staffs soon figured out that the product that was created electronically could also be stored that way. Instead of filing hand-clipped articles from each paper, it became simple to store in the library's computer the computer files that contain each edition of the paper. The year 1985 was a watershed in the installation of electronic library systems at newspapers.[3] By 1990, 67 percent of newspapers with over 100,000 subscribers had an electronic library system in use by reporters, editors, and news librarians, and nearly all others planned to convert.[4]

The reporter or editor who has to find all the stories that the paper published about the debate between the mayor and the water commission can use the electronic library to locate those stories, transfer the important elements of the text directly into a personal computer file, and have all the background readily available for the current story.

With the newspaper backfiles stored in electronic form, the newspaper companies quickly saw the possibilities for selling their newspaper computer files to other people. Today, a newspaper's own library makes its paper accessible to reporters, editors, librarians, and researchers, as well as to the community and the country at large through the sale of these computer files. (Data bases are discussed in detail in Chapter 6.)

In addition to the newspaper backfiles, the news library includes a variety of materials that allow reporters and editors to

- conceptualize their stories (get story angles, do background research, identify interviewees, and do round-up stories),
- analyze previously published materials (check previous stories and avoid duplication), and
- retrieve details and resolve discrepancies in information.[5]

In large news organizations, the news library staff may have satellite stations located in strategic areas of the newsroom, with the library collection on another floor just a phone call away.

For example, the reporter writing about an airplane crash on deadline would search the electronic library for earlier stories published about that company or that type of aircraft. The news librarian would be searching remote electronic data bases for reports of accidents, fines, or problems that may have been written about in other newspapers, magazines, or trade publications from around the country and the world. The reference books in the news library would provide descriptions of that kind of plane, along with the names of and background on the manufacturers of the various components of the craft, the names of airline safety watchdog groups, and lists of the federal agencies that might provide spokespersons for comment. The newspaper library, and the news librarian, then, become central resources in the library stage of the information search.

Broadcast-news libraries have many of the same characteristics as newspaper libraries, with one exception. Along with current reference materials and access to data bases, broadcast libraries may have collections of audio or video tapes of all broadcasts done by the station, often with an electronic index to those tapes. This allows reporters and editors to locate the snippets of tape about a certain topic or person, just as the newspaper reporter or editor can locate a copy of a story. Not all broadcast stations have the room to keep backfiles of tape, however, so these libraries must rely on other types of reference materials, and especially electronic data bases, for background information. The station may belong to regional or national broadcast-news consortia, which provide file tape via satellite upon request, further expanding access to the visual materials needed.

Broadcast-news librarians, writing about their experiences at ABC News in New York during the first days of the Persian Gulf War, detailed the types of reference questions and search methods they had to employ.[6] Producers, correspondents, and researchers relied on the news library for clip files of newspaper and magazine stories, wire service copy, and briefing materials culled from many sources. The librarians provided answers to questions about airport security, Gulf-related terrorism, weapons numbers and characteristics for many countries, and women's roles in the military, and provided transcripts of all briefings by military officials as they became available. Library staff used reference books, telephone calls to experts, transcripts of previous broadcasts and specially prepared files to respond to news staff requests.

Magazine publishers also maintain libraries for fact checking, reference materials, and research assistance. The magazines with the best reputations for accuracy have large staffs of library researchers who use the magazine's own library or libraries elsewhere to check the facts in each article submitted by the authors. These magazine libraries include many of the same sources as the other media libraries mentioned, along with all the back issues of the magazine itself. The researchers take great pride in their ability to check every word of an article, on deadline, for accuracy, fairness, and detail. For instance, for a travel magazine, the researcher had to verify not only the text, but also the accompanying photograph, which showed the silhouette of a bicyclist on a hilltop with a spectacular full moon overhead. The researcher had to use astronomical and weather charts to determine if, indeed, the moon could have been full at that time of year, at that place in the sky, in that country before the photo was cleared to accompany the article.

The library in an advertising or a public-relations agency or department also is designed to meet the information needs of the people writing the ads or news releases, doing the market research, or studying new products, industries, or clients. The library for an advertising department may include tear sheets, pages ripped out of magazines and newspapers that serve as examples of ads for a particular product or service. The library is likely to have files of pictures and photos, in case an artist has to draw a cheetah, for instance, for an ad layout. Industry and trade information is included in the library collection, since the communicators must learn a great deal about the companies, industries, and markets they are interacting with and writing about. Specialized information tools that pinpoint audience characteristics—such as public-opinion polls, survey results, and market-research data—are important components of both advertising and public-relations libraries.[7]

For instance, large public-relations firms regularly conduct background information searches on potential clients before agreeing to represent them. Once they know a client can pay the bills, is a legitimate organization, and presents no conflict-of-interest problems, the agency is able to use the information resources at its disposal to regularly scan major media reports about the client, track industry trends, measure public opinion about the client, decide where to place media messages, and shape the client's public image. The specialized print and electronic information resources in the agency's library are crucial for this day-to-day information gathering.

Media-organization libraries, then, serve a special function. The communicators who are producing messages must have at their fingertips examples of their own organizations' output; materials produced by other communicators around the country or the world; information about industries, products, and audiences for whom the messages are produced; and general fact-finding sources for quick reference.

The libraries within each media organization are supplemented by industry-wide libraries. The Newspaper Association of America (NAA), for instance, has a library in Reston, Virginia. This library is one of the most comprehensive newspaper-business collections anywhere. A wide variety of information is available for anyone who calls or visits with questions about the newspaper industry. The staff of researchers does original research and helps outside researchers use the collection. Many of the library's materials are available for loan to NAA members. The American Association of Advertising Agencies also has a library. Communicators who work for any member agency can call the library with a research question. The telephone staff attempts to answer the question immediately; if that is not possible, they will conduct the necessary search through the association's collections and mail or fax the information to the person requesting it.

Each type of library, then, has its own characteristics and usefulness for the communicator. The variations among types of libraries and among libraries of the same type may suggest that using libraries as part of the communicator's search strategy is a complicated and difficult proposition. On the contrary, once the place of the library in the search process is clear and once the keys for decoding information in libraries are familiar, this part of the search process can be as fruitful and uncomplicated as the other steps in the process. Indeed, as media organizations' own libraries become more sophisticated, the library step of the search process becomes even more central to the communicator's routine.

THE LIBRARY'S PLACE IN THE SEARCH PROCESS

As the search-strategy model illustrates, the role of libraries and data bases in the information-gathering process is an important one. Although communicators may be very familiar with the informal and institutional sources of information included in the model, they may be unaware of the importance of the kinds of materials available in libraries. As repositories of the collected wisdom of civilization, libraries house information that is unavailable in any other form. Materials in libraries can help the communicator understand and identify the issues, the subjects of, and the potential interviewees and audiences for the messages being produced. Library materials can also help the communicator verify information found during other steps of the search process or check the reputations of individuals who may be interviewed later.

In order to identify the library that might be the best available for a particular need, the communicator can refer to several helpful tools. The standard source is the *American Library Directory*. This annual publication is arranged by state and by city within each state, with every library in a city listed, along with such information as the size of the collection, the special collections within the library, the names and telephone numbers of the librarians in charge, and the size of the book budget. More than 33,000 public, academic, and special libraries in the United States and Canada are included. If the communicator is unfamiliar with the kinds of collections available in the part of the country in which he or she works, this tool is a great timesaver.

ijor resource for identifying appropriate collections is the
l Libraries and Information Centers. This multivolume set is
, with supplements, and has a geographic index, a subject
ie index. Public and academic libraries are included as well
:s and collections. The communicator could locate, for in-
st or the most comprehensive collection on the topic of
y using the subject index of this tool.
ost appropriate collection is located, the next challenge is
t efficient use of the material housed there. Every subject
:ture that helps people organize and identify information
This "structure of information" is related to many character-
:he way in which disciplines develop (Chapter 2), the nature
he humanities) of subject area, and the age and acceptability
rea. The structure of information also affects how library
materials relevant to that topic are arranged and made accessible.

Libraries must attempt to collect and organize the entire output of intellectual activity. They must try to help users decode the structure of information for each new subject area. The tools and tactics that are used in this
mammoth attempt sometimes are cumbersome, but, for the most part, they
work. It is up to the efficient information gatherer to unlock and decode
these collections in order to make the best use of them.

Librarians have developed two major methods of categorizing the information housed in libraries into a system of identification and retrieval. These
methods are called classification systems, and they determine how materials
are described in catalogs and arranged on library shelves.

Classification Systems

The Dewey Decimal Classification System. The Dewey decimal system is
used most often in small libraries and in public libraries. It works best for
collections of materials that are not too large and that do not cover too many
different subjects. The reasons for this are more clear when the system is
explained. It consists of ten major categories, or "classes," of knowledge:

000	General Works	500	Natural Sciences, Mathematics
100	Philosophy	600	Technology (Applied Sciences)
200	Religion	700	The Arts
300	Social Sciences	800	Literature and Rhetoric
400	Language	900	Geography, History

Every Dewey number that is assigned to a book consists of three digits
before the decimal point. The first digit is taken from the classes, each of
which is divided into ten "divisions," represented by the second digit of the
Dewey number. So, for instance, the divisions of the class 800, Literature and
Rhetoric are:

800	General Literature	850	Italian, Romanian Literature
810	American Literature	860	Spanish, Portuguese Literature
820	English, Anglo-Saxon Literature	870	Italic, Latin Literature
830	Germanic Literature	880	Hellenic Literature
840	Romance Language Literature	890	Literature of Other Languages

Each of these divisions is further split into ten "sections," to arrive at the third of the three digits before the decimal point in a Dewey number. The sections of the class 810, American Literature, are:

810	American Literature in English	815	Speeches
811	Poetry	816	Letters
812	Drama	817	Satire and Humor
813	Fiction	818	Miscellaneous
814	Essays	819	American Literature in English Not Requiring Local Emphasis

Whether there are any digits after the decimal in a Dewey number depends on the depth and breadth of a particular library's collection; however, there are always three digits before the decimal. So, for instance, all books in a library's collection that are categorized as American drama are on the shelf under the main Dewey number 812. A book such as *Twenty-five Best Plays of the Modern American Theatre* might be given the Dewey number 812.503 in a library with a large American drama collection. The numbers after the decimal allow for fine distinctions between, say, modern drama and colonial drama. Each of the other nine Dewey categories of information is constructed in a way that is similar and logical for that subject area.

The Library of Congress Classification System. The other major library classification scheme is the one developed by the Library of Congress. This classification system is used in academic libraries and in large libraries with very extensive collections on many different subjects. It is a great deal more flexible than the limited Dewey decimal system.

The main characteristic of the Library of Congress system is that it is based on letters. The major categories are:

A   General Works

B   Philosophy, Religion, Psychology

C   History, Auxiliary Sciences (genealogy, archeology, and such)

D   General and Old World History

E,F   History: America

G   Geography, Anthropology, Recreation

H   Social Sciences

J   Political Science

K   Law

L   Education

M   Music

N   Fine Arts

P   Language and Literature

Q   Science

R   Medicine

S   Agriculture

T   Technology

U   Military Science

V   Naval Science

Z   Bibliography, Library Science

Because there are so many more main categories and because the subdivisions under each category are much more specific than in the Dewey decimal system, the Library of Congress classification system can be applied with a greater degree of precision and descriptiveness to each book. For instance, the category P, Language and Literature, can be divided into many smaller categories. The book *Unreliable Sources: A Guide to Detecting Bias in News Media,* which discusses news practices, is given the Library of Congress classification number PN 4888.O25 L44, since the PN 4800 class is for those items dealing with journalism, a subcategory of Language and Literature. The entire classification scheme is outlined in a very large set of volumes that take up a whole shelf in a cataloger's office.

Subject Classification of Information in Libraries

Another major characteristic of information in libraries is the categorization of information by subject terms or headings. The major purpose of subject-headings systems is to allow a standardized method of describing all information in the same general subject area, so that everything pertaining to the topic can be identified. The person searching for information in a library is likely to have a general notion of the topic area that is being researched, rather than a detailed list of authors and titles of materials being sought. For this reason, library staff and indexers tag library records with subject headings as well as with information about who produced the book or article.

As with classification schemes, librarians spend enormous amounts of time developing subject headings that accurately reflect the structure of information in a subject area. There are two main references for subject headings for libraries: *The Sears List of Subject Headings,* used primarily in small or public libraries, and the *Library of Congress Subject Headings,* used primarily in large or academic libraries. There are also special references for specific subject areas, such as *Medical Subject Headings,* which help categorize highly specific collections of materials. The reason for having two subject-headings lists is the same as that for having two classification systems: large libraries with in-depth, specialized collections require a degree of precision and specificity that is unnecessary in smaller libraries.

These subject headings are used in many ways. They appear on the records in the library's card or computer catalog; they are used in the entries of the indexes and the headings in the abstracts that libraries subscribe to in print or electronic form; they may be used to organize materials in files maintained by the library.

Since the communicator is likely to use the larger, more detailed collections in a sophisticated information search, we can look at an example from the subject-headings system most likely to be used in that kind of library. The *Library of Congress Subject Headings* are large red volumes that sit next to most library catalogs or catalog terminals. Because the information in libraries is encoded according to the logic developed by the librarians and indexers in charge, it is useful for the uninitiated searcher to have some tools to help decode that information. If the communicator has to start a library search for information on urban mass transit trends, the subject-headings lists can provide clues to how the librarians and indexers have organized information on that topic. For instance, a typical entry in the *Library of Congress Subject Headings* volume may look like this:

Transportation
    UF   Public transportation
            Transportation—Economic aspects
    BT   Locomotion
    RT   Commerce
            Communication and traffic
    NT   Air travel
            Commuting
            Ferries
            Local transit
            Railroads
            Vehicles
    Energy conservation
    Federal aid
        USE   Federal aid to transportation
    Finance
        NT   Federal aid to transportation
    History
    Law and legislation
    Passenger traffic
    Social aspects

There are some standard rules for interpreting such an entry. The notation "NT" before the items "Air travel" to "Vehicles" stands for *Narrower Term*. These are terms that are slightly more specific than the main subject-heading term but that may also be used for finding information on the topic. The "UF" notation, however, means *Use For* and is placed before terms that are *not* used by the catalogers and indexers in classifying the information. The communicator would waste time by using these terms to look for information. The "BT" and "RT" notations represent *Broader Terms* and *Related Terms* that are acceptable choices as well. The "USE" notation indicates that a term other than the one under which the *USE* appears should be chosen. For example, the entry

> Transportation—Federal aid
> USE Federal aid to transportation

indicates that the term "Transportation—Federal aid" is not used, but that "Federal aid to transportation" is a subject heading under which information will be found.

If the communicator started the search in the *Library of Congress Subject Headings* volumes by looking under the subject heading "Mass transit," the entry would read:

> Mass transit
> USE Local transit

This indicates that the logical choice, "Mass transit," should not be used, but that "Local transit" would yield results on this topic. So for the search for library information on urban mass transit trends, the communicator would learn from the *Library of Congress Subject Headings* volumes that some likely headings to refer to might be "Local transit," "Federal aid to transportation," and "Transportation—Passenger traffic." Since librarians and indexers use inverted words, unusual phrasing, and odd terminology to describe topic areas, the communicator must have some help in decoding the language of the topic. Otherwise, the information in libraries will be locked away under unfamiliar, unusual subject terms.

After a quick look at the subject-headings volumes, the communicator has a better idea of how the organizers of library information have categorized much of the information the library contains. It is not true that *all* library reference tools use these terms. A newspaper index, for instance, may have its own way of describing the topics covered. However, it still may use the Library of Congress subject headings as "see" references that lead the searcher to the appropriate language for the topic, once a start is made. The communicator who has first referred to the *Library of Congress Subject Headings* volumes has clues and leads that will make the search more efficient.

What Library Organization Schemes Mean to the Communicator

The communicator will never have to understand the intricacies of library classification or subject-headings schemes in any detail. However, since all materials in a library are categorized in these ways, it is helpful to have a general acquaintance with how they work. If the communicator is looking for a book on the library shelves, the classification number is a necessary piece of information, along with a general understanding of how to read the numbers on the spines of books shelved around the needed title. It is also helpful to use the subject-headings lists to identify all the terms that may be used to describe and locate information on a topic in the library's catalog and indexes. All of these clues help the communicator decode the structure of the information available in libraries. This introduces the next major step in using libraries: identifying the most useful materials for each new search.

MAJOR TOOLS FOR ACCESS TO INFORMATION IN LIBRARIES

There is a logic to using reference tools during an information search. As the discussion of the bibliographic chain in Chapter 2 suggests, knowledge makes its way into major knowledge repositories in a recognizable and decipherable way. Overviews and summaries of accepted information are found in tertiary sources, such as encyclopedias and handbooks. Secondary sources, such as indexes and abstracts, direct the searcher to the location of information in published material. Primary material, such as books, journal articles, and magazine and newspaper accounts, constitutes much of the original information available on a topic.

The communicator can move through this chain of information in a logical and strategic way. Starting work on a topic, the communicator might recognize the need to define terms by using a dictionary and library subject-headings volumes and to get an overview by looking at an encyclopedia article. Indexes to or abstracts of scholarly journals will lead the communicator to material that is authoritative but perhaps a year or two old. Indexes to newspaper articles will help the communicator locate more recent information about the topic, including the names of some of the major individuals involved in the subject area. These people might be contacted later for interviews. Magazine indexes will lead to popular accounts of the subject. Biographical tools give the communicator clues about the appropriateness or expertise of potential interviewees. Used strategically, the major tools available in a library can greatly increase both the amount of information the communicator has access to and the efficiency with which the communicator conducts the rest of the information search.

The search-strategy model identifies two categories of library sources: one-step tools and two-step tools. The one-step tools contain the needed information. In other words, the communicator can turn to one of these tools and quickly locate a fact, an address, a statistic, or an overview. The two-step tools lead the communicator to the needed information. In other words, the communicator must use the two-step tool to learn where to look for the actual information.

One-Step Library Tools

Encyclopedias. Perhaps one of the most useful of the one-step tools is the encyclopedia. As the first step in the search for an overview of a topic, an encyclopedia article is an excellent choice. A reporter once had to cover the horse shows at a state fair and after reading the article on horses in a general encyclopedia was able to do a creditable job of understanding the various types of horses, interviewing the horse owners, and covering the competitions. Whether for a general overview of a subject area, a brief introduction to the major ideas and events in a field, or a familiarity with the language of a topic, an encyclopedia is an appropriate library tool.

The first thing to recognize about encyclopedias is that there are many different types. Among general encyclopedias, the level of discussion and the detail of articles may be the biggest difference. For instance, the *World Book Encyclopedia* is aimed at a young audience. Hence, the articles are slightly shorter, less technical, and easier for the novice to understand than are the articles in, say, the *Encyclopedia Americana* or the *Encyclopaedia Britannica*. The articles in the *Britannica* are renowned for their authoritativeness (many of the articles are written by the leading scholars in their fields) and for their extensive bibliographies. So the searcher using the *Britannica* will find not only the article itself, but also a list of books or articles on the same topic.

In addition to the various types of general encyclopedias, there are many subject encyclopedias. Since general encyclopedias cannot cover any one topic in great detail, many disciplines have their own specialized encyclopedias, which allow for more in-depth articles, lengthier bibliographies, and longer entries. Some examples are the *Encyclopedia of Major League Baseball Team Histories*, in two volumes; the *Encyclopedia of Governmental Advisory Organizations*, which is a reference guide to 6,000 permanent and ad hoc presidential, congressional, interagency, and other advisory boards; and the *Encyclopedia of Pop, Rock and Soul*, an excellent guide to important events and people in the popular music industry.

A major problem with encyclopedias as a reference tool for mass communication is that there is usually a long gap between editions of an encyclopedia set. Since events and inventions seem to be moving at such a rapid pace, an encyclopedia last revised in 1991 can be sadly out of date five years later. There are now some electronic encyclopedias, which are available through a computer service or on a CD-ROM text storage disc. The subscriber has access to an electronic encyclopedia that is updated as often as once a month. Television and text are merged in another innovation called CDI, which combines a computer with a video and audio system. For instance, a video encyclopedia mixes historical film footage and recordings with text to give the user a vivid account of an event or a famous speech in multimedia form.

Articles in electronic encyclopedias are very short compared with a print version of an encyclopedia, but the advantage is in the recency of the entries. For instance, after the volcano erupted in Colombia, causing mud slides that killed thousands and taking its place as one of the deadliest volcanoes in recorded history, the entry "Volcanoes" in an electronic encyclopedia could be changed to reflect that event. The print version of the encyclopedia would remain unchanged until the next edition. Nonetheless, whether in electronic or in print form, the encyclopedia is one of the best first stops for the communicator using one-step tools.

Dictionaries.   Since the communicator's stock in trade often is the word, the usefulness of a dictionary may seem obvious. Just as with encyclopedias, not all dictionaries are the same. For instance, the *Oxford English Dictionary* is recognized as the most authoritative source for looking up the etymology, or origin and evolution, of words. Many dictionaries include (in addition to the definitions of words) summaries of rules of grammar, perpetual calendars, tables of weights and measures, radio frequencies, constellations, ranks in the armed forces, and a variety of other facts and figures. Some dictionaries are illustrated, so the searcher not only learns the definition of the word *escutcheon,* say, but also sees a drawing of one.

Subject dictionaries are also available. There are, among others, law dictionaries, medical dictionaries, science and technology dictionaries, historical dictionaries, slang dictionaries, and music dictionaries. Since it is necessary for the communicator to have a good grasp of the language of a research topic, dictionaries can be of enormous value. As both timesavers and guides to a field, they can very quickly get the communicator up to speed in an unfamiliar area.

Directories.   Among the most useful kinds of one-step tools in the library are directories. Whether it is the familiar telephone directory, the zip code directory, or something a bit fancier—such as the *Directory of Alternative Communities in the World*—the directory is an important source of information for mass communicators. Because so much time is spent trying to identify the organizations or individuals connected with a particular subject area, directories can be invaluable.

Directories exist for almost any category of people or organizations. Any group with a fairly sizable membership usually publishes a directory. The *Encyclopedia of Associations* is perhaps the best place to begin a search for any type of organization or association. Whether for snowmobilers, matchbook collectors, or chiropractors, if there is an organization, the *Encyclopedia of Associations* is the directory to use to find it.

Large libraries have a good selection of telephone books from around the country and perhaps from around the world. The Yellow Pages for many major metropolitan areas are actually available in data-base form (Chapter 6). The Manhattan and Washington, D.C., telephone books are essential resources to have in every media-organization library because so many people, services, and institutions of national importance are listed in those directories.

Another variety of telephone directory is the reverse directory, also called a "criss-cross," or city directory. More than 1,400 separate city directories are published by the R. L. Polk Company. The most recent edition and backfiles for a particular community are usually found in its public library. The information in city directories is based on telephone or door-to-door interviews with the residents in a community who agree to be listed. The directory records the name of each resident over 18 years of age, as well as the person's address, marital status, occupation, place of employment, and telephone number, and whether the residence is owned or rented. Each business and firm in the area is also cataloged by type, and the owners, partners, or corporate officers are listed. The information is arranged in three sections: a name section, an address or street name section, and a telephone-exchange section. This allows the searcher who has a telephone number, for instance, to trace back to see what person or what kind of residence or business is listed for that number. This tool also gives communicators a good deal of information for checks on facts about individuals found in other ways.

There is one way to learn whether there is a directory for the subject of each search. The *Directory of Directories* or the *International Directories in Print* can help identify directories that cover a variety of subjects. Some examples include the *Thomas Register of American Manufacturers*, which lists products manufactured by approximately 152,000 United States and Canadian manufacturers. A communicator who has to find out what firm makes Joy-Walker athletic shoes for a new advertising account could look up the trade name in the *Thomas Register* and would find a complete entry on the company. Another example is the *Research Centers Directory*, which lists more than 5,000 research programs and centers, including the method of funding, the size of the library connected with the center, the names and telephone numbers of personnel, and the titles of any publications issued by the center. The *Directory of American Scholars* and its companion volume, *American Men and Women of Science*, are very useful for identifying experts in a variety of fields, from the humanities to the physical sciences.

Each of the various *Who's Who* volumes (*Who's Who in America, Who's Who in the Midwest, Who's Who in the Press*) also can be used as directories, as well as sources of biographical information about an entrant. As long as the searcher already has the name of the person who must be located, the *Who's Who* volumes are useful. But if the communicator has to identify someone in a field and does not have an actual name, some of the other directories mentioned may be more helpful.

Publication directories are also of great value. A tool like the *Gale Directory of Publications and Broadcast Media* can help the communicator locate complete information on daily, weekly, monthly, and less frequently published newspapers and magazines, and broadcast outlets. The *Gale Directory* is organized by geographic area in the United States and Canada and by media outlet name or call letters under each location. Market and economic data for each city and town, summaries of population, statistics on agriculture and industry, and maps are included, making the *Gale Directory* of tremendous value for advertisers trying to identify how best to reach a community or learn about the characteristics and media outlets of a town.

There are directories of people, organizations, clubs, firms, institutions, places, publications—you name it, and there is probably a directory for it. The point for the communicator is to know, quickly, where to look for that required address, telephone number, name and title, or membership total. Once the communicator realizes that directories exist in such profusion, their usefulness increases manyfold.

Almanacs and Yearbooks. An almanac is one of the most likely reference tools to find in a media-organization library, even if there are no other references at all. The old-fashioned almanacs gave predictions about the coming year's weather, offered advice to farmers and housewives, included stories and poems, and served as general entertainment books for the families in the early United States. Modern almanacs have a different purpose and character. Most are single-volume, annual compendia of facts, figures, and tidbits of information about a country and society. Most of the information in almanacs is reprinted from other sources, such as census reports, sports statistics, lists of prize winners, data about officials and personalities, and astronomical tables. Most almanacs try to cover popular information, and communicators can choose from several titles. The *World Almanac,* the *Information Please Almanac,* and the *Reader's Digest Almanac* can be found in bookstores as well as in libraries. A large number of subject-specific almanacs, such as the *Almanac of American Politics,* may aid the communicator in finding an item of information or biographical data about a topic or person not included in the more general versions.

Yearbooks of various sorts are also good ready reference tools. Many encyclopedia publishers also publish yearbooks, which cover the latest developments for a particular year. Subject-specific yearbooks, such as the *Statesman's Year-Book* or the *Europa World Year Book,* provide current information on countries and international organizations arranged according to standard subheads: head of government, area and population, constitution and government, religion, education, transportation and communication facilities, and diplomatic representatives. With events unfolding swiftly around the world, communicators may need to have a condensed source of information about an unfamiliar country or organization in order to make sense of information coming in over a wire service or a televised live report. The *United States Government Manual* is the annual yearbook of United States government organization, activities, and chief officers of all agencies within the legislative, judicial, and executive branches.

The *Facts on File Yearbook* is a year's cumulation of the data in the weekly publication *Facts on File*. World news events are gathered in the yearbook under four broad categories: world affairs, United States affairs, other nations, and general. The index has specific entries for every item in the yearbook, so information is easily located. Many professions also have a yearbook. For book publishing, the title is the *Bowker Annual of Library and Book Trade Information*. If the title of a reference tool includes the word *annual* or *yearbook*, the communicator can be fairly sure that the information in the tool is timely and stresses events or statistics of the past year.

Audience and Market Information. A particular type of library information is vitally important for the day-to-day activities of advertising and public-relations professionals: reference tools that include information about the characteristics of audiences and markets. Subscriptions to many of these tools are very expensive, and therefore they may be found only in libraries of advertising or public-relations agencies or departments within a company. Other important audience and market information may be gathered from specialized periodicals, trade association reports, government documents, and other, more easily accessible library sources. These tools provide the communicators with some of the most important information that is used in creating the ads or news releases and messages that influence public opinion and preferences and that eventually affect the kinds of entertainment that the society has available to it through the media.

A number of syndicated research services help the communicator identify the size of a market for a brand and its competitors and potential media outlets for best reaching that market. Two of the major resources for information about audience and consumer characteristics are the syndicated services offered by Mediamark Research Inc. (MRI), and W. R. Simmons (SMRB). Each company reports on results of thousands of interviews annually in which they ask participants to record their demographic characteristics (age, income, education, occupation), product-purchase habits ("Did you buy Heinz ketchup at the store this week?"), media-use habits ("Which magazines do you read regularly?"), and psychographic characteristics ("Do you prefer to read a book or go wind surfing on your day off?"). This information is compiled into a massive data set, published in both print and electronic form, which are used by ad and public-relations specialists to determine what kinds of people purchase which kinds of products and use which kinds of media to learn about new products, styles, trends, and events. When planning how to reach a person who is likely to purchase a 35 mm camera or read a company's advocacy piece, for instance, this kind of information is essential. Another service, produced by the Market Research Corporation of America, offers results of a consumer panel of 7,500 families who keep continuous diaries of their purchases and the effects of promotional activities such as coupons and sales.

Broadcast audience information is available from ratings services. Both Arbitron and Nielsen are in the business of gathering information about audiences for broadcast programming. Arbitron concentrates on measuring local television and local radio audiences, while Nielsen measures the audiences for national network television and local television. (The survey methods used by these services are discussed in Chapter 8.) Libraries receive the multivolume sets that detail audience estimates for hundreds of radio and television markets.

The ratings volumes include a wealth of information about the geographic markets surveyed, the demographic characteristics of the households and of individuals, the time of day when people watch television or listen to the radio, the types of programs that attract the largest audiences, and the time spent by different types of people using broadcast media. While it is not necessary for every communicator to learn to decode the ratings volumes, it is important to understand how this information is used. Ratings information determines the advertising rates charged by broadcast stations, helps communicators understand something about the characteristics of media consumers, and gives a snapshot of the kinds of media programming that are popular or influential among large audiences. The best rule of thumb for the novice trying to use a library's collection of ratings volumes is to ask for help from the librarian or person most familiar with the services.

Another form of information about consumers is psychographic data, which reveal product-specific attitudes, emotions, and behavior. A number of companies conduct psychographic research and make their data available to those who can afford to subscribe. One of the successful psychographic research companies is SRI International, which produces the Values and Lifestyles 2 (VALS 2) marketing system. The VALS 2 system divides consumers into eight types, based on consumption of 170 different categories of products. VALS 2 tries to predict consumer behavior by defining consumers according to their product use and the resources available to them. Yankelovich's MONITOR, VNU's PRIZM, and Donnelley's ClusterPLUS are three other services advertisers and ad agencies may subscribe to for similar psychographic information. In addition, some of the larger firms are developing consumer information systems for marketing research for Europe and Japan.

Other systems, known as *single-source data-gathering systems*, combine electronic monitoring of consumer behavior with traditional consumer research. Two electronic tools are used: television meters, which produce accurate descriptions of who watches TV and what advertising they see; and laser scanners, which record the Uniform Price Code (UPC) symbols on products purchased by panel participants. Three companies have national panels they regularly monitor: Arbitron Ratings Company, with its ScanAmerica system; Information Resources, Inc. (IRI), with its Behaviorscan system; and NPD/ Nielsen, with its Scantrack service.

ScanAmerica households have meters attached to their television sets, and they use "wands" at home to record the UPC symbols of the products they buy. Panelists also record their print media use. Behaviorscan panelists have identification cards with a bar code, which they present to the cashiers at participating stores along with their purchases. The panelists also have their TVs metered. Scantrack uses the TV meter, product scanners, and identification cards. All these information-gathering systems are designed to track precisely what the consumer is watching or reading (exposure to advertising, coupon promotions, and so on) and what the consumer is purchasing. The information is used to determine the effectiveness of advertising messages, promotions, and appeals.

A great many services reveal to advertising and public-relations professionals where ad dollars are spent. These services measure spending by advertisers in various kinds of media, including newspapers (reported in *Media Records*), magazines (reported in *Publisher's Information Bureau, Inc.*), radio and television (reported in *Broadcast Advertisers Reports*), and a combination of ten media (reported in *Leading National Advertisers/Arbitron Multi-Media Service* [LNA/AMMS]). These library tools assist the communicator in planning how to set an advertising budget and in learning something about a competitor's strategy in placing ads. For instance, by using *LNA/AMMS*, an ad professional could learn how much Procter & Gamble spent on advertising for Head & Shoulders shampoo in magazines, Sunday magazines, newspapers, network and spot television, network and national spot radio, cable television, syndicated television, and outdoor sources such as billboards. The reports are available quarterly.

Market information is also an important element of the advertising and public-relations communicator's library-search strategy. Communicators need to understand the markets that will be receiving their messages and the industries for which they are creating messages. Library tools such as *Selling Areas-Marketing, Inc.* (SAMI) provide information about warehouse withdrawals to food stores in defined marketing areas. This gives the communicator an idea of the movement of all dry grocery and household supplies to retail outlets in an area. Other tools such as *Sales & Marketing Management's Survey of Buying Power* and *Editor & Publisher Market Guide* come in handy as well. These publications offer a convenient source of information about population and household data for all major geographical markets in the United States, buying income and spending statistics about markets, and retail sales data by broad product classes. A communicator trying to find and evaluate markets for a new fast food pizza restaurant, for instance, could use these tools to find a table that ranks markets from best to worst on the basis of pizza sales. Both are published annually.

Another tool that has information about industry and commerce in the United States is Rand McNally's *Commercial Atlas and Marketing Guide*. It compiles information about agriculture, communications, manufacturing, population, retail trade, and transportation in American communities. For the communicator trying to decide where to place messages and having to identify the characteristics of a particular market for a new product, service, or industry, this tool is especially useful. For those communicators who do not want to do their own digging for marketing information, the library will probably have directories such as the *International Directory of Marketing Information Sources*, or the annual *Findex Directory of Market Research Reports, Stud-*

ies, and Surveys, which identifies research and marketing reports done in the private sector.

Reference tools and syndicated research services found in libraries can allow the searcher to forgo expensive and time-consuming original research. The United States government publishes reports and documents, including information from the Census Bureau, which are easily located. Specialized trade publications and industry periodicals, indexed in any number of library indexes, also may have useful articles. Even though some of the tools mentioned in this section are very specialized and may be only in advertising or public-relations libraries, it is worth the communicator's time to track down the appropriate reference materials for each search topic.

Two-Step Library Tools

Card or Computer Catalogs. We have already discussed some of the characteristics of catalogs. The catalog for a library is the key to the entire collection of information. The catalog details the holdings of the library and includes information about how each item may be located. The classification systems and the subject-heading schemes discussed earlier are very important elements of a library catalog.

Whether a catalog is in book form, 3- by 5-inch card form, microfiche form, or electronic form, there are some common elements. First, the items in each catalog are accessible in several ways. The main entry, or author listing, includes the most complete information about the book or periodical in the collection (Figure 5.1). In addition to referring to the main entry, the searcher may locate information by looking up the title of the publication (if it is known), a coauthor's name, or a subject categorization. The various subject-headings lists come in handy when using the subject portion of a book, card, or microfiche catalog. A quick peek into the subject-headings lists can help decode the sometimes bizarre word inversions, choice of terms, and filing rules used in subject catalogs.

Electronic catalogs make searching by subject terms less formidable because most sophisticated electronic catalogs allow the researcher to use common terms as search keys, at least initially. Thus the communicator could type the word *wetlands* on the electronic catalog terminal and receive a list of every item in the catalog that has that word somewhere in the record, whether in the book title, the journal title, or the subject-headings section. The electronic catalog might then suggest to the searcher a list of appropriate formal subject headings that would also lead to books and materials on wetlands that do not have that exact term in the record (Figure 5.2).

In any case, the catalog of a library is the most important two-step tool for identifying the holdings of the particular collection. There are, however, some pitfalls in using catalogs, and they can be especially damaging for the communicator. Many times, the most recent items in a library collection have not yet been entered into the catalog. For a communicator trying to meet a recency standard for information, this can be devastating. Catalogs also do

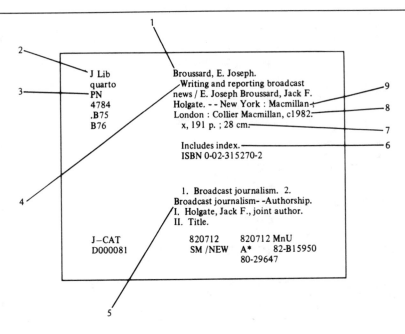

1. Author's name
2. Shelving location
3. Call number
4. Title of book
5. Subject headings assigned to the book and to other catalog cards for this title
6. Notes of special interest
7. Paging, height (in centimeters)
8. Date published
9. Publication place and publisher

FIGURE 5.1   Sample card catalog entry

not detail the specific articles or information located within the books and journals in a library collection. For that kind of help, the communicator must turn to a different set of two-step tools.

Indexes.   Perhaps the most useful of the two-step library tools for the communicator trying to quickly locate library information is the index. An index is nothing more than a listing, usually alphabetically arranged by subject categories, of articles and materials that have appeared in other publications. There are indexes to magazine, newspaper, and journal articles; poems; plays; songs; speeches; pictures; essays; short stories; and a variety of other items that are hidden away in library sources. The index helps the communicator ferret out that elusive item from the piles of sources that would otherwise be lost.

There are some standard indexes that every communicator should know about when beginning the library portion of the search strategy. Basic distinctions between popular and scholarly sources of information must also apply to the use of indexes, and subject headings are also the key to successfully

```
SEARCH REQUEST: A = BROUSSARD E
CATALOG RECORD — NO. 1 OF 1 ENTRIES FOUND

Broussard, E. Joseph
   Writing and reporting broadcast news / E. Joseph Broussard,
      Jack F. Holgate.
   — New York: Macmillan; London; Collier Macmillan, c1982.
   x, 191 p.; 28 cm.
   Includes index.
SUBJECT HEADINGS (Library of Congress; use s = ):
      Broadcast journalism.
      Broadcast journalism—Authorship.

LOCATION: JOURNALISM LIBRARY
CALL NUMBER: Quarto PN4784.B75 B76

LOCATION: WALTER LIBRARY
CALL NUMBER: Quarto PN4784.B75 B76 (copy 2)


TYPE h FOR HELP, e FOR INTRODUCTORY SCREEN, OR r TO REVISE.
AFTER TYPING A COMMAND, PRESS ENTER:
```

FIGURE 5.2   Sample computer catalog entry

using these tools. Once these ground rules are familiar, the indexes listed below help the researcher find information quickly and effortlessly.

Periodical Indexes

1. *The Reader's Guide to Periodical Literature*, 1900 to date (semimonthly): The *Reader's Guide* is probably most familiar to any schoolchild who uses the local public or school library. This index covers material that has appeared in about 180 general and popular magazines. Few technical, specialized, or subject-specific journals are included. Therefore, the communicator must recognize that the information located by using this index will not be very sophisticated or authoritative. However, it is published by one of the largest index publishers in the country, the H. W. Wilson Company, which also publishes a variety of more specialized indexes. So once the *Reader's Guide* is mastered, the communicator should not have too much trouble using other indexes published by this company (for example, items 2–10 in this list). The interpretation of a *Reader's Guide* or other Wilson index entry is fairly standardized (Figure 5.3). Many H. W. Wilson indexes are also available in on-line or CD-ROM format (see Chapter 6).

2. *Applied Science and Technology Index,* 1958 to date (monthly): covers specialized periodicals in those fields.
3. *Art Index,* 1935 to date (quarterly): covers periodicals in the fields of both fine arts and the performing arts; coverage is especially good for photography and photojournalism.
4. *Biological and Agricultural Index,* 1964 to date (monthly): covers specialized periodicals in those fields.
5. *Business Periodicals Index,* 1958 to date (monthly): covers a variety of business and trade publications, many of which are particularly important for communicators trying to find information about industries, markets, population characteristics, trends in business, or biographical information about people in business; also includes many trade publications for print and broadcast journalism, advertising, and public relations.
6. *Education Index,* 1929 to date (monthly): covers periodicals, conference proceedings, bulletins, yearbooks, and book series.
7. *General Science Index,* 1978 to date (monthly): covers general interest science periodicals.
8. *Humanities Index,* 1974 to date (quarterly): covers periodicals and journals in the arts, history, language, and literature.
9. *Index to Legal Periodicals,* 1908 to date (monthly): covers law periodicals and reviews, yearbooks, and annual reviews.
10. *Social Sciences Index,* 1974 to date (quarterly): covers both popular and scholarly publications in political science, psychology, economics, law, geography, and related fields.
11. *Topicator,* 1965 to date (bimonthly): covers publications in the field of journalism and mass communication, including both scholarly and trade publications.
12. *Alternative Press Index,* 1969 to date (quarterly): covers alternative and radical magazines, journals, and newspapers that include such topics as gay rights, socialism, the women's movement, and minority rights. For the communicator looking for information from non-mainstream publications, this index is one of the best sources.
13. *PAIS International in Print,* 1915 to date (monthly, with three cumulations and an annual cumulation, formerly titled *Public Affairs Information Service Bulletin*): covers material in political science, government, public affairs, economics, and sociology. It is especially useful for the communicator looking for public policy information and material. Its expanded coverage now claims to offer an international scope.

Many periodical indexes are also available in on-line or CD-ROM electronic form. (Data bases are discussed in detail in Chapter 6.)

Newspaper Indexes. Articles that have appeared in newspapers are also indexed. It is not necessary to page aimlessly through backfiles or microfilm

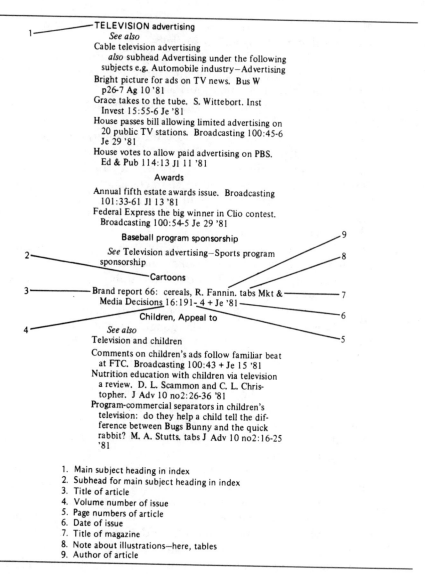

1. Main subject heading in index
2. Subhead for main subject heading in index
3. Title of article
4. Volume number of issue
5. Page numbers of article
6. Date of issue
7. Title of magazine
8. Note about illustrations—here, tables
9. Author of article

FIGURE 5.3 Sample *Reader's Guide to Periodical Literature* citation

SOURCE: *Reader's Guide to Periodical Literature.* Copyright © 1981, 1982 by H. W. Wilson Company. Material reproduced by permission of the publisher.

issues in order to find a particular article about a topic. Major newspaper indexes lead the communicator to the exact information needed to track down even the most elusive of articles. (As mentioned in the section about media libraries, regional newspapers that may once have produced a printed index now may be searchable only in electronic form, since they store their backfiles electronically and there is no market for a printed index. Chapter 6 discusses searching electronic backfiles.)

1. The *New York Times Index*, 1851 to date (semimonthly, with quarterly and annual cumulations): Perhaps the most sophisticated of the printed newspaper indexes, the *New York Times Index* includes not only the date, page number, and column information needed to locate an article, but also a brief summary of the article. For some items, the index actually reproduces a photo, graph, map, or chart that was important in the article, making a trip to the microfilm issues unnecessary. Interpreting a *New York Times Index* entry is a little different from interpreting a periodical index entry, but is just as simple once the basic elements are known (Figure 5.4).

2. *Wall Street Journal Index*, 1950 to date (monthly, with quarterly and annual cumulations): Indexed in two parts, "Corporate News" and "General News," with brief summaries of each article.

3. *Official Washington Post Index*, 1979 to date (monthly, with annual cumulations): a subject and name index containing abstracts of all material of "permanent value" that appeared in the paper.

4. *Christian Science Monitor Index*, 1949 to date (monthly, formerly titled *Index to the Christian Science Monitor*): cites stories carried in the three editions of the paper: eastern, western, and midwestern.

5. *NewsBank Index*, 1970 to date (monthly, with quarterly and annual

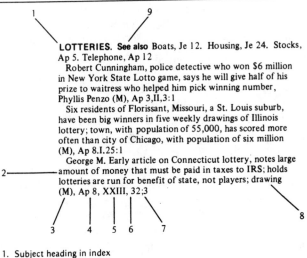

1. Subject heading in index
2. Short summary of article
3. Note about article length—here, "medium"
4. Date of article
5. Section of newspaper in which article appeared
6. Page number
7. Column number
8. Note about visuals—here, "drawing"
9. "See also" reference to related subject headings

FIGURE 5.4 Sample *New York Times Index* citation.

cumulations): Selected articles from more than 450 newspapers are indexed in this printed index, with the full text of the articles available in microfiche. This service is especially useful for the communicator who wants to see what was reported about a subject in various parts of the country but who may not have access to an electronic search service.

6. *Canadian News Index*, 1977 to date (monthly, formerly titled *Canadian Newspaper Index*): offers a subject and name index to Canada's leading newspapers.

Many newspaper indexes are also available in on-line or CD-ROM electronic form.

Broadcast-News Indexes. It is possible to locate some broadcast transcripts, usually on microfilm, by using a variety of broadcast indexes.

1. *CBS News Index*, 1975 to date (quarterly, with annual cumulations): printed index to the four daily news broadcasts and the public-affairs programs on CBS-TV, including presidential press conferences and speeches, "Face the Nation," and "60 Minutes." The full-text transcripts of the programs are issued on microfilm and microfiche.

2. *ABC News Index*, 1969 to date (quarterly, with annual cumulations): printed index to the major ABC news television programs, including "20/20," "Nightline," "This Week with David Brinkley," and "World News Tonight with Peter Jennings." The full-text transcripts are issued on microfiche. Searches by subject, program title, name of personality, and other methods are possible.

3. *Public Television Transcripts Index*, 1987 to date (quarterly, with annual cumulations): printed index to the full-text transcripts of such programs as "The MacNeil/Lehrer Newshour," "Adam Smith's Money World," and other public television offerings. The transcripts are issued on microfiche.

4. *Summary of World Broadcasts by the British Broadcasting Corporation*, 1973 to date (weekly or daily subscription available): Microform only, the set includes transcripts of news broadcasts monitored and translated into English by the BBC from the former Soviet Union, Eastern Europe, the Far East, the Middle East, and Africa.

5. *Television News Index and Abstracts*, 1972 to date (monthly, with a retrospective index to August 1967 issued in microform): printed index to the Vanderbilt University Television News Archives of videotapes of the national evening news as broadcast by ABC, CBS, and NBC. Users may conduct searches by name, subject, reporter, or other methods. The tapes themselves are available from the Vanderbilt Television News Archive in Nashville, Tenn.; the archive will loan tapes, duplicate news broadcasts, or compile items from various broadcasts upon request from the user.

Biographical Indexes.   Earlier in the chapter, directories were mentioned as one useful source of information about people; the backgrounds, expertise, experiences, and activities of individuals are some of the most important kinds of information for certain mass-communication messages. In addition to the directory-type sources, public records, and institutional paper and electronic trails, there are a number of index sources, referred to as *biography master indexes*, that help communicators locate biographical information about individuals.

1. *Biography and Genealogy Master Index,* 1981 to date (currently annual, with cumulations in multiple volumes for 1981 to 1990): compilation from a huge number of biographical directories of the names of people whose biographies have been written. An individual is listed, along with abbreviations indicating where biographical information has been published. For instance, if an individual has been included in a biographical directory such as *Authors in the News* or *Current Biography*, the entry in the *Biography and Genealogy Master Index* will indicate which date and volume of those reference books to consult for the actual biography.

2. *Index to Artistic Biography,* 1973; supplement, 1981: references to biographical information that has appeared in such directories as *Who's Who in American Art* and *Contemporary Japanese-style Painting*.

3. *Index to Literary Biography,* 1975; two-volume supplement, 1983: references to biographical information that has appeared in such directories as *Twentieth-Century American Science Fiction Writers* and *American Writers in Paris, 1920–39*.

4. *Biography Index,* 1946 to date (quarterly, annual, and three-year cumulations): Not really a master index, the *Biography Index* helps communicators locate biographical articles that have appeared in 2,000 periodicals and journals. Also included are references to biographical books and chapters from collective biographies.

5. *Biographical Books, 1876–1949 and 1950–80,* 2 volumes: listing of American books published about people in all fields.

6. *Obituary Index to the New York Times,* 1858 to 1978: references to the immensely detailed obituaries that ran in the *New York Times;* even people who did not appear in the standard biographical directories of the day might, if prominent, have had an elaborate write-up in the obituary column.

7. *New York Times Biographical Service: A Compilation of Current Biographical Information of Current Interest,* 1970 to date (monthly, with annual cumulations): Reprints of major articles and obituaries as they appeared in the *New York Times* are available in this reference tool, which changed to this title in 1974.

8. *Current Biography,* 1940 to date (monthly, with annual cumulations): This magazine-style publication includes articles about people in the news, with brief, well-documented entries and a photo of each person

covered. It is an excellent source for information about people who may not yet (or ever) be included in the more formal biographical sources.

Biography master indexes and many other types of biographical information sources help the communicator supplement the more traditional method of gathering information about people—the interview. If some facts have to be verified, if the person in question will not agree to an interview or is unavailable, or if the person has died, these library tools often are the only methods of gathering the required biographical information that is so important to many messages.

Indexes to Other Kinds of Information. In addition to having indexes to periodical articles, newspaper articles, broadcast transcripts, and biographical information, most large libraries have a variety of indexes to other kinds of materials that are on library shelves. Without these indexes, the searcher cannot dig out the one item needed from that mass of materials. The following is a sample of some of the special indexes available on library shelves alongside the periodical and newspaper indexes.

1. *Book Review Index*, 1965 to date (bimonthly): covers book reviews that have been published in more than 200 periodicals. The communicator may have to know how a particular book was received by the critics before deciding whether to use that book or to interview the author. The communicator can avoid referring to someone whose book got a poor review and reception from peers.
2. *Book Review Digest*, 1905 to date (monthly): covers 100 journals and magazines in which reviews have appeared. *Book Review Digest* is much like *Book Review Index*, except that it includes summaries of the reviews as well as references for locating them. The communicator can save time by using this source because the review is summarized and may have enough information to make tracking down the actual review unnecessary.
3. *Essay and General Literature Index*, 1900 to date (semiannual, with five-year cumulations): covers anthologies on all topics, listing individual chapters or essays within a book and thus allowing the searcher to locate an important essay that is buried in a book with a large number of other articles or essays.
4. *New York Times Film Reviews*, 1913 to date (annual): covers every film review that has appeared in the *New York Times*.
5. *Speech Index: An Index to Collections of World Famous Orations and Speeches for Various Occasions*, 1935–1965; supplement, 1966–1980: Speeches are referenced by subject and by orator, both ordinary and well known.
6. *Oral History Index: An International Directory of Oral History Interviews*, 1990: an alphabetical index to more than 30,000 oral history transcripts

held at nearly 400 oral history centers in the United States, Canada, Great Britain, and Israel.

Abstract Services.   Abstract services are very much like indexes, except for one major factor: abstracts include, along with the information about where to locate an item, a brief summary of the material indexed. Abstract services tend to be more specialized by subject or topic area than general indexes, and the arrangement of information in the abstract service is a little more complicated, but it is fairly easy to learn. And the publications that are abstracted are usually scholarly or specialized, thus favoring the needs of the expert searcher. For the communicator who has to find information quickly, the abstract service can be of tremendous value. It is possible to determine whether the book, article, report, or item is valuable for the particular information need before ever locating the actual item. Since the abstract service summarizes the item, the communicator can make a judgment about the relevance of the item by reading the abstract.

There is one serious drawback for the communicator using abstract services—there is a very significant time delay between the appearance of the material and its inclusion in an abstract service. Because someone has to read and summarize every item that appears in an abstract service, it can be months or even years before an item is included.

Some examples of well-known abstract services are listed, along with some of the less familiar but useful services for the communicator:

1. *Psychological Abstracts*, 1927 to date (monthly): covers international periodicals and is arranged by 17 broad subject categories from parapsychology, marriage and family roles, and mental disorders to personality. This helps the user find the precise section of the service related to the topic being searched, without having to wade through a great deal of unrelated material (Figure 5.5).
2. *Sociological Abstracts*, 1952 to date (bimonthly, with annual cumulations): covers international publications on all aspects of sociology, culture, and related subjects. The journals covered are scholarly, and communicators can quickly get an overview of an author's main ideas and conclusions.
3. *America: History and Life*, 1964 to date (four issues a year plus a cumulated annual index): covers materials on American and Canadian history published throughout the world. Articles, books, films/videos, and dissertations are thoroughly indexed with multiple subject headings, so the communicator has a good chance of locating every relevant item in the service.
4. *Sage Public Administration Abstracts*, 1974 to date (quarterly): covers about 275 periodicals on public policy, bureaucracy, city management, and related subjects. Since many communicators must understand how city management works and how various kinds of city policies differ across the country, this tool can be very helpful.

---

[1]1271. [2]**Conger, Anthony L. & Cole, John D.** [3](Duke U) [4]**Who's crazy in Manhattan: A reexamination of "Treatment of psychological disorders among urban children."** [5]*Journal of Consulting & Clinical Psychology.* 1975 (Apr). Vol 43(2). 179–182. [6]Reanalyzed data reported by **T. S. Langner** et al [7](see **PA.** Vol 52:8150) on the prevalence of psychological disturbances in children from welfare and cross-section homes. Results indicate that the data show no meaningful differences in means or skew and a paradoxical greater heterogeneity among welfare children. Some of the difference in variance is clearly attributable to the differential reliability of final scores, and perhaps the remaining difference is due to between-rater differences. Unless other factors were operating, 2 possible conclusions are tenable: Either welfare children manifest both more health and more disturbance than cross-section children or there are no differences in disorder between the populations. A 3rd conclusion is also offered: The populations do actually differ, but the manner in which the disturbance was viewed, rated, and compared necessarily obscured any differences.[8,9] (15 ref.)—[10]*Journal Abstract.*

1—Record number.
2—Author(s) or editor(s). As many as four are listed; if there are more than four, the first is listed followed by "et al." Succession marks (i.e., Jr., II, III, etc) are not given.
3—Affiliation of first-named author/editor only.
4—Article title, including subtitles: If the original article was written in a foreign language, the original article title is given followed by a slash and the translated title as provided by the source document. If the translated title was not provided by the source document, PsycINFO's translation is given in brackets. The language of the original article is indicated in parentheses.
5—Primary publication title and bibliographic data.
6—Text of abstract.
7—Reference to a previous entry in **Psychological Abstracts.** If an abstract number is unavailable at time of publication, the issue number is given. Consult the Author Index of the **PA** issue noted in order to determine the record number for the article.
8—Summaries included in the primary publication are listed when in language(s) other than that of the article.
9—Number of references is included.
10—Abstract source.

FIGURE 5.5   Journal article abstract from *Psychological Abstracts*

5. *Pollution Abstracts,* 1970 to date (bimonthly, with annual cumulations): covers 2,500 international periodicals on air, water, and noise pollution; waste management; public health; environmental legislation and policies; and related topics. Many technical reports and government documents are also abstracted. This is an excellent tool to use as a way into this complicated subject area.
6. *Criminal Justice Abstracts,* 1988 to date (quarterly): covers about 160 international journals on crime prevention, research into causes of crime and criminality, attitudes toward the penal system, and related issues.

7. *Communication Abstracts*, 1978 to date (bimonthly): covers periodicals and books in the fields of advertising, mass communication, speech and interpersonal communication, broadcasting, and public relations. For the communicator who needs information on the effectiveness of male versus female voice-overs for television commercials, for instance, this service will get into the literature that reports on that kind of research.

Many abstract services are also available in on-line or CD-ROM electronic form.

Large libraries will have more of these services than smaller libraries, and large university libraries will have a greater variety of subject area abstracts than public libraries. Communicators will probably use an abstract service at a middle or late stage in the library search, after they are comfortable with the language of the topic and know exactly what kind of information is needed to fill in the gaps or expand the base of the material already found.

Bibliographies.   A bibliography is a list of publications—books; magazine, journal, and newspaper articles; documents. The Library of Congress publishes a huge bibliography called *The National Union Catalog: A Cumulative Author List* (1956 to date), which lists by author every work published since 1956 that is in the Library of Congress. A bibliography may also be a single publication that includes a list of many information sources on the same topic. The *Bibliography of Bioethics* is an example of an entire volume listing sources on one topic.

One of the more useful bibliographies is a set of reference books called *Books in Print*. There are more than 500,000 books available in print every year. Libraries cannot possibly own all the in-print books, nor can they buy all the books that are printed each year. *Books in Print* can alert the communicator to titles that may be available somewhere, even if the library that he or she is using does not own them. There are several ways to use the multivolume *Books in Print*. The *Subject Guide to Books in Print* is especially helpful when the communicator does not have a particular author or title in mind but wants to learn whether any book is available on a particular topic.

When starting a library search, it is not a bad idea to check to see whether a subject bibliography is available on the topic being researched. So many bibliographies exist that it is foolish for the communicator to do an information search from scratch that may have been done recently by someone else. An index entitled *The Bibliographic Index: A Cumulative Bibliography of Bibliographies* will help the searcher locate bibliographies that have been published as separate books or as articles in 2,200 periodicals. The *Bibliographic Index*, unfortunately, has one important drawback: it is twice removed from the actual information needed. Once a bibliography is found in the *Bibliographic Index*, the next step is to find the bibliography itself, and then still another step is required: to locate the relevant articles or books listed in the bibliography. The astute observer can imagine that the articles may be several months or years out of date. Nonetheless, using bibliographies like these saves enormous effort—effort better spent on locating the information published since the most recent bibliography than on recompiling sources that have already been listed.

Legal Sources. Sources of legal information in libraries constitute an entire category of library tools for the communicator. Many times, information about laws, legal decisions, or interpretations of actions by courts will be found in review articles or commentaries by legal scholars. By using such two-step tools as the *Index to Legal Periodicals, Current Law Index,* or *Legal Resource Index* (on microfilm), the communicator can locate articles or reports that have been written by experts in the field and that have authoritative interpretations of legal information.

Sometimes the communicator may have to find the actual legal decisions or dissenting opinions rather than interpretations of them. If a community is considering instituting an ordinance declaring the vending of violent pornographic magazines and books a violation of women's civil rights, for instance, the astute reporter might want to find out whether there are any other such laws elsewhere in the country that might affect the one being considered. It is not unreasonable to expect a good reporter to do a search for such information in the local law library.

There are certain characteristics of legal information in libraries that the communicator must be familiar with before attempting such a search. The organization of legal information in libraries reflects the organization of the bodies that are producing the laws. Referring to the lessons learned in an American civics class will help a little, but the branches of government that issue legal decisions are not only those mentioned in civics classes.

Three federal and state government bodies can issue laws and regulations. The legislatures of the federal and state governments create statutory law by passing bills that become law when signed by the executive. The administrative agencies create administrative law, consisting of rules and decisions issued by each agency (for example, the Environmental Protection Agency at the federal level issues regulations concerning the disposal of hazardous wastes). The judicial branch of government issues case law, which is found in the court decisions written by judges.

Federal statutory, administrative, and case law applies to every state court and agency in the country. Those statutes, regulations, and case laws written by individual state governments apply only to courts and agencies within that state. In order to determine where to look for information about laws at the federal or state level, the communicator has to understand how the court and regulatory systems are organized at the federal and state levels.

United States statutory law, created by Congress, is found in sessions laws, which collect the statutes in chronological order, and is published in a tool called *Statutes at Large.* These statutes also are compiled in the *United*

States Code, which is organized according to the topic of the law. So if the communicator is looking for any law written and passed by Congress, these are the two most likely tools to use in a law library. If the name of the bill is known, the *Statutes at Large* volumes can be used. If the communicator is looking for *any* law relating to the topic of pornography, the *United States Code* should be used.

Federal administrative law is found in both chronological and topical order as well. The *Federal Register* arranges in chronological order all regulations issued by federal regulatory bodies. The topical arrangement of federal regulations is found in the *Code of Federal Regulations*. Both tools will be in a law library and can be used to locate rules issued by such federal bodies as the Environmental Protection Agency, the Federal Communications Commission, or the Department of Defense.

The judiciary, or courts, make case law, interpret the Constitution, and make other legal decisions. The appellate courts establish precedent, or rules, that all lower courts must apply. Depending on whether a decision was written by a federal court or a state court, the precedent value of the decision applies to either the entire country's courts or just the state's courts. The communicator, when looking for case law, has to distinguish between those laws that apply to only one state or district and those that apply to all the states in the country.

Federal case law is found in a series of case reporters, which organize the laws chronologically, and case digests, which organize the laws topically. Within the federal-court system, however, there are three levels, performing different functions and writing different kinds of laws. These three levels are the trial level, the intermediate appellate level, and the final appellate level.

The federal trial courts are called United States district courts. Each state has at least one federal judicial district, and some states have several districts. The tools that organize the decisions of United States district courts in chronological order are the *West's Federal Supplement* (1932 to date), *Federal Rules Decisions* (1938 to date), and *Federal Cases* (1789–1880). District court decisions are also arranged according to topic in the *West's Federal Practice Digest 4th* (1989 to date), *West's Federal Practice Digest 3d* (1975–1989), *Federal Practice Digest 2d* (1961–1975), *Modern Federal Practice Digest* (1939–1961), *Federal Digest* (1754–1939), and *Decennial Digests* (10-year collections from the digest topics).

The second federal-court level is the intermediate appellate level, the United States courts of appeals. There are 13 federal courts of appeals, each of which covers a particular geographical area known as a circuit. For instance, the Eighth Circuit includes the states of Minnesota, Iowa, Missouri, Arkansas, Nebraska, South Dakota, and North Dakota. Decisions written by judges at this level are also collected in both chronological and topical order. The chronological tools are the *West's Federal Reporter, Second Series* (1924 to date), *Federal Reporter* (1880–1924), and *Federal Cases*. The topical tools are the *West's Federal Practice Digest 4th*, *West's Federal Practice Digest 3d*, *Federal Practice Digest 2d*, *Modern Federal Practice*, *Federal Digest*, and *Decennial Digests*.

The third federal-court level, and the court that sets precedent for the entire country's legal system, is the United States Supreme Court. Again, the decisions of the Supreme Court are arranged in both chronological and topical order. The tools that arrange Supreme Court decisions in chronological order are *U.S. Reports* (the official reporter, 1790 to date), *Supreme Court Reporter* (1882 to date), and *U.S. Supreme Court Reports, Lawyers' Edition* (1790 to date). The topical tools are *Supreme Court Digest* (1943 to date); *Supreme Court Digest, Lawyers' Edition; West's Federal Practice Digest 4th; West's Federal Practice Digest 3d; Federal Practice Digest 2d; Modern Federal Practice Digest; Federal Digest;* and *Decennial Digests.* In addition, Supreme Court rulings began to be transmitted electronically minutes after the decisions were announced, starting with the 1990 session. The venture, named *Project Hermes,* allows news organizations, media trade groups, and legal publishing organizations access to decisions as they are released. (Electronic legal data bases are discussed in detail in Chapter 6.) Each of these tools will help the communicator locate the decisions of the Court with the verbatim wording of the Court's opinion, along with the facts of the case, the names of the lawyers who argued the case before the Court, other legal decisions that were referred to by the justices in reaching their decisions, and any dissenting, or minority, opinions.

Courts at the state level also write decisions that affect state legal activities. Decisions of state courts are collected in a series of state reporters, many of which are published by West Publishing Company. Each state has at least one official high-court reporter; some states have separate reporters for the appellate courts; and a few states have reporters for the trial courts. West publishes a series of regional reporters, each of which reprints the full text of opinions from courts in a specific geographical region: These reporters (all preceded by *West's*) are *Atlantic, North Eastern, North Western, Pacific, South Eastern, South Western,* and *Southern. A Uniform System of Citation* is a standard reference book that lists the reporters for each state and the courts whose opinions are contained in each reporter.

Once the communicator understands the relationship between government organization and the legal research sources that libraries collect, finding the actual court opinions at any level should be fairly straightforward. The communicator must also learn to interpret legal citations before any progress can be made, however. Reading legal citations is a little different from reading citations found in other indexes and abstract services. A citation helps the searcher locate a particular legal document. The reference tool *A Uniform System of Citation* helps the searcher interpret legal citations. One type of legal citation and its various elements is shown in Figure 5.6.

Doing legal research requires a special type of library search strategy. It is not for the novice information searcher. All law libraries have legal-reference librarians who can help the communicator locate the actual legal opinions that often serve as the subjects of news, commentary, and social furor. Most media organizations have a legal counsel who helps professionals make day-to-day decisions about the legality of certain kinds of messages and activities. The legal-reference tools described here are really for the com-

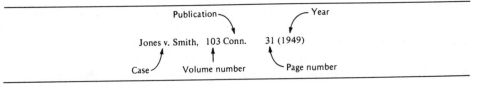

FIGURE 5.6 One type of legal citation

municator who has to understand the atmosphere in which certain public-policy decisions are being made and who has to be able to independently locate and interpret the information that the public might need to make informed decisions.

Picture Sources.   A number of two-step tools in libraries can help the communicator locate pictures. Whether for a feature story on how hospital surgical theaters have changed over time, an article on the flora and fauna of Yellowstone National Park, or an ad for a greeting card company, pictures of both contemporary and historical people, places, and events can be very important for the message. While many media organizations have their own extensive files of visual materials, some items can be found only in special collections. The library reference tools listed here can help the communicator locate the appropriate pictures.

1. *Guide to the Special Collections of Prints and Photographs in the Library of Congress*, 1955: still useful for identifying 802 individual collections in the Prints and Photographic Division of the Library of Congress; includes a subject index.
2. *Index to American Photographic Collections*, 1982: lists 458 private and public collections of photographs in institutions throughout the country; includes a subject index.
3. *Pictorial Resources in the Washington, D.C. Area*, 1976: describes the general picture resources of government organizations and agencies and of private and international organizations.
4. *Illustration Index*, 1980, 1973, 1966, and 1957: Each edition indexes the illustrations that have appeared in various general-interest, historical, sports, and travel magazines.
5. *Picture Sources 4*, 1983: lists picture collections in public libraries, state agencies, museums, universities, newspapers, and stock photo agencies; includes a subject organization and subject index. For instance, the category "castles" includes all collections of pictures of castles. The book is organized by subject and also has a subject index.
6. *Stock Photo and Assignment Source Book: Where to Find Photographs Instantly*, 1984: a complete subject index that helps identify photos in museums, television stations, newspapers, government agencies, motion-picture studios, special libraries, corporations, stock photo agencies, and historical societies. The book also serves as a guide to press and editorial photographers working out of the United States and Europe.

These library tools will help the communicator learn who to contact about permission to reproduce a picture. The picture may be leased or purchased, depending on the policy of the owner. Whether the person in a picture is a public or private individual may also affect the uses to which a picture may be put. The best rule of thumb is to make sure the stipulations of picture use are fully understood at the time of the agreement.

CONSULTING THE LIBRARIAN

The search strategy emphasizes the competence of the searcher. Understanding the bibliographic chain and the conventions of knowledge production as they are reflected in library materials helps communicators achieve this competence. Despite their general ability in libraries, communicators frequently run into dead ends in their searches. Unlike professional librarians, their knowledge of reference tools is limited. In these cases, the best person to consult is the librarian. Not everyone sitting behind a desk in a library is a librarian, however. Many libraries staff their information desks at off times with employees who do not have specific training in the efficient use of library materials. The librarian has a degree and professional training in the methods of organization and use of library collections. The librarian is very familiar with the special characteristics of and collections in the library in which he or she works. And the librarian is the one person who is trained in the area of effective information retrieval.

If the communicator consults a librarian, the librarian will ask for specific information about the research problem. It is up to the communicator to describe precisely what is being sought. The more specific the communicator's request, the swifter and more accurately the librarian can respond. If the communicator needs information about styles of dress in the 1950s, for instance, he or she should *not* ask for information about "costumes."

Since librarians are responsible for organizing and making accessible the information in the library collection, they know how to extract information from the many reference tools on the library shelves. Even if the communicator manages to find a tool that is relevant to the search topic, the librarian may be able to interpret the information it offers. The librarian may also be able to suggest other community resources that the communicator may not have been aware of that can aid in the information search.

Librarians can be of help in identifying library collections that may contain resources not available in the library being used. If the communicator finds several citations for magazine or journal articles in an index, for instance, and then learns that the library does not subscribe to those publications, all is not lost. The librarian may be able to use a fax system to gather the needed item from another collection, or the material may be available in full text in electronic format. The last resort is the interlibrary loan arrangement, which may take several days to two weeks to pan out. Interlibrary loan is obviously not for those materials that are needed to meet a close deadline, but for communicators involved in certain kinds of long-term projects, the time factor is not so important. The specialized item may be worth waiting for.

THE LIBRARY AND THE LIBRARIAN
IN THE MESSAGE-MAKING PROCESS

In many media organizations, librarians are actually becoming part of the message-making team.[8] Media professionals are recognizing that the information-gathering expertise that librarians have can be of great value when information must be quickly located and/or verified. Many large newspapers, for instance, have the news librarian sit in on the daily budget meeting at which stories are assigned, so the library staff knows what the editorial staff will be working on throughout the day and can be ready to offer assistance and resources. News librarians may be assigned to a special projects team working on a long enterprise or investigative project, working alongside the reporters and editors as the project develops. It is not uncommon to see story or by-line credit for librarians who have contributed to a story or project. In particular, media librarians are essential partners with communicators in using the electronic information-gathering systems now available in so many media organization libraries.

Media organizations that have sophisticated media libraries encourage communicators to make better use of those resources that are available. The communicator may not have to refer to outside collections for routine information. The most recent major reference tools; appropriate in-house files of pictures, clippings, and industry and market information; and trained library staff members can meet many information needs on the spot. Similarly, communicators in the field may request information from the media organization library through portable fax systems.

Library collections outside the media organization will be used when information on unusual topics or in-depth material is needed. Fax systems may be used to gather information from community, regional, or national libraries far outside the normal reach of the media library collection. The communicator may have contacts in local libraries who understand the need to meet deadlines and are willing to help with reference questions by telephone or in person. The more personally familiar communicators are with the potential goldmines in libraries, the more likely they are to make effective use of information available there.

LINKS TO THE SEARCH STRATEGY

In this step of the search strategy, the communicator uses both one-step and two-step tools to identify material that is appropriate for the topic being studied. The library step of the search-strategy process requires the communicator to understand the potentials, limitations, and characteristics of information that is available in thousands of collections around the country. The information that is housed in libraries covers the entire range of intellectual output of a society. Whether it is popular, scholarly, legal, biographical, historical, audiovisual, statistical, industrial, or marketing information that is needed, a library is likely to have at least a portion of it. Along with the informal and institutional types of information that the communicator is most familiar with, library sources can add depth, authority, creativity, and uniqueness to any message.

The library, then, becomes an integral part of the communicator's information-gathering task. Confident of the organization of materials housed there, in command of the steps to take in order to decode the information once it is found, and ready to use imagination in ferreting out what is needed, the communicator approaches the library search with a good chance of being successful.

Chapter 6 examines information created, stored, and retrieved electronically. Like material in libraries, this information is identified and retrieved with both one- and two-step tools.

NOTES

1. For the discussion of the history of libraries, we are indebted to Jesse H. Shera, *Introduction to Library Science* (Littleton, Colo.: Libraries Unlimited, 1976), 13–40.
2. Robert M. Finehout, "Treasure It, Don't Trash It," *Public Relations Journal*, April 1986, 8–10.
3. Marcia Ruth, "Electronic Library Systems Reach Watershed Year," *presstime*, July 1985, 10–11.
4. Jean Ward and Kathleen A. Hansen, "Newspapers and Electronic Technologies," *Editor & Publisher*, 3 November 1990, 34–37.
5. Jean Ward, Kathleen A. Hansen, and Douglas M. McLeod, "Effects of the Electronic Library on News Reporting Protocols," *Journalism Quarterly* 65 (Winter 1988): 845–852.
6. Carolyn Schade, "Covering the Persian Gulf War: The First 72 hours at ABC News Library," *American Libraries*, May 1991, 398–400.
7. Elin B. Christianson and Anne M. Waldron, "Advertising Agency Libraries: 30 Years of Change," *Special Libraries* 79 (Spring 1988): 152–162.
8. Thomas J. Colin, "The Facts Checked Round the World: *National Geographic's* Relentless Researchers," *Washington Journalism Review*, November 1984, 31–35; Kathy Foley and Ellen D. Briscoe, "The Newspaper Library in the Information Age: A Personal View from Within," *Online* 13 (November 1989): 15–24; Jean Ward and Kathleen A. Hansen, "Journalist and Librarian Roles, Information Technologies and Newsmaking," *Journalism Quarterly* 68 (Autumn 1991): 491–498.

6

Using Electronic Technologies in Mass Communication

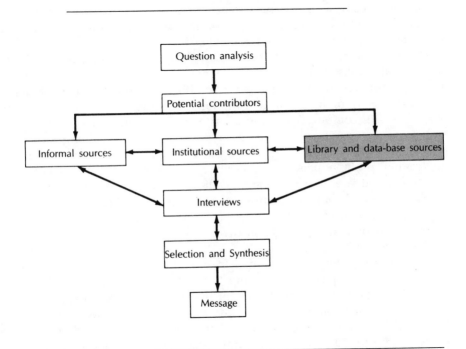

The long-running television program "Saturday Night Live" had a recurring character portrayed by Al Franken. The character, a technology-fascinated reporter, would regularly send in reports to the "Weekend Update" anchor from remote locations through the technology of a "one-man mobile uplink." Franken would appear on the screen carrying a backpack full of electronic equipment, the camera transmitting his image attached with a Steadicam harness to his shoulders and waist. His motorcycle helmet was equipped with a small satellite dish. By pointing his head at the encircling satellite 22,300 miles above the Earth, the character would transmit live pictures from anywhere into which he could cram his equipment-laden frame. Of course, the humor in the routine was that the character would move his head, losing the uplink and causing the picture to turn to snow, or his satellite helmet would be damaged by whatever hostile activity he was witnessing. In one routine, the character confessed that he had been suffering back and knee pain from the weight of his equipment and was now addicted to pain killers.

While this scenario was played for laughs, it is close to reality for today's communicator, who is electronically linked to the world. Cellular telephones allow for voice communication from the most remote locations. Portable fax machines allow for instantaneous transmittal and receipt of print information. Voice mail, electronic mail, and computer bulletin boards link communicators around the world in fractions of a second. Portable satellite–telephone equipment (although not head-mounted!) allowed CNN reporters to continue to report from Baghdad during the Persian Gulf War when all other telephone and satellite links were cut off or denied by Iraqi officials. One reporter evaded United States censorship by sending his stories via his hotel's fax machine late at night. Laptop computers equipped with modems (devices that allow the computer to serve as a terminal for information transmission and receiving) have long been the reporter's means of filing stories from remote locations. Small, easy-to-use videocameras have been used by communication professionals and eye-witnesses alike to record activities from Tiananmen Square to the Persian Gulf to the highway site of a tornado touchdown in El Dorado, Kansas. Portable printers, microcassette tape recorders, pocket-sized short-wave radios, and even equipment that allows for transmission of a still photograph over satellite links have become the tools of the trade.

Aside from the technical gadgetry and gee-whiz attitudes, however, there are some major changes being felt in the way communicators do their work. The promises, and problems, of the information age are being realized in every aspect of communication activity. These developments allow communicators to be better-informed, wiser, and more sophisticated searchers and users of information that is then translated for the audience. The problems involve technical and information overload. Communicators find themselves able to report from almost anywhere in the world, even though they might not be familiar with the context or background of an event they have "parachuted" in to cover. Advertising professionals find so much easily available information about consumers and audiences that it might not be logically collated, understood, and put to use.

The electronic technologies that are available to communicators can be categorized into those which help communicators gather and analyze information before the message is produced, and those which allow for delivery of messages in faster, more efficient ways. We are most concerned here with the electronic technologies that aid in the gathering and analysis of information. Among all the new tools available to communicators, perhaps the most important is the variety of electronic systems called *data bases*.

THE DATA BASE

A data base is a machine-readable file of information that is retrieved through a number of methods. The file may be accessible through a computer–telephone link, searchable in real time through an on-line, interactive link of the searcher's desktop or laptop computer, the telephone, and the electronic file. Or, the data base may be stored on a compact disk which is "played" on a computer equipped with a disk reader, much like the audio disk technology so familiar to music lovers. However, the data-base disk stores text, pictures, graphics, and music, rather than just music. This kind of data base uses a technology called CD-ROM (compact disk–read only memory). Or the electronic file may be available in an audiotext format, in which all the searcher requires is a telephone and the correct number to dial up the information, which is then delivered by a computerized voice. Many people with push-button telephones have learned how to use audiotext services in their communities to learn about the latest sports scores, stock quotes, sales at the local clothing retailer, bus schedules, entertainers' weekend performances, and a wide variety of other community information.

Another form of data base is communicator-produced. Information gathered from many traditional sources, such as public records, interviews, background articles, and research documents may be entered into the media organization's mainframe computer or into a desktop or laptop computer. The information is then searchable in a variety of ways unimagined before the advent of the data-base management software and hardware that makes this possible. Or, the data base may consist of information stored on very extensive magnetic tapes (usually produced by government agencies), which are purchased by the media organization, loaded into the in-house computers and searched and manipulated in a variety of ways the information producers would not have allowed or been able to do in a reasonable amount of time.

The on-line services usually are updated very frequently, in some cases as often as several times a day. Because they are so current, these kinds of data bases are therefore very useful to communicators. Audiotext information systems usually are updated frequently as well, depending on the type of service and the time-sensitivity of the information. The data bases in CD-ROM format usually are updated less frequently, perhaps four times a year. The subscriber receives an updated compact disk with the latest information every three months and returns the old disk to the producer as part of the yearly subscription fee. Communicators may decide to use an on-line service for a search that deals with a very recent event, person, or topic, while a CD-ROM service may be fine for background research or for a topic that has been covered extensively. The data bases that communicators create themselves are updated as frequently as the communicators wish, simply by adding more information as it becomes available.

Electronic data bases contain a huge variety of information, from the complete texts of articles as they appeared in the large daily newspapers, chemical equations, pictures and graphic renderings, demographic information about who lives in a particular neighborhood and how much money people in that area earn, airline schedules, and electronic banking information, to administrative regulations, court opinions, and driver's license registration records.

Data bases may be available to communicators through a media-organization library or through the local public or academic library, or communicators may have their own subscriptions to some of the public services such as *CompuServe* or *Prodigy.* Some data bases are available only through the producer of the electronic files, so the library or individual communicator needs a contract with that producer or service, or needs to purchase the magnetic tapes outright. Other data bases are available through a vendor such as *DIALOG*, which makes accessible more than 400 different data bases. *DIALOG*'s data bases are produced by a wide variety of individual companies and institutions that provide their electronic files to the vendor and receive royalty payments in return. In many instances, the communicator will have access to many types of services and hundreds of data bases.

Types of Data Bases

As we have said, several types of content are stored in electronic data bases. The most complete data bases are the full-text variety. In this type of electronic file, the computer stores the complete text of every article, document, report, biographical entry, directory listing, or other item included. The types of materials vary as much as the individual communicator's uses of the information once it is retrieved. For instance, full-text data bases may include the complete text of:

- scholarly or technical journals
- popular magazines, newsletters
- newspapers
- newswire services
- broadcast-news transcripts
- reference books such as encyclopedias or biographical sources
- directories
- government documents
- public records
- corporate financial statements
- statutes and court decisions.

The data base allows the communicator to locate and then print in full the item as it appeared in the original publication or agency file. This eliminates the need to track down and make a copy of the item in the library or originating agency. Full-text data bases are more expensive to use than some other types of services, but they save the communicator much time.

Another type of data base is the bibliographic file. It yields citations to materials such as magazine and newspaper articles, government reports, scholarly journals, documents, conference proceedings, and so forth. The citation includes the title of the item and the source publication, the date and the page numbers, the author's name, and the document or volume and issue numbers where appropriate. In some bibliographic data bases, a brief abstract of each item also is included. The abstract is short and basically outlines the major contents or points of the article or report. The communicator can compile an extensive list of citations to items by using a bibliographic data base. An additional step is involved, however, because the items must then be located in library collections or agency files, or the information must be faxed from those locations. This is why bibliographic data bases are included in the two-step tools section of the search-strategy model (Figure 1.2). Sometimes local libraries do not subscribe to the publications identified by the data-base search, and the communicator must have information faxed from other collections outside the immediate community. Nonetheless, bibliographic data bases are very useful in identifying materials that might not be uncovered in a search by hand. Even when time does not allow for retrieval of the entire item, a bibliographic data-base search may reveal the name of a new source to interview, for example. Based on the information in a citation and abstract, the communicator may know that the author is someone who should be interviewed.

A third type of data base is the numerical or statistical data base. These files consist of number-based information, such as:

- census data
- demographic data
- marketing and consumer data
- information about publication circulation size
- advertisement placement costs
- audience characteristics for magazines, newspapers, and broadcast stations.

These data bases are particularly important for marketing, advertising, or public-relations professionals, who must quickly gather information about audiences and the media that most effectively reach them. For instance, the information gathered by MediaMark Research Inc. (mentioned in Chapter 5) is available in on-line format. The communicator could locate, electronically, information about how many people in the 18–34-year-old age group are heavy users of shampoo, which magazines they read, their incomes, education levels, and relationship status and determine the best method for advertising a new shampoo brand to those most likely to be interested in trying the new product.

A fourth type of data base is the image data base, which allows for electronic storage and retrieval of visual information. The dramatic increase in the memory storage capability of most desktop computers has allowed this new type of data base to emerge as a realistic and useful addition to text and numeric systems. The materials stored in image data bases may be drawings, photographs, maps, artwork, or even reproductions of a printed page. Some image data bases are stored in CD-ROM format, so the communicator can search for the required image and have it printed or displayed, all from one location. If the communicator is searching an image data base from a remote location, she or he can request that a copy of the image be transmitted over phone lines to a receiving computer, through a satellite link (meaning no phone lines are needed), or through the regular mail system when time is not a factor. For instance, geographic information systems used by marketers and advertisers might include information such as zip codes, census data, locations of individual households, consumer income data, store locations, and a variety of other materials, all represented in map format. Instead of reading tables and charts of raw numbers, the information searcher can see characteristics of a particular neighborhood displayed in a picture. Meteorological data and weather maps can be located, received, and transmitted through the use of image data bases. The Census Bureau released the 1990 census data in conjunction with a mapping system called TIGER (Topographically Integrated Geographic Encoding and Referencing system), which provides a computer street map of the entire United States.

Sources of Data Bases

Electronic data bases are produced by many of the information-producers discussed in earlier chapters. Governments, regulatory agencies, the courts, educational and research institutions, corporations and businesses, public-affairs organizations, and professional and trade associations collect and store information, much of it in electronic form. These institutions may then supply their electronic files to the distributors that offer data-base subscriptions to libraries, businesses, and the public at large, or the institutions may offer the data bases for sale themselves.

For instance, many state governments allow access to public records via on-line data-base systems. The state of Florida has been a leader in the transfer of public records to electronic format. Communicators can search through Dade County civil court records, bankruptcy court records, occupational licensing records, property ownership and assessments, real estate records, automobile registrations, and state Department of Motor Vehicles records through electronic data bases. When the Dade County commissioners tried to change their yearly salaries from $6,000 to $51,000, city desk reporters for the *Miami Herald* did a comprehensive analysis of commissioners' finances using these files. The information was used to profile the life styles of these commissioners. The records helped show that in order to afford the kinds of life styles they were leading, the commissioners had to have substantial outside sources of income aside from their commissioners salaries, undercutting their arguments about needing a raise.

Educational and research institutions provide information for data bases that track government and private grant activity, and scholarly associations supply information to data base producers regarding administrators and researchers interested in serving as interviewees and expert witnesses. In addition, educational institutions are linked throughout the world by specialized services such as *Internet*. *Internet* allows researchers to exchange electronic mail, to share publications and notes, to search each other's computer library catalogs, and to otherwise interact electronically. Many *Internet* data bases are available free or for small search fees.

Many data bases are created from the production of printed publications. The electronic versions of the *New York Times*, the *Wall Street Journal*, the *Washington Post*, and hundreds of other newspapers, newsletters, and magazines, along with reference works and directories, are produced as by-products of the publication of the printed version. Similarly, the Bureau of the Census continues to publish the printed version of the census reports, even though the census data are analyzed and compiled by computer and are available in an electronic version. Electronic versions of the printed materials can be searched in different ways and can allow for more flexible kinds of information gathering than the printed versions. For instance, if a communicator wanted to find classmates of George Bush who graduated from Yale the same year he did, the electronic version of the *Who's Who* could be searched to produce that information. The printed version of *Who's Who* is organized alphabetically by name, and each entry would have to be scanned if the search were done by hand. The electronic version could be searched for each occurrence of the appropriate year and the educational institution's name, locating the president's classmates listed in *Who's Who*.

A data-base producer may create an electronic file that is entirely new, one that does not correspond to a printed version. For instance, a CD-ROM version of the telephone Yellow Pages is available, even though there is no comprehensive printed version of such a massive file. The data base consists of 9.2 million listings from 4,800 United States phone books. A searcher would have to look through all those directories individually to approximate the kind of information file that is represented by the data base.

Because there are so many types and sources of electronic data bases, the communicator may have to refer to a guide or directory in order to learn what might be available for a particular search topic. Several good directories include *Computer-Readable Databases*, the *Federal Database Finder*, the *Directory of Online Databases*, or the *Information Industry Directory*. These directories list as many as 5,600 data bases available from hundreds of producers or vendors, including government sources, along with telephone numbers, addresses, price, and subscription information. Several of these directories also may be searched through an on-line service.

While there is constant movement in this fast-paced technological area, several well-established vendors have emerged as major commercial providers of data bases to subscribers around the world:

- Mead Data Central has developed its full-text services into very extensive, and expensive, systems for communicators and legal professionals, among others. *NEXIS* provides hundreds of full-text news, business, and financial data bases, and *LEXIS* is ideal for locating full-text legal information from United States and state (and some international) sources. *MEDIS* is a collection of medical journals, drug information, and the Medline library.

- *WESTLAW* is a standard data-base service in the legal field. Full texts of federal and state cases and opinions, the *United States Code*, federal regulations, case law from all federal and state appellate courts, and 200 legal periodicals are available on-line.

- *DIALOG* (a subsidiary of the Knight-Ridder newspaper and publishing company) offers more than 400 separate data bases; full-text, bibliographic, numeric, and image files are available, each with its own per-minute fees. *DIALOG* is also a major producer of data bases in CD-ROM format.

- *BRS* is similar to *DIALOG*, offering more than 150 data bases in full-text or citation format. The service is particularly strong in medical, scientific, technical, and business information and is very popular for academic uses.

- *Vu/Text* (also a Knight-Ridder subsidiary) is primarily a full-text news data-base service bureau. Since 1992, the contents of newspapers with Vu/Text contracts have been available through DIALOG.

- *DataTimes* is another full-text news data-base vendor, with an arrangement with another major electronic information-provider, Dow Jones, for combined services. Like *Vu/Text*, *DataTimes* offers full-text access to many regional newspapers.

- *Dow Jones News/Retrieval* is a business, financial, and news information service; since its agreement with *DataTimes*, the two services offer more than 800 different data bases to subscribers.

- *Reuter:file* is a full-text and abstract service offering more than 2,000 international newspapers, business reviews, trade journals, and Reuters newswires. Also included are profiles of 200 countries with analysis of the political, economic, and social cultures, and corporate intelligence files for companies in 33 countries.

- *GEnie* is a product of General Electronic Information Services that provides a flat-rate electronic mail, bulletin board, and computer conferencing system, along with a gateway (an electronic connection between different systems) to *Dow Jones News/Retrieval* data bases.

- *CompuServe* allows for full-text access to many data bases and gateway services to hundreds of others. Electronic mail, bulletin boards, free software exchanges, and moderate pricing make this a popular service for consumers.

- *Prodigy* is the data-base service of Sears and IBM. Unlike many other services, many of the "screens" of information in *Prodigy* include advertising messages along the bottom or in a corner. Like many of the other consumer-oriented services, it offers electronic mail, bulletin boards, access to news, and information in full text and is priced on a flat-rate basis.

Costs of Data Bases

The costs of data-base searching vary depending on the type of service used and the extensiveness of the search. Some on-line services, those searched through a computer–telephone link, incur several charges. The user pays for the amount of time connected to the data base through the telephone link. This is usually not as expensive as a long-distance phone charge, but it is one element of the search cost. The user dials a local telephone number, the signal is switched through an uplink to a telecommunications satellite, and the signal is downlinked to the source data base firm's receiving telecommunications hardware. The connect time is charged on a per-minute basis. The on-line data-base user also pays a per-minute royalty fee for each file searched. This might cost anywhere from $35 to well over $200 per hour, depending on the type of data base, the time of day, and whether the user is searching through a vendor or directly with the data base producer. The last element of the on-line search cost is the per-item charge for each item printed or typed. This may cost from ten cents to as much as $15 per item typed or printed. A typical on-line search through several different files, using a variety of search terms and yielding 15 or 20 printed items may cost $35 to $50, depending on the type of data bases searched.

Some of the consumer-oriented on-line services have devised a simpler search-fee structure, whereby the subscriber pays a flat monthly rate and has unlimited access to the system, including all the data bases, the electronic mail and bulletin board services, and home shopping, banking, and games. These services are usually less valuable for communicators' background research, but they might serve as a method for a communicator in a remote location to gather information and remain in touch with the home organization through a laptop computer and telephone link.

A CD-ROM data base is available through a yearly subscription, sometimes costing thousands of dollars per year. However, once the disks are received and loaded into the in-house computers or stand-alone PCs, the information can be searched as many times as needed with no charge. The producer of the CD-ROM files may update the disks several times a year, and each update is included in the price of the subscription.

Data bases purchased as magnetic tapes for use by a media organization are also quite expensive, usually at least several hundred dollars for the complete file. These files are most likely purchased from the government agency that creates the data base, such as the state department of motor vehicles, or the federal Veterans Administration. There is also the cost of the time and effort of the in-house specialists who must know how to load the tapes into the media organization's computers and translate the files as needed so they can be searched and used by the communicators.

The cost of data bases created by communicators themselves are hard to measure. The software needed to turn a personal computer into a data-base management system is fairly inexpensive; a few hundred dollars will purchase a data-base management software package, which can be used over and over for each new data base created. The cost of the communicators' time and effort to gather the information and load it into the data base is the real element to be considered with this kind of data-base use.

Using Data Bases

As with many other specialized information sources, data bases have a structure and logic of their own. The technical details of information storage and retrieval may differ slightly from one data base to another, but the basic concepts are the same. The data-base user must understand how to decode what is stored in the electronic files in order to successfully retrieve anything of value.

Text data-base systems use a method of language-matching in order to store and retrieve the information in the files. The data-base user provides the terms or concepts, which the computer then tries to locate among the thousands of bits of information in the electronic memory. Each item in the data base consists of words—either the entire text of the items stored or a brief citation and abstract. Items in the data bases may also be "tagged" with descriptors or key words that are provided by the indexers working for producers of the data base or by the vendor's indexers. These are terms the indexers think are likely to best describe the contents of the particular item in the data base. Data-base producers may publish thesauri, or guides, that list all the descriptors or key words that the indexers may choose from when assigning these tags to items in the data base. The data-base searcher has a clue to how information in the data base may be located by referring to the thesaurus of descriptors before starting the search.

The searcher usually has a choice of how to search through the items in the data base. The items, or records, in the data base may be searched by having the computer look at every word in the record, whether it is a bibliographic citation or a complete article. Or, the searcher may use a name and address as the search terms. Or, the searcher can instruct the computer to look through just the descriptors and key words in a record, just the title or author part of a record, or any other combination of search logic.

The computer operates on a system of matching. Every time the computer recognizes one of the requested search terms in the record, that item is identified as appropriate to the search. Search terms also may be combined in a variety of ways, using a system called *Boolean logic*. Boolean logic allows for three main methods of combining terms, using the logical operators "and," "or," or "not" (see Figure 6.1). For instance, the communicator may wish to combine the search terms *acid rain* and *legislation* in order to locate items about recent legislative activities to control that pollutant. After choosing an appropriate data base for the search, the searcher could refer to the thesaurus that might correspond to the chosen data base to see whether the terms *acid rain* and *legislation* are used as key words or descriptors for items about that topic. The searcher could then ask the computer to locate any items in the file that are assigned those descriptors, using the search statement "acid rain and legislation." Or, the searcher could decide to have the computer search for *any* occurrence of the chosen terms in the file and have all of them identified. If the communicator wanted to find articles or documents about both acid rain and coal emissions, the search statement could read "acid rain or coal emissions and legislation." If the communicator wanted articles that did *not* include the legislative activities of Canada regarding acid rain, the search statement could read "acid rain and legislation not Canada." By combining search terms in a variety of ways using Boolean logic, the communicator might locate a completely different set of items with each search statement.

The computer will match the terms chosen and tell the searcher how many items have been located after each search statement is entered. The number of "hits" will depend on the type of data base searched, the terms chosen, and the scope of the request. In the example of the acid rain search, a search in a full-text news and business file such as *NEXIS* might turn up 300 items, far too many for the communicator to economically retrieve and efficiently use. In this case, the searcher would need to revise the search statement to narrow the search, perhaps by including a request for items from the current year only, or items about legislation that has actually been passed rather than just proposed. Or, the searcher might decide to choose a different data base altogether, perhaps one devoted just to tracking legislative activities such as *Legi-Slate*.

If the searcher wants to examine the items identified by the computer

FIGURE 6.1 Boolean Logical Operators

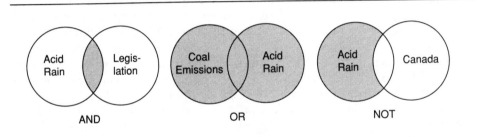

search, there are several options. The items may be viewed on the computer screen in abstract form or in full-text form in a full-text data base. Those items that seem most useful may be printed out on the printer attached to the computer, downloaded, and captured electronically for printing later, or the searcher can request that the producer of the data base print out the items and send them in the mail. In many instances, the communicator might retrieve the necessary information simply by viewing the information on the screen (an interviewee's name, an advertising competitor's choice of a spokesperson) without requiring a hard copy of the item from the data base at all.

The mechanics of a data-base search work the same in virtually all data bases, even though the particulars, such as punctuation and special search characters, differ from one data base to another. What is most important for the communicator to understand is how to best use the power of the computer for information gathering. This recalls the idea, mentioned in Chapters 1 and 2, of conceptualizing the search problem and conducting question analysis. Since the computer is stupid, it cannot make up for what is left out of or misstated in the search statement. The searcher must have a solid understanding of the topic and how materials relevant to the topic are likely to be organized in order to put the computer to work. If the search request is not conceptualized correctly, a great deal of money and time will be spent in vain. Misspelled proper names, incorrect terminology, misspecified numerical or demographic requests all can result in expensive and useless materials. Search terms that are too broad may result in far more items than can be reasonably scanned and evaluated by the communicator on a deadline.

For instance, new reporters at a large midwestern daily newspaper are advised not to use the word *duck* in any search of the paper's own electronic backfiles. The newspaper had run a Pulitzer Prize-nominated series on declining waterfowl populations on the North American continent. An inexperienced searcher using the search term *duck* would locate more than 1,330 stories in the file.

Similarly, a misconceptualized search can cause problems. An inexperienced student searcher wanted to find information about public-awareness campaigns—how they work, what makes for successful campaigns, and who may have produced public-awareness campaigns for various clients. The student knew that many developing countries had been using public-awareness campaigns to promote family planning practices. Instead of conceptualizing the search topic along the lines of public-awareness campaigns or promotional campaigns, the student made the crucial mistake of conceptualizing the search topic as a family planning search. The student chose population research data bases instead of data bases of advertising and marketing literature in which to conduct the search. He used phrases like *family planning* and *population control* instead of phrases like *public-awareness campaigns* and *promotional campaigns*. Thinking that it would be necessary to look for specific examples rather than the broad category of public-awareness campaigns, and forgetting that the computer could locate any occurrence of public-awareness terms in the data base, the student missed an entire body of literature about the topic under consideration.

The searcher must also anticipate every term or phrase that could have been used by the authors of the articles for which the user is searching or by the indexers who tagged the items in the data base. An author may decide to use a common phrase in the title of an article—or may not. An indexer may understand what an article is about and assign key words and descriptors appropriately—or may not. Because of the element of human error or vagary, the searcher must try to be more clever than the system, using every variant of a term (*doctor, physician, heart specialist, cardiologist,* rather than just *doctor,* for instance) in order to be sure of complete retrieval of all relevant items in a data base. This kind of sweeping comprehensiveness does have its drawbacks. "False drops," or retrieved items that fit the logic of the search but are not on the search topic, are more prevalent with a very comprehensive search strategy. But comprehensiveness also ensures that valuable materials will not be missed.

The logic of searching numerical and image data bases has its own demands. If the data base corresponds to printed versions of the audience, demographic, and media information, the data-base searcher must understand how to manipulate the information correctly. If what is needed is a map of housing, income, occupation, and demographic characteristics of a neighborhood within a one-mile radius of the new branch of a bank, the computer must be fed the correct instructions and requirements in order to produce the appropriate materials. Matching specific terms or key words is less crucial in these cases than is accurately specifying to the computer the exact nature of the statistical, demographic, or visual information needed. As with all the other information sources discussed in earlier chapters, data bases will yield information only if the searcher knows how best to tap into what is available.

Some help might be available from the use of gateway systems, which aid the searcher in choosing and searching electronic files. The searcher might have a subscription to one gateway vendor, which allows a user to tap into hundreds of files. The difference is that the user does not have to choose which specific files to search and does not have to know the precise search-statement characteristics to conduct the search. The computer system asks the searcher to describe, in natural language, the topic of the search. The computer might even provide a menu of search terms to help the searcher narrow the topic. The gateway vendor's software then translates those search terms into the appropriate search statement, chooses the files in which there will be the most chance of finding information on that topic, and conducts the search, invisible to the searcher. The advantage of using a system like this is that the searcher need not be an expert in all the intricacies of search commands and search-statement construction in many different data bases. The gateway service does it all for the searcher. The disadvantage of such a system is that the computer may not select the best data bases and may not translate the search request in the most precise or efficient way, resulting in a search that might not reflect the best information available. Also, for communicators' purposes, it is very important to know where information has come from, and a gateway-system search might not be easily decoded for the source and reliability of information.

Working with Data-Base Specialists

In many media organizations, there will be a person, or a group of people, who are specialists in searching electronic data bases. Or, the communicator might use the services of the specialists in a local public or academic library to conduct searches. There is a wide disparity in the resources available to communicators in different industries and among various media outlets within an industry. Some news organizations, for instance, have large budgets for data-base searching and the news librarians conduct searches whenever reporters and editors request them. Other news organizations have yet to enter the electronic-data-base world. Some advertising firms or advertising departments have been using electronic data bases for years; others are still doing research work by hand.

The communicator's main goal is to conduct an efficient and comprehensive search in the best information repositories available. That might include using electronic data bases because so much information is available so quickly. This does not mean that communicators have to conduct the searches themselves, however. It is more important to know that such systems are available and that a community library may have access even if the media organization does not. Requesting the assistance of those most familiar with the intricacies of searching these systems is the first step for many communicators who do not have the time for or interest in learning how to conduct such searches themselves. Uses of data-base searching in media organizations will be discussed later in this ,chapter.

Advantages and Disadvantages of the Data-Base Search

Data-base searching is really just another method of information gathering. Since data-base sources of information are, in many cases, electronic versions of the familiar tools and sources that are found on any good library shelf, data-base sources are included in the search-strategy model with library sources. In addition, more and more institutional sources of information are available in electronic-data-base format. The communicator then can think about doing a data-base search while using more traditional sources. Indeed, in order to be able to conceptualize the problem, it is usually wise for the communicator to conduct not only simultaneous but also preliminary information searches in the informal, institutional, or printed library sources before turning to the data-base search—simply to become familiar with the terms and concepts that help identify the structure of information for the topic.

That strategy is not always possible, however. Although there are printed counterparts for many electronic information sources, the trend is toward the creation of sources that exist only in electronic form. In particular, some public records and government information systems are being converted entirely to electronic data bases, with few paper records to back up the data base. This means that the communicator must know how to balance a search in printed information sources with a search in electronic sources for the right mixture of background.

Another factor that affects when the data-base search is conducted is cost. In many cases, the communicator is trading time for money or vice versa. Although on-line searches may take only a few minutes, the costs still are substantial. A CD-ROM data-base subscription costs a formidable sum for many media organizations or libraries. The costs of purchasing magnetic tapes or creating data bases in-house may be prohibitive for some organizations.

There are a few guidelines for deciding when data-base information is an appropriate choice for the communicator:

- Use a data-base search when the topic or event is so recent that information about it may not have made its way into the printed indexes and library sources yet. Many electronic files are updated daily, so the information is the most current available.

- Use a data-base search when the topic is one that is not well indexed in the printed indexes and library sources. For instance, the search might be on a topic that is fairly well known but for which the printed indexes and sources are clumsy. A search on a subject such as *comparable worth* (the concept of equal pay for comparable work) requires a very round-about search in printed sources but a data-base search could locate every item in which that precise phrase occurred.

- Use a data-base search if the topic is interdisciplinary. For instance, the communicator may have to find information about the psychological and social motivations for juvenile drug addiction. This would require a hand search in several disciplinary indexes (psychology, sociology, medicine, and education literature), using different search concepts (drug addiction, social behavior, motivation research, adolescent or juvenile behavior). A data-base search in several electronic files would automatically link those search concepts and save time.

- Use a data-base search when speed is of the essence and the information must be located as quickly as possible. Remember, however, that it is occasionally faster, cheaper, and easier to use a printed reference book to locate a fact or figure.

- Use a data-base search when the power of the computer to combine items in a unique and helpful way means you can locate, or even create, information that would not be available through a search by hand. For instance, a reporting team might decide that it is worth the effort to gather information from printed public records and load the information into a data-base management system in a desktop computer because it will allow the team to see patterns, trends, and connections that would never be apparent if the individual paper records were searched in isolation.

Question whether a data-base search is appropriate when the information sought is easily available through other methods, is free using another method, or if the topic is so broad that a data-base search would locate far too many items to be usefully and economically retrieved and scanned. The process of narrowing the topic during the question-analysis stage of the search strategy is a crucial one when it comes to deciding whether to conduct an electronic search.

There are several caveats about information gathered from data bases. The lure of electronic information is difficult to resist, but the communicator must approach these information sources with the same skepticism as any other source. Information that finds its way into electronic data bases must be scanned for accuracy, completeness, bias, and recency. The same verification procedures must be used for electronically gathered and analyzed information as for information gathered from more traditional sources. It is very difficult to know how or why certain information gets into a data base. The gatekeeping activities employed by the data-base producers vary from one data base to another. Like any other source of information, data bases and data-base producers have reputations for the quality of their products. Just because something is stored or retrieved electronically does not mean it is accurate or reliable. In many instances, the data-base information is culled from such questionable sources as change-of-address cards filed with the post office, order forms used by catalog retailers, application forms for credit cards, or license renewal forms scribbled by hurried people and transferred to electronic files by overworked and underpaid computer operators. These kinds of files are extremely vulnerable to accuracy and reliability problems.

Another crucial element to remember when using data bases is that unless the file is full text, the communicator is going to have to set aside time to track down every relevant document identified by the data base. This may mean a trip to the local library, a request to have material faxed from a remote location, or even a request through interlibrary loan for something that might take several weeks to arrive.

Electronic data bases have to be put through the same tests of appropriateness as paper documents. If an article appeared in a scholarly publication, it has a different set of characteristics, and potential problems than an article that appeared in a general news magazine. Those characteristics must be understood, and their implications for the usefulness of the information must be weighed.

A search in an electronic file is only as good as the search strategy that was used. If the data-base user does a poor job of supplying the computer with search terms, or if the search problem is not clearly understood, the information gathered from the data base will not be complete, accurate, or appropriate. Entire categories of material can be missed altogether if a poor search strategy is employed. The communicator contemplating data-base searching should either have adequate training or rely on an expert searcher in the media organization or community library.

An additional concern arises when the communicator is searching public records electronically or is compiling a new data base using public information. When does one cross the line into invasion of privacy? Some of the public record systems make it so easy for a searcher to compile a comprehensive record about an individual that it is possible to easily slip into the trap of privacy violation. For instance, it is possible in many communities to use electronic searches to learn about an individual's credit record, bank account, driver's registration, driving violations, any dealings with the court system (civil or criminal), property ownership and taxation, and a myriad of other details of someone's daily activities. This has always been the case, of course, through the use of the paper version of these records. Now, however, the information is virtually instantaneously available to anyone with a desktop computer, modem, and the ingenuity to know where to look. Where once a marketing firm or a team of reporters would have deemed the information too costly and time-consuming to bother with, it is now routinely searched. This concern will be discussed in more detail in Chapter 10.

Finally, there is a danger that with the easy availability of electronic information, the communicator will tend to slight or skip altogether the more traditional and in many cases more important methods of information retrieval. It is still important for the reporter to locate and interview local sources about a particular topic for a story, rather than rely on the national sources located through a data-base search. It is still crucial for advertising professionals to visit the local franchises of the restaurant for which they will be producing ads, rather than rely on the trade journal descriptions located in the advertising data bases. It is still necessary for the public-relations professional to attend the news conference and monitor how the company president's announcement is received, rather than simply conduct a data-base search to see how many papers picked up the story. None of the other steps in the search strategy is replaced by electronic-data-base searching. Communicators in the data-base age must use the same skills of thoroughness, imagination, inquisitiveness, and dogged pursuit of the best information that have served them in the past.

USING DATA BASES IN MEDIA ORGANIZATIONS

Mass communication professionals and their employers have adopted the use of data bases to varying degrees. Some trends appear to be emerging in the application of these systems to the everyday work of communicators in organizations in which data bases are available. We will discuss each area of mass communication work.

News Organization Uses of Data Bases

As of the spring of 1990, 90 percent of the 105 largest newspapers in the United States (those with daily circulations exceeding 100,000) had access to commercial data-base subscriptions. In addition, 67 percent of these newspapers had their own news backfiles stored in an electronic library system that replaced the clipping files that used to fill up filing drawers and crowd the news library.[1] The trend was toward many more medium- and small-circulation papers adding data-base subscriptions and electronic libraries to their news organizations.

It is important to distinguish the commercial data-base subscriptions from the electronic library systems that are available in news rooms. In many newspapers, the entire content of the newspaper is written, edited, laid out, and sent to the printing equipment electronically. Each issue of the paper is also stored electronically, in the newspaper's own mainframe computers or through a service bureau arrangement with one of the large electronic news library vendors such as *Vu/Text* or *DataTimes*. This means that all news workers have access to the newspaper's own backfiles through their terminals. The back issues can be searched electronically using key words and search phrases. Each communicator receives training in the use of the electronic library as part of the orientation to the new job. The reporter or editor's computer screen can be "split" so that the story being worked on is on one side and the electronic library backfiles are coming across on the other. Printers attached to each terminal or scattered around the newsroom can be used to print hard copy of stories found through the electronic search of the backfiles. News workers' searches of the electronic news library system are routine, and the costs are absorbed as part of the operation of a modern news organization. In addition, as the electronic news files age, some news organizations store the oldest material in CD-ROM format rather than having so many years' worth of backfiles in on-line storage. Communicators looking for the most recent backfiles use the on-line system and those requiring archival material go to the CD-ROM reader/printer, which may be in the news room or in the news library.

These same electronic library files may be used to generate income for the newspaper. The newspaper managers may decide to sell the electronic backfiles through the news organization, or they may decide to make an arrangement with one of the large data-base vendors. If the electronic library is installed and managed by one of the large service bureau companies such as *Vu/Text* or *DataTimes*, that company may serve as the vendor of the electronic files. Or, a newspaper may have a vending agreement with several large data-base companies, so that the news content is available through three or four different services. Subscribers around the world may have access to the news backfiles through their subscriptions to the data-base services carrying the newspapers' backfiles.

Commercial data-base services may include many of the news files generated by the storage of news backfiles every day. However, commercial data-base services may include a wide variety of additional information, including information from institutional sources such as the federal government, corporations, or public agencies; from other kinds of publications such as popular, scholarly, and trade journals; from demographic, marketing, and media analysis information sources; and from hundreds of other sources. Unlike access to the electronic news library files, the news staff's access to commercial data bases generally is highly controlled, usually by the library staff. One major reason for this control is cost. In 1990, the average monthly cost of searching commercial data bases at the 105 largest newspapers in the United States was $1,000, with a range from $50 to more than $38,000.[2] Individual reporters, editors, graphic artists, and others in the newsroom usually are not allowed to search commercial data bases indiscriminately, because they do not have the skills and the news organization does not have the budget to allow for unlimited access.

Many news professionals have their own subscriptions to some of the consumer-oriented data-base services as well. For instance, the *CompuServe* data base added a Gulf Crisis News Clip service during the Persian Gulf War. Any subscriber could use the computer–telephone link to receive selected information from the Associated Press, United Press International, and the *Washington Post* newswires, updated every 15 to 20 minutes. Through another part of the *CompuServe* data base, the subscriber could retrieve satellite pictures of the Middle East and accompanying weather forecasts and maps of the region. Several of the bulletin board and electronic mail subsystems also were devoted to sending and receiving messages from the Middle East. Any journalist with a subscription to *CompuServe* could have instant access to the most current information and be able to send messages to or from almost any location.

Data-base use by broadcast journalists is one method of obtaining background information that might not be available from a more traditional news library. Broadcast outlets usually do not have a well-stocked library with easily accessible background information. Both radio and television reporters and producers use commercial data bases as a source of background information, in preparation for interviews with sources, as a source of ideas for stories, and to keep track of what other media outlets in the community are writing about. Unlike their print counterparts, who usually have a news librarian or specialist search for them, broadcast journalists across a wide variety of job functions may have access to data bases. In one study, a quarter of the 66 television stations with data-base subscriptions allowed anyone at the stations who desired it to have access to a data base.[3] News directors, editors, producers, reporters, and researchers might all be able to conduct data-base searches, usually for all types of stories.

Magazine staffers also have access to commercial data bases for their work, again through the library or information center. Fact checking is a very important aspect of magazine work, and some publications have institutionalized fact checking and practice it with a high degree of sophistication. Magazines as varied as the *New Yorker, Reader's Digest, National Geographic, Time,* and *Rolling Stone* have large fact-checking staffs. Virtually every word in a magazine article is potentially subject to a fact check. Studies of fact checkers and their routines have found that reference materials, including data-base sources, are an important resource for many fact checkers. News-oriented data bases are particularly useful since they allow fact checkers to scrutinize dozens of stories with one search. Data bases may also help fact checkers locate interview sources they can contact for verification or clarification of something in a magazine article that requires further information.[4]

Public records stored and searched in computerized form are another major component of data-base use in news organizations. While some states have limited public-record information stored electronically, many have extensive information available for public access. Unlike the commercial data bases, public records might be searched directly by the journalist rather than by the news librarian. Perhaps because the journalist is familiar with using the same files in print format, and also because many of the public records files are available free or for a limited search fee, journalists are more comfortable searching these public records files themselves, without the use of an intermediary. Information from state legislative activities, court proceedings, police and criminal files, corporate financial information, licensing records and a wide variety of additional materials might be available through an on-line data base.

For example, a 1991 spot reporting the Pulitzer Prize went to the *Miami Herald*'s local news staff for its coverage of the Yahweh religious sect. A local real-estate data base and the Dade County property appraiser's tapes helped the reporter and editor track all records and corporate filings for associates, legal counsels, and variations of the names *Yahweh*, *Israel*, and *Temple of Love*. More than 50 properties and corporations were identified, shedding light on the financial activities of the religious group. Reporters at the *Seattle Times* sifted through computerized records on everything from parking tickets to detectives' expense vouchers to show how a police investigation into the deaths of 46 women had been botched.

Another major news use of electronic information is through the purchase of data tapes. Many government files, for instance, can be purchased and loaded into the news organization's mainframe computer, as we have said. In some instances, it may be possible to convert purchased tapes to a format that will run on a personal computer in the news room. In either format, the tapes are then manipulated, searched, sorted, and analyzed by the communicators in ways that would never be practical or allowed if the originating agency had to do the analysis.

Elliot Jaspin, a former newspaper reporter now with the Missouri Institute for Computer-Assisted Reporting, developed a computer conversion program to help journalists analyze purchased data tapes on a PC and also developed a fee-based service that will do data analysis upon request for large files that cannot be transferred to a PC. Jaspin is an advocate of tape purchases for news uses. As a staffer at the *Providence Journal*, he used a state data base of 33,000 state-financed home mortgages to show that the loans benefited wealthy, politically well-connected people such as the governor's daughter, rather than the low- and moderate-income people who were supposed to receive the aid. Other journalists at newspapers around the country have used purchased data tapes to develop stories about hospitals' rates of success in coronary bypass surgery, the apparent effect of curtailed safety inspections of over-the-road truck safety, the prevalence of snub-nosed handguns in street crime, and discrimination on the basis of race by money-lending institutions.[5]

A Washington, D.C., television station and the Missouri Institute for Computer-Assisted Reporting uncovered 3,328 deaths and 52,000 injuries since 1984 associated with medical devices using a $350 tape compiled by the United States Food and Drug Administration (FDA). The FDA has accumulated more than 100,000 reports about medical devices suspected of causing deaths and injuries. In addition to a description of the problem, each computerized record contains the name and address of the manufacturer, the kind of medical device that caused the problem, categorizes each incident as a malfunction, serious injury, or death, and identifies the outcome of any investigation by the FDA. If reporters in New Mexico wanted to find local companies with histories of problems, they could use the data base to identify them. Using the data-base tapes to locate any incident anywhere involving a cardiac pacemaker would also work. Enterprising news professionals could ask and answer a wide variety of questions with the one tape, and hundreds of such tapes are available from federal, state, and local sources.[6]

In yet another form of data-base application, journalists may use their desktop or mainframe computers to create their own data bases. Information generated from searches in printed sources, from interviews, from printed public records, and from the journalists' own observations can be entered into the computer using simple data-base management software such as *AskSam* or *Paradox*. The data base then can be searched, analyzed, and manipulated to create unique information that would not exist in any other form.

For example, two reporters for the Cox Newspapers' Washington bureau created their own data base using records about assault firearms and crime compiled by the United States Bureau of Alcohol, Tobacco & Firearms. The records the reporters wanted to use were filed in a warehouse outside Washington, D.C., in row after row of cardboard boxes. After a long negotiation, the reporters were given permission to enter information from the records into computers using a data-base management software program. The reporters rented six computers and hired workers to help put the information into data-base form. The reporters were able to collate and format the information using the microcomputers, then conducted final tabulations on a mainframe computer. The result was that the reporters were able to determine how often assault weapons were used in crimes, make city-by-city comparisons, determine the preferred gun of drug traffickers and terrorists, and massage the data in several other ways.[7]

The Cox bureau example is an extreme case. In a more conventional application of journalist-created data bases, reporters and editors at *USA Today* have created vast computerized files from interviews, surveys, and the mining of public records. In a series examining crime on nearly 600 college campuses in all 50 states, a special team conducted surveys or interviews with 4,000 students and 700 law enforcement officials and school administrators. The computer data base they created helped them identify a "fear index" by region and helped uncover discrepancies between official reports of crime statistics and what some students reported informally. The senior editor on the project, Robert A. Dubhill, said that it would have taken years to organize the data had it been in boxes and notebooks.[8]

Sometimes news organizations commission research by specialists for the journalists conducting an investigation. Scholars, survey specialists, or experts from the community might be asked to assist the journalist in analyzing data tapes purchased from an agency or might contribute information that is entered into the journalist-created data base. The services of local college or university data-processing departments may be available for use by journalists who need mainframe computer time. Major trade or professional organizations, such as the Missouri Center for Computer-Assisted Reporting or the Investigative Reporters and Editors group might conduct searches or computer analysis of information upon request for members or clients.

For example, the Transactional Records Access Clearinghouse was created to tap into the huge volume of information kept by federal enforcement agencies that is available to the public through the Freedom of Information Act. Two professors at Syracuse University, a former investigative reporter and a quantitative methodologist, make the data base available to news organizations and individuals. Initially, TRAC has focused on data from the Justice Department, the Nuclear Regulatory Commission, and the IRS. One study conducted by the researchers analyzed 5.5 million criminal and civil cases brought in federal courts. Wide variations were found in the level of criminal enforcement from district to district, suggesting that justice was not so evenhanded. Performance of United States attorneys and prosecutors was also analyzed. The study was distributed to 40 news organizations, many of which used the information.[9] Journalists can request information from the data currently available in TRAC's computers.

Communicators also conduct interviews electronically. Many experts and professionals can be contacted through electronic mail or bulletin board systems. A significant number of individuals spend a great deal of time on-line and may be willing to be "interviewed" there. The most effective method of examining the work in progress of some of these individuals might be through their electronic messaging and mail systems. Reaching some people is actually easier through an on-line network than through telephone or personal interviews. Because most electronic mail and bulletin board systems are available 24 hours a day, some interviews (or electronic exchange of messages) can be conducted in the middle of the night or over several days.

For instance, a nonprofit group that investigates fraud, waste and mismanagement and abuse in defense spending and military procurement runs a computer data base and bulletin board. The system is named *SNAFU* and makes military procurement information available to journalists, whistle-blowers, and the public, all for no charge. Documents are searchable by key word, and copies of material can be sent to requesters using an optical character recognition system. An equally interesting feature, however, is the bulletin boards, where users can contact one another, conduct interviews on-line, and leave messages in either an open or confidential communication section of the system.[10]

Computer networks also can help journalists keep in touch with their media organizations. For instance, the NBC computer network runs out of the mainframe computer in the New York headquarters. Most NBC staffers can use PCs or portable computers to access the network from their homes or from on-site locations around the world. The system includes technical and operational reports, rundowns on any problems with the news shows, scripts, bureau plans for operations and daily assignments, program schedules, and stories from the major international news wires. Staffers can send and receive electronic messages. Thousands of wire service stories and scripts can be searched electronically. Hundreds of thousands of videotapes shelved in warehouses are recorded so staff can quickly dispatch them to studios. Video and photo images on compact discs also can be recovered via computer. When Tom Brokaw was anchoring the news from Seoul during the Olympics, everyone on location could communicate instantly with New York as the show came together to make last-minute changes, as when a hurricane in Houston required a program change.[11]

Public Relations Data-Base Use

Researchers in public-relations firms or corporate communications departments may use a variety of data bases to make their messages and activities knowledge-driven rather than assumption-driven. Commercial data bases can be used to gather information from the full range of sources mentioned earlier. Media relations staff might use newspaper data bases to search for press coverage of a company, product, or issue that might be affecting their client or department. Background information or competitive information might be sought for new business development and trend analysis. For instance, a large public-relations firm did an industry analysis using business and industry data bases for a client who wanted to look for new opportunities for investment or purchase. Human resources publications available in data bases help corporate or agency staff explain benefits to employees. Speech writers find tidbits of information to make their clients' speeches timely and interesting using topical or news data bases.

Public-relations professionals also create data bases of information to help the agency or company work smarter. A corporate communications department sometimes serves as the listening post for the company. Someone in the department tracks information using commercial data bases, analyzes that material, summarizes the trends, competitors' activities, legislative activities, and publicity opportunities. The information is then provided to management and employees through on-line bulletin boards, electronic mail, or newsletters.

Sharing information through the use of some of the consumer-oriented data bases is also common. Many public-relations professionals have subscriptions to the consumer-oriented electronic services, and they regularly participate in roundtables and electronic bulletin board conferences with clients, colleagues, and experts in a variety of fields. Because the services operate virtually around the clock, the communicator can "plug in" to activities and decisions at any time.

One of the most important uses of data bases by public-relations professionals is for delivery of news releases. Many news organizations receive public-relations releases electronically, with the information captured by the news room's mainframe computers. Editors might choose a public-relations release, edit it, and send it to the printing presses with no paper version ever changing hands. A number of large companies have their own electronic news-release data-base services. More than 7,000 companies also supply news releases to the *PR Newswire* data base, which then makes the material available to subscribers through a number of major vendors.

Another major use of data bases in public-relations work is to track public opinion and audience information. One of the functions of public-relations work is to affect public opinion. A number of electronic data bases make it possible to locate very current poll information. Using such data bases to track changing attitudes about an issue, trend, or a specific company, the communicator has the opportunity to create messages or to stage events that might anticipate and influence public opinion. Audience and demographic information is also very important, especially for public-relations agency staff who must try to place messages in appropriate media. These communicators can use many of the demographic and audience-information data bases to learn the characteristics of the readers and viewers of the publications and programs that might carry a news release or cover an event.

Advertising Data-Base Use

In advertising, media planners and media buyers were early adopters of data bases for much of their work. The statistical, demographic, and numeric data bases available for advertising planning and buying meant fewer hand-calculations of large sets of numbers. Many of the specialized advertising information sources and syndicated research tools mentioned in Chapter 5 are available in on-line or CD-ROM format. MediaMark Research Inc., Simmons, and many other demographic, audience, and psychographic data producers make their information available to subscribers in electronic form. This means that the communicator can locate information about any combination of advertisement purchases targeted to a specific group of audience members and learn instantly how many people those advertisements will reach, how often the messages need to be repeated, and how effective those ads might be.

An increasing number of commercial data bases are specifically designed to help advertising professionals track industry trends and events. Many of the large data-base vendors mentioned earlier in the chapter offer files that include articles from the advertising trade literature. For instance, if an advertising professional wanted to know if any competitors had signed or tried to sign Madonna as a spokesperson, he or she could use the *PTS Marketing and Advertising Reference Service* data base to locate any information in the trade literature about such a deal. Such data bases can also help the communicator locate information about campaign strategies being used or planned by agencies and advertisers, news and events in the advertising business, new legislative initiatives under consideration that might affect advertisers or clients, and any other industry-related information.

Advertisers also use data bases to track general business and industry trends for clients. If an advertising agency has a soft drink client, the business data bases that include information about the soft drink industry can be scanned regularly for relevant information. Audience and demographic trends related to soft drink consumers would also be of value and could be tracked electronically. For instance, a large advertising agency was trying to win the account of an international hotel chain. The research department of the agency used some of the specialized business and newsletter data bases available through *NEXIS* to locate information about the hotel industry. The information helped the advertising team understand the trends in the hotel industry, how and where hotel companies were expanding and why, and something about how hotel operators saw their own business. These insights allowed the team to create a campaign plan that demonstrated their command of this type of business and the kinds of advertising strategies that would be appropriate. Combined with data-base information about who stayed at hotels and how best to reach them with advertising messages, the information provided a complete picture for the team creating the campaign.

Many advertisers are finding consumer-oriented data-base services a lucrative medium for advertising messages. For instance, the *Prodigy* service includes a small ad on each screen of information that subscribers view. At any point during the on-line session, a subscriber might "open" the ad for more information about whatever product or service is being promoted. Many on-line services also allow for electronic order and purchase of goods and services. Consumers who are equipped with a personal computer, modem, and subscription to such services are a well-heeled target audience for advertisers to try to reach with messages.

As in other communication organizations, advertising professionals also create their own data bases of information for use in-house. Specialized research findings based on surveys, focus groups, or other customized studies can be stored, analyzed, and manipulated using PCs or minicomputers. Many advertising departments and advertising agencies have their own research staffs who regularly conduct specialized research for clients and management. Computer-assisted interviewing equipment and software might be used for a telephone survey of potential target-audience members for a new advertising campaign. The interviewers would conduct the interviews over the telephone while seated in front of a computer work station. Answers to the questions would be entered into the computer and automatically stored as the interview proceeded, and researchers could later analyze the data using the same software. (Interview methods, including computer-assisted interviewing, are discussed in Chapter 7.)

Customized magazine advertising has been created using computerized data bases of subscribers. For instance, *American Baby's* 1.1 million readers can be divided into parents of children in different age groups, with information on a baby's birthday taken from new subscriber cards and stored in computer data bases. Advertisers such as Gerber Foods have run personalized messages geared only to mothers of children in specific age groups. Using selective binding techniques, in which a specific ad is placed in a particular subscriber's issue of the magazine, the company can target parents in just one category, such as those with two- to three-month-olds. A baby-swing manufacturer used the computer data base of subscribers to advertise only to parents with older babies. *Time* magazine merged its computerized subscriber list with L. L. Bean's mail-order list to create a data base of *Time* readers who had been Bean customers or who had requested a catalog. Full-page ads with personalized response-card inserts, including the subscriber's name ink-jetted on the card, were created and sent in a regular issue of the magazine.[12]

Academic Research Uses of Data Bases

Most of the commercial data bases discussed earlier are available to academic researchers (students, faculty, staff) through a number of methods. The academic library may subscribe to a number of on-line vendors and/or may have a variety of CD-ROM data bases available for use. The community public library also might be able to offer electronic search services to users. Sometimes these services are offered on a cost-recovery basis, meaning the academic searcher will have to pay for the costs incurred during the search. Other times, the library will offer electronic searches for free.

The academic researcher can use many of the scholarly data bases to conduct comprehensive literature searches in a subject area or on a particular topic. In many instances, the academic researcher will be doing a search that requires a cross-disciplinary approach. Data-base searches are ideal for this kind of search problem. As mentioned earlier, an electronic search can be structured such that all appropriate disciplinary areas are searched simultaneously, allowing for fast retrieval of material from a wide perspective.

Legal research can be conducted very efficiently using one of the major legal data-base services such as *LEXIS* or *Westlaw*. For instance, a researcher might need information about international trade agreements and other materials dealing with regulation of international investment and trade. A number of the specialized services available in the *Westlaw* data base would help the researcher locate documents such as the texts of actual international trade agreements, rules governing international commercial transactions, international property rights laws, and similar information. Data bases such as *Westlaw* and *LEXIS* also include federal, state, and some international statutes, court documents, and legislative services, allowing the legal researcher to locate all environmental law decisions from the state of Michigan, for instance.

LINKS TO THE SEARCH STRATEGY

In this step of the search strategy, one that did not exist just a few years ago, the communicator takes advantage of new electronic technologies to identify, retrieve, or create information appropriate for the topic. Communicators use material from bibliographic and full-text data bases, statistical and numeric files, image data bases, and a variety of electronic bulletin boards, message systems, and informal electronic networks.

Communicators have become both creators and users of data bases, and they are becoming more sophisticated in their applications of electronic technologies to the search-strategy process as time proceeds. A crucial element for communicators to recognize is that the data base is simply another type of information tool, one that requires application of the same standards of information evaluation and scrutiny as any other source. Data bases can reduce the time and effort spent on routine information gathering and can allow the communicator to find, or actually create from scratch, previously unavailable or inaccessible information.

Unless communicators are well trained in data-base searching and are well versed in the variety of types of data bases that might be useful for a particular search, it is appropriate to seek assistance from an expert searcher within the media organization. For instance, two reporters from the Gannett News Service won a 1991 Pulitzer Prize for their reporting on undetected child-abuse deaths. The researcher working on the story with the reporters did background searches of general information such as Sudden Infant Death Syndrome and specific instances of unexplained infant deaths. She used online data bases from services such as *DIALOG* and *NEXIS* and used special collections at George Washington University and the National Library of Medicine. She created a data base of death certificates from the state agencies and local coroners' offices with infant death records. Her expertise in using computer and traditional information systems allowed the reporters to focus on spotting trends and writing the stories.[13]

As data bases become more familiar to communicators trying to meet the demands of deadlines and requirements for recent and accurate information, there will likely be an increase in their wide availability within media organizations. Even in those media organizations without in-house subscriptions to data bases, communicators may find community libraries or personal subscriptions can provide access to the wide range of services and systems that are becoming so much a part of media professionals' information routines.

Chapter 7 examines the contributions interviews make to the search strategy. Mass communication interviews described in Chapter 7 include individual, group, investigative, and news conference methods.

NOTES

1. Jean Ward and Kathleen A. Hansen, "Newspapers and Electronic Technologies," *Editor & Publisher,* 3 November 1990, 34–37.
2. Ward and Hansen, "Newspapers and Electronic Technologies."
3. Thomas L. Jacobson, "Use of Commercial Data Bases for Television News Reporting," *Journal of Broadcasting and Electronic Media* 33 (Spring 1989): 203–208.
4. Susan P. Shapiro, "Caution! This Paper Has Not Been Fact Checked!," New York: *Gannett Center Working Paper,* undated.
5. Richard P. Kleeman, "Good Hunting in Databases," *The Quill,* September 1989, 16.
6. Chris Szechenyi and Elliot Jaspin, "Casualties of medical technology," *The IRE Journal,* March–April 1991, 4–6.
7. Max Jennings, "PCs Help Reporters Track Good Stories through Mazes of Bureaucratic Statistics," *ASNE Bulletin,* September 1989, 13–17.
8. Jerome Aumente, "Bauds, Bytes and Brokaw: New PCs Revolutionize the Newsroom," *Washington Journalism Review,* April 1989, 39–42.
9. Tracey L. Miller, "Inside TRAC," *Columbia Journalism Review,* March–April 1990, 12–13.
10. Andy Steinbach, "Let Your Fingers Walk through the Pentagon," *IRE Journal,* Spring 1990, 11.
11. Aumente, "Bauds, Bytes and Brokaw."
12. John Motavalli, "Toward an Age of Customized Magazines," *Adweek,* 13 February 1989, 36–37.
13. Nora Paul, "Team Efforts," *IRE Journal,* May–June 1991, 12.

7

Interviewing

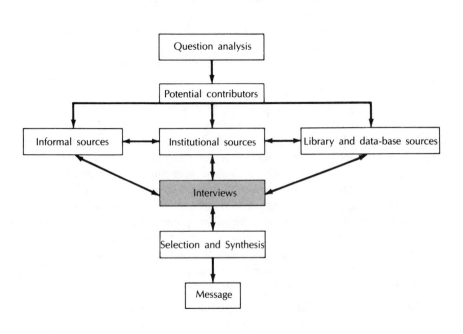

The new high-school teacher in Rabun Gap-Nacoochee, Georgia, had a problem. His students tried to burn the lectern he hid behind, and they did not wait until he turned his back to do it. They sailed paper airplanes, brought their water pistols to class, and in countless other ways told their English teacher from the eastern college that they did not want what he was bringing to them. Eliot Wigginton learned early in the fall of 1966 that he would have to do something different if he were to save himself and his students from disaster. What he hit on was the idea of sending the students to interview the elderly residents of their Appalachian communities. They would record the folklore, the life stories, and the procedures for accomplishing such traditional tasks as building log cabins, dressing hogs, and making moonshine. They would, in the process, restore communication among the generations, preserve information on a way of life that was passing into history, and learn to present what they had found to a world that was waiting for the information. It worked. The students interviewed other residents of their communities and published a magazine that became a regional success. Later, their stories of snake lore, faith healing, soap making, butter churning, planting crops according to signs, and quilting became popular throughout the United States in a succession of *Foxfire* books. The genius of Wigginton's plan for dealing with reluctant students lay in his recognition of how much members of the community can learn from one another and of the role the interview can play in that information-sharing experience.

People traditionally have learned much of what they know about the world from talking with others. Asking a knowledgeable person for information is such a common activity that we hardly recognize it as an information-seeking act. However, people in all walks of life conduct interviews of various sorts daily. For some purposes, people rely uncritically on what they hear from others. For other purposes, they use a variety of sources before accepting information as reliable. Before they enter the mass-communication field, then, people already have informal experience in gathering information through conversation. And, like the young people in rural Georgia, they can refine their interviewing skills, add new techniques, learn additional strategies, and, generally, pass from the ranks of amateur to professional.

Interviewing surely is the most pleasant, as well as the most traditional, method of searching for information. The pleasure is accompanied by perils, however. Experienced communicators have learned to approach the interview with much preparation and much caution. In fact, two social scientists who studied the interview as a reliable reporting resource used a gambling analogy to describe the prevalence of the interview as a journalistic source:

FIRST GAMBLER, arriving in town: Any action around?
SECOND GAMBLER: Roulette.
FIRST GAMBLER: You play?
SECOND GAMBLER: Yes.
FIRST GAMBLER: Is the wheel straight?
SECOND GAMBLER: No.
FIRST GAMBLER: Why do you play?
SECOND GAMBLER: It's the only wheel in town.[1]

For most communicators, the interview is, indeed, addictive. In fact, quitting the interview might give communicators the same withdrawal symptoms that gamblers experience when their gaming is cut off. Despite the hazards of the interview, it deserves its place as a major information source in mass communication. It provides critical elements that can be found with no other method.

Interviews play an essential part in the work of both communicators and communication researchers. Further, interviews are incorporated at more than one point in the processes of both research and media work. For example, researchers may use focus-group interviews to learn of details and issues they intend to examine more extensively through survey interviews later in the research process. (Focus-group and survey interviews are described later in this chapter.) Similarly, a public-relations, advertising, or market research project may use focus group research as a preliminary step in a more elaborate and structured survey research project. News reporters often do a preliminary set of interviews, along with paper and data-base searches, to determine the merit of a story idea and to establish a working framework for a story. In both research-directed interviews and media message interviews, the interviewer may consider the interview a preliminary step in the process or as one of a number of stages in the process. In any case, skilled interviewers assess information from interviews with the same questioning ears and eyes that they employ with print and data-base sources. However limited and potentially flawed, interview sources are critical to most media work and to research on mass communication.

As a trade-off for these critical elements, experienced communicators have learned to compensate for the shortcomings of the interview method. Further, they have learned that interviews differ according to purpose, format, and medium and that the techniques used for interviews also differ, depending on the goals of the participants.

TYPES OF INTERVIEWS

The employment interview is familiar to most adults. Few people are hired on the basis of their résumés alone, although the résumé may present the basic information efficiently. The interview provides a different sort of information to prospective employers and gives an all-important qualitative dimension, allowing potential colleagues to see if they are a good "fit" for working together. Another kind of interview, the helping or counseling interview, also is familiar. Again, the interviewer may have documents that pertain to a client's needs, but additional information is gathered each time the client's "story" is retold. Patients in a clinic often wonder why they are asked to repeat their symptoms to so many people, when the first version is written down in the chart. But the manner of conveying the information tells much of value to members of the medical team, each of whom can follow the story with supplementary questions and can listen and observe the patient as the answer is given. Persuasive interviewing is another form of familiar interview. Some telephone salespeople begin their pitches with what sounds like a consumer survey: "My name is Jill, and I'm taking a fire-safety survey in your neighborhood." In a few moments, however, it is clear that Jill is selling fire extinguishers, not taking a survey. Under other circumstances, the caller may be urging us to vote for his or her candidate or to register to vote or asking us to attend a meeting on neighborhood noise pollution.

Whether a persuasive, a helping, or an employment interview, the format invariably involves the exchange of information. But information itself is the major goal of the type of interviewing that is the subject of this chapter.

In fact, the information interview is a major tool for much of the fact- and idea-finding that goes on in the mass-communication industries. It is used in all types of mass communication and in the production of all forms of media storytelling. For some tasks, the interview is virtually indispensable. For others, it provides, in a single source, some customary and highly prized qualities: authority, human interest, timeliness, and ability to localize, nationalize, or even internationalize the perspective of the message.

THE INTERVIEW AS INTERPERSONAL COMMUNICATION

Newcomers to mass communication frequently are surprised at the amount of interpersonal communication they take part in each day. Having prepared to make messages for the millions, they learn, sometimes with shock, that much of the working day is spent communicating in twosomes or small groups. The interview work that communicators do fits this part of the picture.

Interpersonal dynamics—both verbal and nonverbal—in the interview are complex. If the interview is to be successful, the interviewer must anticipate the dynamics that may develop and be prepared for them. Both interviewers and their subjects have motives and purposes that can be accommodated during the interview. Potential professionals in the field of mass communication may wonder, after seeing a particularly challenging or hostile news interview on television, why anyone ever volunteers to be interviewed. To the viewer at home, the experience looks threatening, sometimes bordering on savage. Yet the interviewer's "victim" volunteered for the experience and may even return soon to go through it all over again. The willingness of interviewees to forgo their psychological security, time, and privacy puzzles those outside the mass-communication professions. Students, for example, frequently assume that their interview requests will be viewed as intrusions and usually are agreeably surprised when the source readily agrees to an interview. Behavior of potential sources is not so surprising, however. Consider that the interview offers a relief from the routine of the day. It offers an opportunity for the interviewee to gain contact with media people, to be recognized as knowledgeable about a subject, to break into the "expert circuit" of sources who are repeatedly called on. The interviewee may gain status or recognition. Understanding for the source's perspective on a public issue may be an additional reward. Finally, the source may benefit from insights about how the media work, and these insights may be useful at another time when the interviewee seeks media attention.

The interviewer's most obvious purpose, of course, is to get information for a message. Beyond that, presenting oneself well is another common goal. The interviewer wishes to perform satisfactorily enough that the source will give interviews again and, perhaps, well enough for the communicator to gain a reputation as a good interviewer. Many interviewers also wish to represent their organizations well, enhancing the reputation of their news, public-relations, or advertising organization.

Interviewer and interviewee alike have legitimate fears as they begin their exchange. Each worries about mistakes. The interviewee may fear being indiscrete, making errors, or disclosing inappropriate or confidential information. The interviewer also has fears: Will I forget an important question? Will I understand the answers to my questions? Will I be able to take accurate notes? Will I be able to recognize errors or contradictions and follow up effectively? In sum, each participant worries about performance during the interview. Once the mutual worries are recognized, the interviewer is responsible for managing the interview so that each person's ego involvement is constructive, threats are reduced, and the relationship is as balanced as possible.

Verbal Communication

One tactic for developing a balanced and mutually satisfying relationship is to focus on the information, rather than on personalities. The interviewer keeps in mind that the audience has particular information needs and the source assists in meeting those needs. Focusing on the information helps reduce tension and the self-consciousness of both participants. Sometimes interviewers discover such high tension in the interviewee that they need to help reduce the stress before the exchange can successfully proceed. At these times, a straightforward question may help to clear the air: "What concerns do you have about our interview that you would like to discuss?" The participants generally can proceed once the apprehensions have been uncovered.

Trust is a necessary component in good interviews. This idea may startle those familiar with dramatized versions of investigative news reporting. But investigative interviews of that sort are a small fraction of the total amount of interviewing done for mass-communication purposes. And even in investigative interviews, much trust is evident. For instance, sources accept the reporter's word that anonymity will be protected if the promise is offered. And reporters trust that the sources will refuse to answer rather than lie.

For interviewers, evidence of trust during the interview can be seen in mutual respect, in self-disclosure, and in concern to make the interview successful. In seeking this evidence of trust, the interviewer attends closely to the covert messages that abound in any such exchange. The subject of the interview, similarly, attends closely to the interviewer's signals. The interviewee meeting an interviewer for the first time often wishes for small talk or personal chatter as a prelude to the business portion of the interview. The source is seeking a context, some reference points, about the interviewer. Some interviewees simply need to learn a few insignificant personal facts about the person who will be presenting questions to them. Other interviewees, however, wish to hear about the interviewer's job, what the information will be used for, or what is new at the "shop." Interviewers who cannot or will not pause for such opening exchanges may find most of their respondents to be rather unresponsive. Of course, the occasional all-business interviewee must be recognized. This person's demeanor generally warns the interviewer: Don't waste time. Don't get personal.

The interviewer has an enormously complex task. Asking the questions and recording the answers are challenging in themselves. But beyond that, the interviewer also is keeping a running tab, an analysis, assessing the quality of the exchanges and the direction that the interview is taking. The interviewer must make adjustments as the interview moves along, a process that succeeds well only after the interviewer has understood what is happening and how it might be altered.

Models of the interpersonal-communication process contain useful elements for this assessment. Typical elements in the models are sender, receiver, channel, feedback, and noise or static. Each element presents a potential for trouble in the process. Typical interview problems result from noise or static in the "system" of the interview. Perhaps the respondent is answering the interviewer's questions in professional jargon, while the interviewer is worried about being able to translate the technical terms into more common language. Perhaps the respondent is worried about giving an answer that is inaccurate or impolitic. Perhaps the respondent fears that the interviewer will make errors in recording and using the answers to questions. Perhaps both are concerned that the interview will be unproductive, that they have wasted their time. Such distractions are not necessarily menacing to interviews. But the skilled interviewer can identify the distractions early in the interview and adopt means for overcoming them.

The concept of covert rehearsal can assist the interviewer. Simply defined, *covert rehearsal* is a mental trial run that allows a person to mentally try out many sentences and responses before letting any of them past the gate, while simultaneously imagining the responses of a conversation partner to each bit of communication.[2] This capacity for rehearsing and anticipating responses assists the interviewer in shifting strategies and perspective as the interview proceeds, empathizing with the subject and shaping questions to fit the developing conversation. The interviewee may reveal signs of insecurity or attempt to change the image projected or show concern that the interviewer may not understand the ideas. The interviewer may read the signs and modify the conduct of the interview accordingly. Of course, the interviewer's signals may be similarly read by the interviewee, who makes adjustments according to the same principles. Ordinary conversation is enormously complex. But the interview, in which answers must be recorded correctly and in context, is even more complex and taxing to the participants.

Along with trust and sensitivity, the interview requires that the interviewee sense the support of the interviewer. That support does not require the interviewer's agreement with the perspective, ideas, policies, and ideology of the subject. Rather, it need reflect only personal support. It is a commitment by the interviewer to listen carefully, to strive faithfully to understand, and to represent the person's point of view accurately. Indeed, studies have shown that appearing to agree with the interviewee is a dangerous practice. The interviewee is so pleased with the evident agreement of the questioner that he or she may overemphasize or exaggerate some points, which may put the veracity or balance of the message at serious risk. Additionally, the subject may not be prepared for the outcome if a personally agreeable interview results in a matter-of-fact or even somewhat negative message.

The spirit of the supportive interview is embodied in an "interview bill of rights," developed with journalistic interviews in mind. Many of the standards set forth in the document are worth considering for other forms of interviews as well.

Rights of the Interviewee

1. The right to an objective listening to the facts presented.
2. The right to an accurate representation of his or her position.
3. The right to a fair and balanced context for all statements.
4. The right to know in advance the general area of questioning and to have reasonable time for preparation.
5. The right to reasonable flexibility as to when to have the interview. (Just as there are times when a reporter cannot be interrupted near a deadline, there are times when others cannot be interrupted.)
6. The right to expect an interviewer to have done some homework.
7. The right to withhold comment when there is good reason without having this translated as evading or "stonewalling," for example, information governed by Securities and Exchange Commission regulations, competitive secrets, matters in litigation or negotiation, information that could damage innocent persons.
8. The right to an assumption of innocence until guilt is proven.
9. The right to offer feedback to the reporter, especially to call attention to instances in which the story, in the honest opinion of the interviewee, missed the point or was in error—and to have this feedback received in good faith.
10. The right to appropriate correction of substantial errors without further damage to the credibility or reputation of the interviewee's organization.[3]

The author of the rights for interviewees has been on both sides of the table. A former journalist, John Jamison was a corporate communication officer for a bank at the time he wrote his article. He included, as well, a set of interviewers' rights:

1. The right to access to an authoritative source of information on a timely basis.
2. The right to candor, within the limits of propriety.
3. The right to access to information and assistance on adverse stories as well as favorable ones.
4. The right to protection on a story the reporter has developed exclu-

sively, until it has been published or until another reporter asks independently for the same information.

5. The right not to be used by business for "free advertising" on a purely commercial story.
6. The right not to be reminded that advertising pays the reporter's salary.
7. The right not to be held accountable for ill treatment by another reporter or another medium at another time.
8. The right to publish a story without showing it to the interviewee in advance.
9. The right not to be asked to suppress legitimate news purely on the grounds that it would be embarrassing or damaging.
10. The right not to be summoned to a news conference when a simple phone call, written statement, news release or interview would do just as well.[4]

Although the concerns of this chapter extend beyond the journalistic interview, Jamison's list of rights illuminates much about the relationships in professional interviews generally. The ground rules reflect means of establishing mutual trust, respect, and consideration. The interview, as interpersonal communication, is more formal, more strategic, and more specific in its goals than is ordinary conversation between two people. However, the qualities that contribute to good conversation also abound in the stimulating interview. They explain, in part, the willingness of sources to give time for interviews and the contribution that interview information makes to the production of interesting messages.

Nonverbal Communication

If the interview were merely verbal questions and answers, it would be extremely complex. But when nonverbal communication is considered, the intricacies are even more pronounced. Some nonverbal elements in any conversation are deliberate, of course. We can frown, smile, back away, and stare deliberately as conscious means of communicating. In addition, both interviewer and interviewee employ a full range of inadvertent nonverbal signals. The interviewer's success at understanding these signals as an integral part of the conversation is critical.

When an interview begins, each person is, in effect, hit with a barrage of nonverbal messages. These involve proxemics (space considerations), kinesics (eye behavior, facial expression, and body movements), paralinguistics (voice quality), and chronemics (time use). Beyond these signals are messages sent via clothing, grooming, hair style, scents, and other aspects of personal style. Considering the richness of the nonverbal system, it is no wonder that interviewers and their sources are content to begin with easy questions while they accustom themselves to the complexities of the nonverbal environment.

But before any questions begin, some space, or proxemic, issues need to be decided. In the United States, interviewers generally avoid the zone reserved for "intimate" acquaintances, roughly 0 to 18 inches. "Personal" distance takes over from 18 inches to about 4 feet, and "social" distance is designated from 4 feet to 12 feet.[5] The participants may negotiate about where to sit. Interviewers generally resist sitting where the speaker can read or even be distracted by the writer's notes. Many interviewers prefer to sit with a desk as a visual barrier, permitting them to keep a notebook on the lap and to write unobtrusively. It is generally recognized that a face-to-face seating arrangement produces better communication than a side-by-side arrangement. If the content of the interview has a confidential aspect, the interview partners may arrange a site away from observers or out of earshot of others. In such instances, the two may sit closer together than is customary in order to avoid being overheard.

Choice of an interview site may be negotiated. Most advertising, public-relations, and news organizations have interview spaces set up for convenience. These provide a distraction-free atmosphere, free of ringing telephones and similar intrusions. Often the interviewee wishes to have the interview in his or her own territory, however. In these cases, the interviewer must adjust to the setting of another person's home or office. These settings may communicate power and authority about the interviewee. Indeed, the setting may be deliberately arranged to project such an image of the inhabitant. Further, the interviewee may be surrounded by associates or, perhaps, family members who wish to have the person's attention. Avoiding distractions is not easy in such settings. Faced with such conditions, the experienced interviewer carefully surveys the scene and selects a chair that will permit note taking and, perhaps, the use of a tape recorder.

Kinesics—including eye behavior, facial expression, and body movement—contribute significantly to meaning in the interview. Interpreting these nonverbal signals accurately is not as easy as some popular-magazine articles might suggest. Some body expressions are universal. A person weeping in one culture is not mistaken for someone laughing in another one. But many gestures and stances do differ from group to group. Lowering of the eyes may suggest evasiveness or lying in one subculture and respect for the conversation partner in another. In observing the kinesics of the interviewee, the interviewer rightly reserves judgment about the meaning of some gestures. When the verbal and the nonverbal messages complement each other, the interviewer is unlikely to be aware of the nonverbal signals. But when, as sometimes happens, the nonverbal content is at odds with the verbal, interviewers tend to believe the nonverbal signals and to continue questioning until they are satisfied that the verbal and the nonverbal messages are consistent.

Eye behavior in the interview provides many cues. A fairly strong and constant gaze may be interpreted as a sign of candor or of deep engagement in the conversation. Beyond a certain point, however, the prolonged gaze is interpreted as a stare, often a sign of intention to dominate or to invade. The rules seem to differ for men and women, with women generally being allowed to gaze for longer periods without being considered rude. Distance is another factor in eye behavior. If people sense they are too close, physically, to each other, they compensate by reducing the amount of eye contact they have with each other. Thus a news reporter attempting to interview a legislator in a crowded hall may be forced to stand too close, under ordinary rules of behavior. To compensate, the reporter and the source will reduce eye contact and will speak in softer tones.

From a strictly practical view, perhaps the most useful nonverbal signals the interviewer can read are the ones revealing that the interviewee may not be sure that the answer is accurate or appropriate. These signals include evasive eye behavior and gestures of ambivalence or puzzlement. Answers that are accompanied by such signals warrant additional probes and follow-up questions. Other practical nonverbal signals are those suggesting that the interviewer has angered the respondent. These permit a quick assessment by the interviewer concerning errors that may have been made in questioning or a particular sensitivity on the part of the interviewee.

Paralinguistics refers to the behavior of the voice—its volume, tone, pitch, intensity—and other vocal signs. These include the hems, haws, groans, um-hums, and other familiar vocalizations. Interviewers are alert to signs of fear, insecurity, boredom, and other emotions that may arise during interviews. Interviewees attend closely to the interviewer's signals, seeking cues that their ideas interest or excite the interviewer and that their responses are acceptable. In the telephone interview, both participants place added emphasis on the paralinguistic factors as a means of compensating for the other nonverbal elements, which are primarily visual.

Time use, or chronemics, is another nonverbal signal system. In the United States, promptness is a highly significant indicator of interest, courtesy, and personal competence. The interviewer who arrives late begins at a disadvantage. If the interviewee is late and the interviewer has been waiting longer than five minutes, the interviewer usually receives an apology and often is perceived to be starting with an advantage in the exchange. Naturally, there are exceptions. The interviewee is accommodating the questioner, a circumstance best not forgotten. And some individuals are chronically late and are not embarrassed by their behavior; they are unlikely to think that they owe the interviewer anything special because of their lateness.

Pacing the interview is one of the principal nonverbal ways that interviewers communicate the appropriate mood, according to sociologist and anthropologist Raymond Gorden: "The most important chronemic technique which the interviewer can control is the length of pauses and the rate of speech in his own conversation and the length of time he waits after the respondent has finished a sentence before he asks another question."[6] Gorden advises the interviewer to set the tone for a relaxed interview by thoughtful, slow speech, rather than using a rapid-fire approach that communicates tension. The resulting tension creates anxiety in the interviewee.

Silence itself is a successful technique, Gorden found in research on interactive in-depth interviews: "Experience and research in social interaction indicate that silence is as meaningful in verbal communication as rests are in a musical score."[7] Interviewees are more spontaneous in interviews characterized by heavy silences. A silent, interested gaze often encourages the interviewee to offer additional points or provocative examples that add greatly to the effectiveness of the interview. In some interview situations, the questioner senses that time requirements prevent the luxury of such pauses. However, even a pause of 20 seconds can be productive. Novice interviewers may fear the silences required by note taking, but evidence suggests these are useful to both partners. Lack of pauses in the interview may be interpreted as evidence of insecurity or anxiety on the part of the interviewer. These feelings are picked up by the respondent. Broadcasting is an exception to these generalizations about silence, for in that activity silence goes against all conventions.

Gorden further advises that pronounced pauses emphasize that the interviewer wants to avoid interrupting. Interviewers should not interrupt, either with words or with disruptive gestures. However, this rule routinely is violated in television-news interviews. Time is precious in broadcasting, and respondents sometimes deliberately refuse to end their sentences because they are schooled in keeping attention and in avoiding additional questions. In some other mass-communication situations, especially where time is critical, the rule against interrupting must be broken. Interviewers often use nonverbal communication to signal the urgency of time.

The richness of nonverbal communication supports the axiom that "you cannot not communicate." Interviewers in mass communication typically attempt to follow professional standards for interviewing. These include open-mindedness, objectivity, accuracy, and a nonjudgmental attitude about people and ideas. With practice, they learn to suppress many of the nonverbal signals that distract the interviewee or disrupt the process. If the interviewee makes them angry, disgusted, or elated, professional interviewers try to maintain a steady, calm, and deliberate demeanor. Television interviewers, in particular, are studies in nonverbal caution. The questioner's nonverbal signals and expressions can be interpreted not only by the interviewee, but also by an audience of perhaps millions watching the exchange on their screens. Their voices may reveal what they hoped to conceal. Television interviewers study tapes of themselves and others as a guide to self-improvement in nonverbal communication, as well as to improve their voices, diction, and images. Interviewers' sensitivity to the systems of nonverbal communication in their own culture may help them to develop the desired qualities of tact and objectivity.

The goal is not to be without personality or viewpoint, but to avoid introducing elements of bias into the interview. For example, interviewers recognize that their own facial expressions or eye behavior may tell the interviewee something that will interfere with the respondent's candid response. They know that their yawn may mean that they have been sitting still too long, but that the person being interviewed probably will interpret it as boredom. In any event, successful interviewers do not *avoid* communicating, but replace bias and opinion with curiosity and interest in the interviewee and the subject. Nonverbal elements play a part in the interviewer's ability to express interest in the topic and the interviewee.

THE PLACE OF INTERVIEWS
IN THE SEARCH PROCESS

Communicators share a number of goals in their information-seeking interviews irrespective of whether they work in news, advertising, or public-relations positions. For example, a corporate official of a firm that manufactures street-sweeping equipment might be interviewed on a given day by a news reporter asking questions about unusual capabilities of a new piece of equipment being marketed, by a member of the firm's public-relations staff who is working on an article for the employee magazine, or by a staff member in the advertising agency that handles the advertising for the firm. Many of the questions they ask will be similar, but some will be distinctive, reflecting the differences in the ultimate use of the information. Their common goal is the gathering of accurate, factual, and comprehensive material that will contribute to an appropriate and interesting message.

Interviews help the communicator to establish a sense of dialogue on a topic. In the case of the street-sweeping equipment example, the interviewer for the company magazine probably would ask questions about the impact of the new equipment on the work force of the firm. The advertising interviewer might be interested in details about the effectiveness of the machine; he or she might even want to operate the equipment briefly to get a feel for the product. The news reporter might be interested in the effect of the equipment on street cleaning in the city, on the firm's profitability, or on the area's unemployment picture. In each of these instances, the interviewer is engaging the company representative in a dialogue that recognizes the ultimate interest of the audience in particular questions about the firm's decisions and behavior.

Some of the compelling human-interest needs of mass communication are met through the use of interview material. Interviews often provide insight about people and consumers and thus stimulate writers to produce copy that engages an audience's interest. The interview need not provide names, addresses, and direct quotes to be influential in this way. It may, more simply, stimulate the creators' ideas in a particular direction. In the advertising campaign for the street sweeper, for example, the interviewer does not expect to quote the company official. But colorful language and ideas, enthusiasm for the product, and interest in how it will be used can stimulate the creative capacities of the interviewer. The enthusiasm and ideas can be transferred from the interviewee to the interviewer and subsequently to the audience.

Authority is another quality that interviews can help contribute to the search strategy. Provided that the interviewees are well chosen, they should be able to present facts, ideas, statistics, and interpretations that add richness and flavor to the message. The writer who is backed by authoritative material can be more bold and more secure in making assertions in the copy than can the writer who is not so buttressed. Writers in every field are conscious that writing around a gap in information results in weak copy. For instance, if the ad copywriter does not have information about the speed and sweeping capacity of the street sweeper, a promising copy angle cannot be pursued.

If controversy or dispute is involved in the content of a message, interviews help the communicator reflect the various perspectives related to the controversy. The writer is able, once the important sides of the issue are uncovered, to present these positions in the news story or ad. For example, the question of mass-transit subsidies interests news and public-relations writers, along with those who advertise transit services. Anyone writing on the subject has to be well versed in controversies connected with the topic.

Preliminary research on most subjects generally turns up conflicting information. Interviews are useful for exploring the disputed material. They also help the communicator to find areas of agreement and to understand the nuances of both agreement and disagreement. For example, in learning about public officials' responses to a proposed federal tax reform, interviews would be essential. Through interviews, the communicator would learn which governors think that their states would suffer and which think that their states would gain from a particular tax proposal. The governors' analyses of the relationships between state tax policy and federal tax policy would emerge from the series of interviews.

Having the most recent information is of the utmost importance in mass communication. Often the interview is the only method by which truly current material can be collected. Some preliminary research may be required in order for the interviewer to choose the source for the most recent information. For example, a public-relations official from one state may need the latest information on flood damage in an adjacent state. Or, a reporter may need a reliable estimate of damage to spruce trees by an infestation of insects. For such tasks, the communicator first must complete research that locates the most competent, up-to-date interview sources, and then proceed to the interviews themselves.

Interviews also provide a setting in which predictions are sought and in which policy pronouncements are made. Mass media are alert to public interest in policy changes, and communicators take advantage of interviews to check on shifts in policy. Similarly, interviewers quiz their sources for interpretations of the significance of what is taking place around them. For instance, a reporter in an interview may ask for facts about a new policy of burning refuse rather than burying it in landfills. Beyond the questions of fact, the reporter may ask for predictions ("Will Carver County residents be willing to separate burnable and unburnable trash?") and for interpretations ("What is the significance for the environment and for the economy of this shift of policy?").

Interviews, then, provide for a continual negotiation between what has been learned and what has escaped the communicator's grasp. Material from interviews helps meet the requirements for context and perspective, for accuracy and completeness, for recency and authority. This material plays a role in the communicator's goal of contributing to a public dialogue. Interviews take place when a solid search of institutional, library, and data-base sources is complete. The search-strategy process we present makes the path clear: the interviewer can always return to resources consulted earlier in the process. But interviews should never take place until the interviewer is well versed in the essentials of the subject.

PREPARING FOR INTERVIEWS

Selecting Interviewees

The first step in preparing for solid interviews is choosing those to be interviewed. Social scientist John Madge classified interviewees into three categories: the potentate, the expert, and the people. Potentates are, of course, those who have authority or power. Experts have special knowledge of a subject. People have experiences in life that allow them to give direct testimony on the effects of the potentate's actions and on the matters the expert studies.[8] Mass communicators frequently are criticized for making casual decisions about who merits interviewing. Interviewees generally are selected for their knowledge, their willingness, their availability, and such personal qualities as lucid expression and the ability to produce interesting quotes. Even if the interview is unlikely to result in quoted material—such as an interview preparatory to the start of an advertising campaign—communicators may be biased toward the colorful, phrase-making respondent. Interesting and colorful interviewees stimulate the creativity of communicators. They help them to get fired up about the topic. But for many communication tasks, the most knowledgeable respondents may not be the flashiest phrase makers. The first rule for selecting interviewees is to choose those with the appropriate facts and experiences. If a choice is to be made between facts and phrases, go with the facts.

Organizations and reference works help communicators in search of reputable sources in diverse fields. For example, the Media Resource Service is a program of the Scientists' Institute for Public Information. It is available to help communicators identify appropriate scientific experts from more than 20,000 scientists. Public-relations offices of universities typically have rosters of faculty members whose research specialties coincide well with communicators' information needs. Publishers issue directories or guides for media organization use, such as the Gale publication *Talk Show Guest Directory.*

Journalists have, in the past decade, taken heavy criticism for their selection of the "experts" they interview on political and policy issues. The use of the golden rolodex, meaning a telephone roster of well-known, uncontroversial individuals willing to appear on TV and to be interviewed for public-affairs news stories, received critical attention in news magazines and journalism reviews. These articles generally suggested that repeatedly consulting the same "experts" showed professional laziness or sloppy work. But scholars also began to examine the social and political significance of sources who make news and who shape news in daily newspapers, television newscasts, news interview programs, and news discussion programs. Scholars' conclusions from these studies stressed the probable political and public opinion consequences of what they found: newspaper interviewees and invited guests on commercial network and public-television public-affairs programs are overwhelmingly white males affiliated with conservative think tanks and foundations, the Republican party and Republican administrations, and elite private universities. However, these representatives generally are not identified as having conservative or right-wing connections; instead, they are designated as "political analysts" or "former" federal government officials.[9]

One academic researcher studying the qualifications of "experts" used as authorities on national network TV conducted a data-base search for experts on Iran. His search identified a UCLA faculty member, Professor Nikki Keddie, who had published eight books about Iran; her record contrasted with that of the network source who appeared repeatedly, who had written no books on Iran but was a native of Lebanon and author of several books about his home country. After obtaining a list of the UCLA professor's books, the author, Lawrence Soley, examined reviewers' comments about the quality of her books, then telephoned her to learn if she had ever been interviewed about her specialty by a network. She had not been used as an expert source. The researcher concluded: "Being female and a professor at a public institution apparently precluded her being used as an 'Iran expert,' even though network owned-and-operated stations are located in the city where she teaches."[10]

Criticism of news media for selection of experts is not limited to national media and political and policy issues. Increasingly, local print and broadcast media have been criticized for relying on the same white, male establishment sources for human-interest sources and for expertise in virtually all news categories. Individuals and organizations have protested to news organizations that excluding women and men of color, for example, presents a distorted picture of the contributions that many members of the community make and contributes to perpetuation of stereotypes. Public-relations practitioners preparing programs, conferences, and public discussions have been challenged similarly to present speakers who more accurately represent the expertise available on the subjects to be discussed.

Evaluating the credentials of those who might be interviewed is a small research task in itself. A potential roster of interviewees develops during the earlier steps of the search strategy. Thus a sensible first step is to review all background material and to make a list of those who have written or spoken on the subject. For example, consider the background research for an advertising campaign on behalf of the Coalition for Literacy. The coalition seeks volunteers to work with functionally illiterate adults. Potential interviewees include officials of the coalition and of other groups concerned with adult illiteracy. Annual reports, newsletters, and boards of directors' minutes of meetings also reveal names of important individuals in this field. Government documents display the names of members of Congress who have shown concern about the problem and the identities of specialists who have testified before congressional committees. Some of these specialists have published articles on the subject in scholarly journals and have been quoted in news magazines. Another type of expertise to be sought is that of people who have themselves experienced the disability of illiteracy. Their expertise may not be evident in the indexes and journals, but members of the literacy organizations probably can help the interviewer locate them. Perhaps some of the formerly illiterate adults have gone on to become volunteer teachers or members of the groups combating illiteracy. The ad campaign may permit a photo, a headline, and a copy block of 350 words for each of several ads to be produced for the campaign. The limited space available makes each bit of material to be included highly significant. The facts, ideas, and experiences presented must be accurate and compelling if the campaign is to succeed.

After a promising roster of potential interviewees is drawn up, the interviewer checks the reputations of those on the list. Some of this checking is done through such standard reference sources as *Who's Who*. In this case, *Who's Who in Education* may include biographical information on some of those who have written on the subject or spoken before congressional committees. Or, the *Authors* volume of *Books in Print* may reveal titles of relevant books written by these people. Some checking can be done through informal and institutional sources. For example, such informal checking can help the interviewer identify persons who are notorious publicity hounds or who are known as liars.

Once the interview roster is ready, the willingness and availability of the sources is determined. Some potential interviewees may be unavailable—out of town or tied up with other responsibilities, for example. Others may be unwilling to be interviewed. Some may have research results that they do not wish to make public yet. Others may prefer to send the interviewer a copy of their testimony before Congress and save the time an interview would take. Some specialists who are unavailable will suggest others as substitutes. However, a good percentage of people on a well-constructed source list should be available. Enriching and supplementing the fruits of the earlier steps in the search strategy is a consistent goal.

Planning Interviews

Careful planning of interviews involves a number of steps and almost innumerable considerations. In some cases, the interviewee stipulates some conditions for the interview. For example, the interviewee may limit the time available to the questioner, may require either a personal or a telephone conversation, may refuse to speak either with or without a tape recorder, or may ask to have another person present. The interviewer will plan the interview around any conditions that were established when the interview was arranged.

Planning for personal and for telephone interviews is similar. Some interviewers believe they get better results from telephone interviews, since the potential distractions of personal appearance, race, and age do not intrude. Some nonverbal cues that are helpful in the personal interview are missing, however, and the interviewer must substitute for these cues. For example, in personal interviews, the listener's facial expression tells the speaker when he or she is puzzled. Watching the note taker tells when the speaker should pause so the writer can catch up. The telephone interviewer may provide plenty of "um-hums" to reassure the interviewee that the listener is still there and may ask to have a pause for note taking. Telephone note taking is speeded up when the interviewer uses a headset and speaker for the interview and a computer or word processor for typing the notes. For extended survey research interviews, computer-assisted telephone interviewing (CATI) software is available. Using this software, telephone interviewers can read the survey questions from the screen and enter codes for the responses directly into the computer. Complex "branching" in questionnaires is simplified and, following completion of the interviewing, results can be speedily obtained with the application of a statistical package.

Interview planning requires a thorough review of all material gathered earlier in the search process. From this review, the interviewer can make a list of needed material and devise a strategy for using interviews to meet the need:

1. What material is agreed on? What patterns of consistency exist?
2. What is disputed? Can inconsistencies be explained or resolved? What is the significance of the disputed facts?
3. What unexplored aspects of the subject should be developed? What is "new" that should be reflected in my questions?
4. What questions are appropriate to each interviewee?
5. What sensitivities and special perspectives should I be aware of in asking questions of each interviewee?
6. What information in my files may need updating or confirming?
7. What human-interest information can be elicited from this interviewee?

In preparing questions that will bring forth information, interviewers naturally stress the content they expect from their interviews. However, interview preparation also involves getting ready for the social and psychological aspects of the interview. Before the questions are drafted, the interviewer considers the situation of the interviewee. Raymond Gorden cites eight inhibitors that interviewers should be aware of in their interview strategies.[11] Four of these inhibitors may make sources unwilling to give information: (1) competing demands for time; (2) ego threats that make the respondent fear loss of esteem or status; (3) standards of etiquette that put some topics off limits in certain circumstances; and (4) trauma, the reluctance to return to a painful situation.

The other four inhibitors affect the speaker's ability to respond adequately: (1) forgetfulness; (2) chronological confusion; (3) inferential confusion; and (4) unconscious behavior. Memory fades, sometimes to be stimulated by conversation about an event. Thus material that is most remote in time may—or may not—be recalled better if it is requested after conversation is under way and the interviewee's recall has been sharpened by reminders about the event. Chronological confusion can take a number of forms. It is common for people to recall two or more events, but forget the order of their occurrence. They also may recall one situation, but incorrectly recall when it arose. For example, a person citing family history might believe that all parcels of the family farm were acquired at one time, since in his memory that has been the case. Inferential confusion results from faulty reasoning rather than faulty memory. The interviewee may not be able to relate his own experience to abstract questions presented in the interview unless the interviewer is patient and provides a step-by-step approach linking the experience of the interviewee with the generalizations. Unconscious behavior also influences interviewees' ability to respond accurately. People under distress or in a crisis frequently are unaware of their own behavior in these circumstances.

Fortunately, mass-communication interviewers can count on other factors that facilitate interviews. Confident interviewers who approach potential interviewees expecting their cooperation find that many people are likely to help fulfill the interviewer's expectation that they cooperate. People appreciate the recognition that interviews bring them, another factor that paves the way. Altruistic appeals to and sympathetic understanding for the prospective interviewee also affect willingness to be interviewed. Interviews can be stimulating new experiences for the respondent. Finally, interviewees who have suffered in a crisis often realize the cathartic benefits of discussing their situations. The news media frequently are criticized for interviews with people experiencing tragedy or crisis. But the testimony of those interviewed does show that many appreciate the chance to have a larger segment of society understand their position.[12] The effects of inhibitors and facilitators will vary, depending on interviewee and subject. The interviewer can attempt to prepare with the recognition that these factors are likely to affect the quality of the interview. The interviewer can be sensitive in determining what questions to ask, what language to use in asking them, in what order to place the questions.

Having assessed both the information needs and the interviewee's potential to respond, the interviewer is ready to develop an agenda of questions. This is a comprehensive list of questions, setting forth everything the interviewer would like to know. Some of these questions might be asked of a number of respondents. Others might be asked of only one interviewee. Except in survey research interviews, open-ended questions are most common. In the closed-ended question, the respondent must select one of the responses provided by the interviewer. For example, most questions asked in Gallup and other polls are closed-ended: "How do you feel about the economy of the United States at this time?" "Very optimistic," "somewhat optimistic," "neutral," "somewhat pessimistic," or "very pessimistic." An open-ended interview question asks, "What is your feeling about the United States economy at this time?" One advantage of closed-ended questions is that a large number of interviews can be analyzed relatively quickly and inexpensively. Open-ended questions have the advantages of completeness, specificity, and depth. In journalistic interviews, open-endedness is stressed, for it leads to spontaneity, interpretation by sources, cues for additional questions, and quotable phrases.

Whether closed- or open-ended, clear questions are required for successful interviews. Social psychologists Eleanor Maccoby and Nathan Maccoby developed six points to assist question writers:[13]

1. *Avoid words with double meaning:* Even such simple terms as *dinner* can confuse and result in error. Residents of a nursing home, for example, may refer to dinner as either the noon meal or the evening meal, depending on custom and social class. The interviewer in such a situation might conclude that people did not know what they were eating, since they gave different answers to the question "What was served for dinner?"

2. *Avoid long questions:* Use a carefully crafted question to open the subject and a series of separate follow-ups that will cover the material. Instead of saying, "Tell me about your experience in Central America, why you decided to go, what you found when you got there, and how you escaped your captors," the questioner should break up the string of questions and begin with, "Why did you go to Central America?"

3. *Specify the time, place, and context in which the interviewee should answer the question:* Once an interview has touched on a variety of topics, the interviewee can easily misunderstand such questions as "Now, once you escaped your captors, you were back in Panama at your company headquarters. What happened at that point?"

4. *Either make explicit all the alternatives that the respondent should have in mind in answering or make explicit none of them:* For example, the interviewer might want to guide the interviewee through some alternatives but could easily fail to suggest the one that matches what the interviewee had in mind. "Once you were safely back in the United States, did you want to call the FBI or the CIA, or did you decide to let your company take over?" Recognizing the incomplete alternatives presented, the source might say, "Well, actually, neither of those." But some respondents might not correct the interviewer and simply evade the question or respond vaguely.

5. *When the interview concerns a subject that is unfamiliar to the interviewee, offer an explanation before presenting the question:* "While you were held captive, some new legislation was introduced in Congress. The provisions include. . . . Do you think that would have helped in your situation?"

6. *It is often helpful to ask questions in terms of the respondent's own immediate (and recent) experience, rather than in terms of generalities:* The respondent may resist such a general question as "Is the State Department doing a good job in these kidnapping cases?" A specific question—"In your case, did the State Department work effectively toward your release?"—is more to the point.

Arranging the questions into an effective agenda is the next step. Many interviewers use a strategy of beginning with reassuringly easy questions. Some may be questions verifying that what has been learned through earlier parts of the search is, indeed, still accurate and up-to-date. While the opening questions may be simple, experienced interviewers are aware of overly broad questions that send the interviewee off the topic or set off an avalanche of irrelevances. Generally, experience suggests that embarrassing, touchy, or ego-threatening questions best be kept until late in the interview. By then, the context is well established, and the interviewer has had a chance to develop a persona as a fair, accurate, and sensitive individual. Touchy questions always bring about the possibility that the subject will declare the interview to be at an end. In that event, the interviewer at least has the earlier portions of the conversation for the record.

Each question in the interview agenda gives rise to additional questions. Some of these are probes, that is, requests for more information based on the idea just stated by the source. Interviewers who are too tightly tied to their own interview agenda may neglect to follow up with appropriate probes. But some interviewers forget their scheduled questions once the follow-ups begin to occur. Rigidly adhering to the question agenda promotes one kind of completeness, at the expense of expanding the topic and developing its new dimensions. Experienced interviewers learn, in time, to walk the line between the two hazards.

Broadcast interviews, especially those on network television, include an intermediary or preliminary interviewing component. Shortage of air time, costs of production, and concerns about what an interviewee might say all contribute to the custom of preliminary interviewing in broadcasting. Staff members scout prospective interviewees, usually by telephone, in a preliminary selection process. Often, potential interviewees are being promoted as sources by their publishers when new books are issued or by movie producers prior to release of a movie. In preliminary interviews, potential network guests are evaluated for their ability to contribute to the program. One author who appeared on the Donahue show said that the program producer spent more than 10 hours on the telephone with her in the three weeks preceding her appearance. Whatever else it might have accomplished, the author concluded, the pre-interview work did not prevent the host of the program from trivializing the author's perspective on her subject.[14]

TV's pursuit of interviewees to fill the time on the news interview programs, talk shows, and documentaries produces hectic schedules for the researchers who, behind the scenes, are responsible for nearly everything except the on-air discussions. While their official work titles may be "writer," "talent coordinator," or "producer," these researchers often are referred to as "bookers," reflecting that part of their jobs that involves contacting potential interviewees. But they also do research on the guest and the event or situation to be discussed, write briefing papers for the on-air talent, and draft questions to be asked in the interview.[15] The topic and lineup of guests for

"Nightline" may change throughout the day, depending on news developments, putting a premium on the researcher's speed and accuracy.

Many potential guests are government officials whose credentials need not be rechecked for each appearance. Others are nominated by publishers, filmmakers, and others promoting candidates for publicity; biographical and promotional material usually comes from the promoter in these cases. Their on-air speaking ability and appearance often requires research—the on-air talent scouts expect interviewees to be able to speak reasonably lucidly, not freeze with fear. Researchers also are on the lookout for frauds, especially since the 1987 hoax by two actors who were interviewed on three network programs posing as sexual surrogates and people with unusual sexual problems. The hoax was widely covered, to the embarrassment of the producers and hosts of the programs.

Columnist Christopher Hitchens, writing of his experience on political talk shows, asserts that some may appear unrehearsed and combative but, in reality, are pretty fully scripted by the time participants are on the air. The White House under Ronald Reagan, Hitchens claims, controlled participation on the programs by refusing to allow administration officials to appear with other interviewees who were considered by the White House to be combative or on the political left. As a participant, Hitchens recalls, he was told what subjects or ideas he was forbidden to mention.[16]

CONDUCTING INTERVIEWS

Because almost all interviewing takes place away from observers' gazes, it is difficult to establish standards for interviewing. The time pressures of broadcast-news interviewing, for example, make that variety of interview too specialized to serve as a model for general interviewing. Thus interviewers are left to develop their art through study, trial, and experience. Substantial scholarly works now are available to guide both novice and experienced interviewers.

Rituals and Routines for Interviewers

Many of the rituals of conversation apply to interviews. Greetings, handshakes, introductions, and occupying a space on the sidewalk or a chair in an office—these have their ritualistic aspects. Rituals assist the conversation and do much to help establish the roles that a pair will play in the interview. Escaping specific roles in interviewing is impossible. The novice who would be natural, rather than act out the roles called for in the situation, is engaging in delusion. "Be natural," communication scholars Eugene Webb and Jerry Salancik agree, is the worst possible advice.[17] To start with, the interviewer begins the exchange with a set of personal characteristics—gender, age, race, voice and speech patterns, and personal appearance. Added to these are the professional expertise, experience, and background study that the interviewer brings to the exchange. The interviewee, too, brings a collection of traits and interview preparation. Each has in mind something to be gained through the interview; each is aware of differences in status and power that must be accounted for if the interview is to succeed. Interviewers, then, must occupy some role and must adjust their behavior during the conversation so that the role develops effectively. As individuals, interviewers learn through trial and error that particular styles are effective with various interviewees. Successful adaptation of a variety of roles is evident when the interviewer can shift at will to accommodate the interviewee's response to various situations.

Out of the trial and error, many interviewers learn rituals that help them whenever they encounter certain predictable responses. For example, the interviewee who exclaims, "You look too young to be doing this kind of work!" may be issuing a challenge to credentials or competence. The young-looking person develops a set of stock phrases designed to establish status without appearing offended: "People often say that to me. But I have been doing this work for eight years now."

Other kinds of rituals may help the interviewee understand the process and, thus, save both time and stress for the participants. For example, by telephoning in advance to arrange an interview, the interviewer can signal a number of characteristics about the interview. By stating the specific topic for which the interview is sought, the communicator acknowledges that the source will prepare for the exchange. Suggesting the amount of time needed for the interview further communicates a concern for effective time use by both parties. At the onset of the interview itself, the questioner can establish that an agenda of questions is ready, indicating that the interviewer has carefully prepared. For instance, "I have six questions to begin with. These concern the new junior-high-school reading curriculum—the need for it, what it is expected to contribute, who will be responsible for it, what it will cost, and so on. When I have finished with those questions, I will ask you what other information is important from your point of view." Interviewers who develop such a ritual find that it helps them to establish their roles as well-prepared, professional communicators. Interviewees, reassured that they will have an opportunity to add what they think is important, concentrate on the questions as they are presented. They can resist the temptation to digress and to inject their pet ideas into the interview at irrelevant times. Further, they find it easy to cast the interviewer into the role of a considerate, open-minded information seeker.

Stock phrases often come in handy. Interviewees frequently try to enlist the interviewer in their projects or seek the interviewer's opinions, especially if he or she might reinforce the interviewees' opinions. Interviewers must resist such invitations, of course, in recognition of the problems of contagious bias as a source of interview error. In some situations, simple evasions will work. At other times, a stock phrase is handy: "I can't disclose my opinion about this to you. Studies show that my neutrality here will give the best atmosphere for an accurate interview. However, you can see that the subject is one that interests me greatly."

When an interviewee strays from the subject, a stock phrase can help to get things back on the track: "I wonder if we could finish talking about the cost of this program, and then get back to the comment about the application process." A timely exit from the interview also benefits from ready phrases. Often, interviewees—who earlier declared that they could spare only a few moments for the interview—tend to prolong it. Many interviewers have expected to spend 20 minutes and have devoted more than an hour to such interviews. Frequently, the interviewee regards the end of the interview as the end of an opportunity to be heard. A reassuring ritual allows the interviewer to leave with an assurance of future accessibility: "You have been more than generous with your time. Let me leave you my office phone number, in case you think of something else I should know." To reassure the interviewee of concern for accuracy, the interviewer can explain: "If I have any questions later, I will telephone to check the facts again."

Sources of Interview Error

The complexity of both verbal and nonverbal elements in the interview makes interviewing a fascinating but error-ridden method of information gathering. With awareness of the leading causes of error, interviewers can develop habits that reduce these errors. According to a study by Gary Lawrence and David Grey, the leading cause of error is failure to get advance information. In this study, news reporters and their sources separately identified problems that had led to subjective errors—that is, errors of emphasis, meaning, or omission. Both sources and interviewers cited insufficient background information as the main cause of subjective inaccuracies.[18] The reporters noted lack of time for adequate preparation as a problem, while the sources attributed the errors to "sensationalism" and insufficient personal contact with the interviewers. In this study, the most serious errors were associated with limited contact between reporter and source. Errors in copy editing, revising, and headline writing also played a role.

Factual errors, as well as subjective errors, plague interviewers. Checking and rechecking are the standard ways advised to overcome these errors. Every name, initial, spelling, time, date, place, number, statistic, and other specific bit of information carries the potential for error. Repeatedly checking for accuracy and telephoning the interviewee after the interview, if additional questions or doubts arise about the accuracy or adequacy of the information, communicates to the interviewee that precision is prized.

While Lawrence and Grey's research referred to news reporting, failure to prepare is likely to cause accuracy problems in interviews of any kind. Other common problems arise from vocabulary differences. Some of these language problems, again, reflect faults in preparation. The interviewer who thinks that the words *science* and *technology* are interchangeable, for example, is poorly prepared to listen accurately to what an interviewee says. The one who does not know the difference between a sociologist and a social worker is likely to make errors of fact and inference. The one who thinks that the words *chicken* and *hen* refer to the same animal will be in trouble when preparing television commercials for a new line of poultry. Interviewers can ill afford to be impatient with distinctions, especially distinctions that are basic to understanding what the source is saying.

The failure of interviewers to control their own prejudices is another source of interview error. The filters through which we approach new information and experience—personal, political, and ideological frameworks—must be accounted for. Successful interviewers learn to compensate, to some degree, for these and other filters. Some interviews simply are boring to some people who are assigned to them. In such cases, the disinterest in the topic must be set aside, and careful attention must be given to the subject and the interviewee.

The bias of the interviewer is contagious. Numerous researchers have established that interviewers' attitudes are reflected in what an interviewee says during an interview. An early study showed that people applying for welfare benefits attributed their economic problems to a variety of causes—alcohol and the economic system, for example. The interviewer who was a prohibitionist recorded three times as many subjects blaming alcohol for their problems as did his colleague, a socialist. The socialist, in turn, elicited twice as many responses blaming the economic system as did his colleague.[19] Interviewer bias is communicated in a variety of ways. Facial expression, eye contact, and enthusiastic "um-hums" while the respondent is talking may play a part in encouraging the interviewee to continue in the same vein. Loaded questions have a similar effect. These are questions that virtually dictate the answer the interviewer wants or expects. For example, the interviewer might ask: (1) "Did you feel terrible regret after the accident?" or (2) "What were your feelings after the accident?" The interviewee understands that "yes" is the expected, perhaps socially acceptable, answer to the first question. Through awareness of the covert rehearsal process described earlier, the interviewer can learn to control the most bias-inducing behavior. Studying video- or audiotapes of interviews can help the interviewer identify practices that bias the interview.

When the interviewer sets up the formal question agenda, attention can be given to questions that are biased in their language or their perspective. But many interviews follow the agenda somewhat loosely, and, in any case, follow-up questions and probes arise spontaneously. It is in the follow-up questions that bias is likely to be most strongly communicated. Interviewing specialists invariably caution that the interviewer never should disclose opinions, show anger, or argue with the interviewee. Despite that caution, dramatized versions of news reporters doing interviews typically depict the interviewer as opinionated and argumentative—and successful because of it. Nevertheless, the interviewer who slips out with, "But don't you think. . ." has violated standards that have been established with good reason. The interviewer is not advised to be passive in the presence of controversy but to learn follow-up techniques that avoid introducing bias. Rather than saying, "But don't you think. . ." the interviewer can observe, "I see. Tell me how you respond to Ann Swanson's view that the landfill will destroy the environment."

The double-barrelled question also may arise as a follow-up, although the questioner would not have included it in the formal agenda. The double-barrelled question is confusing because it asks the respondent to answer two items simultaneously. The practice always is subject to producing an answer that is commonly misunderstood.

The interviewer's pattern of note taking also might communicate a bias. Undoubtedly, the interviewee is aware of note taking. When the interviewer takes notes sporadically, rather than steadily, during the interview, the respondent may take cues from the note taking itself. That is, the interviewee observes that some answers seem worthy of notes, while others are ignored. Wanting to be effective, the respondent stresses those ideas on which the interviewer is taking notes. Of course, interviewees frequently misinterpret the significance of the note-taking pattern. But that does not change the fact that selective note taking can introduce an element of bias into the interview.

Race and gender are additional factors that affect accuracy in interviews. A number of studies show that people's answers are affected by whether they are interviewed by a member of their own race or a member of a different race. Both blacks and whites tend to be more frank with interviewers of their own race and seem to try to avoid answers that might offend members of the other race. This is particularly so when the interview questions deal with racial issues.[20]

It should be emphasized that race alone does not account for differences in interview responses. Perceptions of power, authority, and status affect the interaction of interviewer and interviewee. Hence, while the interviewer cannot change race, it is possible to try to avoid interview error by paying close attention to any context in which race may be involved. For example, if the interviewee senses that he or she is perceived stereotypically, the effect on the answers is likely to be greater. Interviewers should be aware that subjects may be significantly affected by differences in the race of interview partners. There are no easy formulas for avoiding interview error arising from these differences.

The effects of gender on interviews have had much less attention from researchers. Clearly, the same sorts of stereotypical thinking that affect the interview dynamics between blacks and whites are at work in interviews between men and women. Again, relative power in the interview situation affects the exchange. In general, women are perceived to lack the status and power that men possess, and, for the interviewer, this can work either to advantage or to disadvantage. For example, a powerful man being interviewed by a woman may be entirely relaxed because he usually is surrounded by women who take direction from him. He may actually answer questions more candidly with a female interviewer than with a male. However, if some of the questions seem difficult or searching, he may become more upset with the woman than he would with a man. The interviewee may have been expecting more deferential treatment. Unprepared for the interviewer's direct and professional approach, he might resist questions that he would have answered if the interviewer were male. This example is but one of many responses related to gender. Like race, gender does not operate in isolation from such other factors as power, status, social class, and age. Interviewers in mass-communication work recognize the power of such factors to affect the accuracy of their interviews. With experience and sensitivity, they develop techniques to help compensate for those factors that cannot be changed. They also recognize that such factors cannot be overcome entirely.

Whether intentionally or not, sources contribute to interview errors. Faulty memory is a frequent source of error. The passage of time, along with wishful thinking, often causes people to recall inaccurately. Checking with other sources—documents, records, other individuals—can help the interviewer identify such inaccuracies and perhaps even correct them.

Misunderstanding questions is another source of interview error. It is the interviewer's responsibility to set each question in a context, to use clear language, and to watch closely for signs that the question was misunderstood. If the interview was recorded, the playback may reveal the presence of misunderstood questions. A recommendation from Lawrence and Grey's study suggests that interviewers routinely ask their sources, "What is the significance of this?" as a check on context and interpretation.

Intentional falsehood also occurs in interviewing. Respondents have been known to claim credit for the work of others, to deny participation in activities they fear would look bad, and to misrepresent their views or policies. The desire for respect, celebrity status, and popularity affects some interviewees. Outright lies come chiefly from naïve people. Partial disclosure, slanting to meet a situation, and evasion are some practices of more sophisticated sources who wish to evade the truth. Mitchell Charnley and Blair Charnley, experienced journalists and educators, state that interviewees commonly lie out of self-interest. They cite these examples:

> Falsification to cover complicity in shameful or criminal behavior.
> Reluctance to admit having been on [welfare].
> Fear that the truth will "look bad" to family, friends, or employer.
> Hope of looking wealthy, well-traveled, or well-educated.
> Desire to get public attention, "free publicity."
> Distrust of the reporter or of the use to which the story is to be put.
> Attempt to tell the reporter what "the reporter wants to hear."[21]

Even the most skilled interviewer cannot avoid all lies, but good preparation empowers the interviewer to follow up with detailed questions that can help uncover lies and distortions.

News reporters in Washington, D.C., advise journalists that federal officials lie frequently and that uncovering deception by officials takes energy and ingenuity, along with more traditional tactics such as checking the numbers and statistics, observing at the scene, consulting opponents, and interviewing ordinary people affected by government policies and directives.[22]

A standard procedure in social science interviews is verifying results. The person supervising the interviewing phase of a research project selects a subsample of each interviewer's completed questionnaires and calls or writes to confirm that the respondent did, indeed, participate in the interview. Confirming the accuracy of the interview record generally is not the issue in social science research verification. To the contrary, the accuracy of information gathered in the interview is of greater concern in the journalistic print interview. Traditionally, individual news reporters have been expected to verify material collected during their own interviews. Recent challenges to the tradition have appeared. Publications, especially magazines, increasingly employ researchers (often called *fact checkers* even though their accuracy checks also cover inference, fairness, and ethics) to confirm both interview information and material from published sources.[23] In addition, periodicals accepting free-lance articles ask writers to submit interview records citing the interviewee's name, title, credentials, and telephone numbers and bibliographies of supporting materials along with their articles.

One form of accuracy check traditionally has been taboo in the daily news industries—showing a news story to the quoted sources before it is published. In the growing concern for accuracy, this taboo has been called into question. Steve Weinberg, investigative reporter, author, and teacher, concludes that the conventional wisdom needs to change. After a decade of showing advance copy to interviewees so they could review the accuracy of their contributions, Weinberg began telling other journalists that the practice had helped him to produce stories that were more thorough, fair, and accurate.[24] In training student journalists, George P. Kennedy at the University of Missouri requires a similar accuracy exercise for staff of the campus daily.[25]

Being Interviewed

The importance of—and hazards of—the journalistic interview have led some organizations to provide interviewee training to representatives for their organizations. These range in scope from elaborate and expensive seminars in which executives are coached in answering (and evading) reporters' questions to modest pamphlets containing guidelines for dealing with reporters. In the category of the elaborate seminar, experts work with seminar members to teach them interviewing skills. In these sessions, videotaped mock interviews often are used to help teach public figures how to present themselves as authoritative, candid, and likeable. Probably more common are the pamphlets that organizations publish to tell employees what the firm's public-relations office is prepared to do to assist the employee in having a successful interview and to coach employees who may unexpectedly be called upon to do media interviews. One university news service explains, "You have the stories. We help you to become storytellers." A media guide issued by the news service advises the individual called by a reporter to "take control; don't answer questions until you're ready," to write down the reporter's name, affiliation, and phone number, to find out the subject of the story, the deadline, and the role the reporter expects of the source before agreeing to the interview. To prepare, the interviewee is advised to use the interview to "tell your story," to remember the public is the audience, to limit the number of points to be made, to keep language simple and avoid jargon, to anticipate questions and prepare short, concise answers, to collect material that will help the reporter understand the story, and to rehearse with someone trusted. The interviewee should tape the interview and review it afterward, then call the reporter to correct any misstatements or confusing communication. Rather than waiting for the reporter to ask the "right" question, this news service suggests that the interviewee "make your main point early and often." Other advice to interviewees: Don't evade, lie, or answer questions that are unclear; don't comment off the record. If the story that emerges contains errors, call the reporter to correct the errors so mistakes will not be repeated in subsequent stories.[26]

MASS-COMMUNICATION INTERVIEWS

Group Interviews

Up to this point in the chapter, only two-person interviews have been discussed. However, group interviewing also is prevalent in mass-communication research and in the mass-communication industries. One form of group interview is known as the focus group. In focus groups, an interviewer meets with a small group of interviewees who have agreed to discuss a topic or a product. The interviewer has a schedule of questions and presents these to the interviewees, probing for details and encouraging those in the group to respond to other interviewees' comments. Subjects for discussion arise from the group, as well as from the interviewer. A special strength of the focus group is its capacity to raise issues and to enlarge the scope of the discussion. In academic research, for example, focus group interviews may precede survey research, assisting those doing the study by identifying important questions and issues that might have been neglected otherwise. Also, focus group participants may correct researchers' misinformation and may suggest appropriate sets of responses to be offered in closed survey questions. Focus group interviews are prominent in advertising and marketing research and less frequently used in news and public-relations work. Potential members of focus groups can range from grade schoolers, gathered to taste and judge a new snack, to retired people who discuss the services of travel agencies.

The moderator of a focus group lets the discussion range while it is moving productively and producing useful comment. Tasks include making certain that main points are covered, being receptive to new points that arise, and making sure that each respondent has a chance to talk. The moderator also has the task, at the outset of the discussion, of telling the group how the interview works, of setting up recording equipment and explaining its use to members, and of collecting any permissions that are required of the participants. Focus-group sessions typically are tape-recorded and transcribed for ease of later analysis. Group members are told the method of recording and the subsequent use of their comments. Paying participants a small sum is a typical practice.

The advertising industry makes frequent use of focus-group interviewing. As in the example mentioned earlier, a travel firm's ad agency may wish to learn what services are especially appreciated by retirement-age people, who constitute a sizable proportion of those who travel and who use travel agencies. For this purpose, interviewees may be sought from among those who are retired, have traveled recently, and are in a particular income bracket. The ideas gleaned from the focus-group discussion may be used as the basis for an advertising campaign directed at the retired. An intermediate step might be using the discussion points as the basis for a survey that would provide numerical data on the major questions.

Group interviewing is used in news reporting also. For news work, where direct quotes generally are required, group interviewing presents some difficulties. Even if the session is tape-recorded, identifying the voices accurately is difficult. Under some circumstances, however, group interviewing has advantages. The news reporter may find that individuals are unwilling to be interviewed for attribution but are willing to have their stories told as a part of the group's story. For a story on alcoholism, members of Alcoholics Anonymous may relate their experiences to one another while the reporter listens. Employees of an adoption agency who counsel groups of unmarried mothers or adopting parents might permit a group interview, on the condition that individuals' names not be used. Temporary residents of shelters for battered women may tell their stories in a group, with similar restrictions on publication of their identities.

Having permission to tape-record the discussion is important in such group interviews, although the recording generally is flawed by extraneous sounds and inaudible voices. As a precaution against the flaws in the tape, the reporter usually takes as many notes as possible. Further, the reporter may, at the end of the session, pass around paper and a pencil, requesting names and telephone numbers to be called for later clarifications and as a check on accuracy. While this may seem to violate the "anonymity" provision, group members may have come to trust the reporter during the meeting, and some may be willing to be called so their comments can be clarified or verified before the story is written. In addition, telephone calls may elicit other important information that did not emerge during the group interview.

Investigative Interviews

Multiple interviews are the rule for investigative journalism. In addition to extensive use of records and documents, investigative journalists try to run down all relevant leads and double- or triple-check all facts. Good investigative reporters are characterized by their excellent information-finding skills and their tireless checking of often dull material. Interviews often lead to additional sources that must be checked out. The investigative report perhaps provides the widest range of interviewees of any type of reporting. Brian Brooks and his colleagues cite the following potential interviewees for a story on under-the-table political contributions: enemies, friends, losers, victims, experts, police, and people in trouble.[27] Neighbors, co-workers, government officials, waiters and bartenders, and relatives of those involved or affected by the story also are potential sources.

Experienced investigators advise the same detached stance that is standard for other interviews. Clark Mollenhoff, one of the most successful investigative reporters, puts it this way:

> Although the proper interviewing technique will vary with the circumstances, it is usually best to assume a simple inquisitive stand that seeks fact and explanation while avoiding personal antagonism. It may occasionally be wise strategy to play ignorant, but it is never an advantage to BE ignorant about the facts, the specific terminology, or the relevant law when interviewing a subject. There is no excuse in crucial interviews for failing to examine in advance all relevant public records and the public testimony and documents that may be related to the subject to be discussed.[28]

Reporters Judith Bolch and Kay Miller agree on the need for an objective stance and self-control for investigative interviews. They advise:

> Maintaining an objective stance is necessary not only when the reporter dislikes his subject. The same nonpartisan position should be evident when interviewing a person you admire about a topic you support. Just as you don't argue with someone whose position you oppose, neither do you use the interview to applaud someone whose cause you favor. In the story, the facts can speak for themselves. This does not mean that you should be cold or unsympathetic to the interviewee's circumstances. Indeed, some very successful investigative reporters advocate a strong display of understanding for the subject's field and problems. Just remember not to use the interview as a forum to promote your own opinions.[29]

Since investigative reporting implies the revelation of what is hidden because it is illegal, unethical, or unsavory, interviewees may agree to be interviewed only on an "off-the-record," or "deep-background," basis. Reporters, of course, want to work with all interview and document materials on the record. When it is clear that the interview cannot be conducted on that basis, reporters have a number of choices. One is to tell the potential interviewee that other sources who will go on the record will be sought. Another is to negotiate with the source and to arrive at a clear understanding of what is to be used for direct quotation, what may appear in paraphrase form, and what can be used in an unattributed statement for which the reporter must take responsibility. Obviously, the negotiation with the source benefits the reporter in many instances. The source, asking for an off-the-record interview perhaps did not understand that "off" means that neither the information from the interview nor any "leads" from it are to be developed. In any case, before the interview begins, both participants should have a precise understanding of the terms under which it is being conducted. Journalists wisely avoid off-the-record interviews. The journalist is at risk that the source will use the occasion to tell lies or manipulate the coverage.

In most news organizations, reporters work under policy guidelines that the organization has established for off-the-record material. Whenever questions about interview or publication propriety arise, reporters are expected to check out the question with editors before agreeing to special limitations on the interview.

News Conferences

News conferences range in style and size from the televised presidential news conferences, with hundreds of reporters assembled, to informal sessions, with one source and a handful of questioners. The news conference undoubtedly is the journalist's least-favorite method of news gathering. From the viewpoint of the source, the news conference is a timesaving convention. But from the reporter's perspective, there is little to recommend it. If the news conference is televised, reporters for newspapers find that their questions and the answers to them have been broadcast on television before they can write their own stories. Follow-up and clarification questions are difficult at large news conferences. Reporters who have prepared particularly well often do not reap the benefits of their preparation. They may not have a chance to ask their questions, and, if they do, they reveal the lines of their inquiry to competitors.

Despite the limitations of news conferences, they continue to be a standard method that busy or celebrated people use for giving information to the media. Behind the scenes at press conferences, the work of public-relations staff members is critical. For many conferences, public-relations staff have prepared handouts that give the essential information about the announcements to be made that day. In these packets, reporters find the basics related to the announcement—names, titles, dates, places, and decisions—that free them to ask more substantial and interpretive questions than they otherwise would be able to ask. From the viewpoint of the public-relations staff, these information packets are designed to promote accuracy in the news reports that follow the conference.

Grant Winter, a television journalist, emphasized the particular needs of the broadcasting industry in his advice to public-relations people on how to improve broadcast-news conferences. Planning for broadcast equipment, including phone jacks, lights, microphones, tripods, and parking spaces for trucks is part of the public-relations specialist's responsibility. Handouts recommended by this reporter include news releases, biographies of speakers, texts of speeches, and visuals such as charts. Winter also asks that a speaker be available for separate one-on-one interviews following the news conference and that the public-relations office be prepared throughout the remainder of the day for follow-up questions by telephone. He points out that without opportunity to do a check for accuracy before broadcasting, a story can be scrapped rather than used on air.[30]

Questions in the news conference should be short. Reporters who seem to be making speeches instead of asking questions draw the anger of their colleagues. So do the unprepared, whose questions do not advance the topic but require the source to repeat information that the well-informed reporters have already acquired. Well-prepared and attentive listeners are in the best position to present important follow-up questions during the news conference.

Verbatim Interviews

In the verbatim interview, the dialogue of the interview is reproduced for the reader. The interviewer's question is printed as it was asked, followed by the response. The technique is used principally in magazines, usually with a source who is very newsworthy or who is expert on a current topic. For example, such interviews in *Newsweek, Omni, U.S. News & World Report*, and *Playboy* usually present the views of political figures, celebrities, or experts on a topic of controversy.

The interview itself is preceded by a short introduction that establishes the context of the interview and gives background material on the interviewer and the topic.

Survey Interviews

Survey interviews are widely used in many facets of mass-communication work. Advertising and public-relations professionals made extensive use of survey research earlier than news workers did. In the 1960s, Philip Meyer led the way for journalists' use of surveys in his studies of Detroit residents' views of the crisis in race relations. Subsequently, he was influential in persuading news organizations that they could effectively use social-science methods to improve the information in news reports. In his book *Precision Journalism*, Meyer proposed a plan for journalists' use of scientific methods in reporting.[31] The same methods had been in use for decades in other organizations that provide media content—for example, national polling organizations, such as Gallup, that serve individual metropolitan, state, or regional clients.

Survey interviews both differ from and resemble other types of interviews in a variety of ways. In scientific interviewing, the interviewees are selected according to principles of tested sampling procedures. The interviewers are trained to work from identical interview forms. Most often, the questions are structured so that the answers can be analyzed statistically. Standards for interviewers are similar in survey research and in other, less formal methods, however. All the cautions about advance preparation, careful use of language and nonverbal communication, and self-control apply.

Much mass-communication survey research is done by the firm needing the information. However, some is commissioned by the media and executed by research firms that specialize in particular types of research. In addition, media organizations subscribe to the reports issued regularly by other research organizations. For example, a newspaper may use survey research to develop material for news reports and may regularly publish the Gallup opinion columns, but may commission an independent firm to do its readership or marketing studies. (The use of polls and surveys is discussed in detail in Chapter 8.)

LISTENING TO AND RECORDING INTERVIEWS

In many circumstances, we think of listening as a passive and perhaps even restful activity. But effective listening during interviews is an active and even exhausting activity. Great concentration is required to listen efficiently and attentively, while using another part of the brain to keep track of the overall course of the interview and to keep the agenda of questions in mind. Research suggests that listening is a highly complex task and that few people are trained to listen. A typical student may have a dozen years' instruction in reading and writing but no formal training in listening, despite the fact that typical adults use about 45 percent of their daily communication time in listening, 30 percent in speaking, 15 percent in reading, and 10 percent in writing.[32] Professional communicators may spend even more of their typical day's time in listening when they interview extensively. They quickly learn that the demands of concentration and analytical listening can be exhausting, far more tiring than using reference works in the library, for example. For that reason, they try to avoid scheduling more interviews in a day than they can complete without making errors that arise from fatigue.

Interview error arises from inefficient listening habits, as well as from fatigue and such other factors as noise and distracting environments. In his early studies on students as listeners, communication researcher Ralph Nichols learned that students operate at only 25 percent of their potential listening efficiency.[33] From these studies, Nichols developed guides to effective listening. Some of his points pertain well to listening in interviews:

1. Avoid overstimulation: do not get too excited about what the respondent seems to be saying until comprehension of the point is complete.
2. Listen for central ideas and be able to discriminate between fact and principle, idea and example, evidence and argument.
3. Give the speaker conscious attention, indicating by eye contact, posture, and facial expression that you are attentive, all of which help the interviewee to express himself or herself clearly.
4. Resist distractions, either by improving the physical conditions or by concentrating effectively.
5. Have several systems of note taking and adapt to the speaking style of the interviewee.

Interviewers have some advantage over listeners to speeches or lectures. They can learn to recognize when listening has lapsed or become inefficient and can ask to have something repeated or spelled out. Indeed, active listeners habitually pay attention to their own listening efficiency and try, in an interview, to overcome faults.

The "listening attitude," in which the listener is open to hearing the speaker's ideas, contrasts with the "going through the motions" attitude of some interviewers, according to communication researchers George M. Killenberg and Rob Anderson. Using listening rules is effective only when the interviewer shows an attitude of genuine interest in the ideas of the speaker, they write. Killenberg and Anderson examine three kinds of journalistic listening: listening for new information, listening in a discriminative style to discern differences between statements and positions, listening for personality aspects of the interviewee. All three may be taking place simultaneously during an interview, of course, but one may be dominant in particular kinds of interviews. Informational listening involves getting a clear record of factual material, checking perceptions about that material, and learning the interviewee's central ideas and the style in which they are expressed. Discriminative listening is important in interviews in which discrepancies in information or interpretation are being explored. The authors suggest that interviewers adopt a style of "sensitive skepticism," as contrasted with cynicism, avoid arguing with the interviewee, be alert to the interviewee's reasoning fallacies, identify one's own personal biases and how they could affect effective listening, and be on guard against becoming bored with what seems on the surface to be the "same old stuff" on a particular subject. For "personality" listening, which takes place when interviewing well-known or celebrated people, the authors suggest that interviewers avoid premature judgment about the interviewee's character or intelligence, focus on supporting the individual's willingness to tell of personal experiences, and on nonverbal cues given in the interview.[34]

In some fashion, all interviews are recorded. A few—but very few—interviewers claim to record interviews in their memories. They claim to have such excellent and complete recall that they do not need notebooks and tape recorders. But by far, the vast majority of interviewers use notebooks and tape recorders, as the occasion requires. Broadcasting interviewers, of course, record their interviews and make notes that help them decide what to select for the broadcast itself. Notes also help the reporters and editors review the context of film clips or sound bites that are part of the broadcast.

For many interviewers, the tape recorder is standard equipment. For both personal and telephone interviews, interviewers ask the source's permission to record. Secretly recording a conversation is considered unethical, and under some circumstances in some states, it is illegal. When recording equipment was a novelty, interviewees feared it and often resisted being recorded. Today, however, recording equipment of all sorts is commonplace. Many interviewees have tape-recorded family history or have made videotapes of family weddings. Familiarity with recording techniques has demystified the operation. Interviewers confidently request permission to record, and permission usually is granted.

Most interviewers use recorders in conjunction with note taking. This procedure is followed for a number of reasons: Recorders sometimes fail; batteries go dead; tapes become snarled; extraneous noises obliterate some of the questions and answers. As a precaution against battery failure and tape snarls, interviewers carry spare equipment. But valuable interview time is lost when equipment fails, and interviewers frequently take notes rather than tinker with balky equipment. Even when the recording equipment works perfectly, recorded interviews present some disadvantages. One is the time needed to review the tape and to select material from it. Experts advise interviewers to use a tape recorder with a counter so they can take note of the number at which various parts of the interview can be located. For example, in an interview with an expert on diet and heart disease, the interviewer might keep a record that "question on cholesterol begins at 294" and thus save the time needed to search the tape when seeking a particular answer. Or, a reporter might record the numbers at which particularly clear and interesting quote material is located—for example, "quote on R's efficiency at 133."

Typically, interviewers select relevant portions of the taped material, relying on it to confirm or check their notes. In some circumstances, however, the interview may be fully transcribed. Among these are investigative interviews, especially when publication of material may result in lawsuits or in charges that the report misquoted or misrepresented a person. Often publication of such a news story is delayed while a verbatim transcript is produced and examined by editors and legal staff. The result may be a news story, accompanied by a full transcript of the interview or by selected questions and answers from the transcript. Another kind of transcription is made by an interpretive reporting specialist, who records numerous in-depth interviews when working on a major story. He personally transcribes these interviews into his own computer files. In doing so, he contends, information that would have escaped his attention or seemed unimportant during the interviews often proves to be highly significant when heard while listening closely to a tape or reading a transcript. However, today, for most mass-communication purposes, transcription is considered too time-consuming and expensive.

For research purposes, transcribed interviews play an increasingly important role. Examples of studies in which extended interviews by academic researchers with media practitioners as interviewees include a study by communication researchers Jay G. Blumler and Carolyn Martin Spicer employing interviews with more than 150 writers, producers, and others on the creative staffs of television comedy and drama programs.[35] James S. Ettema and Theodore L. Glasser, communication researchers, also used transcribed in-depth interviews in their study of prize-winning reporters who discussed evidence and ethical issues in their stories.[36]

Even if the interview is not transcribed or listened to in its entirety, the taped version offers several advantages. If dispute arises over what was said, the tape offers evidence that can be conclusive. For example, one news reporter had preceded his interviews with substantial research and had traveled throughout the newspaper's circulation area interviewing officials about a controversial problem. After his long series of articles started appearing, the officials called to object that they had been misquoted. Although they had agreed to the taped interviews, the pressure on them was so intense that they nevertheless denied their own words. The reporter had retained all tapes of the interviews and had notes detailing which official appeared at which place on each tape. He used the tapes to convince his editors of the accuracy of his work.

Taped interviews also help the interviewer to get exact quotations that reflect the style of the speaker and the flavor of the interview. This is a mixed advantage. Even excellent speakers and conversationalists use rambling sentences and snarled syntax. Strict interpretation of the exact quotation rule often leaves communicators with no directly quotable material. The tape, however, provides an excellent basis for solid paraphrase and for quotable fragments of sentences. A further advantage in using the tape recorder for interviews lies in its educational value. Interviewers can analyze their performances in the interviews, noting those techniques that were effective and those that should not be repeated in subsequent interviews.

For much interviewing, the taped interview is the backup to the version in the notebook. Taking accurate and full notes is one of the greatest challenges to interviewers. Even after years of practice, many interviewers wish for better note-taking skills. Using shorthand is recommended even by interviewers who do not know a formal system. Those who are skilled in one of the established shorthand systems can record interview answers with ease. If they take notes excessively, however, they face the same time-consuming transcription problems associated with taped answers. Whatever system is used, interviewers constantly try to refine it for speed and accuracy.

Respondents recognize when interview notes are being made, but the skilled interviewer does not allow the speaker to be distracted by the process. In telephone interviews, if the interviewer has a computer terminal, the notes can be made as the interview proceeds. The almost soundless clicking of the keyboard generally can be heard on the other end of the line but is far less distracting than a typewriter. In personal interviews, the interviewer tries to sit facing the interviewee and may prop the notes on the arm of the chair or against a crossed leg. If the notebook rests on a table at which both participants are seated, the interviewee may become curious about what the interviewer is putting into the notes. Some interviewees even try to read the notes as they are being made or ask what is being written. To avoid development of such curiosity, interviewers try to keep their notebooks inconspicuous. Another method of keeping respondents' eyes off the notebook is to maintain steady eye contact with the interviewee. With practice, interviewers can learn to write without looking at their notes. Once steady eye contact is established, the focus is off the notes. To keep from getting lost on the notebook page, the writer can place the thumb of the hand holding the notebook along the margin where the next line of notes is to be made.

As noted earlier, the interviewer should not give cues about what is valued in the interview. The interviewer can avoid this error by taking notes on all answers. This practice not only contributes to completeness and helps establish the context of the interviewee's answers, but also avoids giving cues that some of the interviewee's ideas are not worth writing down.

If interviewees are distracted by any of the procedures of recording and making notes, it is considerate to explain the process and answer questions that arise. Some interviewees, for example, worry about what use is made of a recorded interview. They can be assured that once the communicator's work with the tape is finished, the tape is erased and used in subsequent interviews. If the tapes routinely are saved until any controversy about the accuracy of the material is resolved, the interviewee can be informed of that.

Once the main part of the interview is concluded, some time is devoted to reviewing the notes with the interviewee. At this time, all factual items—times, dates, places, costs, statistics, proper names—are rechecked. Main ideas also are repeated to the interviewee as a check on important points that may be used in a news story, an advertising campaign, or a public-relations release.

As soon as possible after the interview—before driving away in a car or during a bus ride back to the office—the interviewer once again reviews the notes and adds material or observations that are missing. Memory fades quickly, so the earliest opportunity is taken to write down ideas or observations that complete the picture or help to establish significance or context.

LINKS TO THE SEARCH STRATEGY

In this step of the search strategy, the communicator uses interviews to gain essential information that is not available through other methods. The earlier search-strategy steps prepare the interviewer to select appropriate sources and to develop questions for interviews that will generate new information.

Interviews are critical steps in the search strategy. For some essential material, interviews are the only source. Further, they provide a check on the accuracy, completeness, recency, and perspective of information located through other sources. Frequently, they alert the communicator to gaps in the information gathered in earlier steps in the search strategy. A stimulating interview fosters the communicator's creativity. An interview with ordinary people helps the communicator stay in touch with audience needs. Interviews with experts give authority and confidence to the message. Interviews are fraught with problems of accuracy and reliability, as are other information sources. Interviewers can be alert to the danger points in interviewing and take measures to overcome the hazards. They can check interview material against other sources—from institutions, libraries, data bases, and other interviews. Good interviewers practice a healthy skepticism about information from all sources, including interviews.

Chapter 8 examines a particular type of interview method—the survey. This type of scientific data-collection interview has unique characteristics, advantages, and disadvantages for communicators.

NOTES

1. Eugene J. Webb and Jerry R. Salancik, "The Interview; Or the Only Wheel in Town," *Journalism Monographs*, November 1966, 1.
2. J. Edward Hulett, Jr., "A Symbolic Interactionist Model of Human Communication," *AV Communication Review* 14 (Spring 1966): 18–19.
3. John Jamison, as quoted in Robert U. Brown, "Shop Talk," *Editor & Publisher*, 28 May 1977, 56.
4. Brown, "Shop Talk."
5. Edward T. Hall, *The Hidden Dimension* (New York: Doubleday [Anchor Books], 1966), 110–120.
6. Raymond L. Gorden, *Interviewing: Strategy, Techniques and Tactics*, 3d ed. (Homewood, Ill.: Dorsey Press, 1980), 316.
7. Gorden, *Interviewing*, 320.
8. John Madge, *The Tools of Social Science* (Garden City, N.Y.: Doubleday [Anchor Books], 1965), 155.
9. Jane Delano Brown, Carl Bybee, Stanley Weardon, and Dulcie Murdock Straughan, "Invisible Power: Newspaper News Sources and the Limits of Diversity," *Journalism Quarterly* 64 (1987): 45–54; Jeff Cohen, "ABC's 'Nightline' Serves as a Soapbox for Conservative Elite," originally published in *Newsday*, reprinted in *Star Tribune*, 28 February 1989, 11A; Marc Cooper and Lawrence C. Soley, "All the Right Sources," *Mother Jones*, February–March, 1990, 20–27, 45–48; Barbara Garmarekian, "In Pursuit of the Clever Quotemaster," *New York Times*, 12 May 1989, 10Y; Charles Rothfeld, "On Legal Pundits and How They Got that Way," *New York Times*, 4 May 1990, 10B; D. Charles Whitney, Marilyn Fritzler, Steven Jones, Sharon Mazzarella, and Lana Rakow, "Geographic and Source Biases in Network Television News 1982–1984," *Journal of Broadcasting and Electronic Media* 33 (1989): 159–174.
10. Lawrence C. Soley, "The News Shapers," University of Minnesota, mimeo, 1989, 42–43.
11. Gorden, *Interviewing*, 91–104.
12. Gorden, *Interviewing*, 109–116.
13. Eleanor E. Maccoby and Nathan Maccoby, "The Interview: A Tool of Social Science," in Gardner Lindzey, ed., *Handbook of Social Psychology*, vol. 1 (Reading, Mass.: Addison-Wesley, 1954), 449–487.
14. Arlene Rossen Cardozo, "Application of Jurgen Habermas' Ideal Speech Situation to the Journalistic Interview in the U.S." (Ph.D. diss., University of Minnesota, 1990), 107–109.
15. Ron Givens, "Talking People into Talking," *Newsweek*, 17 July 1989, 44, 46.
16. Christopher Hitchens, "BLABSCAM: TV's Rigged Political Talk Shows," *Harper's*, March 1987, 75–76.
17. Webb and Salancik, "The Interview," 11.

18. Gary C. Lawrence and David L. Grey, "Subjective Inaccuracies in Local News Reporting," *Journalism Quarterly* 46 (Winter 1969): 755.
19. Stuart A. Rice, "Contagious Bias in the Interview: A Methodological Note," *American Journal of Sociology* 35 (1929): 420–423.
20. Howard Schuman and Jean M. Converse, "The Effects of Black and White Interviewers on Black Responses in 1968," *Public Opinion Quarterly* 35 (Spring 1971): 45–68; Shirley Hatchett and Howard Schuman, "White Respondents and Race-of-Interviewer Effects," *Public Opinion Quarterly* 39 (Winter 1975): 523–528.
21. Mitchell V. Charnley and Blair Charnley, *Reporting*, 4th ed. (New York: Holt, Rinehart and Winston, 1979), 272.
22. Anthony Marro, "When the Government Tells Lies," *Columbia Journalism Review*, March–April, 1985, 29–41.
23. Susan P. Shapiro, "Caution! This Paper Has Not Been Fact Checked! A Study of Fact Checking in American Magazines," undated working paper published by the Gannett Center for Media Studies, Columbia University, New York.
24. Steve Weinberg, "So What's Wrong with Pre-publication Review?" *The Quill*, May 1990, 26–28.
25. George P. Kennedy, "What? Show the Story to a Source—In Advance?" *presstime*, March 1986, 40–41.
26. *Media Guide*, University Relations, University of Minnesota, Minneapolis, 1991.
27. Brian S. Brooks, George Kennedy, Daryl R. Moen, and Don Ranly, *News Reporting and Writing* (New York: St. Martin's Press, 1980), 394–395.
28. Clark R. Mollenhoff, *Investigative Reporting* (New York: Macmillan, 1981), 18.
29. Judith Bolch and Kay Miller, *Investigative and In-Depth Reporting* (New York: Hastings House, 1978), 61.
30. Grant Winter, "Improving Broadcast News Conferences," *Public Relations Journal*, July 1990, 25–26.
31. Philip Meyer, *Precision Journalism* (Bloomington: Indiana University Press, 1971).
32. J. Vernon Jensen, *Perspectives on Oral Communication* (Boston: Holbrook Press, 1970), 113.
33. Ralph G. Nichols, "Do We Know How to Listen? Practical Helps in a Modern Age," *Speech Teacher* 10 (March 1961): 156.
34. George M. Killenberg and Rob Anderson, *Before the Story: Interviewing and Communication Skills for Journalists* (New York: St. Martin's Press, 1989), 95–117.
35. Jay G. Blumler and Carolyn Martin Spicer, "Prospects for Creativity in the New Television Marketplace: Evidence from the Program-Makers," *Journal of Communication* 40 (Autumn 1990): 78–101.
36. James S. Ettema and Theodore L. Glasser, "Narrative Form and Moral Force: The Realization of Innocence and Guilt through Investigative Journalism," *Journal of Communication* 38 (Summer 1988): 8–26.

8

Using Polls and Surveys

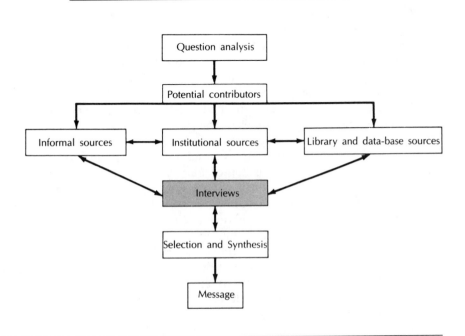

Levi Strauss & Company has learned that an alarm clock, a stereo, and jeans are the three most important items that college students say they need for campus living. The market research firm of Yankelovich Clancy Shulman has found that 66 percent of people who like to shop for clothes still find the experience frustrating and time-consuming. A *New York Times*/CBS News poll finds that the vast majority of those families with children who were polled (80 percent) eat dinner together on a typical weeknight, debunking the stereotype of the modern, frenzied family. A survey of office workers' attitudes finds that only 39 percent of workers think their organization's management meets standards of honesty and ethical behavior when dealing with employees. Teenage girls, according to a Rand Youth Poll, have $73.95 a week to spend, and one third of that amount is spent on clothes.

All these tidbits of information were generated by the use of a poll or survey. Whether for a public-relations study, a marketing plan, a news story, or an advertising campaign, information from polls and surveys plays an important role in the repertoire of sources for communicators.

THE POLL AND THE SURVEY

Surveys or polls measure a number of variables for a sample of a population at one period of time. Several words in this definition need clarification because they are used with more precision than in everyday usage. For instance, a *variable* is a concept that can be measured and that changes. Several common variables are opinions, attitudes, behavior, knowledge, or intentions, all of which can be measured by a well-constructed survey questionnaire. A sample of any group is a small, representative group that can be used as a measure of the larger group. Unless a pollster wishes to conduct a census (that is, poll every member of the group), a sample is the appropriate group to which the survey questions can be addressed. The *population* is the group of people to which the survey results can be applied, or generalized. This is the group that the pollster or survey researcher is trying to learn something about. A common error is to assume that *population* always refers to the entire population of the United States. That may sometimes be the group the pollsters wish to learn about, but not always. The population may be all adults of voting age in the state of Vermont. Or, it may be all women from 18 to 35 years of age with annual incomes of $15,000 or more. Or, it may be all trial lawyers in the Eighth Circuit. Or, it may be all college students who own motorcycles. In other words, the population may be defined in whatever way accurately describes the group of people the researchers want to study and the group from which the sample is drawn.

The final major element in the survey definition is the notion of time. This refers to the fact that results of any survey or poll are correct for only the time during which the survey or poll was taken. The clichéd but accurate analogy is that a poll or survey takes a "snapshot" of attitudes or opinions at one point in time. The results cannot predict future attitudes, behaviors, intentions, or characteristics. Events may intrude that cause members of the population to change their minds, thus making the survey results invalid as a predictor of future attitudes, behavior, or intentions. This idea will be further explored later in the chapter.

THE SEARCH STRATEGY AND THE POLL
OR SURVEY

The search-strategy process incorporates the poll or survey at many points. At the question-analysis stage, the communicator may determine that a major piece of required information is public-opinion data or results from a poll of some kind, thus requiring a particular kind of search at later stages. Communicators may take informal, or straw, polls at the initial stage of information gathering for a topic. By talking to friends, associates, or people on the street about a new project, communicators may gather informal impressions that can later be examined in a more formal manner. Institutions produce, sponsor, and use polls and surveys for many reasons, and the communicator can tap into these institutional sources for access to poll data. Libraries and data bases store both the reports and documents produced as a result of survey work and the tools to help the communicator locate polls done by many different organizations. Surveys, at least the kind that communicators are interested in, are based on interviews. Thus the interview step of the search strategy figures prominently in the production of poll and survey information. Finally, the information from polls and surveys must undergo very stringent evaluation and analysis because the data must be reliably produced in order for the communicator to use the information confidently. So the search-strategy process includes elements of poll and survey information at each step.

USES OF POLLS AND SURVEYS

Communicators encounter four common uses of poll and survey information. Surveys help to:

1. Provide editorial and news content for the news media;
2. Form the basis of marketing or advertising research;
3. Measure public opinion for public-relations, governmental, or political uses; and
4. Build social-science theory.

Earl Babbie, in *The Practice of Social Research*, describes surveys in this way:

> Surveys may be used for descriptive, explanatory, and exploratory purposes. They are chiefly used in studies that have individual people as the units of analysis. . . . Survey research is probably the best method available to the social scientist interested in collecting original data for describing a population too large to observe directly.[1]

Communicators rely on surveys and polls for a variety of information. For instance, advertising and marketing professionals regularly use surveys to:

1. Learn about consumer behavior;
2. Gauge demand for new or existing products and services;
3. Define demographic and psychographic characteristics of various groups of consumers; and
4. Test new advertising or marketing campaigns.

News professionals use surveys and polls to:

1. Learn about their communities;
2. Provide information about voter preferences during election campaigns;
3. Learn how to make their news products more appealing to the public; and
4. Offer interesting and unusual insights on the events that affect society.

Public-relations specialists use polls and surveys to:

1. Gauge public opinion about the companies, industries, or groups they represent;
2. Learn how new approaches or trends may affect the public perception of clients; and
3. Plan methods of communicating about client interests in an effective way.

Philip Meyer, in *Precision Journalism*, identifies seven kinds of information that a survey or poll can collect:

1. Opinions
2. Attitudes
3. Changes in attitudes
4. Personality
5. Knowledge
6. Behavior
7. Background variables.[2]

Meyer's approach is decidedly journalistic, but the kinds of information he refers to can be of equal value to communicators in advertising or public relations. Meyer also includes a list of demographic variables that are of interest to survey researchers. Characteristics such as religion, race, sex, education, income, and occupational status can be important in understanding how different groups respond to survey or poll questions.

Survey research is especially useful for studying problems in realistic settings, rather than in a laboratory. The cost of surveys is reasonable considering the amount of information they provide. Further cost control is possible by choosing among the three major methods of gathering survey data: mail, telephone interview, and personal interview. These three methods will be discussed in greater detail later in the chapter. Surveys allow a large amount of data to be collected with relative ease from a variety of people. Many variables can be examined (demographic or lifestyle variables, attitudes, behavior, intentions), and statistical methods help to analyze the data that are collected. Because many reputable organizations conduct surveys, much information to help the communicator may already exist, thus reducing the need to do a survey from scratch. The use of surveys and polls in mass communication is increasing as the reliability and sophistication of polling methods improves. However, some major questions must be answered when the communicator considers using information from a poll or survey.

Organizations that Conduct Polls and Surveys

A major question that must be asked before using information from a poll or survey is, "Who sponsored this survey?" Many organizations, public and private, conduct surveys. Some—such as Gallup, Roper, and Harris—are professional polling organizations that have large staffs and budgets and conduct generally reputable polls. Besides these familiar professional polling companies, there are a huge number of independent polling organizations that offer their services to various constituents. For instance, an organization called Teenage Research Unlimited does syndicated studies at six-month intervals to monitor teen buying habits, media preferences, and life styles. The Rand Youth Poll is a source of similar information, conducted by the Youth Research Institute. Every large metropolitan area has survey-research firms that conduct polls and surveys on contract bases. Scanning the Yellow Pages directories in large cities will reveal the abundance of such firms. These professional polling organizations run the full range—from top notch and reliable to fly-by-night and very unreliable.

Other survey-research organizations are affiliated with educational institutions. The Survey Research Center (SRC) is a part of the Institute for Social Research at the University of Michigan. The SRC is well known for its thorough and lengthy survey-research studies. The National Opinion Research Center at the University of Chicago was the first national survey-research organization for social research in the public interest. Most major public research universities have units that conduct surveys and polls both to use within the institution and to meet social research needs. For instance, the Center for Urban and Regional Affairs at the University of Minnesota sponsored a survey of senior citizens who left the state for warmer climates during the winter and learned that those 83,000 "snowbirds" who leave for a median of eight weeks a year spend $150 million outside the state. This provides important information for state planners and economic decision makers. The American Council on Education has cosponsored, with the University of California at Los Angeles an annual national survey of first-year college students to learn about incoming students' career interests, values, attitudes, and intentions. The group has data for a 25-year period, allowing for comparisons across a generation of college students.

Many surveys and polls are conducted by governmental agencies at all levels. The vast decennial census is a form of survey that is used to apportion seats in the House of Representatives and to help the federal government set social policy.[3] The information gathered from the census is of major importance in planning for the needs of the nation. Missing just one person in the 1990 census meant a loss of up to $1,500 annually in government funding to the community where that person lived. At least $38 billion is allocated by federal, state, and local governments each year based on census data. In fact, so much rides on the decennial census figures that in 1988, anticipating problems with the 1990 census, New York, Chicago, and other urban areas filed a joint lawsuit charging that Census Bureau methods undercount major metropolitan community populations. The lawsuit, still being fought in 1992, sought to force the bureau to adjust its figures based on a post–1990 follow-up survey.

In addition to these challenges, the 1990 census was the first conducted in the era of desktop and laptop computers. Along with the traditional paper reports, 1990 census data were released on microfiche, computer tapes, floppy disks, and CD-ROM (compact disk–read only memory). Thousands of private marketing and research firms, media organizations, advertisers, government, and public utility agencies, public interest groups, and countless others can use the census data to learn about population shifts, life styles, health and welfare of groups within society, travel and work patterns, housing characteristics, and a myriad of other descriptive details about life in the United States. An enormous multimillion-dollar information industry has evolved around the sorting, analysis, packaging, programming, customizing, and combining of census data and information culled from thousands of such sources as lists of car purchasers, magazine subscribers, and change-of-address filings.

The Census Bureau conducts other regular surveys. For instance, the Census Bureau surveys 60,000 households each month to collect employment and unemployment data for the Bureau of Labor Statistics in the Current Population Survey (CPS). The CPS also includes some questions asked only once a year. In October, the CPS asks about demographic characteristics of students in the household; in March it asks about household income and other household characteristics. The Census Bureau also conducts the ongoing Consumer Expenditure Survey, the main purpose of which is to update prices for the market basket of goods used to calculate the Consumer Price Index. The American Housing Survey, conducted by the Census Bureau every other year for the federal Department of Housing and Urban Development, surveys 50,000 households to collect structural and financial information about housing units, as well as demographic data about the people who live in those units.

Other agencies and levels of government also conduct polls and surveys, as part of their information-gathering routine and to monitor changing public attitudes and needs. For instance, the annual Health Interview Survey conducted by the National Center for Health Statistics (part of the United States Department of Health and Human Services) is a principal source of information about the health of Americans. Demographic factors related to illness, injuries, disabilities, the costs and uses of medical services, and similar information are collected from survey respondents. The United States Department of Agriculture conducts a regular survey that asks about food commonly eaten by individuals, the amount per day, and per meal or snack. Governmental agencies are prolific in their generation and use of information based on survey or poll data.

Another major sponsor of polls and surveys is business at all levels. Whether for marketing, advertising, public-relations, or social research reasons, large and small businesses and corporations conduct their own or commission surveys to plan for their corporate futures. A major research firm like Yankelovich Clancy Shulman does a large number of market research and public opinion polls for corporations. They will track customer attitudes toward a client's products, analyze customer data, and define and solve a variety of marketing problems based on survey information. Large corporations may conduct surveys about their products and consumer attitudes for their own, internal proprietary purposes and then repackage and release the information in the form of a public-relations "report to the public." For instance, Chivas Regal, which sells an expensive scotch, called a press conference to release its "Chivas Regal Report on Working Americans: Emerging Values for the 1990s." The commissioned survey included results detailing working Americans' values and attitudes, including the desire to return to a simpler society with less emphasis on material success. Clearly, Chivas commissioned the survey to learn more about the attitudes, values, income, and activities of potential scotch customers, then repackaged the information for presentation to the media. Drawing media attention to Chivas' marketing survey also draws attention to the company's interest in positioning its product in the most favorable spot to appeal to potential customers.

Special interest groups, such as lobbying organizations, political action committees, and associations, also conduct polls or commission professionals to do them. For instance, a Washington advocacy group called Democrats for the 90s commissioned a poll in 1990 to learn more about registered voters' attitudes toward Congress, the president, political concerns, leadership, the economy, and other national issues. The Democratic party used the results to identify areas of Democratic opportunities and weaknesses in planning political strategy for the decade. The Times Mirror Center for the People and the Press conducted a poll during the Persian Gulf War that found strong public backing for both military censorship and for efforts by the press to report what was happening. Many lobbying groups or special interest groups have particular purposes in commissioning a survey—finding support for a particular program or activity, for example—and the resulting data must be even more cautiously studied for signs of bias than is usually the case.

Obviously, politicians and political parties conduct polls, especially around election time but also at other times. The professional pollsters who are hired by politicians or political parties provide vital information about the voting intentions of the electorate, the voters' moods and attitudes toward public policy, and the issues that voters believe are important to society. Pollsters who are identified with one politician or party are also identified with a particular viewpoint, however, and their survey-research methods may tend to be biased in favor of that view. In addition, politicians and political parties conduct extensive private polling during a campaign period. Some of these polls, such as tracking polls, are highly specialized efforts with very high risks because the samples are so small and the voting intentions being tracked are so volatile. These, and other dangers of political polling, will be discussed later in the chapter.

Finally, media organizations conduct polls and surveys. Whether they actually do the survey research themselves or contract with professional organizations for the work, media organizations have abiding interests in polls and surveys as sources of both editorial and marketing information. Indeed, there are a number of media consortia, groups that pool their resources and expertise to conduct polls on a regular basis as a source of news and information. Some of these consortia are CBS News/*New York Times*; Media General/Associated Press; ABC News/*Washington Post*; NBC News/*Wall Street Journal*; and CNN/*USA Today*. These major media organizations conduct their polls using established survey-research standards, and they have the budgets to do reputable jobs. Budgetary concerns contributed to the development of network television's cooperative election-night polling, starting with the 1990 congressional and state elections. Declaring a truce in the networks' traditional election-night competition to be the first to declare the winner in each state's races, the network news departments of ABC, NBC, CBS, and CNN formed a cooperative venture to conduct voter surveys and produce vote projections on election night. Network executives estimated that the venture saved the news departments $9 million a piece during the 1990 elections, with little perceptible effect on the information delivered to viewers.[4]

Many media organizations also have long traditions of conducting statewide polls. For instance, the *Des Moines Register's* Iowa Poll is the oldest continual state poll in the country, having started in 1943. The Iowa Poll reports on four to six surveys conducted annually and allows a glimpse of midwestern attitudes on current issues, and cultural and social values.

In addition to using polls and surveys to provide news content, media organizations conduct market surveys to learn how their audiences feel about the news product—the newspaper, the television operation, the radio station. These studies help the media organizations shape the news product to meet readers' or viewers' needs and demands. The surveys also allow consumers to feel that they have a say in shaping their news outlets because the polls demonstrate that the media organization is soliciting its audience's response.

Advertising and public-relations professionals also conduct polls and surveys as regular parts of their information gathering about consumer and public attitudes, concerns, and demands. These surveys are often proprietary; that is, the data are not available to the public because they reveal information about marketing or advertising strategy, but the ad and public-relations staff can make extensive use of the information. In addition, advertising and public-relations professionals rely heavily on survey data collected by private survey-research firms. Sources such as *Simmons Study of Media and Markets*, an annual compilation of 20,000 survey interviews with consumers conducted by a private firm, are extremely important for advertising purposes.

Where to Locate Poll and Survey Information

Before communicators can evaluate a poll or survey for its appropriateness as an information source, they have to find one. Archives of public opinion data can be located through several computerized data bases, searchable directly by the user. The *Public Opinion Location Library (POLL)* data base, produced by the Roper Center, helps users locate survey results from studies conducted by Gallup, Harris, Roper, the major media organizations (newspapers, news magazines), and others. The Roper Center research library is dedicated exclusively to locating, organizing, and indexing public opinion data. Two other computerized data bases for locating public opinion data are the *Variables* program at the University of Michigan's Inter-University Consortium for Political and Social Research and the *Public Opinion Item Index* of the Institute for Research in Social Science at the University of North Carolina. Published sources of public opinion data include compilations of polling data as well as articles and reports of polls. Magazines such as the *Public Opinion Quarterly, Roper Reports, American Enterprise,* and *American Demographics* regularly carry articles of interest to communicators looking for survey data. Tools such as the *Social Sciences Index, Sociological Abstracts,* the *New York Times Index,* the *TV News Index and Abstracts,* and the *Reader's Guide to Periodical Literature* include references to survey data under subject headings such as "public opinion" or "polls and surveys." Some major reference tools to help identify polls and surveys and some major sources of survey research follow.[5]

Major Polls and Research Firms

1. *ABC News/Washington Post Poll,* 7 West 66th Street, New York, N.Y. 10023: A cooperative venture since February 1981, the *ABC/Washington Post Poll* consortium conducts an average of one major-topic poll per month. It maintains a mailing list for reprints of poll results.
2. *CBS News/New York Times Poll,* CBS News, 524 West 57th Street, New York, N.Y. 10017: Collaborating since 1976, when they began with a series of surveys during the presidential elections, CBS News and the *New York Times* now conduct national telephone surveys covering general political, social, and economic topics. The consortium maintains a mailing list for reprints of poll results.
3. *The Gallup Organization,* 53 Bank Street, Princeton, N.J. 08542: The Gallup Organization has conducted polls since 1935. It began as a political poll, but now includes social and economic issues. The firm also conducts custom research for private clients in the United States and overseas. It does polls for *Newsweek* magazine; the *Gallup Youth Survey* is available through Associated Press; and Gallup poll press releases, done twice a week, are available by subscription through the Los Angeles Times Syndicate.
4. *Louis Harris and Associates,* 630 Fifth Avenue, New York, N.Y. 10111: Louis Harris and Associates was founded in 1956 and conducts public-opinion research surveys on many subjects for many types of

clients. The Information Services Department answers questions about the firm's surveys and sends reprints of news releases. Harris Survey reprints are also available by subscription from Information Services. The Harris archive at the University of North Carolina includes previous poll information.

5. *Los Angeles Times Poll*, Times Mirror Square, Los Angeles, Calif. 90053: Begun in November 1977 to survey the California population, the *Los Angeles Times Poll* conducts national telephone surveys in addition to California state polls. It maintains a mailing list for reprints of poll results.

6. *NORC: A Social Science Research Center*, 1155 East 60th Street, Chicago, Ill. 60637: Established in 1941 as the first national survey research organization for social research in the public interest (formerly called the National Opinion Research Center), much of the research of NORC is conducted with government or foundation support. It has conducted an annual *General Social Survey* since 1972 (except 1979) to monitor trends in social values in the United States. NORC is affiliated with the University of Chicago and publishes the *NORC Reporter*.

7. *NBC News/Wall Street Journal*, NBC News, 30 Rockefeller Plaza, New York, N.Y. 10020: The *NBC/Wall Street Journal* collaboration began in 1988. The consortium conducts national telephone surveys on political topics, economic and social issues.

8. *CNN/USA Today*, Turner Broadcasting System, One CNN Center, P.O. Box 105366, Atlanta, Ga. 30348–5366: Another relatively recent collaboration, this group conducts national polls on political, social, and economic issues.

9. *Opinion Research Corporation*, P.O. Box 183, Princeton, N.J. 08542–0183: The Opinion Research Corporation has done survey research since 1938 on social, economic, and political subjects, all of which is available. They also do marketing research among consumers, executives, and professionals.

10. *The Roper Organization*, 205 East 42nd Street, New York N.Y. 10017: Social and political attitude surveys, market research, and public policy issues are covered in the polls of the Roper Organization. Its data are archived, among other places, at the Roper Center for Public Opinion Research at the University of Connecticut, Storrs Campus.

11. *SRI International*, Values and Lifestyles 2 (VALS 2), 333 Ravenswood Avenue, Menlo Park, Calif. 94025: SRI International measures consumers' attitudes about products, politics, work, education, and lifestyle characteristics, and includes information about consumers' available resources. It divides Americans into eight types, based on self-images, aspirations, and the products they use. Its surveys are especially useful for marketing and advertising communicators.

12. *Yankelovich Clancy Shulman*, 8 Wright Street, Westport, Conn. 06880: Marketing and consumer research regarding social values and attitudes is conducted for corporations, government, and media organiza-

tions. The firm also will customize research for corporate clients and assist in solving marketing problems.

Periodicals and Newsletters

1. *Gallup Poll Monthly* (monthly): detailed results of recent polls. The publication includes wording of questions and findings from polls conducted by Gallup on a vast array of topics and issues.
2. *American Enterprise* (bimonthly): magazine that publishes nontechnical, readable articles about public opinion on current topics in politics, economics, and social issues.
3. *Public Opinion Quarterly* (quarterly): scholarly publication of the American Association for Public Opinion Research, with detailed articles on survey methodology as well as analysis of poll results. Each issue usually contains a section called "The Polls," which presents results from many polls on selected topics.
4. *Roper Reports* (10 times a year): publication of results of Roper polls and of survey results.
5. *World Opinion Update* (monthly): results of American and foreign polls conducted in 100 countries on foreign and domestic affairs.

Collected Sets and Reference Tools

1. *Findex: The Directory of Market Research Reports, Studies, and Surveys:* annual guide to published, commercially available market and business research. This is a source for market research, rather than for general-interest public-opinion polls.
2. *Gallup Poll: Public Opinion Annual Series:* three volumes containing results from 1935 to 1971; two volumes containing results from 1972 to 1977; and annual volumes since 1978 collecting all statistical data from the Gallup polls.
3. *Harris Survey Yearbook of Public Opinion:* results of Harris surveys from 1970 to 1973 presented in chart form.
4. *American Public Opinion Index:* annual index published by the Opinion Research Service in Louisville, Ky., since 1981. The index includes many types of polls and refers to a companion microfiche publication called *American Public Opinion Data.*
5. *Index to International Public Opinion:* annual volumes reporting data collected from many of the major public opinion research organizations in 15 countries and geographic regions. The volumes include sample results and question wording.

Evaluating Polls and Surveys

Types of Survey Interviews.   One of the crucial questions facing the communicator trying to evaluate the usefulness and reliability of information from a survey is "How was this survey administered?" Three common methods are used to gather survey data: the face-to-face interview; the telephone interview; and the mail questionnaire. Each has its advantages and disadvantages, and each poses evaluation questions for the communicator.

The face-to-face method of survey interviewing involves trained interviewers meeting individually with the survey respondents and asking the survey questions in person. This method can accommodate longer and more complex questions and questions that require the respondent to react to visual images (charts, drawings, photographs). Well-trained interviewers can take notice of how the interview is proceeding by observing respondents' nonverbal behavior.

Some disadvantages of the face-to-face interview method are that the labor and transportation costs for the interviewers' training and travel to and from the respondents' locations are very high. Respondents are difficult to locate because many people are not willing to allow strangers into their homes. Interviewer selection is critical because the appearance, age, race, sex, dress, or nonverbal behavior of the interviewer may have subtle effects on respondents' answers to survey questions. For instance, when conducting the door-to-door census, the Census Bureau is careful to choose interviewers whose background and race are appropriate for the neighborhoods in which they will be conducting interviews. Because of the costs and the importance of interviewer training, the face-to-face interview method is less popular than it once was.

The communicator who is evaluating a survey or poll that was done using the face-to-face interview method must answer several questions: How were the interviewers selected? Were the interviewers chosen to avoid the bias of race, age, sex, or other social factors? How were the interviewers trained, and were training sessions conducted using the actual questionnaires? How was the work of each interviewer checked? What instructions did the interviewers receive regarding the selection of respondents? All these elements are important guides to the quality of the firm doing the survey and to the reliability of the information gathered by the poll or survey.

The second method of survey interviewing is the telephone interview. The advantages of the telephone survey are that reduced long-distance telephone rates make costs reasonable, return calls are simple, the nonresponse rate is low because interviewers can keep calling back until the respondent is home, and interviewers can collect a large amount of data in a short time.

For many years, the biggest drawback of the telephone survey was that poorer or less-educated people were less likely to have telephones and therefore would not be included in the survey sample. That problem is less prevalent now, but higher local telephone rates may affect this in the future. Also, random-digit dialing techniques (whereby a computer is instructed to create a roster of random telephone numbers within a certain exchange) have reduced the problems of new listings and unlisted numbers, which were inaccessible when interviewers had to rely on the telephone directories. However, telephone interviewers still face respondents' suspicions of telephone interviews; visual questions are not possible through the telephone interview method; and long or complicated questions are inappropriate. Another drawback of the telephone survey method is the increasing prevalence of telephone answering machines, voice mail systems, and caller identification technology; all allow potential respondents to avoid the telephone survey taker.

Communicators evaluating a poll or survey based on telephone interviews must ask if the questionnaire and individual questions were short enough, if the telephone banks were staffed in a central location (telephone interviewers who work at home are subject to less supervision, obviously), what instructions the interviewers had regarding who in the household to interview, and how many call-backs were standard procedure for the survey.

The third kind of survey method, the mail questionnaire, is the least expensive of the three because it involves fewer personnel to administer. A survey questionnaire is simply mailed to each member in the sample, and the respondents must choose to fill it out and mail it back. Advantages aside from cost include the ability to cover a wide geographic area, to provide anonymity to the respondents (which encourages candid responses), and to use less highly trained staff.

There are a number of disadvantages of the mail questionnaire. The response rate is usually very low because recipients tend to forget to mail the survey back, throw it out, or otherwise fail to complete a usable questionnaire. There is no way to know exactly who filled out the questionnaire if it is received in usable form. For instance, a questionnaire sent to corporate executives may be filled out by secretaries, even though executives were specifically needed as respondents. Also, the responses may be skewed because only those people who were really interested in the subject of the survey took the time to fill the questionnaire out, thereby introducing some bias into the results.

Communicators evaluating results of a poll based on a mail questionnaire must ask what the response rate was (the lower the response rate, the less reliable the results), whether follow-up questionnaires were sent out to those who failed to respond the first time, whether there was an attempt to monitor who actually filled out the questionnaire, and how self-explanatory the instructions to the respondents were. The mail survey obviously does not allow the respondent to ask questions of the interviewers or pollsters, so clear instructions to the respondent are crucial.

Types of Survey Samples.   A survey or poll is usually conducted using some sample of the population that the pollsters wish to learn about. Communicators must be very careful to evaluate the sampling techniques employed in any poll or survey they are contemplating using. There are various types of samples, and some are more reliable than others.

The sample may be chosen by nonprobability or by probability sampling methods. Nonprobability sampling methods include all those in which respondents are selected without randomness, without the requirement that every person in the population have an equal chance of being interviewed.

One type of nonprobability sample is the *available sample,* in which the interviewers choose as respondents people who are readily accessible. Using people passing by a street corner as respondents is an example of this type of sample. One problem with an available sample is that there is no way to determine who the respondents represent. There is an unknown chance of error; that is, it is impossible to tell if the respondents represent a larger group, and the results of the survey are not generalizable.

In choosing a *volunteer sample,* the interviewers select as respondents those who volunteer for the survey. Using students who volunteer to complete a survey questionnaire is an example. The "900 number" telephone surveys sometimes sponsored by radio or television stations also are examples of volunteer samples. In addition to volunteering for the survey, the respondents in these phone-in surveys are also *paying* to participate. One difficulty with this method of choosing a sample is that people who volunteer for things usually have different characteristics from those of the general population; they have more education, higher intelligence, greater need for approval, and other psychological characteristics that make them unrepresentative of a larger group.[6]

For a *quota sample,* the interviewers choose respondents based on prearranged categories of sample characteristics. For instance, the survey interviewer is instructed to interview 50 men and 50 women for the survey, and when those quotas are met, the sample is complete. This sampling method, again, does not allow the pollster to measure how representative those respondents are of the larger group being studied. The chance for error is very high.

To make up a *purposive sample,* the interviewers select respondents from subgroups in the population because they have specific characteristics or qualities. For instance, an interviewer in a grocery store may be instructed to interview only those people who say they eat yoghurt and will not administer the survey to any others. Again, this sampling method does not allow the interviewer or the pollster to know how representative those respondents are of the larger population being studied.

Probability sampling methods allow the survey researcher a much better chance of accurately choosing representative respondents. It is the only method that makes it possible to estimate the amount of error that the sample will produce. A random sample is the result of a probability sampling method. The term *random* does not suggest haphazardness. A *random sample* is set up systematically, so that every member of the population being studied has an equal chance of being included in the sample. For certain types of random samples, however, such precision is not possible; in instances where an *equal* chance is not possible, the researchers design the study so that each member of the population has a *known* chance of being included in the sample. There are three types of random samples typically used by those conducting a probability sample survey.[7]

A *simple random sample* is used when the goal is to obtain a random selection of members of a broadly defined population. For instance, a random-digit dialing technique that generates telephone numbers within a certain exchange area should produce a simple random sample of individuals within a geographic area. Because the computer is generating the telephone numbers that interviewers will call, unlisted or new telephone numbers can be included along with long-established, listed numbers. Therefore, every residential phone in that exchange area has a chance of being chosen.

A *stratified random sample* adds another step to the process, with the goal of having the sample take into account certain characteristics of the population. For instance, if the researcher knows that the population being studied includes subgroups of individuals from various age groups, it is possible to draw random subsamples from each age group so that each is proportionally represented in the total sample. The combined stratified random sample will then better represent the population the researcher wants to learn about.

A *disproportionate random sample* is similar to the stratified random sample approach. Several subsamples are randomly drawn, but the goal is to have each subsample be *disproportionate* to the size of each group in the actual population. This allows the researcher to attempt to better represent the views of subgroups than would be possible with a simple random sample. For instance, if the researcher is interested in comparing different racial groups' attitudes toward the mayor's new tax proposals in a community, it might be desirable to draw subsamples of equal size for each racial group, even though the community does not include an equal number of each racial group as a whole. A simple random sample from the community at large would yield a much smaller number of racial minority group members than would the disproportionate random method. The disproportionate random method would allow for more accurate comparisons and conclusions about each group's attitudes.

The key to recognizing a probability sample is to look for descriptions of the accuracy of the poll's results. The communicator trying to evaluate the information from a poll or survey must know what kind of sample was used. If the sample was one of the nonprobability types, the results are less reliable than those from a probability sample. But nonprobability samples are often easier and cheaper to use, so many surveys are conducted using them. If the survey was based on a probability sample, the results are more likely to be reliable, although several other factors, such as the wording of questions, must be considered.

Even the most carefully selected random sample will almost never provide a perfect representation of the population that is being studied. There will always be some degree of sampling error. *Sampling error* is the range of variance from actual total population characteristics or question response patterns within which the results of a particular survey may fall.[8] For instance, a political poll may indicate that Jones has 44 percent of voter support; Smith has 46 percent; and the rest of the voters are undecided. The stated sampling error is plus or minus 4 percent. This means that Jones may have as much as

48 percent support or as little as 40 percent. Smith may have as much as 50 percent support or as little as 42 percent. In other words, because of the sampling error, the race is too close to call.

Several things determine the sampling error in a random-sample survey. One major factor is the size of the sample. A general rule is that the larger the sample, the smaller the sampling error. After a certain level, however, any increase in the sample size results in such a small decrease in the sampling error that it is not worth the effort or expense to increase the size of the sample. This is why most major polling organizations use a random sample of 1,200 to 1,500 respondents. This results in sufficiently small sampling error (2.5 to 3.5 percentage points) so that a larger sample size is justified. Also, when a stratified random sample or a disproportionate random sample is used, the results may include an analysis of subsamples, or responses from smaller groups within the larger sample. The margin of error for subsample results is *always* larger than the margin of error for the total sample; again, this relates to the size of the subsamples. Always look for subsample margin-of-error figures when examining results that summarize a variety of subsample findings.

Another major factor in determining the sampling error is the extent of variation within the population on topics in the survey. The more likely it is that members of the population hold very different views or are very different from one another, the larger the sampling error because it is harder, even with a random sample, to be sure that *all* the different viewpoints will be represented by the sample.

A third major factor in determining the sampling error is the level of confidence used with the analysis of the survey results. The *level of confidence* refers to the odds that the results of a specific survey are within the estimated sampling error range.[9] In other words, are the survey researchers 90 percent, 95 percent, or 99 percent sure that the sample data represent the population from which the sample was drawn? Typical confidence levels are 90 percent, 95 percent, and 99 percent. There are tables that help the survey researcher determine how large a sample is needed to achieve results with a plus or minus 4 percent sampling error and a 95 percent level of confidence, for instance. These tables are not needed by the communicator who is trying to evaluate someone else's survey, but are needed by the communicator who is planning a media survey.

The communicator who is evaluating information from a random-sample poll, then, should look for the statement about the range of sampling error and the level of confidence. If these figures are stated, the communicator can be sure the results are based on a probability sampling method. Meyer suggests that a common goal of pollsters is to conduct a poll with a sampling error of no more than 5 percent at the 95 percent confidence level.[10] If the communicator is evaluating a poll with those kinds of figures, the data are likely to be more credible than those from a poll with higher sampling error and lower confidence levels.

Some general rules about how types of samples affect the usefulness of poll and survey information, then, are:

1. Look for a probability sample if the results are generalized to a larger population.
2. Look for a stated range of sampling error and level of confidence; the lower the sampling error range and the higher the level of confidence, the more credible the data.
3. Understand that nonprobability samples are cheaper and easier to conduct and may be used more frequently. Sports writers' rankings of football teams, call-in talk-show survey results, person-on-the-street interviews, and postcards mailed to fan magazines all can be called "surveys"—but if the individuals answering the questions are not part of a sample drawn randomly from a known population, the results cannot be generalized to the larger population being studied.

Types of Survey Questions.   Another major area of concern for communicators attempting to evaluate survey information is the kinds of questions that were used in the questionnaire. The types of questions, the wording of questions, and the placement of questions in the overall design of a questionnaire can dramatically affect the results of a survey.

There are four basic types of questions, some of which are more appropriate for survey questionnaires than others. The first type of question is the *stimulus open/response open* question. An example might be: "What do you believe are the major problems in the city?" This question, or stimulus, does not give any direction to the respondent, thus leaving the answer, or response, completely open-ended. The respondent can choose to concentrate on any problem and can answer in any way that seems comfortable.

The second kind of question is the *stimulus open/response closed* format. This might be: "What do you believe are the major problems in the city?" with a list of 12 problems from which to choose. The question is still very broad and undirected, but the respondent must choose from among a finite number of answers.

The third kind of question is the *stimulus closed/response open* format. An example would be: "Unemployment is one problem facing our community. How do you feel about it?" This very specific question directs the respondent to a particular issue. However, the response is still open-ended. Respondents can answer in their own language in any way that comes to mind.

The last type of question, which is most often used in polls or surveys, is the *stimulus closed/response closed* format. The question might be: "Unemployment is one problem facing our community. How do you feel about it?" with a list of seven answers, ranging from "very concerned" to "not at all concerned." Both the question and the choice of answers are very thoroughly outlined. There is no room for the respondents to answer in their own words.

Stimulus closed/response closed questions are used most often in surveys and polls because they provide data that are easily tabulated and analyzed. Since all respondents must choose from one set of answers, the researchers can prearrange for the coding, or analysis, of each questionnaire. When interpreting information from a poll or survey, the communicator can request a questionnaire and can determine whether the questions were mostly closed-ended or open-ended. Open-ended questions are harder to code, and a good explanation of how open-ended items were coded must accompany the interpretation of the survey information.

One type of closed-ended question requires a *dichotomous* (yes/no, agree/disagree) response. This response form allows for little sensitivity to the degree of conviction that a respondent may have about a particular issue or question, but it is the easiest response to tabulate. The *multiple-choice* format is another closed-ended question type. Good multiple-choice questions include all answers and answers that are mutually exclusive. For instance, a multiple-choice question that asked, "How long have you worked here?" and listed answers of "less than 1 year," "1 year to 5 years," "5 to 10 years," and "more than 10 years," leaves the person who has worked there for 5 years with two answers. How will that person decide which answer to choose? This kind of sloppy response design should alert the communicator to other potential problems with the survey information.

Another kind of closed-ended question form is the scale. *Rating scales* provide the respondent with five or seven answer choices, ranging from, say, "strongly agree" to "strongly disagree" or "very fair" to "very unfair." *Semantic-differential scales* provide five or seven answer choices, ranging from, say, "good" to "bad" or "uninteresting" to "interesting." Both of these types of scales allow the respondent to express some degree of feeling or conviction about a question.

The *checklist* and the *rank order* round out the types of closed-ended questions. With the *checklist*, the respondent chooses from a set list all the items that may be appropriate. The rank order allows the respondent to indicate first choice, second choice, and so forth. All these closed-ended question forms allow for fairly consistent and unambiguous coding of responses. The communicator can be alert to those forms of questions and responses that seem inappropriate, poorly constructed, or inconsistent when evaluating the survey or poll information.

The wording of questions is another major area of concern in evaluating polls and surveys. Question bias, clarity, length, and construction can cause crucial differences in results from polls and surveys. Communication researchers Roger Wimmer and Joseph Dominick have developed several rules about question wording:[11]

1. Questions should be clear, using everyday language and avoiding jargon.
2. Questions should be short, thereby reducing the likelihood of being misunderstood, especially in telephone interviews.

3. Questions should not ask more than one thing. An example of a double-barrelled question might be: "This product is mild and gets out stubborn stains. Do you agree or disagree?" The respondent might agree with the first part of the statement, but disagree with the second.
4. Questions should avoid biased words or terms. An example might be: "In your free time, would you rather read a book or just watch TV?" The respondent is likely to infer that *just* watching television is a less desirable activity. In a question such as "Where did you hear the news about the president's new tax program?" the word *hear* biases against an answer such as "I read about it in the newspaper." There are even more insidious examples of bias in questions, a result of the survey sponsor's having an interest in seeing the survey produce a certain set of answers. Questions can be written to signal the respondent about *exactly* what the interviewer wishes to hear.
5. Questions should avoid leading the respondents' answers. A leading question might be: "Like most Americans, do you read a newspaper every day?" People who answer "no" place themselves in an un-American group! Another example might be: "Do you believe, along with many others, that abortion is murder?" The leading question tells the respondent what the appropriate or expected answer is.
6. Questions should avoid asking for unusually detailed or difficult information. A detailed question might be: "Over the past 30 days, how many hours of TV has your family viewed?" Most respondents would not be able to answer that question without considerable calculation. A simpler way of gathering the same information would be to ask, "About how many hours a day does your family spend watching TV?"
7. Questions should avoid embarrassing the respondent whenever possible. It is difficult to judge which kinds of questions will be embarrassing to every person, but some questions will embarrass almost everyone. For instance, questions about level of income are usually perceived unfavorably. In fact, many survey researchers place those questions at the very end of the questionnaire so that if the respondent is offended by the question, the rest of the interview is not spoiled.
8. Questions should not assume level of knowledge on the part of the respondent. Many surveys include "filter questions," which help the interviewer decide whether that part of the questionnaire is pertinent to the respondent. The filter question might be: "Have you taken a written driver's license examination within the past five years?" If the respondent answers "no," then the questions that deal with proposed changes in written driver's license exams are best not answered by the respondent.
9. Questions should avoid abbreviations, acronyms, foreign phrases, or slang. Respondents are less likely to be confused when simple, familiar language is used. Also, certain slang phrases may connote some kind of bias on the part of the interviewer, which will influence the respondent.
10. Questions should be specific about the time span that is implied. For instance, a question may ask about the respondent's approval or disapproval of a $20 billion program for road and bridge improvement. Unless the question specifies the number of years over which the money will be spent, the respondent has no way to evaluate the program's impact, and the answer given will be meaningless.

11. Where appropriate, questions should attempt to gauge the intensity of feeling the respondent has about a topic. For instance, a question may ask for the respondent's preference for one product over another. Some respondents may not feel particularly intense about their preference for either, but just to be polite, they will give an answer. If an intensity question were included ("How strong is your preference for Product A?"), those who were less intense could indicate their ambivalence.

The communicator who is considering the use of information from a poll or survey should have the questionnaire in hand in order to apply these standards of evaluation to the questions. Any indication that the questionnaire was poorly prepared or that the questions were improperly written should alert the communicator to the possibility that the information gathered through the survey may not be reliable.

The order in which questions appear in the questionnaire can also affect the reliability of the results. Don A. Dillman, in his book *Mail and Telephone Surveys*, states, "The major contributions that question order can make to data quality are to ease the task of the respondents and to reduce any resistance to participation."[12] Dillman recommends that questions be grouped by topic and within topic by consistent formats. The first few questions in a questionnaire are crucial in preventing termination of the interview and in relaxing the respondent. Questions relating to personal characteristics (age, education level, income level) should come in the last section. Topic questions that are likely to be objectionable should be placed just before the personal items. If the communicator detects confusion in the placement of questions or identifies questions that are likely to be offensive to respondents, the survey results may be suspect.

Interpreting Poll and Survey Information

As the discussion so far has indicated, the communicator can develop some basic skills in evaluating and interpreting information from polls and surveys. When communicators are considering using poll or survey information, they should have the answers to the following questions:

1. Who sponsored or paid for this poll, and who conducted it? As we have already indicated, serious bias can enter into a survey design if the sponsoring agency or the firm conducting the poll has a particular ax to grind.
2. Who was interviewed? What population was sampled?
3. How were people selected for the interviews? In other words, was it a probability or a nonprobability sample? If a nonprobability sample was used, the results cannot be generalized to a larger population.
4. How many people were interviewed? What was the size of the sample? What were the sizes of any subsamples or specific groups for which results were analyzed separately?
5. If a probability sample was used, what was the range of sampling

error and the level of confidence for the total sample? What were those figures for any subgroups within the sample?

6. How were the interviews conducted? Were they mail, telephone, or face-to-face interviews? Were the interviewers trained personnel or volunteers? Were they supervised, or were they working on their own?

7. What were the actual questions that were asked? What kind of response choices did respondents have (response open or response closed)?

8. What was the wording of questions? Were there biased, loaded, double-barrelled, or ambiguous questions?

9. When were the interviews conducted? The results of a survey are good only for the time at which the questions were asked. Also, outside events may affect respondents' answers to questions. For instance, during the 1990 United States Senate election in Minnesota, the Minneapolis *Star Tribune* tracked the two candidates' appeal to voters with regular surveys. On the Sunday before the election, the *Star Tribune* published a front-page story showing incumbent Senator Rudy Boschwitz with a 9-point lead over the underdog candidate, Professor Paul Wellstone. The poll had been completed on Saturday afternoon. However, events over that weekend and the Monday before the election proved the pollsters wrong. In those three days, media attention was drawn to a letter mailed by Boschwitz supporters (on Boschwitz's letterhead and carrying his signature) to members of the Minnesota Jewish community. Despite the fact that both candidates were Jewish, the letter accused Wellstone of not being a strong supporter of Jewish community members' interests and questioned the religious upbringing of the Wellstone children (Wellstone's spouse was Christian). Many members of the Jewish community were outraged, and the debate spilled into the media coverage of the campaign in its final days, when even many non-Jewish citizens in the state expressed their dismay at the tactics. On election day, voters turned out in huge numbers, and despite the poll findings gathered just three days earlier, Boschwitz was defeated and Wellstone went to Washington. Outside events clearly affected the reliability of the survey results.

10. What was the response rate for the survey? If fewer than 70 to 80 percent of the sample respondents were actually interviewed, the chances are high that the nonresponse pattern is systematic rather than random. That is, persons of a certain type within the sample may have tended not to answer the questionnaire, rather than persons scattered throughout all types within the sample. If this is the case, then sampling error cannot be accurately predicted.

11. How and when were the data analyzed? Were subgroups within the sample analyzed separately from the entire sample? What were those results?

12. What was the purpose of the survey or poll? Who is going to use the results for what purpose? Depending on the purposes of the poll, certain data might be withheld, selectively disclosed, or otherwise manipulated by the poll sponsors.

These general questions must be sufficiently addressed before the communicator can interpret the results of any poll or survey.

CAVEATS TO THE COMMUNICATOR

Even the most careful scrutiny of information from polls and surveys cannot altogether ensure against error or misinterpretation. When communicators use polls and surveys as the basis of media messages, particularly news stories, several problems can arise. Greg Schneiders, a public-opinion professional, has identified three ways that a media report about a poll can mislead or misinform the public.[13] These three problem areas are sampling error, nonsampling error, and reporting error. Sampling error is the polling flaw most familiar to the public. Unless the communicator accurately interprets the results, taking into consideration the sampling error tolerance, and points out the range of sampling error to the audience, very misleading and downright incorrect interpretations can result. For instance, in the spring of 1990, Nicaragua held presidential elections. United States pollsters uniformly forecast a sweeping victory for the Sandinista candidate and incumbent president, Daniel Ortega. In fact, when election results were in, the opposition candidate, Violeta Chamorro, had won with a 15 percent lead over Ortega. The polls were off by 28 to 30 percent. One explanation for the discrepancies, when the fiasco was later analyzed, appeared to be due to sampling error. Pollsters conducted most of their interviews in the urban areas of Nicaragua, but massive numbers of rural residents actually turned out to vote. This meant that the sample, even though drawn randomly, did not accurately represent the group of people who actually voted. None of the media reports about the poll results before the election mentioned that the samples were primarily drawn from the urban areas. Thus the poll findings were misleading and the media reports to the audience were not complete.[14]

Sampling error is also proving difficult for advertising and marketing uses of poll and survey data. Late in 1990, a number of researchers and market professionals revealed that refusal rates for marketing research surveys reached close to 50 percent in some parts of the United States.[15] Marketers and advertisers fear that if fully one half of the members of their random sample refuse to participate, those who *do* agree to answer their questions may not be truly representative of the groups they most want to learn about. This kind of systematic bias, even in random samples, can wreak havoc with survey results.

The second way that a poll or survey can mislead, according to Schneiders, is by nonsampling error. Polling results can be skewed by questions that are poorly worded, are too vague, are too specific, or have any of the other poor characteristics that have already been mentioned. These kinds of nonsampling errors are more insidious and more difficult for the public to understand or appreciate than sampling errors, which are usually reported by the polling source. Because polls are really snapshots in time, their results are susceptible to misinterpretation or overinterpretation. In fact, these nonsampling errors are the most prevalent kind of errors that communicators must deal with in reporting on polls and surveys.

Even the respected polling organizations can fall prey to nonsampling error. During both the 1989 and 1990 national elections, a number of respected polling organizations experienced embarrassing miscalls in some state gubernatorial and large metropolitan mayoral elections. For instance, a pre-election poll by the *Washington Post* showed the Virginia governor's race clearly going in favor of L. Douglas Wilder, a black candidate running against a white candidate, J. Marshall Coleman. The *Post* had Wilder ahead by 11 percentage points just days before the election. When the actual results were in, Wilder squeaked out a victory, but by a margin of one quarter of one percentage point. What happened?

Social scientists know that survey respondents are reluctant to answer a question in a way that might seem "socially unacceptable." Perhaps the members of the *Post* sample were reluctant to tell the survey takers that they intended to vote for the white candidate, for fear of appearing racist in their choice. But when voters actually went to the polls, they voted differently than their answers had indicated to pollsters. Survey methods cannot compensate for results based on untruthful answers from respondents. Similarly, pollsters found that Dianne Feinstein's support as a 1990 candidate for California governor went up if the interviewer was a woman. Concerns about question wording and the timing of surveys also must be considered part of nonsampling error.

The third way that polls mislead is through reporting error, according to Schneiders. Press interpretation plays a huge role in how a particular poll is perceived by the public. Through oversimplification, inept interpretation, or downright incorrect reporting, polls can be very misleading. For instance, a poll may show candidate Jones with lagging support among women, with Smith leading Jones among women by 55 to 41 percent. Jones might be ahead among men, with Smith trailing 52 to 40 percent. Through media reports, this might be characterized as Jones' "gender gap" with women. However, the figures could just as easily be characterized as Smith's "gender gap" with men.

Communication researchers G. Cleveland Wilhoit and David Weaver suggest several ways that communicators can improve their reporting of survey and poll results:[16]

1. Avoid generalizing beyond the sample. It is tempting to write about the public in general when the sample includes, for instance, only registered voters. Headline writers are often more at fault than the person

writing the story because they must reduce the results to a few dramatic words. But accurate headlines and stories can be written that avoid this problem.

2. Avoid treating insignificant differences as real. If differences could be due to sampling error alone, they should not be treated as real or significant findings. This happens especially during election campaigns. Candidate Jones is described as being ahead of Candidate Smith, even though just a few percentage points separate them and the difference could be explained by sampling error.

3. Avoid drawing firm conclusions from only a few response categories, questions, or surveys. It is important to take into account all the answers to a particular question to arrive at an overall conclusion. For instance, a question may include several options for response, but the communicator may concentrate on only one of those options in drawing a conclusion. Or, a conclusion may be drawn by relying on only one or two questions if there are several in a survey on the same topic. Or, one survey is used to draw a conclusion when findings from several related surveys were available. All these methods of drawing conclusions leave the communicator open to error and misinterpretation.

4. Try to describe the sampling error, sampling method, and population characteristics in a clear, understandable fashion. Give information about how many people were included in the sample and when the interviews were conducted.

5. Use side bars, tables, charts, or graphs where appropriate to better explain the results. Information describing how the survey was conducted and figures on sampling error, confidence level, and population characteristics might be better placed in an accompanying sidebar rather than incorporated in the body of the story for a newspaper poll. Graphs or charts may be more effective than a simple voice delivery in expressing the survey results on a television broadcast.

6. Do not treat poll or survey results as something fixed or static. Results are snapshots of constantly changing feelings and beliefs. It is up to the communicator to correctly interpret those feelings and to make it clear that the results apply to only one period of time.

These suggestions should help the communicator when making decisions about how to present and report on poll and survey information. Applying these simple rules of scrutiny and interpretation can help the communicator avoid misleading the public and misinforming the audience.

A striking example of faulty press scrutiny of poll information comes from an Ann Landers "survey" of readers of her regular newspaper column. The columnist asked her readers in a 1989 column, "Has your sex life gone downhill since marriage? If so, why?" She claimed to have received more than 141,000 responses, about evenly divided between men and women readers. The overwhelming majority of the respondents, 82 percent, said that sex after marriage was much less satisfactory. Media reports immediately seized upon the information; Landers appeared on the "Oprah Winfey" television talk show to discuss her "findings," local radio and television commentators around the country referred to the results, and newspapers wrote wry articles incorporating the figures.

The first thing that should jump to the communicator's attention is that the sample was a volunteer sample; readers who saw the column chose to respond. Therefore, the results cannot be generalized to any larger population, regardless of the number of responses Landers claims to have received. There was no way to know who really responded and how representative they were of the population of married couples she claims she was learning something about. Landers assumed married couples responded, but in fact the results could have included many responses from unmarried persons or many responses from the same person. A volunteer sample just does not allow for any interpretation of who is represented. Second, the question wording was outrageously biased in favor of the dissatisfied response—using such phrases as "gone downhill" and "If so, why?" clearly cues the respondent to the answer that is expected. Media reports of these, and similar, survey results do audience members a disservice if they do not include a critical explanation of the spurious nature of the findings.

Journalists are not the only communicators prone to misinterpret or misrepresent the results of surveys or polls. In what has to be one of the most serious polling and research mistakes of modern marketing, the Coca-Cola Company decided, in 1985, to change the formula of its long-standing favorite cola. The outcry was immediate and fierce. Coca-Cola claimed to have done about 180,000 to 200,000 blind taste tests, pitting three or more "new" Coke recipes against the "old" formula. However, only 30,000 to 40,000 of these tests involved the specific formula that eventually became the "new" Coke. The company claimed that the blind taste tests showed support for the "new" version of 61 percent to 39 percent. However, those figures were not consistent in the overall testing.[17]

Equally damaging was the fact that the interviews done during the taste tests never indicated to the respondents that the old formula would be taken away entirely. The polling did not take into consideration the public's attachment to the general idea of Coke as a uniquely American icon. The idea of intensity of feeling was not considered. If questions had attempted to determine the respondents' intensity of preference, the researchers may have found that the 61 percent who said they preferred the new formula were not intense about their preference. However, the 39 percent who preferred the original formula may have been *very* intense about their preference. Questions also could have attempted to determine which group included the heavy Coca-Cola drinkers. Perhaps the 39 percent who preferred the old formula represented a large proportion of individuals who drink a lot of Coke, whereas the 61 percent who preferred the new formula were not heavy Coke drinkers. Thus, offending the 39 percent meant offending the people who drink the product the most and feel most intensely about it.

The market reaction against the new Coke surprised even the most seasoned pollsters. Clearly, the survey research conducted by the company had been incomplete and had missed measuring the emotional attachment of respondents to the original Coke. The company, in a stunning marketing reversal, announced within several months of introducing the new Coke that the old Coke would return to the shelves under the name Coca-Cola Classic. Coca-Cola Classic quickly trounced new Coke in the marketplace. National advertising for new Coke disappeared, although the company continued to quietly market the beverage locally in several regions of the country. In 1990, in another attempt to steal some brand share away from Pepsi, Coke tentatively started market testing a renamed and repackaged version of the "new" product, rechristened Coke II. Officials announced, however, that the company had no intentions of withdrawing Coca-Cola Classic.[18]

Controversy over polling and sampling methods has also caused problems for the television industry. In the February 1990 "sweeps" period, during which the Nielsen ratings service (and others) gathered information about television viewership, it appeared that 2.2 million fewer viewers were watching television than the previous February. The television networks pointed to the use of "people meters" as the culprit. People meters keep a record when a television set is on and the stations to which it is tuned. But it also requires family members to punch in and punch out personal code numbers when they start and stop watching. Nielsen claims that with a national sample size of 4,000 households, it is providing a refined demographic data base upon which television networks and advertisers can rely.

However, the networks claimed that in a study done for a broadcast-industry trade group, fewer than one half of the homes in the Nielsen sample were from Nielsen's list of predesignated homes; the rest were alternates. The networks worried that the sample was unrepresentative of the viewing population because so many people in the initial sample refused to have the people meter in their homes. Besides, the networks claimed, the people meter methods were so intrusive that natural viewing patterns were interfered with in the process of taking the survey. Because millions of dollars of advertising revenue depend on the figures generated by the ratings services' data, the networks invited rival research firms to compete with Nielsen in offering a service that measures network television audiences.[19]

Political polling methods have also come under scrutiny. Techniques such as tracking polls result in findings that can be very misleading. Tracking polls are used heavily by political campaigns, and in recent presidential elections they also have been used by the major polling organizations. The daily polls try to monitor shifts in support for candidates. The polls are based on a rolling sample in which, for example, groups of 100 individuals are interviewed on four consecutive days. The total sample across those days is 400, but much can happen between the first and fourth day of polling. Also, tracking polls may fail to measure last-minute changes of heart or major solidification of voter preference. The Gallup organization was embarrassed during the 1988 presidential primary in New Hampshire because it stopped taking its tracking polls at 4 P.M. Sunday evening, but voters did not make up their minds until Monday or Tuesday, election day. Gallup predicted a Robert Dole victory over George Bush, but Bush won the Republican primary.

These caveats should not suggest that polls and surveys are so susceptible to error and inaccuracy that they should not be used by communicators
at all. On the contrary, many media organizations are relying on polls and
survey information much more than in the past. The sophistication and
reliability of poll and survey information have increased, and the public
fascination with such information has been an encouragement to media organizations. News, both print and broadcast, features regular coverage of poll
and survey information. During nonelection times, media organizations report on or conduct polls that measure the public mood about events that
affect our collective lives. During election periods, media polls help voters
learn which candidate is popular or ahead or in touch with the electorate.
Polls and surveys can provide a light-hearted and interesting look at our
communities and ourselves. Marketing, public-relations, and advertising professionals rely on polls and surveys to help them learn more about the
groups they wish to reach. Whether measuring the appeal of a new product
or the effectiveness of a particular message, these professionals rely on the
detailed information that surveys can give them.

Communicators are not entirely alone in evaluating results from polls or
surveys. Many times, the expertise of survey researchers, either in universities or in survey-research firms, can be called on. Large media organizations
hire their own survey-research experts, who may be willing to help the
communicator interpret the results of a poll conducted by someone other
than the media organization. Professional associations of survey researchers
hold annual meetings and publish guidebooks and articles to enlighten the
beginner. These associations also have codes of research ethics and polling
practice. Groups such as the American Business Press, the National Council
on Public Polls, and the American Association for Public Opinion Research
encourage their members to adhere to guidelines regarding the conduct of
research, the reporting of results, and relations with the media requesting
findings. The communicator can also count on the support and assistance of
a network of other media professionals skilled in survey research.

LINKS TO THE SEARCH STRATEGY

In this step of the search strategy, the communicator may be using information from surveys conducted by others or may be planning and conducting
original survey research. The communicator is likely to encounter poll and
survey information in any other step of the search strategy. Some of this
information is publicly available through library and data-base sources or
from material shared by sources. Some survey material is proprietary and
available only with permission from the institution that commissioned the
study. Survey and poll information is used for both the content of news,
advertising, and public relations, and for understanding message audiences.

Evaluating and interpreting poll and survey information are additional
challenges to the communicator. Using information generated at other steps

in the search process can be helpful in alerting communicators to potential problems in poll or survey information.

Chapter 9 examines the challenges presented in selecting and synthesizing information. Specific techniques for evaluating material and for understanding the context of information are introduced.

NOTES

1. Earl Babbie, *The Practice of Social Research*, 3d ed. (Belmont, Calif.: Wadsworth, 1983), 209.
2. Philip Meyer, *Precision Journalism* (Bloomington: Indiana University Press, 1979), 139.
3. Peter Francese, "People Patterns: Marriage Helps Keep Poverty at Bay," *Advertising Age*, 8 August 1985, 32.
4. Richard L. Berke, "TV Networks Join on Voter Surveys," *New York Times*, 7 November 1990, A1.
5. Many of the sources described can be found in Tom W. Smith and Frederick D. Weil, "The Polls—A Report: Finding Public Opinion Data: A Guide to Sources," *Public Opinion Quarterly* 54 (Winter 1990): 609–626.
6. R. Rosenthal and R. L. Rosnow, *Artifact in Behavioral Research* (New York: Academic Press, 1969).
7. G. Cleveland Wilhoit and David H. Weaver, *Newsroom Guide to Polls and Surveys* (Washington, D.C.: American Newspaper Publishers Association, 1980), 21.
8. Wilhoit and Weaver, *Newsroom Guide*, 26.
9. Wilhoit and Weaver, *Newsroom Guide*.
10. Meyer, *Precision Journalism*, 119.
11. Many of the rules for question wording and some of the examples used come from a good discussion of this topic in Roger D. Wimmer and Joseph R. Dominick, *Mass Media Research: An Introduction* (Belmont, Calif.: Wadsworth, 1983), 113–120.
12. Don A. Dillman, *Mail and Telephone Surveys: The Total Design Method* (New York: Wiley, 1978), 218.
13. Greg Schneiders, "Sorry: Wrong Numbers," *Washington Journalism Review* (September 1984): 47–50.
14. Norman Ornstein, "Why Polls Flopped in Nicaragua," *New York Times*, 7 March 1990, A15.
15. Randall Rothenberg, "Surveys Proliferate, But Answers Dwindle," *New York Times*, 5 October 1990, A1.
16. Wilhoit and Weaver, *Newsroom Guide*, 77.
17. *See*, for instance, Jack Honomichl, "Missing Ingredients in 'New' Coke's Research," *Advertising* Age, 22 July 1985, 1, 58; Richard W. Stevenson, "The Revival of the 'Old' Coke," *New York Times*, 12 July 1985, 25, 39; Nell Henderson, "Coca-Cola Apologizes to Real Thing's Fans," *Washington Post*, 12 July 1985, B1, 2; Letters to the Editor, "Coke Damaged Research," *Advertising Age*, 12 August 1985, 2.
18. Randall Rothenberg, "New Coke by a New Name: Coke II to Make Test Debut," *New York Times*, 7 March 1990, C17.
19. Randall Rothenberg, "Black Hole in Television," *New York Times*, 8 October 1990, C1.

CHAPTER

9

Selecting and Synthesizing Information

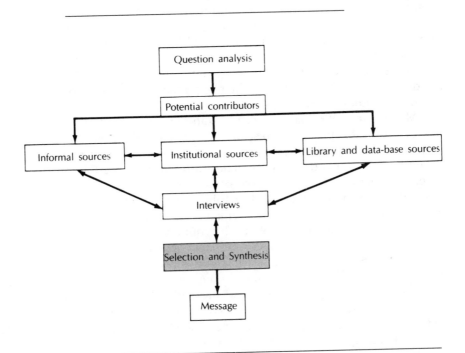

There is little doubt that the most challenging work in the search-strategy process often is evaluating, selecting, and synthesizing information. Of course, evaluation and selection do not occur only after all or most of the information has been collected. Rather, selections are made during earlier parts of the search strategy, when the searcher, either deliberately or casually, takes or avoids a particular route. For example, a news reporter may decide a potential interviewee is not reliable, based on previous experience with the person or on the individual's reputation for accuracy and truthworthiness. The reporter seeks and interviews others instead. Or, a public relations specialist may discover conflicting information in newspaper data-base reports and decide to seek original documents or more reliable statistical information from primary sources. Still, there is a special time of reckoning just before the communicator gets ready to create the message. This chapter, then, examines the judgments made in selecting and synthesizing information.

From the broadest perspective, information can be seen as a reflection of the ways that power is distributed in a particular society. The phrase "information is power" has become so commonplace as to be considered by some to be a cliche. That the idea is commonplace supports its importance. At the same time, the idea that information reflects power has received more limited attention. But the organizations and public bodies, and occasional individuals, possessing the power to create information to serve their needs contribute mightily to an overall shaping of the information environment. It is here, in various power centers, that some subjects and issues are studied and promoted at great public or private expense, while other subjects and issues remain unexamined. Often, it is the same power sources that have the capacity, described in Chapter 2, to influence public discussion through their information subsidies to the mass media.

Major information subsidies, for example, come to media and other businesses through reports and research by governmental bodies. A media subsidy can be a significant factor in mass communication when the communicator depends on an outside source to produce the information and when information from the source comes free or at low cost to the communicator. Without the producer and distributor of the information, the communicator would have no access to the material, because it did not exist, because the information was unavailable to the communicator, or it was too expensive (however that might be judged). A clear example is found in the federal census, which has no competitor in the realm of describing the United States population. The census constitutes an enormous information subsidy, since it provides information essential to private and governmental decision making. Even the largest private corporation could not produce the equivalent of the federal census. News, public-relations, marketing, and advertising organizations depend upon it as a low-cost provider of useful data. At the same time, the 1990 census was criticized as inaccurate in counting the homeless, immigrants, and illegal residents, and people of color. Municipal officials claimed large numbers of their residents never received census forms. While advertisers probably found the census results adequate for their purposes, some mayors and advocates for the homeless loudly criticized it for specific inadequacies that would affect their work. News workers continue to rely on census figures, too, but also produce stories about the challenges to its accuracy.

Governmental support for some research also creates a form of information subsidy. For example, federal research support has been provided disproportionately for medical research that applies only to the health of white males. The medical reporter or public-relations writer seeking information on, for example, the role of low doses of aspirin in preventing heart attacks, discovers that the studies on this subject generally cover white males only.

The research subsidy for studies of a minority of the population thus limits the communicator's ability to write accurately about the population as a whole. Writers of popular articles frequently are criticized for failing to notice that a study involves a specific population and for erroneously assuming the information applies to the population generally. Other writers, however, accurately observing that federal research money has disproportionately subsidized research benefiting some people, have developed news and public-relations stories that expose these discrepancies. Some writers, however, have inaccurately applied research results to the population at large, rather than to the limited group to which the results apply.

The concept of information subsidies is an essential framework communicators can use in the broad evaluation of material they have uncovered for their messages. Questions that arise from this concept include:

Who paid to produce this information?

For what purpose was it produced?

What interests or viewpoints are reflected in the production of the information?

What interests or viewpoints are omitted in the production of the information?

What kind of information subsidy is involved when a communicator uses this information?

Realistically, communicators hardly can avoid using information that is somehow shaped by the interests, prejudices, or shortcomings of influential and highly organized information-producers. Communicators rarely do the primary research on a subject; they rely heavily on what has been produced elsewhere. At the same time, if alert to the power contexts associated with information, communicators have many opportunities to avoid some of the most damaging effects of accepting information at face value, as if its origin and limitations were of no consequence. Communicators, in addition, can give a "reality check" to heavily subsidized information that contradicts what has been learned through observation, interviews, and other methods. Communication scholars, of course, frequently conduct original research. But even they must refer to earlier research by others whose methods and results require evaluation similar to processes used by media writers.

The requirements to understand and adjust for the influence of various power centers come into play during the final process of judging and synthesizing information. But they also are critically employed at the question-analysis stage of research when the communicator is defining the subject and planning a search strategy and during the search process itself. Many communicators never state specifically how they evaluate material and select some information while ignoring or discarding other material. In this chapter, we identify some standards for judging information and suggest how some of the standards can be applied. Beyond that, we recognize that selection processes take account of the fact that the search undoubtedly produces volumes of material that never will be visible in the message as such. Some of the material will be discarded as inappropriate, irrelevant, or low in quality. Other material will be useful for confirming or verifying information that will be presented to audiences.

SELECTING AND APPRAISING INFORMATION

Critical Thinking

Increasingly, it is clear that we live in a fact-innundated world. Making sense of the facts has become such a challenge that educators from preschool through higher education have gone to work on the problem. What they are trying to teach frequently is called *critical thinking*, although other terminology includes *creative thinking* and *better thinking*. Popular books and magazine articles have covered the subject, and expensive better-thinking seminars are offered to train adults to think clearly, draw reasonable inferences, and synthesize material. Emphasis is on the idea that thinking can be learned, that critical thinking is not synonymous with high intelligence, and that critical thinking can be developed at nearly any age.[1] Information specialist Robert Berkman, advising information seekers on the importance of critical thinking, wrote, "Critical thinking means not just believing something because everyone says it's so, or because something is repeated often or it is the first opinion you hear. Critical thinking also means questioning, probing, and looking for connections between data until you yourself are convinced of the truth of the matters under investigation."[2]

Language can be a cue that helps to invoke the critical thinking mode. Communicators involved in writing about the 500th anniversary of Columbus' voyage to "India" should have noticed that some publicists described the trip as "the discovery of America," while others referred to it as "Columbus' invasion of the Americas." Such a clear signal that sources operate on different assumptions should alert communicators to the dangers of adopting the perspective and language of one of the sources without raising critical questions. What can be learned when one examines the difference between *discovery* and *invasion*?

On the other hand, some language can be deceptive rather than illuminating. Writer Andrew Sullivan gives examples of political action committee (PAC) names that can confuse the unwary: Americans for Constitutional Freedom represents *Playboy* magazine; Citizens Organized for the National Interest defends Israel; the Center for Peace and Freedom lobbies for the Strategic Defense Initiative ("Star Wars"). Sullivan's examples are among hundreds cited in *PACS Americana*, a book by Edward Roeder, who also provides a computer program to help uncover the true purposes of PACs with deceptive names.[3]

Accepting numbers and statistics as accurate can be another pitfall. Numbers may tantalize the unsuspicious in a variety of ways. One rule is that when any administrator, activist, journalist, or scientist serves up a numerical estimate of risk that looks too precise to be true, it probably is. This warning applies to guesses or estimates provided by sources during interviews, to numbers emerging from computer models, to projections of how many will develop cancer, and how many will die following a nuclear accident.[4] The critical thinker asks, how can this figure be calculated? How did the expert arrive at this figure?

Communicators also are warned to examine vested interests. For example, the Environmental Protection Agency appointed a 16-member task force to investigate the health effects of second-hand cigarette smoke. But the Associated Press identified six of the appointed members, including the chair, as people with ties to the tobacco industry and members of the Center for Indoor Air Research, financed by three large tobacco firms. A seventh member with ties to the industry was appointed at the urging of a large tobacco company.[5] Instead of simply announcing the names of the appointees, the reporter provided a critical analysis of the appointments and alerted the public to the presence of tobacco officials as members of a scientific inquiry panel. Similarly, the roles of former high federal officials were examined for conflict of interest. Jeff Gerth and Sarah Bartlett reported that Henry A. Kissinger, Brent Scowcroft, and Lawrence S. Eagleburger formed Kissinger Associates, Inc. and began to consult for high fees from multinational companies, while continuing to serve on United States government advisory boards and to advise presidents on subjects closely related to the interests of clients for whom they consult. The authors asked, "In a field as subtle as foreign policy, can people like Mr. Kissinger and his associates wall off what they know of confidential Government discussions from what they can legitimately advise their corporate clients? And when people of their stature help shape Government decisions, can they ignore what they know of their corporate clients' interests?"[6]

Evaluation of visual information presents additional complexities. The popularity of small videocameras has meant that TV stations frequently receive copies of footage shot by bystanders at accidents or witnesses to earthquake, tornado, or hurricane devastation. As amateur camera operators became increasingly successful at having their video material used by TV stations, some stations and networks began to advertise for amateur footage. After a witness videotaped what appeared to be a brutal beating by police officers in Los Angeles, amateur photographers began to submit additional footage of police–resident encounters to TV news departments. While the photography and public interest in the material may suggest the tapes should be aired, news directors need to develop methods for checking out the origin and context of the tapes. Both ABC News and NBC News were taken in by an amateur video supposedly showing the Chernobyl nuclear power plant in the Soviet Union just after reactor meltdown. The networks were victims of a hoax in which an amateur submitted footage of a cement plant fire in Trieste, Italy.[7] Checking an atlas might have shown the network news departments what was wrong with the video: Chernobyl is a small town on a flood plain, whereas the pictures showed mountains in the background. Further, the

footage showed a large city with European-style housing, not Russian architecture. Aerial photographs also present a challenge. A satellite photography
specialist has warned TV networks that some interpreters of satellite photos
should not be trusted. CBS and ABC accepted faulty interpretations of photos as evidence that two nuclear reactors at Chernobyl had melted down,
only to return to the air acknowledging that only one had done so. Since
communicators generally do not have expertise in decoding aerial photography, critical thinking is to be applied in examining the credentials and expertise of those purporting to be specialists at understanding aerial photos.

These examples briefly illustrate the essential role of critical thinking in
helping communicators avoid thoughtless acceptance of anything declared to
be a fact. Further, critical thinking can lead to significant news stories that
transcend routine announcements and appointments. Critical thinking involves skills that can help the communicator do superior work on seemingly
routine assignments, in which appraisal and selection of information are the
unseen but essential qualities that contribute to an exceptional report.

According to librarian Mona McCormick, critical thinkers possess several
skills that help them in their selection of information gathered as the result of
a search strategy. McCormick's list of skills refers primarily to helping searchers evaluate information gathered from libraries or data bases.

> Critical thinkers are able to:
> *Identify main issues:* The main points of a paper or argument may be
> perfectly clear, or hidden in obscure language, or possibly never stated at
> all. Until the main ideas have been identified, the searcher cannot begin to
> test them.
> *Recognize underlying assumptions:* Analysis of ideas must go beyond the
> argument to the assumptions upon which the major points are based. Some
> assumptions are generally accepted; others are subject to doubt or may be
> untenable.
> *Evaluate evidence:* One must test claims to *see* if they are true. This in-
> volves discovering if the facts are relevant, if the facts support the conclu-
> sions drawn, if the data are adequate (are there enough?), and if important
> data have been omitted.
> *Evaluate authority:* Who is the author, and what are the author's qualifica-
> tions? Who is the publisher, and does the publisher have a point of view?
> *Recognize bias:* Listen for the drums of propaganda, and be aware of
> emotional appeals, labeling, and name-calling.
> *Understand the problems of language:* Recognize generalities, ambiguities,
> vague terms, cliches, and equivocations, and question definitions.
> *Relate information to ideas:* This has some of the elements of evaluating
> evidence. A connection must be made between information, facts, figures,
> however correct, and the way they contribute to ideas or concepts. Other-
> wise, information is never used to reach a conclusion.[8]

Even though this list of skills refers primarily to information gathered
from libraries or data bases, many of the critical thinker's skills are equally
important for identifying the best interviewee, the most accurate marketing

research, the most professionally conducted poll, or the most reliable eyewitness testimony. By honing the skills of critical thinking, the communicator is able to recognize appropriate information during the search itself and is prepared to select the best information during the winnowing process.

The basic tenets of critical thinking are embedded in the culture and can serve as norms for the selection of information. Communication researchers Winston Brembeck and William Howell, referring to the standards for evaluating persuasive arguments, identify six American norms for critical thinking that are similar to the skills identified by McCormick:

1. Orderliness—when the argument is arranged in an orderly manner
2. Clarity—when the argument is clearly stated
3. Directness—when the argument is straightforward and unobtuse
4. Concreteness—when the argument is grounded in solid ideas or examples
5. Specificity—when the argument refers to specific and precise ideas or examples
6. Accuracy—when the argument is seen to have the following attributes of accuracy:
   a. simple and clear wording
   b. recognition of opposing views
   c. compared items are really comparable
   d. representative statistics
   e. fair representative examples or illustrations
   f. support for generalizations
   g. quotes from reliable and qualified authorities
   h. avoidance of concealment or deception
   i. acknowledgment of all relevant facts
   j. appropriate documentation[9]

These norms for critical thinking about persuasive arguments can also be applied to critical thinking about most types of information gathered by communicators. The critical thinker asks whether the information gathered meets the norms that society has defined, the audience expects, and the profession requires. For instance, concern about missing children has caused many groups to warn that as many as 1.5 million children disappear each year and that strangers kidnap as many as 50,000 of them. These figures come from concerned-parents' organizations, children's groups, and other unofficial sources. A careful check of verifiable information sources (FBI missing-persons reports, official law-enforcement figures) shows that there are fewer than 30,000 open cases of missing children nationwide, including runaways and children abducted by a parent, and fewer than 100 active cases nationwide of children taken by strangers.[10] The communicator preparing a news story or a public-service announcement would need to carefully examine the figures from unofficial sources and look for "reliable and qualified authorities" and "appropriate documentation" before using any statistics on the number of missing children.

Climate of Opinion

Just as communicators recognize the culture-bound norms for critical thinking, they also operate within a climate of opinion that affects their selection of information. The crafting of messages and the information gathering preparatory to that crafting is done in a political, social, cultural, and temporal climate. At each step in the search-strategy process, the communicator makes decisions about the appropriateness of the information for the audience, the message content, and the message purpose. Information that has language or visual images that might have been appropriate for one time period could be jarringly out of place in another.

For instance, cigarette smoking used to connote sophistication and glamour, and many mass-communication films and photos reflected that cultural standard. However, as more evidence about the effects of cigarette smoking came to light, smoking was no longer equated with elegant or debonair people. Similarly, words such as *girl* for a woman, *liberal* for a person with a particular political point of view, or *evangelical fundamentalist* for a person with a certain religious point of view have connotations that change, depending on the geographic location, the time period, and the context. In selecting information for the content of a message, the communicator must take into account the connotations that the information might have.

The media also exist within a climate of opinion. Professionals working for a broadcast station or newspaper, an advertising department or agency, or a public-relations firm recognize that the public has well-articulated opinions about the mass-communication media. Selection of information for messages takes place within the context of what the audience expects and requires of the media. Polls consistently rate the advertising industry near the bottom of the scale in public confidence. News professionals do not fare very much better.[11] Communicators concerned about the public image of the media must identify, articulate, and consistently apply rigorous standards of information selection and appraisal in order to overcome the charges of inaccuracy, incompetence, fraud, unfairness, and bias that are regularly leveled at the profession.

Standards

The standards that communicators can apply to the selection and appraisal of information include concerns for evidence, credibility, audience factors, legal and ethical factors, and social taste, values, and conventions. Each of these areas of concern has been studied and, in some cases, codified for the assistance of communicators trying to apply consistent selection standards.

Evidence. Traditionally, the obvious use of evidence is in the deliberation process. Courts of law and legal professionals (lawyers, judges) are concerned about the admissibility of evidence, the appropriateness of evidence to the making of a case, and other judicial standards. The discussion of evidence as presented by rhetoricians and scholars of debate concentrates on the types of data that can be considered as evidence, the sources of evidence, and the classification of evidence for the purposes of effective persuasion or debate.[12]

For mass communicators, the use of standards of evidence takes on a slightly different hue. Evidence can be in the form of written materials (articles, books, letters, court records), oral communications (interview testimony), or personal observation, knowledge, or experience. The communicator can apply traditional tests of evidence to all the information that is gathered through the search-strategy process. When skillfully applied, these tests of evidence can alert the communicator to potential problems or inconsistencies in information, to gaps in the information being collected, and to areas that require further investigation.

The tests of evidence, as they apply to mass-communication information gathering, are:

1. Clarity	**7.** Sufficiency
2. Verifiability	**8.** Internal consistency
3. Accuracy	**9.** External consistency
4. Recency	**10.** Comparative quality
5. Relevance	**11.** Contextuality
6. Reputation	**12.** Statistical validity[13]

Clarity. During an interview with a person who witnessed a hold-up, a reporter discovers that the witness can be clear on only two points about the robbery and the perpetrator. The reporter would have to evaluate the testimony of the witness on the basis of clarity and may decide that the evidence is not trustworthy. Or, an advertising account executive might decide that the advertising campaign goals of the client advertiser are unclear, requiring further information gathering before planning the campaign.

Verifiability. A famous author may write an autobiography that includes a number of impressive claims about his or her education, achievements, and financial success. The communicator may be unable to verify that the author actually attended the schools because the school enrollment and alumni records do not include the author's name. Or, an interviewee may provide personal testimony about a particular event on the condition that the communicator not reveal the source of the information, making independent verification of the information difficult, if not impossible. Information that cannot be verified is suspect.

Accuracy. For an article about the research programs of countries studying Halley's Comet, the writer would want to get the most accurate information about each country's activities. The writer might reject information about the research programs from other journalistic accounts on the basis of the accuracy test and decide to contact the various research agencies directly. Or, background information for an ad comparing airline routes and frequency of flights would require accurate route and flight figures.

Recency.   A public-relations firm working on the problem of airport noise for an airport commission needs the most recent figures on the number of plane takeoffs and landings since deregulation of the airline industry. Information about how recent plane activity compares with prederegulation activity would be useful as well. Or, an ad campaign for a brand of pizza requires the most recent information about consumer preferences and media habits of pizza eaters. A marketing study two years old would be rejected on the basis of the recency test.

Relevance.   An advertiser evaluating market research about consumer characteristics must decide whether the research is relevant to the product or service being advertised. A study of people who buy chicken may or may not be relevant to the advertiser of turkey. Or, a reporter writing about the nation's *fiscal* policy may reject the notion of interviewing an expert on *monetary* policy based on the relevance test. The testimony of a movie celebrity about the farmers' plight might be rejected in favor of an agricultural economist's view based on the test of relevance.

Reputation.   People, institutions, and records have reputations. A reporter might try to arrange an interview with a government official who has a reputation for being candid and forthright on the issue of tax reform. The same reporter might avoid another official because of his or her reputation for stonewalling the press. Or a public-relations practitioner might rely on the *Rand McNally Commercial Atlas and Marketing Guide* for figures on retail trade in the United States because of its reputation for recent and accurate information.

Sufficiency.   A news release being prepared by a public-relations firm about a new synthetic growth hormone requires that the communicator anticipate all the questions that the audience will have about the product. The communicator must have information about the effectiveness of the product in stimulating growth, the cost of treatment, the side effects of the hormone if administered improperly, and the product test history. Incomplete information in any of these areas will send the communicator back to the search process on the basis of the sufficiency test.

Internal Consistency.   The communicator might decide not to use a particular document because the figures for average household income used on page 15 are inconsistent with those on page 38, indicating a serious internal-consistency problem. Or, the testimony of an interviewee varies widely over the course of a three-hour interview, suggesting that the interviewee is being inconsistent in his or her own story.

External Consistency. Two reports on the implications of a change in real-estate taxes come to different conclusions about the projected tax on an $80,000 house, alerting the communicator that there is an external-consistency problem with the evidence. This suggests that further information is needed to clarify the inconsistency. Or, an advertising firm conducts its own research about the market for a new brand of jeans, and the conclusions differ from those of an industry-wide research project on the same product, suggesting an external-consistency problem.

Comparative Quality. Decisions about what constitutes "good" information or the "best" information are necessary at some point. An advertising researcher might decide that of two studies of teen-age athletes, the one that specifically addresses athletes' leisure activities is the most useful. Or, a reporter might decide that among all the interviews she conducted with "experts" on the subject of health-care costs, two stand out as being the most informative and containing the newest or freshest perspectives.

Contextuality. All information exists within a particular context. An interviewee's comments at one point in an interview cannot be taken out of the context of the rest of the interview. Isolated figures in a report about the incidence of police loafing on the job cannot be taken out of the context of the rest of the report, which might indicate that the problem is not widespread. Both the context and the time period within which information exists must be recognized and respected by the communicator gathering information for messages. If the context or time period cannot be determined, the information is suspect.

Statistical Validity. It is not necessary for the communicator to become a statistician in order to test the validity of statistical information. Simple questions about the method of gathering the statistics, the method of analyzing the data, and the standards for reporting the results are within the communicator's ability. A reporter might question whether the results of a social survey discussed in an academic paper were based on a random sample. Or, an advertising researcher might have to determine whether a market study includes standard tests of reliability for statistical data.

The communicator applies the tests of evidence to information gathered during the search-strategy process. After evaluating information using these tests, the communicator may decide that additional information of a certain type is needed or that more authoritative, recent, relevant, or accurate information is required to round out the perspective of the message. The communicator can return to the standard sources of information in order to locate the necessary information, as the models discussed in Chapter 1 indicate. The tests of evidence give the communicator some independent measures of the appropriateness of material gathered to that point in the search.

In addition to the communicator's judgment about the evidence, there are concerns about the acceptability of the evidence to the audience. The communicator, after all, is gathering and preparing information for an audience, and the evidence that is amassed for the purposes of the message must be consistent with audience characteristics. The communicator might ask some questions:

1. Will the audience understand and accept the evidence in the message?
2. Is the evidence instrumental in making the case or in supporting the claim of the message?
3. Does the evidence coincide with the beliefs and attitudes of the audience? If not, substantially more information than what is usually needed will be required to make the point, because the audience will be predisposed to disbelieve the message.
4. Is the evidence at an appropriate technical and intellectual level for the audience?
5. Will the audience know and respect the source of the evidence?[14]

Depending on how the communicator answers these questions, the information search steps may have to be retraced in order to be sure that the information and the evidence gathered are appropriate for the needs of the audience.

Credibility.   Another major component in the selection of information for messages is the credibility of the sources used. There are many facets to any discussion of credibility and the media. Audience members have access to all kinds of information from sources other than the media. The public has some standards for what is credible, authentic, fair, unbiased, and acceptable information. There is also an implicit recognition on the part of the public that communicators should operate by the same credibility standards as those held by the general populace. That is not necessarily the perception the public has about the media, however.

Studies regularly find that public confidence in the media and media professionals is low.[15] The confidence that people have, or do not have, in media institutions and media practitioners can be explained in part by a measure of the credibility of these institutions and practitioners. Studies going back to the 1930s have indicated that the credibility of the media is of concern to the general public, and more recent studies have reinforced the finding that there are problems with media credibility. As news, advertising, and public-relations methods and techniques become more sophisticated, there is the danger that public confidence will fall even lower, a reflection of public suspicions of high-tech, complex methods of information gathering and dissemination.

For these reasons, it is imperative that communicators develop standards of credibility for their own information selection. If media professionals are regularly seen to be gathering and presenting high-quality, credible, and accurate information, public concerns about media behavior will have to focus elsewhere.

Traditionally, decisions about the credibility of information involved a concept called *ethos*. Classical theorists used this concept to describe the personal characteristics of a speaker, such as authoritativeness, trustworthiness, likability, and dynamism. In an age of a mass society made up of many divergent sources and types of information, it is less likely that individuals have personal knowledge of the specific ethos of particular sources of information. Therefore, it becomes necessary to rely on some generalizations and associations between individuals and the institutions they represent or the information they provide.

Communicators have two concerns about credibility when selecting information for messages. They must be aware of the credibility of the source of the information: the news reporter must judge the authority and trustworthiness of the interviewee or the report; the advertising professional must judge the credibility of the testimony of consumers of a product or the conclusions of market research; the public-relations practitioner must judge the believability of opinion research. And communicators must also be aware of their own credibility to the audience. They have to select and present information that will be credible and useful to the recipients of their messages. Their messages must be crafted carefully and consistently in order to build public confidence in the credibility of the information presented.

Communicators can rely on some indexes of credibility when selecting information for messages. That is, they can rely on some basic principles regarding the believability of information that they collect and from which they select. All information, whether personal testimony or documents, can be examined for its trustworthiness and appropriateness for each message. Individuals can be judged on standards of authority, expertise, skills, ethical qualities, or institutional affiliations. Documents or records can be judged for their accuracy, consistency, and tone. Rhetoric researchers Robert Newman and Dale Newman list 14 indexes of credibility, and although they are specific to journalistic concerns, they may be applied to information gathered for advertising or public-relations purposes.

Situational Tests
1. Tension. The lower the tension associated with an event, the higher the credibility of reports about it.
2. Accessibility. The more accessible the situation being reported on, both to the reporters and their audience, the more credible the reports.
3. Freedom to report—absence of gag rule. The more freedom a witness has to report things as he sees them, the greater his credibility.

Documentary Tests
4. Authenticity. The greater the presumption of authenticity, the higher the credibility of a document.
5. Internal consistency. The higher the internal consistency of an author, the more credible his testimony.

6. Carefulness of generalization. The more careful the generalizations of a writer, the higher the credibility of his testimony.
7. Reluctance. The greater the damage of his own testimony to a witness, the more credible it is.

Characteristics of the Writer
8. Expertise. The greater the relevant expertise of an author, the higher his credibility.
9. Objectivity. The greater the objectivity of an author, the more credible his testimony.
10. Accuracy record. The more accurate the description and prediction record of a source, the higher the credibility of his testimony in general.

Tests of Primary Authorities
11. Eyewitness principle. The greater a witness' personal observation of a matter to which he testifies, the higher his credibility.
12. Contemporaneity. The more contemporaneous the report of a witness, the more credible his testimony.

Tests of Secondary Sources
13. Selection of primary sources. The more discerning a writer's selection of primary sources, the more credible his testimony.
14. Accuracy of citation. The more accurate the citations of a writer, the more credible his testimony.[16]

Each of these factors may contribute to the credibility of information collected by communicators for messages. Reporters regularly select interviewees on the basis of their records of past reliability (accuracy record). Advertising professionals are interested in information from the actual consumers of products or services for which they produce ads (eyewitness principle). Public-relations practitioners like to have recognized experts as spokespersons for their company or position (expertise). Selection of information implies the application of standards of credibility to all material gathered in preparation for a message.

Audience Factors. All communication is persuasive in some way. Messages persuade the audience to pay attention to and give credence to the information contained in the words and pictures. In selecting information for messages, communicators consider the information needs of the audience and the persuasive needs of the message. As has been stated before, audience members have information needs that can be anticipated by the astute communicator. When analyzing information gathered for a message, the communicator can ask, "Will this information meet the needs of the audience to whom this message is directed?" "Will the newspaper reader go away wondering why the story didn't include that figure for farm income?" "Will the potential customer go away wondering why the advertisement for the computer didn't have any statement about the memory capacity of the new model?" If there is reason to believe that the information base is insufficient for the needs of the audience, the search for additional information begins.

Similarly, there is competition for the attention of audiences. In their information selection, communicators want to choose material that will be persuasive, present that material in attractive ways, and succeed in moving the audience. The information-selection process, then, can also take into account the need to make messages that are going to hold their own in the flood of information that engulfs audience members every day. The news story that includes attractively presented data on the changes in neighborhood housing based on census information will be more effective than the same story based on the tired old pontifications of the city alderperson who was elected on a promise to improve housing. The ad that includes information about the health benefits of ground turkey over ground beef (leaner, fewer calories, higher nutrition) will be more effective with a health-conscious audience than an ad that does not have that information. The public-relations video release to cable-access stations that includes a summary of an independent scientific study confirming the safety of a company's methods of disposing of hazardous chemical wastes will be more credible than the release that includes only company spokespersons' assurances. Audience considerations play an important role in the communicator's decisions about information gathered through a search strategy.

Legal and Ethical Factors.   Whenever the communicator is faced with assessing information for use in a message, there is concern for the legal and ethical ramifications of using that information. There are also legal and ethical considerations in the gathering of the information in the first place. A considerable body of law and a great deal of traditional practice inform the communicator's decisions about the legal and ethical collection and use of information. Chapter 10 will deal with some of these considerations in more detail. It is important to mention here, though, that the selection process does include some restraints and obligations on the part of the communicator.

The advertising substantiation rule requires that any claim made by an advertiser be defensible with information *in hand*. This means that the communicator cannot make any claim in advertising copy for which there is insufficient supporting evidence or information. A judge might require that the advertiser produce the substantiating information in court and may even require the advertiser to run expensive and embarrassing retractions if the information is not forthcoming. For these reasons, it is imperative that any claim be fully supported by background information.

Similarly, news professionals have an obligation to defend their reports before editors and, eventually, the public. The background information must be sufficient to support any conclusions or observations the reporter arrives at in order to avoid charges of both unethical and illegal news practices. Unfounded claims can be cause for libel action. A solid, thorough, and complete search for background information and complete documentation of all evidence is the reporter's best defense against such charges.

Appraisal and selection of information, then, includes an obligation to keep an eye on the legal and ethical concerns that might arise from the collection or use of information that the search process has uncovered.

Taste, Values, and Conventions.   Among the many complaints against the media, perhaps the most vehement involve charges that the media violate simple standards of taste and public values. It is certainly true that mass-communication activities are pervasive and inescapable. The media reflect the culture and the society in which they exist. For example, the advertisements of half a century ago reflect what we would consider to be an unacceptable level of racism and sexism. News stories from that time also reflect a great deal about what was important to the public and about the issues that gripped the nation. The act of placing a message in the public arena takes on considerable significance when cast in the light of creating a historical record of a time and place.

Selection of information for messages takes place within the strictures of social and cultural values and expectations. The communicator chooses information for the news story or the ad with public taste and values in mind. Of course, it is impossible for the communicator to remove himself or herself from or to stand aloof from the culture in which the messages are being created. As such, the information component of each message is a reflection of the values and norms of the individual communicator, the communicator's media organization, and the society at a particular time.

There will always be attempts to change the boundaries of public taste, and many of these attempts will be successful. Advertisements that once were considered too risqué to appear anywhere in the United States now grace the billboards of every highway. When the risks of offending public taste seem to be overshadowed by the potential for public good, the communicator faces making a choice about information gathered and placed in the public arena. Some audience members might be offended by the investigative reporter's persistent interview methods in order to gather the information needed for a report, but the resulting story might mean that an act of crime or corruption is uncovered and corrected. Some audience members might be aghast at the inclusion of information about family planning clinics in a public-service announcement about preventing teenage pregnancy, but that information might be vital to the message. The communicator, in conjunction with editors, supervisors, clients, or company officials, will make those decisions regarding public taste and values as they relate to information gathering and use. Informed by consistent standards, ethical and legal practices, and concern for the community, the profession, and the media organization, those decisions are more easily made.

SYNTHESIZING INFORMATION

Selecting and evaluating information leads to the final step in the search-strategy process—synthesizing all the selected information. The communicator has been engaged in a continual process of information synthesis through each step in the search, but as with evaluation and selection, there is a point at which synthesis becomes the main focus of activity. This involves scrutiny of all material that has been selected to identify common themes, agreed-on facts and views, differences of opinion, discrepancies in interpretation, and so on. The reporter might discover through the synthesis process that it is necessary to write a side-bar (that is, a short, accompanying piece to the main story) in order to fully explain the ramifications of the new medical procedure being reported on. The advertising account executive might decide that it is necessary to produce both print and radio ads for the new product after reviewing all the marketing studies about the target audience's media habits.

Much of the synthesis process involves what can be called *prewriting*. Prewriting has been described by a number of authors and refers to the steps that any writer goes through before actually sitting down to write: conceptualizing the topic, planning the approach, sorting the information, and mentally writing the story, ad, public-relations release, or other message.[17] The prewriting process, then, is the point at which the communicator begins making decisions about what the gathered information means and how that meaning can be conveyed to the audience. Synthesizing all the facts, opinions, views, and themes in the gathered information is an implicit part of developing the interpretation of the information for the message and the audience.

Synthesis may involve a one-shot message, such as a short news story or a retail ad intended to run for a brief period in local newspapers. But it also can involve hundreds of pieces of information, gathered over a long period of time from diverse sources. For example, a scholar writing a history of journalism, advertising, or public relations has extensive and varied sources to consider when interpreting a subject. So do reporters working on investigative stories or interpretive series for which extensive research is undertaken. In one such investigative project, a number of reporters for the *Houston Post* produced research connecting savings and loan failures in Texas, California, Florida, and Oklahoma to figures in organized crime and CIA-connected people. The complex synthesis included tips from anonymous sources, anonymously provided documents, criminal law cases, commercial data-base searches, law-enforcement reports, bankruptcy filings, corporate annual reports, lawsuits, tax appraisals, partnership agreements, and interviews with investors, real-estate brokers, banking experts, private investigators, FBI agents, and United States attorneys.[18]

In the case of the savings and loan project, great quantities of material were collected before the first story ever ran. Since information continued to be added by various staff members, careful examination of the collected material was required prior to each subsequent story published. The unfolding of the story illustrates the idea that the communicator may need to retrace the path through the search-strategy model numerous times. This is the case not only in investigative journalism but also in message preparation for advertisements and public relations. The advertising campaign strategist may decide that although the information in hand is complete in providing an overview of the industry and the product category, additional information is needed to understand how a consumer is going to react to the new product. The advertising specialists on the team might not be able to craft an adequate message without that additional information about realistic consumer attitudes. Or, the reporter might notice that all the selected information for a story about declining drug use among teens concurs on the general trend, but lacks enough data about why the trend is occurring. The reporter's interpretation of the story would have to be based on speculation without additional information from sociologists, drug rehabilitation experts, and psychologists studying adolescents. The synthesis process would allow each of these communicators to first identify what additional information is needed and then focus the resulting search.

Even when the synthesis process does not identify gaps or inconsistencies in the gathered information, the communicator can benefit from a systematic review of all selected information. Aware of the need to form appropriate messages based on complete information about the topic, the audience, and the purpose of the message, the communicator uses the synthesis process to begin mentally crafting the message. This helps the communicator plan how the message will begin, decide what information is the most important for the audience, design the look or sound of the message, organize the logical progression of facts and/or persuasive arguments in the message, and so forth. When the communicator finally reaches the stage of actually writing the message, all the information will be organized and logically presented for the most effect.

The synthesis process, then, is the final step in the information-gathering and -selection procedure before producing a mass-communication message. The selection, evaluation, and synthesis of information collected through a systematic and comprehensive search strategy are formidable tasks for the communicator working under quick deadlines. However, any good search process will turn up more information than will be appropriate for or fit into a message. Therefore, sharp evaluation and synthesis skills will serve the communicator well.

LINKS TO THE SEARCH STRATEGY

In this step of the search strategy, all the previous activity in the search strategy is reviewed. Preliminary selection and evaluation of information have been done at each earlier step, but the communicator makes final information decisions at this point. The importance of critical thinking in a fact-inundated world is stressed. Critical thinking can help communicators avoid gullibility and transcend the limits of a seemingly routine assignment.

The search-strategy model identifies standards for selection such as evidence, credibility, audience needs, and legal, ethical, and taste issues involved in information evaluation. The communicator may also seek to understand and compensate for the influence of information subsidies that may distort the evaluation and synthesis process. For instance, information provided to the communicator by such major information providers as governments, political parties, and industries can be evaluated for its capacity to influence the assumptions of the communicator and the approach taken in producing the message.

The synthesis step of the search strategy requires the communicator to account for the accumulated meaning of the material gathered. This involves asking, "What does this material mean?" "Can I summarize the main point of this material?" and "How does the material fit in relation to the other information collected throughout the search process?" The communicator identifies common themes, discrepancies, and points that need to be verified or labeled as contradictory. The selection and synthesis step of the search strategy, then, provides the last chance for the communicator to identify missing material, catch errors, and make final decisions about the shape of the message.

Chapter 10 examines the social responsibility context in which all messages are produced. The chapter will review the societal perspectives, professional and organizational perspectives, and the individual perspectives on social responsibility and legal obligations that influence the production of media messages.

NOTES

1. Janet Elder, "A Learned Response," *New York Times*, Special Report, Education, Section 4A, 6 January 1991, 23.
2. Robert I. Berkman, *Find It Fast* (New York: Harper & Row, 1990), 250.
3. Andrew Sullivan, "Noms de PACs: A Lobbying Group's Name Won't Tell You Its Game," *Minneapolis Star and Tribune*, 24 September 1986, 19A. Originally published in the *New Republic*.
4. Malcolm W. Brown, "Big, Precise Numbers Are Very Likely Estimates," *Minneapolis Star and Tribune*, 10 September 1986, 14C. Originally published in the *New York Times*.
5. Associated Press, "Six Panelists on Smoking Are Linked to Tobacco," *New York Times*, 10 November 1990, A9.
6. Jeff Gerth and Sarah Bartlett, "Kissinger and Friends and Revolving Doors," *New York Times*, 30 April 1989, A1.
7. George Warren, "Big News, Little Cameras," *Washington Journalism Review*, December 1990, 37–39.
8. Mona McCormick, *New York Times Guide to Reference Materials*, rev. ed. (New York: Times Books, 1985), 186.
9. Winston L. Brembeck and William S. Howell, *Persuasian: A Means of Social Influence*, 2d ed. (Englewood Cliffs, N.J.: Prentice-Hall, 1976), 193–194.
10. Diane Griego and Louis Kilzer, "Experts Say Data on Lost Children Exaggerated," *Minneapolis Star and Tribune*, 23 May 1985, 17A–18A. Originally published in the *Denver Post*.
11. For instance, Gallup has conducted five surveys since 1976 asking the question, "How would you rate the honesty and ethical standards of people in these different fields?" "Very high," "high," "average," "low," or "very low." The

results, which show little change from 1976 to 1985, put advertising practitioners third from the bottom, with 59 percent of respondents judging their standards low or very low, just above insurance salesmen and automobile salesmen. Newspaper reporters are twelfth out of 25. Television reporters or commentators did the best, coming in ninth out of 25.

12. See, for example, Robert P. Newman and Dale R. Newman, *Evidence* (Boston: Houghton Mifflin, 1969); James C. McCroskey, *An Introduction to Rhetorical Communication*, 4th ed. (Englewood Cliffs, N.J.: Prentice-Hall, 1982); Austin J. Freeley, *Argumentation and Debate: Rational Decision Making*, 4th ed. (Belmont, Calif.: Wadsworth, 1976); Douglas Ehninger and Wayne Brockriede, *Decision by Debate*, 2d ed. (New York: Harper & Row, 1978); J. Vernon Jensen, *Argumentation: Reasoning in Communication* (New York: Van Nostrand, 1981).

13. After Jensen, *Argumentation*, 135–136.

14. Jensen, *Argumentation*, 134.

15. Mitchell V. Charnley, "Preliminary Notes on a Study of Newspaper Accuracy," *Journalism Quarterly* 13 (1936): 394–401; Maxwell E. McCombs and Laura Washington, "Opinion Surveys Offer Conflicting Clues as to How Public Views Press," *presstime* (February 1983): 4–10; Eric Zanot, "Public Attitudes Toward Advertising," *Proceedings of the Annual Conference of the American Academy of Advertising* (East Lansing, Mich.: The Academy, 1981): 142–146; "Confidence in Institutions," *Gallup Report*, no. 238 (July 1985): 3, 10, 12; *Newspaper Credibility: Building Reader Trust* (Washington, D.C.: American Society of Newspaper Editors, 1985).

16. Newman and Newman, *Evidence*, 87–88.

17. See, for example, Wallace Kaufman and William Powers, *The Writer's Mind* (Englewood Cliffs, N.J.: Prentice-Hall, 1970); David L. Grey, *The Writing Process: A Behavioral Approach to Communicating Information and Ideas* (Belmont, Calif.: Wadsworth, 1972).

18. Steve Weinberg, "The Mob, the CIA, and the S&L Scandal," *Columbia Journalism Review*, November–December 1990, 28–35.

10

Social Responsibility
and the Search Strategy

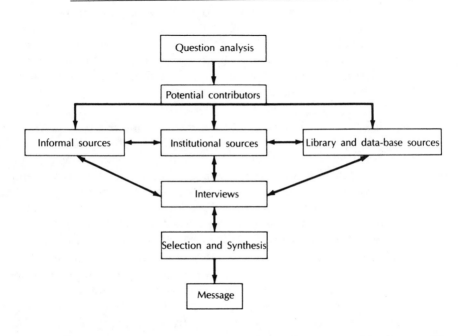

Dilemmas about the proper use of information are as old as the command-ments, which forbid lying and false witness. But the complexity of new information technologies and their capacity to bring words and images at the tap of a few keystrokes are keeping critics and ethics specialists well occu-pied. Communicators, faculty, critics, and consumers increasingly raise ques-tions about media practices. Critical commentary abounds in the popular press, as well as in books and in trade and academic journals.[1] Those who seek examples of questionable use of information find it easy to assemble bulging files of clippings, in which various offenses are outlined. Further, the various branches of the mass-communication industries continue to criticize each other and governments as well for the way they dispense or withhold information from the public.

Contemporary accounts of legal and ethical issues reflected in the popular and trade press recently have involved:

- *Theft of news video from satellites.* TV stations that gather reports for their own use (and for resale or sharing with cooperating stations) have charged that competing stations have stolen their video footage from the satellites that transmit the video from station to station. Such charges include those by CNN that NBC took its coverage of the Beijing uprisings in China and by CONUS, a large network of cooperating stations, that ABC, CBS, and CNN pirated its material on a Colombian airline crash in New York. Professionals pondering the problems posed by such allegations find that lawsuits probably are too cumbersome and costly to be practical. The prescription: professional ethics should be developed.[2]

- *Deceptive advertising.* A Volvo advertising campaign seemed to promise that a Volvo car could survive a monster truck attack that left competing cars crumpled. Extras hired by the ad agency for the crowd scenes at the car-crushing exhibition became curious about the welding they observed at the taping. They noted the strengthening of the Volvo and the weakening of the structure of competitors' cars, then contacted state officials. The Federal Trade Commission also investigated. The penalty: Volvo paid a fine, ran corrective ads admitting the fraud; the ad agency resigned the account.[3]

- *News room espionage.* A Florida TV station became suspicious that someone outside its news room was accessing its computer system and tampering with its news log and its schedule of stories to be broadcast. The unauthorized entrance into the station's computer was linked to the home computer of a former staff member, who had joined the news staff of a competing station. The outcome: an arrest for conspiracy to break into another station's computer.[4]

- *Video news releases.* Video press releases imitate TV stories produced by station staff members but in reality promote—usually in a subtle way—a product, point of view, political candidate, or politician. Audiences can be misled, not only about the origin of the message, but also about accuracy of claims and the effectiveness or safety of the promoted product or of a politician's record. One such release identified an antibiotic and showed a physician praising the drug. The video release failed to identify side effects, which by law would have to be addressed if the promotion had been an ad rather than a press release. Hundreds of TV stations receive such video press releases without charge; provision is made for stations to localize the release by substituting the voice of their own reporter for the voice on the tape.[5] A Nielsen Media Research survey of 200 TV stations in

1988 showed that 93 percent of the stations could receive such releases through satellite downlinking facilities and, further, that nearly 75 percent of those stations were willing to use the releases.[6] Magazine "advertorials" and newspaper special sections present similar information problems for audiences. The dilemma: media get free "features" while sponsors get free promotions, the public is misled, and federal regulators don't know how to apply standards where they are needed.

- *Putting interns in unethical situations.* At firms offering internships, students frequently learn insider lessons on the ethical and legal standards of some in media industries. For instance, some investigative news units in TV broadcasting have asked interns to give false or concealed identities in order to place them inside organizations under investigation. An intern at a newspaper was asked to conceal her identity as part of an extensive set of investigative interviews. Another intern in a newspaper advertising department was instructed to conceal his identity as an intern when he asked to have advertising rate cards of competitors mailed to his home address. The competitors' rates then were used as the basis for preparing an advertising pitch that would undercut the competition. The result: student interns learned that corporations think it is acceptable to ask interns to seek information illegally or unethically, aware that interns are in a poor position to challenge these directives or to protest the ethics involved.

These examples illustrate problems of ethics and law in the collection of information. They are but a small portion of the entire measure of ethical and legal issues that involve information use, which include privacy violations, entrapment, eavesdropping, plagiarism, stealing information, violating a promised confidentiality, and concealing a conflict of interest when collecting or using information. Such information-gathering issues present considerable challenges, all of which have been made more complex by the development of new information technologies.

This chapter, then, concentrates on questions of law and ethics as aspects of social responsibility that are chiefly concerned with the gathering of information, rather than its dissemination. Legal obligations include those that bind all communicators to a set of either negative or positive obligations. The law embodies in specific ways many social and political values that are held in high esteem in a particular culture. Each communicator and communication firm or organization is equally bound to obey the law. Ethical obligations, in contrast, represent self-control and self-enforcement on the part of individual communicators, their professional associations, and the organizations for which they work. Ethical obligations are voluntary. And they are much more often a matter of dispute than legal requirements. For example, United States law prohibits the advertising of tobacco over the airwaves. In recognition of the dangers of tobacco to health, some United States and

Canadian publications, believing it is unethical to advertise harmful materials, refuse to accept tobacco advertising. The management of the Minneapolis Metrodome stadium refuses to allow tobacco advertising inside the stadium. Both decisions lie in the ethical realm, rather than the legal realm. But the United States government, which enforces the prohibition of tobacco advertising on radio and television, has exerted pressure abroad to permit the advertising of United States tobacco products on the air in countries that might import American tobacco products if the demand can be developed. Legal, yes, since Congress has not prohibited such activity. Ethical? No, say opponents of this government action. Are newspapers and magazines that profit from tobacco advertising giving enough coverage to United States government promotion of tobacco abroad? No, say opponents, who point to the vested interest publishers have in keeping advertisers happy.

Getting agreement about what is socially responsible communication—or socially irresponsible communication, for that matter—is more difficult than finding the cases, however. It is generally conceded that socially responsible communicators are not content merely with staying on the right side of the law. While the law embodies a significant portion of society's values, individuals and organizations that want to be considered ethical must go beyond the rough requirements of the law itself and adopt higher and more thoughtful standards.

Throughout the process of information search, assessment, and synthesis, communicators face many situations that challenge their personal senses of ethics and fair play as well as their organizations' policies and the social and political expectations of society at large. Communicators generally are sensitive to their responsibilities to society. That is not to say that carrying out these responsibilities is simple. Conflicts abound. As the examples cited suggest, the action that promotes an overall social good may harm, or appear to harm, one's organization, reputations of oneself or one's profession or organization, and the public's right to accurate information. Communicators, in formal conferences and in casual conversation, are giving increased and serious attention to social responsibility in their fields.

The scrutiny goes far beyond self-examination. The mass-communication industries and the professionals who carry out responsibilities within them are the subject of substantial scrutiny and criticism from other quarters. Undoubtedly, the concern reflects widespread agreement that mass-communication organizations are among the most powerful of American social institutions. Power is accompanied by a public demand for responsibility. Since the American media system is the least regulated media system on the globe, these demands for accountability suggest that public opinion and self-regulation are expected to offer constraints. The debates about what constitutes social responsibility are both intricate and subtle. As the examples that introduce this chapter suggest, they often reflect legitimate competing social, corporate, and personal values.

As information technologies have grown more elaborate and more widely available, the challenges to use information responsibly have increased. Both audiences and message makers are afflicted by information overload. Communicators, for their part, have experienced changes in the way they must work and in the demands society makes on them. Communicators must be competent, at the very least, with the equipment of the computer age. They must recognize that the production of information itself has grown dramatically, that some information is easily and inexpensively accessible, while other information is difficult to get and costly. Some information is "sponsored" and disseminated for the purpose of shaping public attitudes; often, this is the material that is both cheap and readily accessible. New information technologies allow communicators to "find it in a data base" and to assume the information meets appropriate quality standards. But electronic information can proliferate in print and electronic forms and can be incorporated virtually endlessly without verification or close scrutiny by those who use it. Communication scholar Anthony Smith noted that for much of today's media, writing is less concerned with authorship than with such information-centered tasks as comparing material from data bases, manipulating ever-expanding bodies of information, and serving as the intermediary between the reader and a constantly expanding store of information.[7]

The gap between any particular bit of information and the eventual audience is expanding. Society may well be expecting greater accountability from communicators at the very time when they are incorporating into their messages an increasing amount of information gathered by others. Along with increased skill in assessing information, communicators need more training in the responsibilities they face in their field. In addition, the reputations of individuals and of media organizations, and their overall credibility with the public, hinges in part on how they handle information.

Media organizations have all the legal and ethical obligations that are typical of other businesses. But beyond those, they have special responsibilities related to the way they collect and select information, represent reality, and entertain with their stories. This brief treatment of responsibility focuses on conduct connected with the gathering and selecting of material for mass-media messages. It concerns the legality and ethics that attend all activities that take place during the search strategy. Many other issues are significant but do not specifically concern the process of search strategy: fair hiring and employment practices, language and images as instruments of discrimination, conflicts of interest, and marketing decisions that ignore some audiences. Even thus restricted, this discussion can treat only in cursory fashion some of the issues that communicators and media organizations confront.

THE SOCIAL RESPONSIBILITY CONTEXT

The anthropologist Edward T. Hall has written, "Culture is communication and communication is culture."[8] Individuals and institutions create culture through communication, which, in turn, influences individuals and institutions. We all exist—or are caught together—in the web of culture that we spin. To be sure, mass communication is but one force in the culture-making enterprise. Both interpersonal and public communication play significant roles. But the pervasiveness, prominence, and power of mass communication have grown steadily in the past century. The recent information-age developments contribute to an increasing influence of mass communication in society. Communicators can expect that substantial attention will be directed to the manner in which they gather and use information. That attention will come from other social institutions, from media organizations, and from individuals. As in the recent past, individual communicators will continue to offer criticism and suggestions. Much of their comment reflects the common sense that communicators themselves must live in the world they help to construct. At root, their criticism reflects a concern for accuracy and fairness, a concern they share with other critics and commentators.

Mass-media messages constitute what scholar Gilbert Seldes has called "the public arts." These are the popular art forms, stories, songs, and dramas that are produced by teams of professionals for presentation to the public as a whole. Writing in 1956, Seldes was early in recognizing society's essential interest in the nature and quality of mass-communicated art. These arts, Seldes wrote, "are matters of public concern, subject to public opinion," and "even *outside of law* the public has sovereign rights over them, since these arts, no less than the institutions of government, belong to the people." Seldes foresaw that revolutionary changes in entertainment and communication were likely to affect fundamental social values and reminded his readers that they should give serious attention to these arts. Further, he urged the managers of all cultural institutions to use the public arts to protect the national cultural heritage.[9]

In recognizing the power of the public and of those who direct cultural institutions, Seldes and other observers have accepted the principle that in democracies, the public responds to mass communicators informally and indirectly rather than through bureaucracies and elected officials. Government regulation of the mass media has been feared and restricted in the United States as in no other industrialized nation. This circumstance has put unprecedented power and responsibility in the hands of mass communicators in the United States. With some exceptions, those who gather and select information for the public are free to perform this work without interference from government. But they also are answerable for their actions to public opinion and to the law. These circumstances ensure that the social responsibility debate on media performance will be lively and enduring.

Inevitably, this debate proceeds on limited grounds. What is comfortably forgotten is that media systems everywhere, no less in the United States, are among the principal instruments of social control. The messages distributed may discomfort individuals in the other major power centers. Occasionally, these messages may lead to the removal of a football coach, a chief executive officer, or even a president. But the power centers themselves remain and, in fact, are sustained in power at least in part by the mass-media system.

Together, news, advertising, and public-relations activities work as maintainers of existing social, political, and economic arrangements.

The Societal Perspective

A closer look at responsibility from a societal perspective considers the relationship of the mass-media systems to other major systems and the reputation the mass-media organizations and professionals have with the public.

Scientific study of public opinion shows that major institutions have ups and downs when public confidence in these institutions is measured. Overall confidence in major institutions fell, for example, beginning in the mid-1960s. The drop in confidence was felt in the mass-communication fields, along with other major sectors. In fact, some observers blamed the news media, in particular, for the public's reduced confidence in such institutions as the federal government, the military establishment, and business. Irrespective of that charge, public opinion about the trustworthiness of mass communication varies from one period to another. In addition, opinion about those in print and broadcast news, in advertising, and in public relations differs.

Recent studies of credibility, reputation, and ethics of the news media have produced findings that may seem in conflict. The amount of recent study on this topic alone suggests that organizations commissioning rather expensive research had reason to be concerned about the public's response to newsmaking. One study commissioned by the American Society of Newspaper Editors showed that daily newspapers and television news had comparable credibility ratings. They were judged high in credibility by 32 percent, medium by 43 percent, and low by 25 percent of those polled. Among the journalistic practices most heavily criticized were deception and invasion of privacy. Overall, the national representative sample of adults agreed, with only 6 percent disagreeing, that the investigation of corruption and abuses of power is important. However, solid majorities disapprove of such techniques as clandestinely recording conversations, failing to identify oneself as a reporter or posing as someone other than a reporter, paying people for information, and running stories that quote sources who cannot be identified.[10]

Another study of the public's response to the news media concentrated on "believability" of the news media. It found that, while individuals may disapprove of particular reporting methods, overall that disapproval has not translated to disbelief in the information presented by the news media. There is no believability crisis, this study said. Further, neither print nor broadcast technology has a believability advantage with the public.[11]

A study that specifically examined the perceptions about people in a variety of fields was conducted by the Gallup organization. This study looked at perceived ethical standards in 1981 and again in 1990, asking respondents how they rate the honesty and ethical standards of those in medicine, religion, teaching, engineering, mass communication, Congress, and various sales fields. Opinion held quite steadily during the nine-year period, with pharmacists, clergy, medical practitioners, and college teachers enjoying the best reputations with the public. For individuals in those fields, 50 percent or more of those polled rated practitioners as very high and high in their ethical standards. Television reporters/commentators, journalists, and newspaper reporters all declined slightly in ethical credibility, from a range of 30 to 32 percent receiving high rankings in 1981 down to 24 to 32 percent in 1990. Ranking near the bottom of the list were advertising practitioners, who shared status with stockbrokers, insurance salesmen, and car salesmen. In 1990, ratings of "high and very high" were as follows: stockbrokers, 14 percent; insurance salesmen, 13 percent; advertising practitioners, 12 percent; and car salesmen, 6 percent. Senators and members of Congress were judged as having high or very high standards by 24 percent and 20 percent, respectively.[12] It is important to note that the study is about public perception of ethics and honesty, not about the actual behavior of members of these groups. In addition, those occupations with the lowest ratings all involve selling or promoting goods or services, a fact that may influence opinion about these groups.

While the Gallup study shows the public regards journalists' ethics somewhat more highly than those of elected officials, and other studies show support for the watchdog role of the press, it is unclear whether these opinions will hold up during national emergencies. Journalists have been troubled and perhaps mystified by the strong public approval for United States government restrictions on coverage and censorship of reports on military actions in Grenada, Panama, and the Persian Gulf. Indeed, in those episodes, media reporting became more of an issue than the invasions.

A practicing attorney with a media law specialty, Patrick M. Garry, argues that the public has become more alienated from a monopolized and concentrated press that fails to provide a forum through which the public can communicate about important issues. Media ethics should not simply examine the conduct of investigative reporters, he argues, but should also focus on the need for public participation in the social dialogue. He explains public approval of press bans: "It is not surprising today that the American public mistrusts a press perceived as aloof and inattentive. Indeed, during the invasion of Grenada, the public supported Reagan's ban on the press because it felt that the press would only have sabotaged the invasion. In the midst of such distrust, the media will never be able to satisfy the public's demand for ethical journalism. A democratic public alienated from an institutional press will continually retaliate with ethical complaints against the media."[13]

Privacy rights are emerging as a major issue that divides the populace from many media practitioners. Seeking relief from invasions of privacy, individuals and organizations are asking for privacy legislation at both state and federal levels. Individuals are beginning to understand and to fear the electronic information trails that they make when using their Social Security numbers, student identification numbers, and bank account numbers. Credit ratings and financial transactions, especially, are a concern, along with such information widely available in computer files containing driver's license information. For example, after a man described as an obsessed fan stalked and killed an actress in California, that state passed a law making confidential the personal information in Department of Motor Vehicles files, the source of the fan's information. Marketing specialists, who purchase electronic files of driver's license and auto registrations in most states, oppose such laws. In Iowa, after a woman was attacked in a parking lot, her name, address, and place of work were published in a news story about the attack; the state's attorney general complained that the woman's assailant had learned everything he needed to know in order to attack her again. He proposed legislation to put crime victims' addresses off limits until after an indictment is issued.

Other nongovernmental electronic files are issues, as well. Privately maintained data bases include files on individuals who have filed malpractice suits or worker compensation claims, been evicted from a residence, or taken a landlord to court. Credit bureaus have files on nearly 90 percent of American adults, whose records are linked into the computer systems of the three biggest national credit bureaus. Critics claim that credit files frequently are inaccurate and that they are notoriously easy to access, as demonstrated by a business reporter who obtained Vice President Dan Quayle's credit report and by other reporters who imitated the research by collecting reports on other prominent individuals.[14]

In recognition of the public's growing concerns about privacy, newspapers in major cities have changed their policies of always publishing a full name, age, address, and occupation for individuals in news reports. The precise scene of a crime also may be omitted in favor of a general block location (3000 block of Grand Avenue), for example.

The practice known as "outing" in which a magazine or newspaper asserts that an individual is gay has brought about much discussion both in the alternative and the mainstream media. A national magazine, *Outweek*, makes it a practice to disclose the homosexuality of public figures who are generally thought to be heterosexual. Those who practice outing claim that it will contribute to acceptance of gays in the straight community; they expect mainstream media to pick up the stories when the stories involve celebrities. But editors interviewed for an article in *The Quill* said that in their view, sexual preference has no news value unless it directly affects the performance of a public official.[15]

As noted in the Gallup study, the low rating of advertising ethics perhaps reflects its relationship to sales, as well as popular assertions that advertising tends to manipulate audiences. The Gallup rating is consistent with findings in numerous studies that show a public critical of advertising practices and strategies. In 1989 business executives who were polled placed advertising executives number eight among 16 professions.[16] Advertising researchers cited below have done considerable research on public perception of deception in advertising. Summarizing from studies done in 1939 and 1964 by Bauer and Greyser, William Weilbacher reported that about half the population was skeptical of the truthfulness of advertising.[17] Franklin Carlile and

Howard Leonard, in their survey of opinion about advertising, learned that 51 percent of respondents judged half or more of advertising messages to be deceptive.[18] Eric Zanot reviewed 38 studies of opinion about advertising, conducted over a 50-year period. Overall, the studies show a decidedly negative public opinion toward advertising.[19]

Many factors contribute to public views of media responsibility or irresponsibility. The skill with which communicators gather and select information for mass-media messages undoubtedly plays some part in their reputations. While some studies of news and advertising suggest the relationships between public opinion and specific practices, the significance of information gathering as a factor in media reputations has not been sufficiently studied.

Societal criticism of media performance is a prod to media improvement. Many representatives of other institutions provide such criticism. For example, when a judge in a criminal trial grants a motion to change the location of the trial because news coverage has made a fair trial impossible in the local community, that decision may represent an implicit criticism of media behavior. When a consumer or competitor draws public attention to an advertisement that presents what is believed to be a harmful advertising claim, the criticism is clear and direct. Journalism educators also criticize the mass-communication industries. They provide public criticism through articles, books, and letters to editors. In another forum, the classroom, they criticize existing standards of collecting, verifying, and selecting information, and they attempt to teach students improved methods of collecting information and of judging information to be put into the public arena.

These societal criticisms and suggestions generally reflect a social responsibility perspective. In the United States, the social responsibility perspective affects many, if not all, major institutions. Corporations, educational institutions, churches, civic associations—to name a few—are exhorted to act in a socially responsible manner. This demand for social responsibility is rooted in the recognition that there are limited means for getting institutions to act in the best interests of society in spite of their self-interest. Scholar Wilbur Schramm expressed the choices this way:

> There are only three great instruments which society may use to encourage or prod the mass media to responsible performance. These are government and its various regulatory bodies, national, state, and local; the media themselves, their individual personnel, and their formal and informal associations and administrative organizations; and the general public, with its formal and informal organizations and associations.
>
> If we ask where, among these, responsibility lies for the kind of mass communication we have in this country, and for any change we want to bring about in mass communication, then quite clearly the answer to that responsibility is shared. Neither government, nor media, nor the public can be counted on to do the job alone, and on the other hand, none of them is exempt from responsibility for doing it. What we are looking for . . . is a desirable balance of responsibility among them. . . .[20]

Communicators and Professionalism. Professional education and licensing have been traditional means by which society has sought to ensure reliable practice from those who bear important social responsibilities. For law, medicine, accounting, and other fields of expertise, specific training is followed by examinations, state licensing, and administration of oaths that include promises to live up to the standards established for the profession. Degrees, oaths, and licenses are not required of communicators. Thus society can make no legal claims that communicators have violated their professional oaths.

Another way to view professionalism suggests that a profession is established when those who work in a field form associations, set standards for competence, and draw up codes of ethics. Using these criteria, communicators in some fields may appear to qualify as professionals. However, these standards still provide no means for society to reach out to discipline an errant professional. The unethical physician may lose the license to practice, and the corrupt attorney may be disbarred. But American society can impose no professional sanctions against communicators. Further, the First Amendment restrictions against regulating free expression appear to establish a perpetual stand-off. Communicators cannot be licensed or dis-licensed. In that sense, they cannot attain, at least formally, the status of professionals. Society cannot punish communicators for violations of their own ethical codes. But communicators are not exempt from standards established for all people. That is, they may be held accountable if they defame an individual or publish false and deceptive advertisements.

Another way of looking at professionalism is to examine the professional as an independent practitioner. It has been said that professionals are those who are free to follow the standards of the profession without answering to supervisors or being compromised by a profit-seeking management. Again, communicators almost always fall outside this definition. Most work in highly structured firms and know their places on the organization chart. They report to a succession of supervisors; management almost invariably has profit as a goal—if not the leading goal. The traditional idea of the physician or lawyer in private practice fits this notion of the independent practitioner. But contemporary realities are that, increasingly, such traditional professionals as doctors and lawyers also practice in complex corporate structures. Their actions are scrutinized by managers of the organization, their peers, outside agencies that pay patients' and clients' bills, and various advocacy groups. Within their organizations, they adhere to agreed-on procedures and protocols. Their independence has been dramatically reduced. From this perspective, mass communicators are almost as free to practice independently as are those in the more traditional professions.

A further perspective on professionalism takes into account the specific theories and skills needed to practice and the value that society attaches to the exercise of these skills. It is clear that some communicators enjoy high status, while others are reviled. The editors of the prestige press and the pornography kings alike fit the definition of communicator. The skill and value test for professionalism seems to apply best for individuals, not for the communication field as a whole.

Overall, communicators cannot make a clear claim to professional status. Nor can society administer the rewards and punishments to communicators that it does to those in traditional professions. Without the power to control entry into the field and to withdraw the license to operate, society and its major power centers operate in more subtle and invisible ways to influence the communication industries and those who work in them.

Legal Aspects of Information Gathering. Society is not powerless. Prior restraint by government of communication is prohibited by the First Amendment, but communicators have legal obligations for their conduct in collecting and publishing information. On the one hand, society facilitates the individual's and thus the communicator's access to information that concerns public affairs. A variety of state and federal laws provide for open records and open meetings as a means of ensuring that the public's business will be open to scrutiny. But on the other hand, communicators act outside the law when they break into offices or homes, steal documents or trade secrets, give false identities, invade privacy, maliciously defame individuals, violate copyright, or publish false and deceptive advertisements.

Fortunately, such challengeable actions are fairly rare. As gatherers and assessors of information, communicators are expected to understand and adhere to their legal obligations. Further, their organizations have legal staff and other supervisors who advise when legal questions arise. A few examples should clarify the relationship of these issues to the information-gathering process.

Example 1. A reporter-photographer team is assigned to cover a family whose son has been taken hostage. Family members rebuff the news team's efforts and refuse to provide photos and information about the young man. To escape the pressures and the scrutiny of news reporters, family members depart for a hideaway while they await developments. A neighbor stays in the house to watch the property and to take in newspapers and mail. In the family's absence, the reporter and photographer seek information from the house-watching neighbor. They enter the house to interview the neighbor. While the reporter converses with the neighbor, his partner removes from the family's living room several photographs of the hostage and other family members. The family returns to find their son's picture, along with other family photos and a story, on the front page of the newspaper. The family complains that newspaper staff members illegally entered their home, took property, and appropriated the property for commercial gain. In this matter, the news gatherers were acting illegally merely by entering the house and taking the photographs. Even if they subsequently were advised by their attorney not to use the material, they are guilty of intruding illegally. Illegal entry in news reporting is very rare, especially in the form described here.

However, new surveillance and information technologies provide a variety of opportunities for other forms of illegal intrusion—electronic eavesdropping, concealed photography and voice recording, and tapping private data bases or other electronic files protected by privacy statutes. As technology continues to provide new techniques, legal issues such as intrusion and appropriation probably will become more significant. Reporters and their legal advisers will find themselves faced with new variations on the old temptation to collect information illegally.

Example 2.   As part of a public-relations campaign, staff members decide to use direct-mail solicitation in a fund-raising campaign. Preliminary research shows that members of three national organizations are top prospects as large contributors. One organization, however, carefully guards its membership list, and there is no legitimate method for obtaining the list. A free-lance writer in the community happens to work occasionally for the organization. The free lance is applying for a position on the public-relations staff and, during his interview with the firm, implies that he could provide the membership list and would try to do so if he were to become a staff member in the organization. When he does join the staff, he brings along a photocopy of the prized material. The writer is guilty of stealing, and the firm is guilty of receiving and using stolen property.

Example 3.   A weekly newspaper employs an artist to sell and design ads for small retail firms. The artist recognizes that various well-known cartoon characters could be used to gain attention for her potential advertising clients. She bases her sales techniques on a series of her sketches, which incorporate well-known cartoon characters. The merchants regard the ads as very successful; the publisher values the additional advertising clients; and the artist-salesperson is pleased to be launched on a new career. However, the artists whose cartoon characters have been copied are not happy. They begin to file suits for infringement of copyright. The law is on their side.

These examples merely suggest some actions that are illegal. They are illegal for communicators and noncommunicators alike. Because communicators' messages reach a large number of people, communicators' violations of the law are much more conspicuous and significant than are similar violations by the populace. For example, the advertising artist violated copyright in using the cartoon characters in the ads she prepared. Countless other artists have done the same thing when preparing posters to promote attendance at community events. Only in rare instances will the poster makers receive letters from the copyright holders' lawyers. As a practical matter, the poster makers are ignorant of the copyright law, and the copyright holder does not discover the violation. The First Amendment offers many protections to mass communicators, but it does not free them from requirements to obey all the laws applicable to other persons.

Advertising and the Law.   Unlike news, advertising content is subject to regulation by federal, state, and local laws. Federal laws are the most powerful form of regulation. The purpose of regulating advertising is to protect the public from ads that are untruthful, discriminatory, and deceptive, all of which may constitute unfair competition. Two important aspects of regulation affect those who gather and select information for advertising. One aspect involves illegal content. It is, for example, unlawful for those advertising available jobs or housing to discriminate in the ad on the basis of gender, race, or national origin. The contrast between news and advertising in this instance is fairly clear. For instance, since employment discrimination is illegal, a publication is acting against federal law if it discriminates on racial grounds when it hires employees. If it prints advertising that allows a real-estate firm to announce its illegal discrimination, the publication is acting illegally. However, the publication is protected on First Amendment grounds if it prints articles or editorials advocating that same form of discrimination.

A second aspect of advertising regulation has to do with claims made about services and products. The Federal Trade Commission (FTC) regulates national advertising of products and services involved in interstate commerce. It is concerned with the overall "truth" of ads, including omission of important facts, false statements, and inaccurate implications. For information collection and assessment, the FTC substantiation rule is of paramount importance. The burden of proof is on the advertiser. Those who cannot substantiate their claims must stop making the claims. In some cases, the FTC will require corrective advertising that informs the audience of false claims made in earlier advertisements.

After a decade of relatively little interference, the FTC in 1991 put advertisers and ad agencies on notice that it would pay closer attention to their claims and respond quickly to deceptive ads. Auto ads, such as the Volvo ad cited in the chapter introduction, and food ads making dubious nutrition claims have come under particular scrutiny. The FTC ordered Kraft General Foods, for example, to stop running an ad for Kraft Singles claiming that each slice of cheese had as much calcium as five ounces of milk.[21] A consumer watchdog group, the Center for Science in the Public Interest, uses public-relations campaigns to draw attention to ads it considers deceptive. It gives out "lemon" awards yearly, citing specific false information or implications and correcting the deceptions. Auto, food, cigarette, airline, and beverage company ads were cited for 1990.

Obviously, the substantiation requirement can involve communicators in a fairly comprehensive search strategy, including many of the evaluation standards discussed in Chapter 9. Advertising departments and agencies employ staff whose legal expertise and research skills help meet substantiation requirements.

While the FTC is the major federal regulator, other bureaus also regulate advertising in ways that affect information gathering. Federal legislation gives more than 30 agencies other than the FTC the power to monitor advertising messages. Among other subjects, these agencies oversee the protection of slogans, trademarks, and brand names; the eligibility of advertising matter to go through the postal system; the protection of copyright; and the safeguarding of the American flag and currency against reproduction for commercial purposes.

The relationship between the media and society defies easy summary. Mass communication is among the powerful social influences in the United States. Mass communicators serve both as watchdogs on and as promoters of other institutions. In turn, mass communicators' behavior is scrutinized and evaluated by other institutions. The reputation is mixed, with some communicators and some industries enjoying substantially more acceptance than others. Some communicators emphasize their obligation to monitor and criticize government and other power centers; they like to think of themselves as independent of the institutions they scrutinize. Others stress the consensus-building role the mass media play; they tend to incorporate the perspectives of other major power centers into their work as they promote ideas and products. Because of the diversity of media functions, no one-sentence capsule can adequately characterize society's response to mass communicators' performance. However, it seems clear that society is increasingly critical of many actions by communicators that are related to the use of information.

The Professional and Organizational Perspectives

In addition to the social responsibility imperatives, communication organizations and professionals engage in self-criticism and set standards for their own conduct as information gatherers. Communicators acknowledge society's criticisms of mass communication and of communicators' behavior. In many respects, the standards of the media reflect society's broad demands. For example, respect for accuracy, completeness, human dignity, and fairness are held in common by society and mass communicators. But some communicators' values may differ from those of other Americans. For example, communicators may give more support to free press and other First Amendment guarantees than do citizens in general. Further, news workers may view social conflict as a mechanism that supports democracy. Not incidentally, conflict is a major ingredient in the recipe for news.

Communicators do not take all the critical cues that society offers, nor do they limit their criticism of media to the criticisms offered from the outside. Rather, communicators develop insider perspectives on responsibility that should be viewed as important parts of the larger critical picture. The most conspicuous evidence of this lies in the proliferation of professional codes of conduct in the past 65 years. Codes exist for all mass-communication activities and at all levels. Some are fairly longstanding, such as the 1922 Canons of Ethics of the American Society of Newspaper Editors. Others are recent, such as a set of guidelines for local advertising in auto sales. Some codes reflect ownership and management requirements; others originate with the practitioners. Other codes are established for entire industries. Overall, the prevalence of codes undoubtedly reflects communicators' sensitivity to criticism from outside as well as inside communication industries.

Codes in the News Industries.   In the newspaper, magazine, and broadcasting industries, particularly, codes have expanded in number and in scope. Codes have been adopted by the American Society of Newspaper Editors, the Society of Professional Journalists, the Associated Press Managing Editors Association, the National Association of Broadcasters, the Radio and Television News Directors Association, and the Magazine Publishers Association. In addition, the managements of individual publications frequently establish codes to which their staffs are expected to adhere.

John Hulteng has summarized the major thrust of news codes as follows:

> Journalists must observe a responsibility to the public welfare; their impressive power should be employed for the general good, not for private advantage.
>
> Journalists should provide a news report that is sincere, true, and accurate; accounts should be thorough, balanced, and complete.
>
> Journalists must be impartial; they should function as the public's representatives, not as the mouthpieces of partisan groups or special interests.
>
> Journalists must be fair; they must give space or air time to the several sides of a dispute; private rights should not be invaded; corrections of errors should be prompt and wholehearted.
>
> Journalists should respect the canons of decency, insofar as those canons can be identified in a society with ever-changing values.[22]

Not all ethical concerns in news are related to the gathering and assessing of information. Some concern conflict of interest: being a candidate for public office while working as a reporter or accepting free tickets, trips, or meals from news sources. Such obvious conflicts are pretty generally prohibited. On several important information-gathering issues, however, professionals in the news industry are significantly divided. Ralph Izard surveyed members of the Society of Professional Journalists, the Associated Press Managing Editors Association, and the Radio and Television News Directors Association and reported important disagreements on key issues of information gathering.

Respondents did not agree on whether to use information obtained by eavesdropping outside the location of a secret meeting, for example. There was disagreement about using information obtained in an interview with a member of a grand jury who had been sworn to secrecy. There also was disagreement about using information obtained from the sealed record of a closed courtroom hearing provided by a confidential source. Those surveyed did agree that they would use information obtained from the transcript of a grand-jury proceeding provided by a confidential source. Izard concluded, "Questions about what the public has a right to know and how far reporters should go in getting that information continue as troublesome ethical issues for American journalists."[23]

The information-gathering phase of news reporting is a veritable mine-field of ethical disputes, the main ones of which we will now describe. To describe is not to resolve, however. Reporters and editors make the day-to-day decisions that finally establish what is acceptable journalistic practice.

Theft.   Gathering and using information that is not obtained legitimately is considered to be theft. Journalists have criticized one another for a variety of such actions. For example, stealing information from the files of other professionals or from businesses and using it to develop a story is both illegal and unethical. Using material that others have stolen or accepting anonymously "leaked" information or documents is another problem. Plagiarism is more common than many editors suspect. And, as journalists increasingly use information from a variety of printed and electronic sources, the risks of plagiarism increase.

Deception.   When information gatherers fail to accurately identify themselves and their purpose, they are engaging in deception. Overall, such actions undoubtedly are rare. They probably are most commonly practiced as part of investigative reporting. In these instances, journalists often justify such practices as taking a position in a business or joining an organization as a way to obtain evidence and information that they claim could be found no other way. In other words, the end justifies the means. A prize-winning team of investigative reporters at WCCO-TV, for example, uses hidden microphones and cameras and places its investigators as "employees." And the *Chicago Sun-Times* went so far as to rent a building, obtain a license, and open a bar as a way to obtain evidence that city and state inspectors took bribes in return for certifying substandard health and safety equipment. The journalists used hidden cameras and microphones to record the transactions. Their investigative stories were nominated for the Pulitzer Prize, but their methods initiated an intense debate. They did not win the Pulitzer Prize.[24]

Leaked Information.   Ordinarily, journalists cite their sources for facts, opinions, and predictions. Their audiences have some opportunity to assess the sources' credibility, expertise, and any vested interest in the information provided. When news sources wish to leak information to the news media without taking responsibility for it, reporters and editors are on guard. Persons leaking information about corruption, for example, may have genuine concern for the public welfare. Others may be motivated by partisanship or desire for personal gain or revenge. Irrespective of the leakers' motives, the information provided may be flawed or distorted. Those who are accused must try to defend themselves without knowing the identity of their accusers, a violation of the American spirit of fair play. Some journalists use leaked information only as the lead to on-the-record facts that can give them solid stories. For example, a source may tell the reporter that a corrupt practice can be uncovered by examining a particular set of public records. The responsibility for presenting the information then rests on the reporter's skill in mining the public records and interpreting them, rather than on assertions of wrongdoing leaked to the reporter.[25]

Correcting Errors. Factual errors are inevitable in daily journalism, and virtually all news organizations require their staffs to make prompt corrections of such errors. Fact checking in national magazines, both weekly and monthly, helps magazine journalists avoid many errors that otherwise would require correction. The fact-checking techniques used in magazines may be employed increasingly in the future in daily journalism. Improved reference libraries and on-line information services should permit more fact checking before publication, notwithstanding the pressures of daily news work. Correcting factual errors for the benefit of the public is an important and fairly obvious goal. However, incorporating the corrections into the news library's files and data bases also is important, so that subsequent users of the files and data bases do not repeat the original error. As news organizations increasingly use information from other organizations and provide their own reports to others, fact checking and correction of errors will grow in importance.

The growth of codes in journalism testifies to a professional spirit that has developed steadily in news work. Despite the proliferation of codes, however, those who work in the news industries face many legal, ethical, and social responsibility challenges that leave them uncomfortable. Straightforward acceptance of a particular "rule" often requires that the journalist abandon or compromise a report that seems to be in the public interest. The methods through which reporters gather their information are major contributors to such dilemmas.

Codes in Advertising. Like news, advertising has responded to both external and internal criticism. Advertising codes reflect some of the specific criticisms directed at the field. For example, codes take cognizance of the charge that advertising is deceptive, fosters unfair stereotypes of people, presents false testimonials for products, and gives misleading price claims. The codes do not, for the most part, attempt to deal with the broader criticisms of advertising—that it persuades people to spend beyond their means, debases the language, saturates the environment, and exploits peoples' personal insecurities.

Codes and standards abound in advertising. Professional associations of advertisers have codes. The creative code of the American Association of Advertising Agencies is an example of this sort of document. The code is endorsed by a variety of other advertising groups, such as the Advertising Federation of America, the Advertising Association of the West, and a variety of industry groups. Those subscribing to this code state that they will not knowingly produce advertising that contains:

1. False or misleading statements or exaggerations, visual or verbal.
2. Testimonials which do not reflect the real choice of a competent witness.
3. Price claims which are misleading.

4. Comparisons which unfairly disparage a competitive product or service.
5. Claims insufficiently supported, or which distort the true meaning or practicable application of statements made by professional or scientific authority.
6. Statements, suggestions or pictures offensive to public decency.

In the code, the American Association of Advertising Agencies states that clear and willful violations are to be referred to its board of directors, which has authority to annul membership in the organization.

The advertising industry also has a two-tiered self-regulatory mechanism. Advertising that appears deceptive can first be referred to the National Advertising Division (NAD) of the Council of Better Business Bureaus. Beyond that, cases that are not satisfactorily resolved through the NAD can be appealed to the National Advertising Review Board.

Individual advertising agencies and corporate advertising departments also have codes and standards to help employees recognize and deal with ethical questions. A survey of employees in such agencies and departments found that most did face ethical decisions on the job. Some decisions concerned the ethics of information gathering. One such problem involved requests for confidential information concerning competitors. It is considered unethical to give one client information that has been generated for another account. One respondent in the study wrote of a situation that

> involves a client request for market research which borders on industrial espionage. Usually, after careful questioning of objectives, we can determine that the purpose of the study is unethical, and turn down the client's request. Again, this refusal on our part to conduct the study for ethical reasons can cause client resentment.[26]

Mass-media industries also have codes concerning truth in advertising. Television, radio, magazines, newspapers, and films use the advertising industry to promote their wares. As part of that activity, they have established codes for the accuracy and taste of their own advertising. In addition, these media are in a position to accept or reject ads submitted to them. The most specific and stringent of these standards are found in broadcasting. Further review is conducted by networks and by individual broadcasting stations.

Industries, trade associations, and professions have adopted codes pertaining to their own groups. Drug manufacturers, automobile dealers, attorneys, and the insurance industry are examples of groups that have codes for their own advertising content. For example, associations of car dealers have established standards for accuracy in advertising interest rates, prices, monthly payments, availability of models, and trade-in provisions. Some of these code provisions cover the same points as do state or federal law. The Federal Trade Commission, for example, considers incomplete advertising of credit terms a deceptive practice. Thus the car dealer has to be concerned with both legal requirements and code requirements when advertising interest rates on auto loans.

Codes in Public Relations. Public-relations practitioners, like advertising specialists, work closely with clients. Legal and ethical decisions often arise as clients and publicists discuss information-gathering strategies. When the client and the practitioner cannot agree about a social responsibility issue, it generally is the client who wields greater power. The practitioner has the power of persuasion, and, in a number of cases, the law may be on the side of the public-relations specialist. For example, the Securities and Exchange Commission monitors the way in which corporations report their financial affairs. Information about stock offerings is scrutinized for accuracy and omission of important facts. The object is to ensure that investors can get accurate information before they buy securities. Public-relations practitioners, along with lawyers, stockbrokers, and accountants, increasingly are being held responsible for the accuracy of information they communicate to the public.[27] When public-relations practitioners find themselves on the losing side of an important ethical question, it is not unusual for them to resign their positions as a matter of principle.

The code of the Public Relations Society of America, in fact, recommends precisely that course of action. It is the only major code for communicators that does so. The code contains 14 provisions, the final one of which states:

> A member shall, as soon as possible, sever relations with any organization or individual if such relationship requires conduct contrary to the articles of this Code.

Other provisions of the code that are related to the information aspect of public-relations work are:

> A member shall adhere to truth and accuracy and to generally accepted standards of good taste.
>
> A member shall safeguard the confidences of both present and former clients or employers and shall not accept retainers or employment which will involve the disclosure or use of these confidences to the disadvantage or prejudice of such clients or employers.
>
> A member shall not engage in any practice which tends to corrupt the integrity of channels of communication or the processes of government.
>
> A member shall not intentionally communicate false or misleading information and is obligated to use care to avoid communication of false or misleading information.
>
> A member shall not make use of any individual or organization purporting to serve or represent an announced case, or purporting to be independent or unbiased, but actually serving an undisclosed special interest or a member, client or employer.

The public-relations code, like those for advertising and journalism, reflects the concerns of society as well as of the practitioners who adopted the codes. Provisions of all the codes are designed, at least in part, to offer the public reasons to have confidence in the intentions and integrity of communicators. The codes represent standards, not descriptions of the way all communicators practice their craft. In the words of public-relations researchers Scott Cutlip and Allen Center, "Practical people know that the adoption of a code of ethics does not automatically bring morality to a calling, but such codes do reflect a concern among the leaders for raising the ethical levels, and they provide yardsticks of measurement."[28]

An international code of ethics for public-relations practitioners has been proposed. The prevalence and power of transnational corporations (those companies with units and divisions in many parts of the world) suggest that international public-relations ethics standards should be established. "The ultimate goal should be development of a universal, multilaterally honored code of ethics endorsed and subscribed to by professional communicators in all transnational corporations worldwide," Kruckeberg writes. Communicators worldwide share many ethical perspectives, and they should work together to develop standards, publicize them, and encourage compliance. He cites four key issues that he deems important in the international arena: graft and corruption issues, such as payoffs for doing business; consumer issues, such as the Nestle infant-formula promotion in Third World countries; human safety issues, such as the Bhopal chemical disaster in India; political/humanitarian issues, including business practices in South Africa and elsewhere.[29]

Professional Associations.   Standards for communicators' conduct are a significant concern reflected in communication associations. In their meetings and in their professional publications, association members show their concern about questions of ethics. *Advertising Age* publishes its selections of "ads we can do without," and the *Columbia Journalism Review* carries a regular column of "Darts and Laurels" praising or criticizing reporting decisions. Longer articles in these and other journals discuss information questions in the context of social responsibility.

Individual media organizations also have taken steps that show their awareness of communicators' responsibility. In 1985, about 30 daily newspapers had appointed reader representatives, or ombudsmen, to their staffs. These representatives hear readers' complaints about the way in which news is gathered and presented. They investigate the complaints and explain the circumstances of and rationales for editors' decisions. Finally, they offer their own views about the merits of the disputed information.

Overall, mass-media organizations are moving toward openness and willingness to admit that many decisions are not clear-cut. Admitting to errors of judgment seems to be more prevalent than in the past. Philosopher Sissela Bok is among those arguing that the news media must consider their information-gathering methods more seriously and be more open about those methods:

> The press and other news media rightly stand for openness in public discourse. But until they give equally firm support to openness in their own practices, their stance will be inconsistent and lend credence to charges of unfairness. It is now a stance that challenges every collective rationale for

secrecy save the media's own. Yet the media serve commercial and partisan interests in addition to public ones; and media practices of secrecy, selective disclosure, and probing should not be exempt from scrutiny.[30]

The Individual Perspective

We turn now to considerations of the individual communicator, whose information-finding routines play such an important role in modern life. Some praise and much criticism accompany these actions. News is acknowledged as providing important surveillance in the world, serving as the social glue that keeps society together, and fostering the discussion required for political health. Advertising is accepted as a necessary component in the modern market economy. Public relations is credited with helping to bring a variety of views before the public and with mediating among competing interests. But criticism of these fields is strong. News, its critics charge, ratifies the assumptions of those in power and helps them to perpetuate their power, while ignoring reality as experienced by most of the population. Advertising, it is said, contributes to materialism, wasteful consumption, and the corruption of the electoral system. Public relations thrives by creating and manipulating images on behalf of those with narrow interests, failing to give public-interest information a priority.

Mass communicators, then, do their daily work in a decidedly ambivalent atmosphere. In very general ways, American society's Judeo-Christian values offer major constraints. Lying, stealing, and bearing false witness are universally rejected, at least in the abstract. Despite such guides, mass communicators find themselves confronting conflicting obligations. Media ethics researchers Clifford Christians, Kim Rotzoll, and Mark Fackler have identified five duties that confront communicators:[31]

1. *Duty to ourselves:* Personal integrity and conscience are paramount.
2. *Duty to clients/subscribers/supporters:* Those who pay the bills either to produce the message or to receive it command various obligations.
3. *Duty to one's organization or firm:* Loyalty to the organization takes various forms, including some that may be unpopular for the moment but may be in the long-term interest of the organization.
4. *Duty to professional colleagues:* Workers in the same field stand together, often against others in the organization, when upholding work standards they believe in.
5. *Duty to society:* Social and public good often are balanced against all the other four considerations when communicators reflect on their duty. Advertising dangerous products, producing pornographic and violent messages, ignoring public officials' flouting of the law, and similar acts are examples of communicators' conflict with the social good.

In confronting social responsibility issues, communicators typically face a number of these conflicting duties. The duty to oneself includes the need to abide by one's own moral standards. But this may conflict with more worldly ambitions—desire for recognition, advancement, and financial security. The duty to the organization may be at odds with loyalty to colleagues or to the profession.

Finally, even assuming that each communicator is willing to forgo all other obligations and decide on behalf of the social good, it is no simple matter to decide what is in society's best interests. This is particularly the case if communicators have been instilled with the idea of their own moral neutrality, with the notion that they are neutral agents who transmit information for which others bear the real responsibility. To some extent, responsibility does reside elsewhere. For example, communicators are not responsible for errors in the federal government's unemployment statistics. But if common sense or experience warns that the statistics may be manipulated or erroneous, communicators are responsible to seek additional information and to bring it to the public. Scholars writing about communication ethics agree that individuals in this field should not regard themselves merely as agents of those who wield economic and political power.

Inevitably, individual communicators will reach different conclusions about some social responsibility issues. This is the case because neither society nor the media organization can fully shape the varied individuals who become mass communicators. Each has a unique background of ethnic, social, and economic origin; education; religion; genetics; and family tradition. These factors mean that individuals will analyze social responsibility issues differently and apply standards in distinctive ways.

THE SEARCH STRATEGY AND SOCIAL RESPONSIBILITY

The search strategy for mass communicators is designed to give them a powerful concept for approaching the critically important work of collecting and selecting information. The model for information search helps communicators meet their responsibilities to society to obtain the best information available. It helps them to meet their responsibilities to their organizations by giving an efficient, time-conscious method for gathering and verifying information. It helps them to meet responsibilities to colleagues and to the professions, many of whom will rely on information publicized by others in the field.

Finally, the search strategy is designed to help communicators meet a variety of responsibilities to themselves. By outlining extensive and varied methods for locating information, the search-strategy model provides many legitimate methods for getting material that less skilled communicators might try to obtain through unethical means. The search-strategy process also provides communicators with personal power that accompanies a respected skill. In this case, being highly skilled as an information gatherer in an information-overload society brings credibility to the communicator. Further, the search strategy is a conceptual tool to be used in explaining the communicator's standards to others. When the public, colleagues, or supervisors challenge the information on which a message is based, the communicator can present an ordered, rational account of the information-selection process.

Within communication organizations, the search strategy provides a method and a terminology to help colleagues conduct information searches and to assess the results. Using the standards and methods available in the search strategy, supervisors can evaluate the skill and expertise of information gatherers on their staffs and of free lances who present their work for sale. Critics and scholars can use the model in research related to mass-media messages.

The search strategy offers no remedy for information-gathering offenses originating in greed, naked ambition, low taste, and insensitivity. But perhaps most communicators' flaws are laid to other deficiencies. These include ignorance about the information universe, lack of skill in collecting information, and absence of evaluation standards. These flaws, intellectual rather than moral in origin, can be amended by education and practice. The search strategy is designed as a powerful tool to improve the practice of mass communication. However, like any powerful tool, it can be used for social harm as well as social good.

Ultimately, personal, organizational, and public ethics return to the center of the picture. The new information age offers possibilities that frighten many: invasions of privacy, irresponsible use of information, and growth of the information-poor as a segment of society. Improved information-gathering methods in mass communication are small, but significant, parts of this picture. Despite improvements in information-gathering techniques, the important questions of privacy, responsibility, and equity remain to be addressed by lawmakers and judges and the electorate.

NOTES

1. Periodicals devoted to media ethics include the *Journal of Mass Media Ethics*, *FineLine—the Newsletter on Journalism Ethics*, and *Media Ethics Update*. In addition, virtually every other communication journal carries articles on media ethics. Books on media and information ethics issued since 1980 have included: Sissela Bok, *Secrets: On the Ethics of Concealment and Revelation* (New York: Pantheon Books, 1982); Clifford G. Christians, Kim B. Rotzoll, and Mark Fackler, *Media Ethics: Cases & Moral Reasoning*, 3rd ed. (New York: Longman, 1991); Thomas W. Cooper, *Communication Ethics and Global Change* (New York: Longman, 1989); Deni T. Elliott, ed., *Responsible Journalism* (Beverly Hills, Calif.: Sage, 1986); Conrad C. Fink, *Media Ethics in the Newsroom and Beyond* (New York: McGraw-Hill, 1988); Eugene Goodwin, *Groping for Media Ethics* (Ames, Iowa: Iowa State University Press, 1983); Howard Gossage, *Is Advertising Worth Saving?* (Urbana: University of Illinois Press, 1986); Larry Gross, John Stuart Katz, and Jay Ruby, eds., *Image Ethics: The Moral Rights of Subjects in Photographs, Film, and Television*, (New York: Oxford University Press, 1988); John L. Huteng, *Playing It Straight: A Practical Discussion of the Ethical Principles of the ASNE* (Chester, Conn.: Globe Pequot Press, 1981); John L. Hulteng, *The Messenger's Motives: Ethical Problems of the News Media*, 2nd ed. (Englewood Cliffs, N.J.: Prentice-Hall, 1985); Richard L. Johannesen, *Ethics in Human Communication*, 3rd ed. (Prospect Heights, Ill.: Waveland Press, 1990); Stephen Klaidman and Tom L. Beauchamp, *The Virtuous Journalist* (New

York: Oxford University Press, 1987); Dean Kruckeberg and Kenneth Starck, *Public Relations and Community: A Reconstructed Theory* (New York: Praeger, 1988); Edmund B. Lambeth, *Committed Journalism: An Ethic for the Profession* (Bloomington: Indiana University Press, 1986); John C. Merrill, *The Dialectic in Journalism: Toward a Responsible Use of Press Freedom* (Baton Rouge: Louisiana State University Press, 1989); Philip Meyer, *Editors, Publishers and Newspaper Ethics,* (Washington, D.C.: American Society of Newspaper Editors, 1983); Philip Meyer, *Ethical Journalism* (New York: Longman, 1987); Philip Patterson and Lee Wilkins, *Media Ethics: Issues and Cases* (Dubuque, Iowa: William C. Brown, 1991); Wesley G. Pippert, *An Ethics of News: A Reporter's Search for Truth* (Washington, D.C.: Georgetown University Press, 1989); William L. Rivers, Wilbur Schramm, and Clifford Christians, *Responsibility in Mass Communication,* 3rd ed. (New York: Harper and Row, 1980); Robert Schmuhl, ed., *The Responsibilities of Journalists* (Notre Dame: University of Notre Dame Press, 1984); Lee Thayer, ed., *Ethics, Morality and the Media* (New York: Hastings House, 1980).

2. Lou Prato, "Satellite Thievery: Can Ethics Stop It?" *Washington Journalism Review* 12 (April 1990): 12.

3. Jennifer Lawrence, "How Volvo's Ad Collided with the Truth," *Advertising Age* 61 (12 November 1990): 76; Barry Meier, "New Volvo Ad Calls Old One a Phony," *New York Times,* 6 November 1990, C1 and C15.

4. Michael Hoyt, "The Tampa Media–Espionage Case," *Columbia Journalism Review,* May–June 1989, 27–32.

5. Michael deCourcy Hines, "TV News Gets a Subtle Sales Pitch as the Press Release Goes Electronic," *New York Times,* 21 April 1987, 8.

6. Randall Rothenberg, "Playing the B-roll Bop," *The Quill,* September 1990, 29.

7. Anthony Smith, *Goodbye Gutenberg* (Oxford: Oxford University Press, 1980), 118.

8. Edward T. Hall, *The Silent Language* (Greenwich, CT: Fawcett, 1963), 169.

9. Gilbert Seldes, "The Public Arts: Our Rights and Duties," in Wilbur Schramm, ed., *Mass Communications,* 2nd ed. (Urbana: University of Illinois Press, 1975), 587–593.

10. *Newspaper Credibility: Building Reader Trust* (Washington, D.C.: American Society of Newspaper Editors, 1985).

11. Michael J. Robinson and Andrew Kohut, "Believability and the Press," *Public Opinion Quarterly* 52 (Summer 1988): 174–189.

12. Gallup Opinion Survey, Feb. 8–11, 1990.

13. Patrick M. Garry, "The Democratic Challenge to Media Ethics," *Media Ethics Update* 3 (Fall 1990): 1, 12.

14. "What Price Privacy?" *Consumer Reports,* May 1991, 356–360.

15. Mitchell Hartman, "When to Say Someone Is Gay," *The Quill* November–December 1990, 6.

16. "Ad Execs Stumble in Ethics Poll," *Advertising Age* 14 (August 1989): 39.

17. William Weilbacher, *Advertising* (New York: Macmillan, 1979), 153.

18. Franklin Carlile and Howard Leonard, "Caveat: Venditor!" *Journal of Advertising Research* 22 (August–September 1982): 20.

19. Eric Zanot, "Public Attitudes Toward Advertising," *Proceedings of the Annual Conference of the American Academy of Advertising* (East Lansing, Mich.: The Academy, 1981): 146

20. Wilbur Schramm, "Who is Responsible for the Quality of Mass Communications?" in Schramm, *Mass Communications,* pp. 648–660.

21. Kim Foltz, "F.T.C. Signals Its Concerns over Deceptive Campaigns," *New York Times,* 14 February 1991, C15.

22. Hulteng, *Messenger's Motives*, 24.
23. Ralph S. Izard, "Judgment Issues Split Respondents," *1983 Journalism Ethics Report* (n.p.: National Ethics Committee, Society of Professional Journalists, 1983), 7.
24. Steve Robinson, "Pulitzers: Was the Mirage a Deception?" *Columbia Journalism Review* 18 (July–August 1979): 14–15.
25. Goodwin, *Groping For Ethics in Journalism*, 121.
26. Kim B. Rotzoll and Clifford Christians, "An Inquiry into Advertising Practitioners' Perceptions of Ethical Decisions—The Advertising Agency," *Proceedings of the Annual Conference of the American Academy of Advertising* (East Lansing, Mich.: The Academy, 1979): 28.
27. Scott M. Cutlip, "Attendent Responsibility: Public Relations and the SEC," *Public Relations Journal* (January 1985): 26–31.
28. Scott M. Cutlip and Allen H. Center, *Effective Public Relations*, 5th ed. (Englewood Cliffs, N.J.: Prentice-Hall, 1978), 586.
29. Dean Kruckeberg, "The Need for an International Code of Ethics," *Public Relations Review* 15 (Summer 1989): 6–18.
30. Sissela Bok, *Secrets* (New York: Random House [Vintage Books] 1984), 264.
31. Christians, Rotzoll, and Fackler, *Media Ethics*, 18.
32. Anthony Smith, *Goodbye Gutenberg*,

Afterword

The search-strategy approach presented in this book is directed both to those who produce mass-media messages and those who do research about the mass media. It emphasizes that any society has an important stake in the quality and the nature of the media messages the public receives and that no media message is better than the information on which it is based. It recognizes that communicators and library or information-science professionals use many similar methods in unearthing the information they seek and also that some methods are distinct for each of these professions. At the same time, it seeks to provide communicators with some of the methods that traditionally have been used principally by knowledgeable information specialists. Communicators and communication researchers thus stand to have their methods enriched and systematized.

The search-strategy model has been presented as a memorable visual device, to be drawn on conceptually whenever the user needs to use an information strategy or to evaluate a strategy already put into place. The model presents in graphic form the main elements of the search process and the relationships among these elements. Further, it provides a vocabulary through which communicators and researchers can discuss information strategies. It seeks to make specific and explicit many routines that have become habitual in information search and also to make visible the many new routines that electronic information technologies make possible.

Both message makers and researchers in mass communication need to examine bodies of knowledge arising from a wide variety of academic fields and institutional settings. Increasingly, interdisciplinary thinking is less a convenience and more a necessity. The search strategy provides a conceptual tool that assists those who need to work with such varied kinds of knowledge. It is intended, also, to help those who use it learn to appraise the quality of secondary information, to detect subtle bias, and to recognize inconsistencies and discrepancies that need to be detected.

Question analysis, undertaken at the outset of the search strategy, is important in forming the intellectual foundation for the remainder of the searcher's work. Having identified the important questions and the context for the message, the communicator goes ahead to examine contributions to be made by *informal sources and observations, institutional sources, library and data-base sources,* and *interviews.* Typically, these examinations do not take place in a linear fashion; rather, the communicator moves among these sources, raising new questions, confirming or discarding material, checking on reputations and sources of bias, updating information no longer current, seeking human interest and story-telling material that will engage the audience. *Evaluation, selection,* and *synthesis* take place as the media writer or scholar closes the information-search stage and enters the writing phase.

In their work, communicators are exhorted to accept their work as socially and politically significant and to regard their decisions about information use as significant for society as a whole, for the media and educational institutions in which they work, and for their individual senses of self-worth. A skillfully performed search for and selection of information should help communicators meet these social, professional, and personal goals. But proficiency is not likely to wipe out every information offense that can be committed in the complex new information society of which we are parts. As Anthony Smith wrote, mass communication is less about single-handed authorship than about the "refining of past knowledge, in reformulation, in recirculation, in reordering the vast human storage of information that springs from the collective intellectual activity of the species."[1] This book is consistent with a reformulation perspective on media messages. Since material of varied quality and perspective is incorporated in the communicator's messages, the degree of communicator responsibility is not unlimited. It should be understood that the search strategy is a conceptual tool, not a panacea. It should be seen as an improvement over random, casual, and haphazard practices, not as a solution to all media flaws.

NOTE

1. Anthony Smith, *Goodbye Gutenberg* (Oxford: Oxford University Press, 1980), 315.

General Index

A Topical Tool Index, which arranges library and data base sources by broad subject areas, follows this general index. The general index includes authors, titles, and subjects.

Topical Tool Index

Communicators sometimes need to gather information within and across disciplines. To address that need, library and data-base tools are arranged here according to broad subject areas. Of course, there are hundreds of tools that are useful for each of these topics; only those tools covered in this text are included here. Consult the *Computer-Readable Databases* guide for other relevant electronic information sources.